# Implementing X.400 and X.500:

## The PP and QUIPU Systems

For a complete listing of the *Artech House Telecommunications Library*,
turn to the back of this book . . .

# Implementing X.400 and X.500:
## The PP and QUIPU Systems

Stephen E. Kille

Artech House
Boston • London

**Library of Congress Cataloging-in-Publication Data**
Kille, Stephen E.
Implementing X.400 and X.500: The PP and QUIPU Systems / Stephen E. Kille.
p. cm.
Includes bibliographical references and index.
ISBN 0-89006-564-0
1. Electronic mail systems--Handbooks, manuals, etc. 2. Computer networks--Standards--Handbooks, manuals, etc. I. Title.
II. Title: QUIPU implementation of X.400 and X.500.
TK5105.73K55 1991 91-21436
004.692--dc20 CIP

**British Library Cataloguing in Publication Data**
Kille, Stephen E.
Implementing X.400 and X.500: The PP and QUIPU Systems
I. Title
384.34

ISBN 0-89006-564-0


**685 Canton Street**
**Norwood, MA 02062**



**International Standard Book Number: 0-89006-564-0**
**Library of Congress Catalog Card Number: 91-21436**

**10 9 8 7 6 5 4 3 2 1**

*To My Parents*

# Contents

# List of Figures

# List of Tables

# Preface

Open Systems Interconnection (OSI) is spreading widely, and will soon be a major component of operational networking. This book does not try to discuss the pros and cons of OSI, but simply presents implementations of X.400 and the OSI Directory, which are two key OSI applications, by use of their system manuals. A major reason for writing this book is to make these two manuals more readily available in a convenient format. X.400 based Message Handling is the first OSI service to see a large number of implementations and operational services, and is widely viewed as the "flagship" OSI application. The OSI Directory (X.500) is seen as a key infrastructure component for networking services. Unlike the case of X.400, there is no equivalent existing service to the OSI Directory, and so use of the OSI Directory is growing rapidly within the international research community. Some consider that the OSI Directory will soon be as important or more important than X.400. PP and QUIPU are implementations of X.400 and the OSI Directory respectively, and are interesting for a number of reasons:

- They are openly available (effectively public domain), and thus available to anyone who is interested.
- They are widely used in the research community, and therefore many are familiar with them.
- They have been demonstrated as viable for operational service in complex environments.
- They are early implementations of the 1988 OSI standards, and so not many other implementations are currently available.
- They are full implementations — many early implementations took very significant shortcuts.

The manuals contained in this book document the systems in some detail, and give a useful insight into the problems of such systems. In principle, the manuals are openly available, and easily accessible to anyone interested. However, in practice, this is not always the case. Those with access to appropriate networks will print single sided copies of the documentation. Those without access need to obtain the software distribution, which contains a copy of the manual and is an expensive way to obtain only the documentation. Bringing the manuals into a book provides a much more convenient and economical format. The manuals have been included in their entirety and with only minor editing to make them suitable for book form.

The PP and QUIPU software is updated on a timescale which is too short to have the associated manuals released simultaneously in book form. Those concerned with detailed aspects of the software, will usually need to obtain the very latest versions of the manual. In a book of this form, one can choose to publish released manuals only, which would guarantee being significantly out of date. This book is based on manuals which are intercepts on major releases (PP 6.0 and QUIPU 7.0), both of which are expected in Summer 1991. Thus, this book is broadly in line with the versions of the software in use, although there will be some detailed alignment problems.

In addition to the two manuals, there is an introductory chapter. This gives a technical and historical overview of the two systems, and sets the two manuals in context. The author, as system architect and project manager of development of the two systems, suggests the expected evolution of the systems, and analyzes some of the design choices. These notes give a personal view on the direction and success of the two systems. This material is important to the general reader, but is not really appropriate for a system manual.

## Acknowledgements

Producing openly available software leads to a very satisfying level of cooperative help, and this book is due to the work of many people, with contributions to both the code and the text of the manuals from all over the world. Two people deserve special credit. Julian Onions of X-Tel Services has played a central role in the PP implementation, and is responsible for much of of the system. He has worked patiently and carefully through the long development cycle. Colin Robbins of X-Tel Services developed the core of the QUIPU system and now leads development and support activities. His methodical approach has retained sanity when updates have been contributed from many sources.

The many contributors have already been detailed in the PP and QUIPU Manuals; however, a few people deserve special mention. Marshall T. Rose of Performance Systems International, has provided the ISODE (ISO Development Environment), which is a key component of both PP and QUIPU. His energy, enthusiasm, and refusal to compromise on quality have been invaluable. Peter Cowan of X-Tel Services has made a key contribution to PP. Alan Turland of Edinburgh University Computer Service and Mike Roe of Cambridge Computer Laboratory have written significant components of the QUIPU DSA. Many others have helped to write, document, debug, and deploy the systems.

Professor Peter Kirstein of University College London, Hugh Smith of Nottingham University, and Jim Craigie of the Joint Network Team have made important contributions to providing a framework in which these two developments could happen.

Thanks to Paul Barker and David Goodman of University College London, Ian Kille of British Telecom, Julian Onions, Colin Robbins, and Marshall Rose for helpful review comments on the first part of this book.

I would like to thank my parents, to whom I dedicate this book, for being there when I needed them. Last, but not least, I thank Alison for her help with everything, for a lot of fun, and for changing my life over the last year.

Steve Kille
London, April 1991

# Part I

# Introduction

# Chapter 1

# Background

## 1.1 OSI

This book is about the implementation of two OSI (Open Systems Interconnection) applications, and so in some senses OSI is fundamental to the material presented here. This book is not an OSI tutorial, and the reader will need to be familiar with OSI in order to gain full benefit from this book. For a rigorous theoretical introduction, the book by Knowles, Larmouth and Knightson is useful [KLK87]. For a more practical introduction, the Open Book by Rose is recommended [Ros89]. This book also describes the ISODE implementation, which is discussed further in Section 1.3. As the ISODE is used by both PP and QUIPU, Rose's book is a sensible companion to this one.

### 1.1.1 X.400 Message Handling

Use of electronic mail services is now established as an important service in many environments. This has been achieved by a range of different message protocols and by centralis ed "email" services, leading to a situation where there are islands of electronic mail connectivity. There is a clear need to have a common international standard, which can be used as a mechanism to glue together the disjoint services in order to provide a single coherent global electronic mail service.

The CCITT X.400 recommendations on message handling services have versions published in 1984 and 1988 [MHS84, MHS88a]. These recommendations describe how message transfer agents (MTAs) can operate collectively to provide an end-to-end Message Transfer Service. They specifically describe how the message transfer service can be used to provide an interpersonal messaging service between human users. X.400 specifies an interface, and is very appropriate for gatewaying onto systems which do not follow X.400 internally. A general introduction to X.400 can be found in the NCC Book [Chi89]. For those familiar with X.400(1984), Manros's book is a useful introduction to X.400(1988) [Man89]. For further information, it is best to read the first parts of the standard itself.

### 1.1.2 The OSI Directory

The need for a global directory service to support a variety of applications has been seen for some while. Some of these requirements are:

**Message Handling Systems** During the development of the 1984 X.400 series recommendations for message handling systems, many people foresaw the requirement for directory services [Whi84]. These requirements have resulted in a complex specification of usage in the 1988 version of X.400 [MHS88a]

**OSI Applications** The whole approach to naming and addressing within OSI assumes the availability of a directory service [CCI88b].

**White Pages Service** There would be substantial advantage in upgrading the current telephone directory system to give online access. The French Minitel system has shown the feasibility of this.

Because of such requirements, a standardised OSI directory service has been specified as CCITT X.500 series recommendations / ISO DIS 9594 [CCI88b]. This is known generically as the "OSI Directory". The OSI Directory standard gives a clear and general introduction to X.500. Rose's The Little Black Book gives a useful discussion of some aspects of the directory, and in particular problems related to use of the OSI Directory [Ros91].

## 1.2 Deployed Systems

Over the last decade, there has been massive activity in the deployment and operation of computer networks. A good overall picture of this activity is given in John Quarterman's book The Matrix [Qua90]. In the international research community, TCP/IP based networking, especially that related to the DARPA/NSF Internet, is particularly important and is dominant in the international research community, both academic and industrial. Operational issues, and the relationship to existing systems will often be discussed in the context of this environment. There have been a range of systems and services deployed to provide both messaging and directory type services. From a user's standpoint, the OSI Services are just one more set of services to be added to the already existing services. This is particularly true for messaging, where there are many existing systems, often based on the RFC 822 format specification [Cro82]. The dominance of these existing systems has certainly delayed the deployment of X.400. Another factor is that many early implementations of X.400 have been very minimal. Thus, while the protocols may be more powerful, the local facilities and management options on the systems have been restricted. This has lead to a situation where X.400 based systems do not offer an overall improvement of service. There are now quite a number of X.400 products on offer, but the number of systems in service is very small in comparison to older non-X.400 systems.

The situation for the OSI directory is somewhat different. There are a number of deployed databases and directory services, but none really fulfill the role of the OSI Directory. Existing services fall into two categories:

1. Name service type functions, which enable lookup of precisely specified names. These may be widely distributed. A good example of this is the domain naming scheme[Moc84].
2. Centralised database services

There is a significant requirement for a large scale distributed database which provides searching capabilities. There is a particular requirement to look up users to determine information such as electronic mail addresses and telephone numbers. Because the OSI directory fills this niche, its deployment has been able to proceed much more rapidly, as there is a vacuum. This expansion is particularly notable in directory pilot exercises in the UK and the US, which are discussed in Section 2.10.

## 1.3 ISODE

The ISODE (ISO development environment), whose principal is Marshall T. Rose of Performance Systems International, is a key component of the two systems described here. The ISODE is an implementation of the OSI upper layers. It contains: the layer services of session and presentation; the ACSE, ROSE and RTSE application service elements; FTAM and VTP applications; and ASN.1 handling tools. A key choice in ISODE is to be able to operate over a TCP/IP network. It does this by use of a mapping defined in RFC 1006 [RC87, RC86]. This has enabled OSI applications, including PP and QUIPU to be deployed ahead of provision of a global OSI network service.

The ISODE is openly available, which puts it effectively in the public domain. QUIPU is packaged as a part of ISODE, and there is a symbiotic relationship between PP and ISODE. All three systems can be regarded as being a part of the same family. The ISODE has been a very popular implementation of OSI, and has been taken up in many quarters. A number of manufacturers are using ISODE in their products.

## 1.4 Availability

The availability of PP and QUIPU are described in their respective manuals. The expected procedures for the releases are included. The contact addresses are correct. It is posssible that the prices may be altered.

As far as possible the manuals are presented in their original form, although some small changes are made for this book.

The QUIPU manual is a pre-release of the manual for version 7.0 of the code. The manual is usually packaged as Volume 5 of the ISODE manual [Ros90a]. The common ISODE introductory material is retained as it contains useful pointers to the rest of the ISODE. Any differences between this book and version 7.0 will be noted clearly in the version 7.0 release.

The PP manual relates to version 5.3 of the code. Version 6.0 is expected to be broadly similar. This manual is usually packaged as a four-volume set. Each volume is presented as a part of this book. Any differences between this book and version 6.0 will be noted clearly in the version 6.0 release.

# Chapter 2

# QUIPU

## 2.1 History

The OSI directory service has a much more complex functionality than any previously existing services. While there have been directory services which have tackled some of the problems of scale and distribution, these have used much simpler name structures, and have not provided the powerful searching facilities of the OSI directory. At the other end of the spectrum, many existing database systems deal with the searching problems, but this is usually done in a very centralised manner. Thus, despite the massive requirement for the OSI directory, the specification has been made without real practical experience of the problem. This is very much in contrast to the development of X.400 [MHS84], which was done on the basis of a good deal of previous relevant messaging experience. The initial planning of QUIPU began in 1986 when it was seen as important to experiment with the OSI directory prior to the provision of large scale services. The first version of QUIPU was developed to facilitate such experimentation, and it has evolved from this base.

The QUIPU directory service was initially developed under the INCA (integrated network communication architecture) project, which was an ESPRIT research project comprising GEC (prime contractor), ATM, Nixdorf, Olivetti, and University College London (UCL). UCL was a subcontractor to GEC. INCA investigated a wide range of areas, including support of multimedia workstations, and provision of a range of networking technologies such as the Olivetti broadband net. Other aspects of the project are discussed in [KK87]. The directory service activities were a small component of this project, with all of the work being done at UCL.

It is worth noting the etymology of QUIPU. It must be remembered that QUIPU was originally developed as a part of the INCA project. The Incas of Peru did not have writing. Instead, they stored information on strings, carefully knotted in a specific manner and with coloured thread, and attached to a larger rope. These devices were known as "Quipus." The encoding was obscure, and could only be read by selected trained people: the Quipucamayocs. The Quipu was a key component of Inca society, as it contained information about property and locations throughout the extensive Inca empire.

The ISODE system was used by the QUIPU system from the start, to provide the OSI services required by the OSI directory. QUIPU is now being issued as a part of the ISODE, and the ISODE applications have been adapted to use QUIPU for their directory requirements. This integration is discussed later. The close interrelationship of QUIPU and ISODE has been mutually beneficial.

The early QUIPU prototype was successful, and was used to give the first demonstration of distributed X.500 at the ESPRIT Conference Week in November 1988. This demonstration involved DSAs (directory system agent) in four countries, using both directory access protocol and directory system protocol. The viability of the system as being a suitable basis for operating a pilot service was demonstrated. Following the initial development under INCA, the QUIPU system was developed under contract to the Joint Network Team, to provide a system for use in the (then) planned UK academic community pilot. This funding has been ongoing, and has led to vastly improved functionality and robustness of the system. Strong authentication services have been expermented with in QUIPU, in collaboration with the Locator project [CHI+87]. This includes both directory provision of security, and directory use of security.

The QUIPU development, and this book, are primarily concerned with the DSA side. QUIPU specifies a C API (application program interface), to facilitate implementation of DUAs (directory user agent). There are a number of DUAs which are notable:

- DISH (the DIrectory SHell) which was implemented along with QUIPU is a useful tool for testing the directory and for management functions. A number of other sample DUAs were implemented with QUIPU.
- Performance Systems International implemented a number of DUAs for use in the US White Pages Pilot. The most well known of these are FRED, which is a front end to the DISH program emulating the older Internet WHOIS service and the X Window System[1] XWP program.
- Brunel University was funded by the Joint Network Team to produce DUAs for UNIX[2], and MS-DOS[3]. The UNIX DUAs are distributed with QUIPU.

The evolution of QUIPU is now very much tied up with the deployment of QUIPU in directory pilots around the world, as described in Section 2.10. These pilots are being very successful, and as QUIPU is the dominant implementation in these pilots, this also reflects the success of QUIPU.

[1]The X Window System is a trademark of the Massachusettes Institute of Technology
[2]UNIX is a trademark of AT&T Bell Laboratories.
[3]MS-DOS is a trademark of Microsoft Corporation.

## 2.2 Design Overview

There were two overriding concepts in the original design of QUIPU: simplicity and flexibility. The former is important to facilitate rapid implementation with relatively small amounts of effort. The latter is important to allow experimentation with a variety of problems associated with provision of directory service. Evolution has lead to some increase of complexity. QUIPU is implemented in the C programming language, to run initially under the UNIX operating system.

An application, which might be a user interface or an OSI process, accesses the directory through a DUA. In QUIPU, the DUA is provided as a C API, which is structured in a manner aligned to the directory Abstract service of the OSI directory. This gives the application straightforward access to the *full* directory service. The DUA interface is described in more detail in section 2.8. The DUA code below the API is kept as small as feasible, so that the cost of simple directory usage is as low as possible. If a DUA wishes to do caching, this should be done above the API. Extensive caching is done by the DSA (directory system agent), and so DUA caching is often not needed.

## 2.3 The Memory Database

The memory-oriented database of QUIPU is one of its most distinctive features, and it is useful to examine the reasoning behind this choice. Probably the hardest decision in designing a DSA is the choice of database. A tempting choice is to use a commercial database to provide this base functionality. Unfortunately, the directory data structures and those supported by conventional database packages do not match at all well [Kil85], and so this possibility was rejected. The design of a special purpose database system was a daunting task, particularly when the required parameters were not at all well understood. We therefore chose to map the DSA database directly onto memory, using C structures which correspond to the form of the DIT (directory information tree). The master data is read from disk at machine start time, and updated back to disk when modify operations occur. This approach has the following advantages:

- It is straightforward to implement.
- There are no "unnatural" restrictions due to database keying approaches.
- It will give high performance for small volumes of data.

Superficially, the approach seems to place severe restrictions on the volume of data which a DSA can hold. However, the use of virtual memory means that the operating system will give a good deal of support to allow extension. The continuing rapid drop in the price of memory chips has also made this approach seem increasingly favourable. This basic approach has been evolved in three ways:

1. Significant tuning, in order to minimise the memory cost of each entry. Reducing this size has been the key to improving performance.
2. A special memory allocation mechanism, optimised for QUIPU, which significantly improves the paging characteristics.
3. A mechanism specified whereby large attributes can be stored in a file on disk, rather than in memory.
4. Addition of indexes on specific attribute types over a subtree of variable depth. This allows for common searches to be optimised.

These approaches allow for DSAs of up to 100 000 entries to be built, which is substantially greater than the initial system. Experiences with this approach are analyzed in Sections 2.10 and 2.12.

## 2.4 The Disk Database

The master database for each DSA is held on disk. A text format for this database was chosen for the following reasons:

- As the data is only accessed by the DSA at startup, the format of the data can be chosen to be convenient from a management standpoint.
- It is easy to create from external sources by ad hoc means.
- It can be inspected without the use of special tools.
- Errors can be "patched" by use of a text editor.
- It is convenient for post-processing and reformatting.

This format must represent various basic items as text. These representations are used in a number of places throughout QUIPU, and the full format is specified in the QUIPU manual. The key features of this syntax are summarised here. First, a means of defining local representations of ASN.1 object identifiers is given [ISO87], which is used to represent attribute types: for example, CN represents the attribute type for "Common Name". Attribute values have an attribute syntax which is implied by the attribute type. Attributes are represented as:

<attribute-type> = <attribute-value>

Multiple attribute values are separated by &. For example:

```
object-class = Person & Organizational Person
```

This example defines an object class attribute with two values, both encoded as object identifiers. The text encoding of name is a simple extension from this. Relative distinguished names (RDN) are specified as a hierarchy separated by @, with the most significant component on the left. In the unusual case where the RDN has multiple attributes, the components are separated by %. For example (simple RDNs only):

```
@C=GB@O=University College London@CN=Steve Kille
```

In the QUIPU directory, we introduce the concept of entry data block (EDB) as a fundamental unit of data. This approach is a simplification of the full generality of data distribution in the standard OSI directory. An EDB is the total information for a full set of sibling entries, which includes RDNs and all attributes. Each non-leaf entry, including the root of the directory information tree (DIT), can be considered to have an EDB, which defines its children. The EDB is the fundamental component for distributed operation within QUIPU.

```
MASTER
910402104424Z
cn=Steve Kille
objectClass= top & person & organizationalPerson & thornObject & pilotPerson
cn= Steve Kille &\
        Stephen E. Kille
sn= Kille
description= Researcher into Distributed Applications and OSI &\
        PP and QUIPU project leader
telephoneNumber= +44 71-380-7294
userPassword= {CRYPT}PWFUF
uid= steve
mail= S.Kille\40cs.ucl.ac.uk
drink= Pinta - Brakspears
roomNumber= G24
photo= {FILE}
userClass= csresstaff
homePhone= +44 71-350-2888
lastModifiedTime= 910118135033Z
lastModifiedBy= c=GB@o=University College London@ou=Computer Science@cn=Steve Kille
homePostalAddress= {T.61}35 Elspeth Road $ London $ SW11 1DW
personalTitle= Mr
acl= others # read # attributes # telephoneNumber$surname$objectClass$userClass...
        others # compare # attributes # userPassword &\
        self # write # attributes # userPassword
mhsORAddresses= {ASN}303430326104130267626 20a1308676f6c6420343030a207....

cn=Paul Barker
objectClass= top & person & organizationalPerson
sn= Barker
telephoneNumber= +44 71-380-7366
userPassword= {CRYPT}TFFWNB
```

Figure 2.1: Example EDB File

Each EDB is stored in a file, such as the example given in Figure 2.1. After the preamble, a list of entries is separated by blank lines. The first line of each entry is its RDN, followed by the remaining attributes. Note how a photograph attribute is held by reference to an external file, and how the mhsORAddress attribute has its data entered as an ASN.1 string, by using the ASN.1 basic encoding rules, and then printing the result in hexadecimal.

The whole DIT is represented by the use of a UNIX directory tree. The directory names are given by the appropriate string-encoded RDN, and the EDB is stored in an eponymous file. Recursively, the children of non-leaf nodes are stored in subdirectories, each named by a string-encoded representation of the associated RDN.

This structure is relatively easy to generate and manipulate, which was the prime objective. It also makes restructuring the DIT, sometimes known as "aboriculture," relatively easy and has also allowed for ad hoc replication of parts of the DIT to be accomplished in a straightforward manner.

The basic database structure has been extended in the light of initial experience. First, a file *EDB.map* has been added, which maps the full RDN onto a shorter key. This has two roles:

- Provision of a convenient short directory name in a local database.
- Portability to systems where directory names have length or character set restrictions.

The second extension is to add a hash-indexed form of the EDB, which allows for updates to happen a good deal more rapidly. For loading purposes the text EDB has been acceptable, but writing out a whole EDB for a change to a single entry was too costly.

## 2.5 DSA Internal Structure

The DSA operates with all of its data in memory which it initialises from disk, and so is inherently slow in starting up. For this reason, the DSA process configuration needs to be fairly static, and so it would not be possible to start a DSA process to serve a single request. However, it is important for the directory to be responsive and to have a high availability, which led to the decision to allow the DSA to perform its own internal scheduling, described later. The major structures, implemented as C data structures, are now described.

The first internal structure is the DIT itself, which is simply built up as a collection of entry structures. There is one structure for each entry, linked analogously to the DIT. It has the following main components, which are built up at load time:

- The relative distinguished name.
- All the attributes (in the entry or inherited).
- Whether the entry is master, slave, or cache information.
- Access Control information, linked into all of the relevant places.

- Links to parent, child, and sibling entries. The last two are maintained as B-Tree structures.
- Soundex keys for appropriate attributes.
- Optional alias pointer.
- Information on cache time.

The second structure is a list of OSI associations to DUAs and DSAs. These indicate the state of each connection, and the identity of the remote system. Use of these links ensures that only one association is active between a given pair of DSAs. It is also reasonable for DSAs with high levels of interaction to maintain associations for a long time. This tends to improve performance, as the initial cost of connection setup and authentication is saved. Associated with each association is a list of "task" structures. Each task is associated with an operation which has been invoked over the association. Each task has information giving the state of the task, and a list of "operation" structures, to be invoked on remote DSAs. These operation structures are cross-linked to the associations, and each has an associated state. Every task and association has a priority, based on the user specified priority, but also related to the nature of the task. For example, large searches are given lower priority. Information in the task/operation structures is represented by C structures which correspond to the parameters, results and errors of the ROS operation. These are designed to be convenient to manipulate, as distinct from the network representation which is not.

Two distinct modules operate on this collection of structures. One is a network module, which manages associations. Pending OPDUs (operation protocol data units) are built up from relevant structures in the operations/tasks, and sent out onto the net. Conversely, inbound activity is detected, and OPDUs are read in incrementally. When complete, they will be decoded into the relevant C structures. All of this activity must be done asynchronously, for which the ISODE gives full support. In general, servicing network activity is given priority, which is important to allow rapid servicing of high priority simple queries. The second module processes the queries. Tasks are examined, and processed to generate either results or necessary intermediate operations. Scheduling is blocked, so that long search operations are interrupted in order to prevent significant delays in other operations.

A basic design decision was to place as much of this complexity as possible in the DSA. For this reason, a QUIPU DUA will by default contact a single DSA, and that DSA will do all of the complex scheduling, which means that this sort of complexity does not need to be repeated in the DUA. Thus from the DUA standpoint, the DSA will always chain queries on, and only return DSA Referrals in exceptional circumstances.

When a QUIPU DSA talks to another QUIPU DSA, which it can tell by the supported application contexts determined from the DSA's entry in the DIT, it uses a special version of DSP (directory system protocol), known as QUIPU DSP. This allows the DSA to optimise for the manner in which another QUIPU DSA behaves. In particular, it can recognize that replicated data is being supported systematically.

The QUIPU DSP supports an operation call *getEDB*, which enables copies of EDBs to be transferred between QUIPU DSAs. This systematic replication is important, in order to provide good searching performance and high availability.

QUIPU uses a private approach to represent knowledge information in the DIT, which means that knowledge information can be entered remotely by use of a QUIPU DUA. The presentation address of a DSA is stored in the DSA's own entry. This simplifies management, but care must be taken to prevent deadlock. This is done by careful naming of DSAs: usually by choice of a name higher in the DIT than the information managed in the DSA. There is a definite advantage to having the DSA's own entry mastered in the DSA itself. In particular, this allows the DSA to represent a range of management information in its own entry. To prevent the deadlock described earlier, this information is always "spot-shadowed" out to a DSA which will make the information available to other DSAs.

A final key extension in QUIPU deals with multiple lower layers, such ar connection oriented network service, connectionless network service, or TCP/IP. It will recognise that different DSAs operate over different stacks, and perform appropriate application level relaying (chaining) in order to overcome the lower level discontinuities.

## 2.6 Security

The QUIPU implementation uses simple authentication by default. There is also some support for strong authentication, which is based on public key cryptography [CCI88a]. Work has been done to allow both for provision of authentication by the directory, and for use of authentication by the directory.

Access control is one of the areas omitted from the current version of the OSI directory standard. To build a real implementation, where modification of data is performed remotely by users and managers, it is essential to have access controls on the data. The design criteria were that:

- It should not require changes to the directory access protocol.
- Functionality should be high.
- The structure should be reasonably intuitive.
- The storage overhead should not be unduly high where the requirements are simple.

The first requirement is met by defining access control as a single valued attribute, which is "known" by the directory. The key to the approach is the relatively small number of access categories from none to write. These are encoded as an integer, with each level of access implying the lower ones. These access levels are associated with different pieces of information:

- The entry itself (controlling creation of new attributes).

- Specified attributes.
- The children (controlling access to the subtree).

QUIPU has four possibilities for specifying who is being controlled, with the first two being optimised encodings of common cases. These possibilities are:

- The entry itself.
- Public rights.
- Subtree (e.g., all names (DUAs) in an organisation).
- A list (e.g., a manager list).

Defaulting is done carefully to ensure that memory is not wasted, and duplicated information is handled by reference in order to avoid repetition. In addition to these optimisations, the QUIPU DSA also takes care to save storage, by avoiding duplication of data at load time. If an entry does not explicitly have an ACL attribute, one is pointed to which corresponds to the default actions.

The ACL attribute is a key component of correct caching. When one QUIPU DSA reads from another QUIPU DSA, it will always choose to read the ACL (even if the originating DUA did not request it). Then, results can be cached and used correctly on the basis of the (cached) ACL attribute. Also, the ACL can be used to determine the list of attributes present in the entry, so that a caching DSA can tell if it has all of them. Non-QUIPU DSAs will not return the ACL attribute, and so information will not be cached in this case.

## 2.7 Schemas

An area of the standard which causes particular problems is that of schemas. The balance of control between directory, Application, and Management is a delicate one. If the directory does not provide sufficient functionality, management will not be possible. If it overly constrains the structure, it may prevent reasonable usage.

The first aspect of schemas is matching of attributes — attribute syntaxes. QUIPU supports three types of attribute syntax:

- A number of standard syntaxes, for which optimised internal encoding and matching is supplied. These standard syntaxes are defined in the OSI directory, X.400, and the COSINE and Internet X.500 schema [BK91].
- Some special syntaxes, defined for QUIPU specific attributes.
- A general ASN.1 syntax, which can be used to represent any syntax. This means that all attributes can be stored, and retrieved correctly without knowledge of their exact syntax. Matching is permitted and will be done consistently, but may not be done correctly for some syntaxes.

Support of attribute syntaxes must be reflected in code. The approach is modularised so that a new syntax can be added by simply defining a new set of routines to be linked into the DSA. This makes it straightforward to add support for new private attribute syntaxes.

The second level of schema is controlling which attributes are present in a given entry. In line with the OSI directory standard, QUIPU understands object classes. An entry may belong to multiple classes, not necessarily in an (object class) hierarchy. All such object classes must be known to the QUIPU DSA that masters the entry, which it determines from a local table. The definitions of the object classes will allow the DSA to derive a list of mandatory and optional attributes for a given entry. QUIPU defines its own object classes and attribute types for storage of QUIPU specific information. It is also possible to define an object class with no object identifier, which allows for any attribute to be stored.

The final aspect of schemas is controlling the structure of the tree. While the OSI directory has considered the relationship of objects in the tree, no specific mechanisms are provided to deal with its structure. Two significant requirements have been identified:

- The manager must be able to control the shape of the tree, in terms of object class hierarchy.
- The user must be provided with an efficient mechanism to determine the (potential) shape of the tree.

QUIPU defines a tree structure attribute to solve these problems. Each value of the tree structure attribute holds a list of object classes, and represents a single potential type of entry. This is in line with the latest developments in the OSI directory specification. For example, a tree structure value might permit:

quipu object + person + organisational person + MHS user

The object class of entries in the DIT directly below the node containing the schema attribute must be in the tree structure list. This gives managers the facility to control the shape of the DIT.

In the standard, an attribute is associated with a single entry. In many cases, it is useful for an attribute to be "inherited" by its children. For example, a telephone number may be common to an entire organisation. QUIPU provides a mechanism to specify an inherited attribute. This also allows for defaults to be specified. This is particularly important for attributes such as the access control list. This inheritance mechanism leads to a significant performance gain due to reduction in the size of leaf entries, as well as reduced management overhead.

## 2.8 DUAs

One of the main reasons for developing QUIPU is to make it available to applications. For this reason, the procedural interface is defined clearly, and documented in some detail in the QUIPU manual. Clearly, the structures required by this family of operations are complex. This is a reflection of the level of functionality available from the OSI directory. To facilitate the user of QUIPU, a utility library has been provided, with procedures and structure definitions to help in this task. It includes routines to: allocate structures; free structures; fill structures with default values; build structures from string representations; compare structures; and print structures.

The procedural interface has been used as the basis for a number of DUAs. A good example of this is the POD user interface, shown in Figure 2.2. Most of the key DUA work, apart from DISH, has been done by those outside the QUIPU project, and so although some DUA information is included in the manual, DUA issues are not discussed in detail here.

A key component in the evolution of QUIPU has been the specification of "user-friendly naming" [Kil90c]. This approach allows the user to provide a free-form string version of a name, which is then searched for in the directory in a standardised fashion. For example the input:

```
Kille, UCL, UK
```

would be used to generate a series of searches, which leads to the identifying of the unique distinguished name:

```
Steve Kille, Computer Science, University College London, GB
```

This approach has enabled the directory to be integrated with a number of applications in a user-oriented manner. It has been used with message handling to support distribution lists, and integrated with OSI applications such as FTAM to look up presentation addresses.

## 2.9 Conformance

QUIPU supports the X.500 directory access and directory system protocols (DAP and DSP) and the associated services. QUIPU can act as a top level DSA, and supports all of the attributes and object classes defined in X.500. No formal conformance testing has been done, and no test suites are known of at the time of writing. No protocol deficiencies are known. The openly available release of QUIPU does not fully support the security related services. The QUIPU DSA does not correctly follow nonspecific subordinate references, but will pass them on to the DSA.

## 2.10 Deployment and Interoperability

The QUIPU implementation was installed in many countries during 1988, and a demonstration configuration established. The first deployment as a pilot system

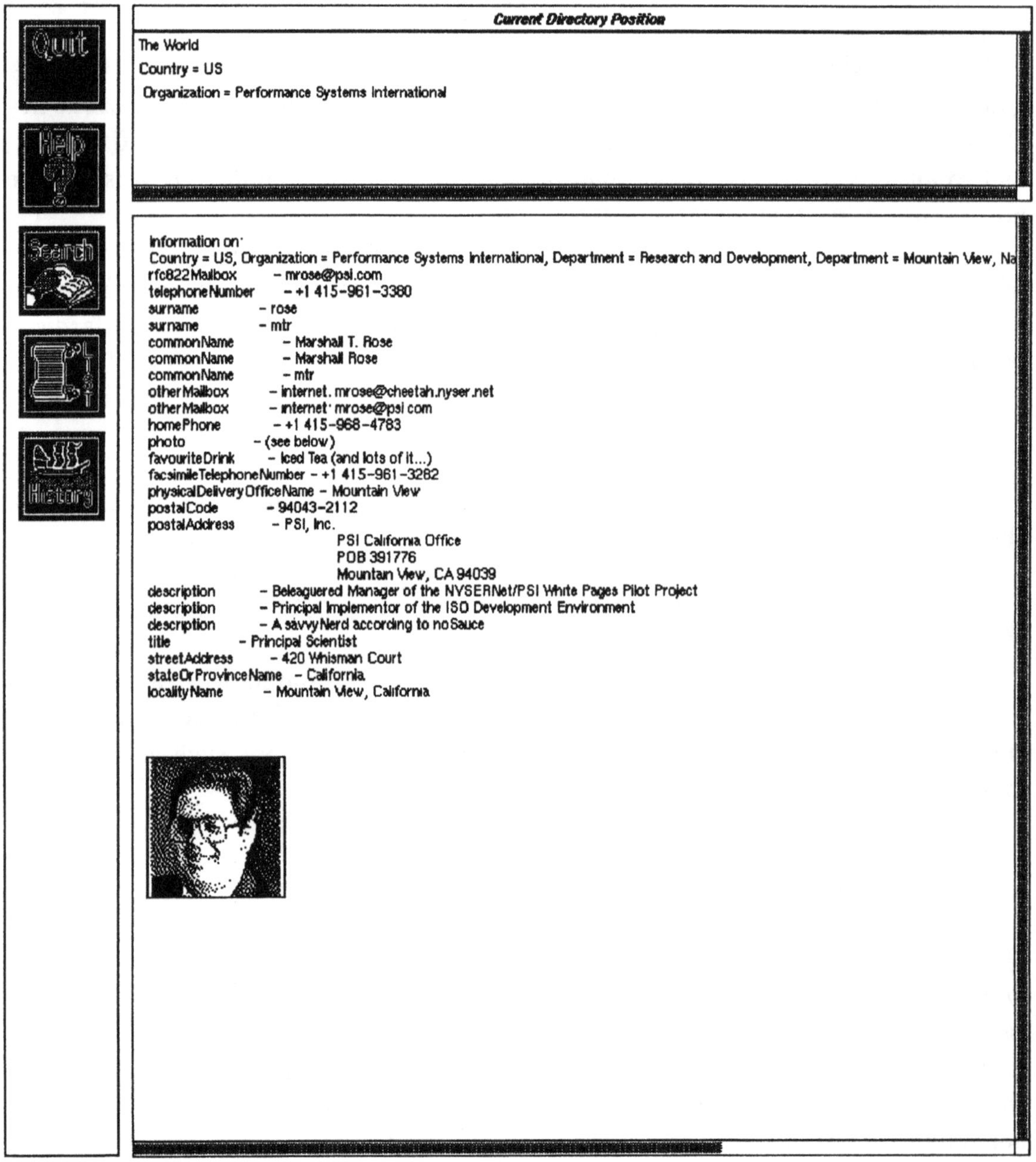


Figure 2.2: Example Use of the POD DUA

was undertaken by NYSERNet Inc, on NYSERNet (New York scientific, educational and research network), which is one of the component networks of the DARPA/NSF Internet. This project was originally known as the NYSERNet White Pages pilot Project, and is now the PSI White Pages Project [Ros90b]. This was done as a pilot service, prior to establishment of a service for the Internet as a whole. A new DUA called FRED, which emulates an existing internet interface, was implemented and made available to participating organisations as a part of ISODE. The pilot started in July 1989, and in April 1991 contains over 76 organisations, 67 DSAs and and 250,000 entries. It is expanding steadily.

A pilot has been established in the UK academic community, which commenced operation in December 1989 [Cra89]. The Joint Network Team is in the process of giving hardware to all UK universities to run DSAs on. These systems are operated as services for the entire university. In addition, there are other sites in the UK: commercial sites and academic systems not supported by service centres. The QUIPU system is being extended for this pilot, and high performance DUAs for the naïve user are being developed at Brunel University. The pilot currently contains about 65,000 entries in 31 organisations using 36 DSAs.

These two pilots are part of a broader picture of establishment of directory pilots in the research community. There is now directory activity in at least fifteen countries. The overall directory contains over 400,000 entries on over 300 Organisations in over 200 DSAs. The PARADISE (piloting a researchers directory service in europe) project is being funded by COSINE to provide the glue between the national pilots in order to build a coherent European and International directory service [Goo91]. There is an emerging international directory, with a steady increase of data volume, quality of data, and level of real usage. The majority of this activity is based on the use of QUIPU.

Basic protocol interoperability of QUIPU has been demonstrated, with four to five other implementations. Some of this has been done in the context of the pilot, with other implementations providing either DUAs, or DSAs managing a clearly delineated subtree of the DIT (typically a single organistion). In other cases, this has been by separate protocol interoperability tests. The test have shown good protocol interworking, both for directory access and directory system protocols. Use of ASN.1 compilers has ensured that there are relatively few detailed protocol errors. There has been relatively little experience with interaction between different implementations where the distributed operations are complex. This is partly due to problems in bringing other implementations up to a suitable state, and partly because it is difficult to be effective in this area when working only to the standard.

## 2.11 Expected Evolution

QUIPU was built to be used, and it is expected that evolution of QUIPU will be very much tied in with the evolution of the operational pilot activity. A group has been established by the Internet Engineering Task Force to consider the problems of deploying the OSI directory, and to specify the technical infrastructure needed for such an activity. The work of this group is summarised in a paper by the author [Kil91a]. Much of the technical work is derived from experience with QUIPU, and so QUIPU can be seen as driving the technical evolution of the pilot. There will be some differences with the way in which QUIPU currently works, and so QUIPU will need to be extended to support the following three options: the OSI directory as defined in the standard; the OSI directory with Internet extensions; the OSI directory with QUIPU private extensions. The choice will depend on what the remote DSA supports.

There are a number of areas in which it is certain that QUIPU will be extended. The most important ones are:

- Alignment to the new work coming out in the 1992 version of the OSI directory. The major aspects of this are:
  - A number of small extensions to the abstract service.
  - Attribute subtyping, to enable definition of an attribute type hierarchy.
  - A means for specifying DIT structure.
  - Schema publication.
  - An extended information model to associate attributes with multiple entries.
  - Replication and knowledge management.
  - Access Control.
- QUIPU will certainly move to provide a means for managing schema within the directory. Any work will be aligned to the 1992 standard. An initial scheme may be developed which does not include all of the 1992 complexity.
- Some management facilities have been added in to QUIPU, and it is clear that a lot more are needed. The design of the new features planned is described in [Kil90a]. This includes work to specify authorisation for different users of the directory.
- There is a good deal more work to be done on replication and caching. There needs to be some experimental evaluation of the new spot-shadowing support, in order to see how this should be evolved. Cache operation needs careful tuning and parameterisation in order to be sensibly optimised.
- In addition to upgrading the access control to the 1992 standard, there is some critical functionality which is neither in the current QUIPU approach nor in the new standard. This is a feature to restrict searching, so that users outside an organisation may not systematically trawl the database in order to get a full organisational listing, but can still search for information on the basis of non-exact keys. This sort of control is demanded by many potential users of the directory.

- There is a need to integrate fully the strong authentication services, and to develop a security policy approach which ties together issues of access control and management.
- Some parts of the directory are used for service provision, and others for experimentation. There is a need to register the quality of both data and directory service provision, in order that these valid, but different, types of usage can smoothly coexist.

## 2.12 Analysis of Design Choices

Finally, a few of the design choices made for QUIPU are revisited. The reflections here are a personal view of the author.

### 2.12.1 Database Choice

The memory-oriented database choice seems to have worked out well. The cost per entry is something like 0.5 kbyte. This is quite affordable for most applications. Read operations come back very quickly, even for very large DSAs. The main speed concern is the search operation. Raw searching has been tuned substantially, and on a reasonable-sized machine will operate at five to ten thousand entries per second. Where the indexes can be used, the search rate is much faster and fairly independent of DSA size. There is also an issue of DSA startup time, as the DSA can only load at a rate of a few thousand entries per minute. Thus, larger DSAs are feasible, particularly if the major DUA usage can be tuned to the way in which attributes are indexed. The database will scale to a size of about 100,000 entries without undue problem. This is large enough for the majority of organisations. The database does not have logging and rollback facilities you would find in a conventional package.

We had initally planned that the database usage would give a good feel for the type of database needed for a DSA. Following operational experience, the problem seems ever harder. It is not at all clear what form of alternative database might be used.

It would have been a good idea to have specified a procedural interface onto the local database, even though the definition of this interface would have evolved substantially with QUIPU. This would have allowed the database to be decoupled, and would have facilitated testing with alternative approaches. It would also have allowed for useful standalone testing of the database.

### 2.12.2 DUA/DSA split

Keeping the DUA simple and putting all scheduling into the DSA was a good initial choice. More sophisticated DUAs need asynchronous access, and gain an increasing understanding of the directory in order to deal smoothly with failures and to enable rapid searching of a larger portion of the DIT. However, most DUAs still prefer to work with a single DSA, although this may change with the next stage of increase in DUA complexity.

### 2.12.3 Procedural DUA

We chose to document the DUA API (Application Program Interface) clearly, and make our main efforts on DSA support. A few demonstration DUAs were included with the initial QUIPU. This choice worked very well: a lot of sites have built DUAs over the QUIPU API, and our effort has not been diluted. It may be useful to add support for the standard XDS API, which has been defined more recently than the QUIPU API [XDS90].

### 2.12.4 Extensions to X.500

Some have criticised QUIPU for deviating from pure OSI, and implementing extensions. The critisism is unfair, as QUIPU can be operated without the extensions. However, the extensions have been a key to QUIPU's success. There is a need to operate over TCP/IP networks, and to have replication and knowledge management. Many of the QUIPU extensions are likely to become de facto agreements for directory usage in the research community. The QUIPU specific access control has been an essential component on many sites where QUIPU has been deployed.

### 2.12.5 Number of Associations

It was initially assumed that a QUIPU DSA would have a very small number of associations, and that the scheduling facilities would be used only occasionally to deal with the case when two queries arrived together. In practice, there has been a much higher degree of parallelism. DSAs have been seen to reach the maximum number of associations (62 at UCL). DUAs often retain associations, and multicasting complex searches often lead to a big fanout. There is also a steady traffic for maintenance of replicas. There is a need to reconsider some aspects of the design in this area.

### 2.12.6 Schema Management

No facilities for schema management were provided in the initial QUIPU. This was partly because it would be hard to devise a management approach which met all the needs. In practice, distribution of tables has been awkward but quite tractable. It is clear schema distribution needs to be automated, and folded back onto the directory. This should allow for both standard and private schema.

### 2.12.7 DIT Structure

There was functionality in QUIPU to control the DIT structure. Minimal use of this has been made in the operational pilot: most pilot managers removed this attribute, and then followed a reasonable structure without directory enforcement. It will be interesting to see if the new functions of the standard to do this get used. It is not clear that there is a real requirement for this sort of functionality.

### 2.12.8 Access Control

The access control has caused more discussion than any other aspect of QUIPU. The approach is complex, and has had more criticism about difficulty of administration than about lack of function. The 1992 standard is a good deal more complex, and it is likely to cause a lot of difficulty to administer cleanly. The main user request has been for controls to manage multi-entry operations (especially search), which has not been addressed by either QUIPU or the 1992 standard.

### 2.12.9 Attribute Inheritance

The function to allow inheritance of attributes was added later. It has provided substantial benefit, both in terms of performance, and manageability of the directory.

## 2.13 Conclusions

In summary, the QUIPU development has been very successful. Many of the original design choices have been shown to be reasonable, or at least amenable to appropriate evolution. In many ways, QUIPU has been too successful, as it is unfortunate that the worldwide OSI directory pilot is largely based on this single implementation. It is clear that QUIPU's use will grow, and that the system has scope for a good deal more evolution.

# Chapter 3

# PP

PP is a message transfer agent oriented towards support of the X.400 series recommendations [MHS84, MHS88a]. PP is implemented in C to run under the UNIX operating system. There has been extensive experience with a number of sophisticated text-based message transfer systems, usually based on the RFC 822 standards [Cro82, Kin84, All83, Pre85]. Many emerging X.400 systems, while offering the superior X.400 protocols, in many respects offer a poorer service than the older systems. PP was evolved when a group of us aimed to draw on the results of earlier work and create a message transfer system with high functionality. The major goals of PP are:

- Provision of a clean interface for message submission and delivery, so that a wide range of user agents may be supported.
- Support for all of the message transfer service elements specified by the 1984 and 1988 versions of X.400.
- Support for some services not provided by X.400.
- Specific support to facilitate the handling of multimedia messages.
- Robustness and efficiency required to support high levels of traffic.
- Scheduling of message delivery in a sophisticated manner, to optimise local and communication resources.
- Provision of a range of management, authorisation and monitoring facilities.
- Reformatting between body part types in a general manner.
- Support for multiple address formats (initially two).
- Use of standardised OSI directory services [CCI88b].
- Support for message protocol conversion in an integrated fashion.
- Full access to the message transfer service for applications other than interpersonal messaging.

The rest of this chapter discusses the features of PP in more detail, and explains how they are used to achieve the listed goals.

## 3.1 History

PP began in 1985 when a group of people wished to produce a system to supports X.400. It was clear that existing RFC 822 MTAs were not going to be extensible to do all that we wanted. We had looked at some existing X.400 systems, and these did not seem to be a suitable basis for our work. PP arose as the solution to the problems raised in these discussions. The ideas for the basic structure draw heavily on the MMDF system [Kin84], and it is fair to say that MMDF is the parent of PP. The initial coding proceeded steadily.

PP received its first public airing at CEBIT (Hannover Fair) in March 1989, where it carried ODIF over X.400, and converted it into local format by use of private conversion tools. It interworked with a number of X.400(84) systems at this point. This was as a part of the ESPRIT PODA project. PP 4.0 was released at the very end of 1989 to 15 beta sites. Three more beta releases were made during 1990 to an increasing number of beta sites. The first openly available release was PP 5.0 in September 1990. Funding for PP has been from a number of sources, the most significant being the UK Joint Network Team.

## 3.2 Design Overview

The PP MTA makes extensive use of UNIX processes to provide the modularity which is fundamental to PP. The aim has been to make each process perform a single function. This allows for flexible construction of complex processing, and minimises side effects. The overall process structure is illustrated in Figure 3.1.

PP has a *single* queue. This is important for the following reasons:

1. It increases robustness.
2. It facilitates uniform handling of errors.
3. It simplifies management.

There are two critical processes with complex functionality. All of the others are "dumb." The first key process in PP is submit. Submit takes an incoming message (local or remote), and places it in the queue. Submit will perform all calculations of the processing required for a given message, and determine how it will be delivered. Early checking ensures that errors are detected at the earliest point, and that later processes can be implemented in a more straightforward fashion. The initial checking includes all management and address verification. Messages may be passed to Submit either by a user agent or by a protocol server known as an inbound channel.

The second key process is the QMGR, or queue manager, which schedules all operations within PP. The QMGR holds the full queue status in memory, and controls the processes which perform the work. By centralising this information in a single process, a range of useful scheduling and management options are made

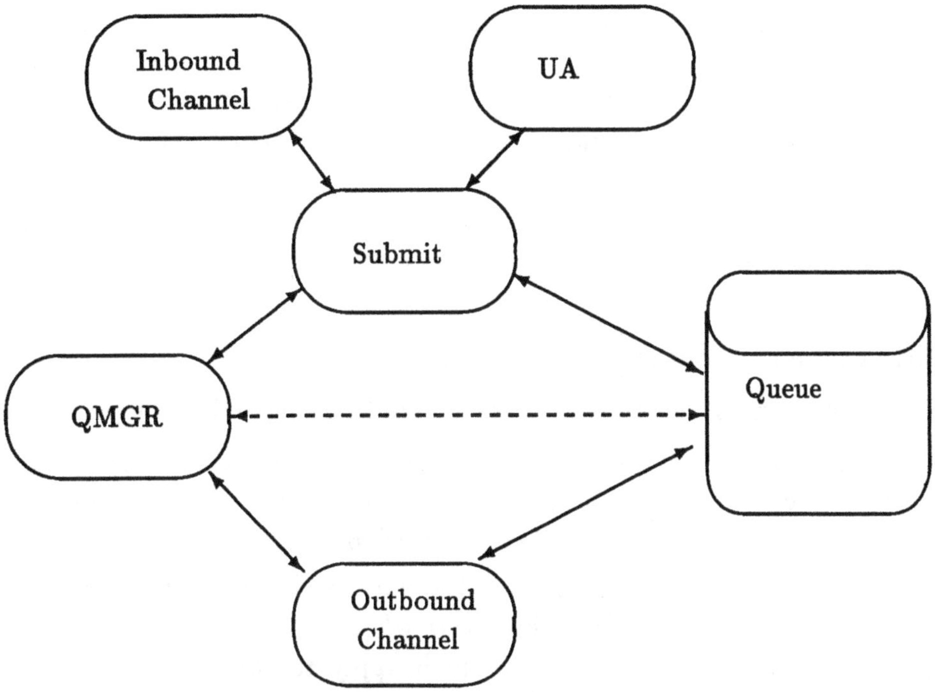


Figure 3.1: PP Process Structure

available, and performance is also improved. The major components controlled by the QMGR are channels, which perform one of two functions:

1. Delivery of a message, either locally or by use of a message transfer protocol (e.g., the X.400 P1).
2. Manipulation of the message within the queue (e.g., to carry out a format conversion).

For a given MTA, there is a single queue and a single QMGR. There may be multiple instances of the Submit process acting at any one time. Channel processes and UA processes are generic (i.e., there are different types), and there may be multiple instances of any specific channel or UA.

## 3.3 Queue Structure

For each message in the queue, there are two components:

1. A file containing the control information for processing the message. This roughly corresponds to the envelope information of X.400.
2. A UNIX directory [1] containing the message as it arrived and zero or more processed forms of the message, together with any associated delivery notifications.

[1]The term UNIX *directory* is used explicitly to distinguish it from the OSI directory.

The control file is text encoded, as there is a big advantage in being able to view and manipulate a queued message by use of a text editor. While this should definitely not be a normal event, it is hard to design management tools for every eventuality. The queue encoding format is designed to be generic, and not tied to a specific protocol. This is important when attempting to support a range of protocols. The key element of the control file is a single line of information for each recipient. The more important parameters associated with each recipient are:

- A unique (integer) key.
- The address of the recipient in one or more forms.
- The sequence of channels which the message should be passed through.
- The status of processing for the recipient, which would include the formatting channels which have been applied, whether the message has been delivered to that recipient, and any delivery notifications needed.

The recipient parameters which change while the message is being processed are encoded in a fixed format, to maximise robustness when a control file is altered. There are also a large number of parameters which apply to the whole message. These include parameters to represent all of the X.400 message transfer service:

- The message originator, using the same encoding as a recipient, to facilitate error returns.
- The message ID.
- A list of encoded information types.
- Deferred delivery date.
- Trace information.

In addition, there are various services not supported by X.400:

- Control of logging on a per message basis.
- Provision of message delayed delivery warnings at a user controlled interval.
- Specification of non-delivery timeout (this can be represented in an extension feature of X.400(1988)).

An example address file is given in Figure 3.2.

The message itself is stored within a UNIX directory, which contains several things:

- A UNIX directory called *base*, which contains the message as submitted.
- Zero or more additional UNIX directories, which contain modified forms of the original message. These UNIX directories are labeled according to the sequence of modifications (channels) which have been applied.
- Zero or more delivery notifications, which are referenced from the control file. Several recipients can share one delivery notification. The advantages of storing the delivery notification with the original message are discussed later.

```
Start-of-MsgEnvPrm
Message-type User-Mpdu
Message-size 971
Return-interval 72
Content-type p2
Encoded-info EncTypes="hdr.p2,ia5"
Original-encoded-info EncTypes=ia5
cont-return true
Inbound-channel x400in
Inbound-mta dec
MsgId string="91516161700991/157870@JOCKEY" Country=GB
   Admin="GOLD 400" Prmd=DIGITAL
Trace Country=GB Admin="GOLD 400" Prmd=DIGITAL
   arrival="Tue, 17 Jul 1990 19:31:08 +0000" action=0
   End-of-block
Trace mta="bells.cs.ucl.ac.uk" Country=gb Admin="gold 400"
   Prmd="uk.ac" arrival="Tue, 17 Jul 1990 21:40:07 +0000"
   action=0 End-of-block
Queued-time "Tue, 17 Jul 1990 21:40:09 +0000"
Origs rno=000 status=done reform-done=000 outchan=x400out
   outmta=dec ext-id=0 resp=false mta-rreq=basic
   usr-rreq=basic type=x400
   orig="/G=ANDREW/S=BUSH/OU=SWS/OU=E00/OU=EUR/O=DIGITAL/
      PRMD=DIGITAL/ADMD=GOLD 400/C=GB/"
   x400="/G=ANDREW/S=BUSH/OU=SWS/OU=E00/OU=EUR/O=DIGITAL/
      PRMD=DIGITAL/ADMD=GOLD 400/C=GB/"
   rfc="ANDREW.BUSH@SWS.E00.EUR.DIGITAL.DIGITAL.gold-400.gb"
   End-of-addr
Recip rno=001 status=pend reform-done=004
   reform-list="p2explode,p2to822,822tojnt,822flatten"
   outchan=gb-janet
   outmta="central-administration.cambridge.ac.uk"
   ext-id=1 resp=true mta-rreq=basic usr-rreq=basic type=822
   eits="ia5,hdr.822-jntmail" content=822
   orig="/S=SANDHAM_D/OU=ADMIN/O=CAM/PRMD=UK.AC/
      ADMD=GOLD 400/C=GB/"
   x400="/S=SANDHAM_D/OU=ADMIN/O=CAM/PRMD=UK.AC/
      ADMD=GOLD 400/C=GB/"
   rfc="SANDHAM_D@central-administration.cambridge.ac.uk"
   End-of-addr
```

Figure 3.2: Example PP Address File

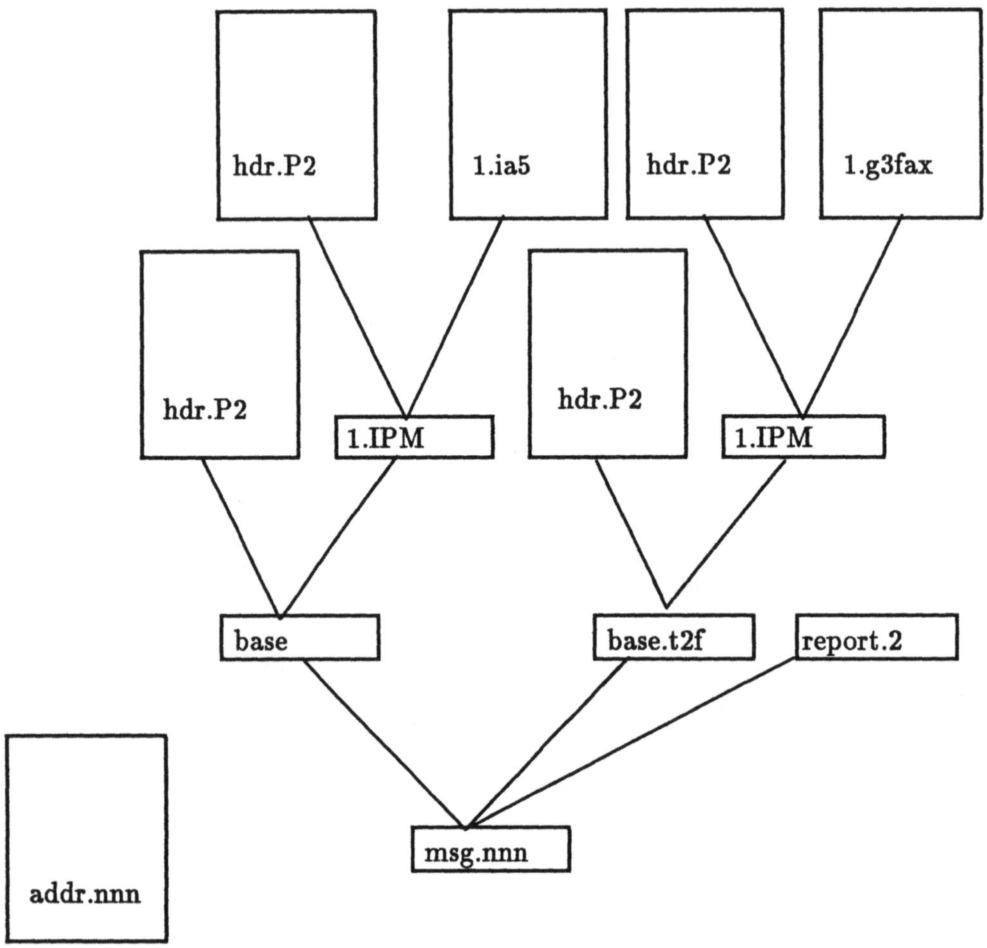


Figure 3.3: PP Queue Entry Structure

A PP message content is stored as UNIX directory. An example is given in Figure 3.3. The message header (P2 or equivalent), and each body part are stored as files. Forwarded messages are stored as subdirectories — the format definition is recursive. Each component is labeled according to its type. Body parts also have a number, so that sequencing can be preserved. For example: a file called "3.ia5" would be the third body part containing IA5 text; a file called "hdr.P2" would contain a heading encoded according to P2. This structure is not constrained to interpersonal messaging (IPM), although IPM is the major target. The main reason for this structure is to facilitate reformatting. By putting the various components into separate files, reformatting can be carried out in a straightforward manner. It is expected that a PP related user agent would also use this structure, as it appears to offer a good basis for flexible construction of Multimedia messages.

## 3.4 Message Submission

The process of message submission is now considered in a little more detail. A message is submitted by either a user agent (local submission) or by an inbound channel, which interacts with Submit through a protocol. The current version of this protocol uses a UNIX interprocess communication (IPC) mechanism (pipes or sockets). The encoding of the current protocol is text based, with parameters equivalent to the queue structure.

The first stage of message submission is for the submitting process to initialise a Submit process. Then all the per-message parameters will be sent to Submit, which will perform validity checks and initial management checks. Submit then acknowledges these parameters, and address checking begins.

PP currently recognises two forms of address: RFC 822 address, and X.400 O/R address. Both of these are handled using a text encoding. For X.400, this uses the RFC 987/RFC 1148 [Kil86b, Kil90b] domain-oriented encoding. A submitting process will select the appropriate form, and then offer each address in turn. There are two modes of interaction:

1. Any errors will be passed back to the submitting process. This is useful for user agents, and interactive protocols such as SMTP [Pos82].
2. A successful response is always passed back to the submitting process, and delivery notifications are generated if necessary (these reside in the queue for later processing). This mechanism is useful for protocols such as X.400 P1, X.400 P3, or JNT mail protocol [Kil84].

Address checking will first determine the MTA to which the message should be sent. After the MTA is determined, an outbound channel is selected. Where an MTA is accessible by multiple channels, channel binding attempts to minimise protocol conversions. Management checking is also carried out at this point, as it is sometimes important to control channel choice for administrative reasons. This includes application of authorisation controls, so that routing can be regulated on the basis of host, network and user. A description of the general approach from which the PP implementation is derived is given in a paper by Kille and Brink [KB85].

Following the determination of the outbound channel, the reformatting requirements are calculated. This will result in a sequence of channels, which will perform the correct series of protocol and body part reformatting on the message in question. This is a surprisingly difficult calculation to make, but it can be done in a reasonably general manner. All of the submission time checking is discussed further in Section 3.9. This will be clearer when more of the PP system is understood.

When all of the recipient addresses have been accepted, the transfer of the content takes place. There is a separate transfer for each component of the initial message stored in the queue. For example:

- An RFC 822 message is submitted as two files.
- A P2 message is submitted as one file.
- A local submission of a complex UNIX directory hierarchy is submitted directly.

Submit understands the P1 level aspects of RFC 1148 [Kil90b, Kil86a]. This means that it can map addresses between the two forms, and will correctly handle trace and message identifiers. Finally, any remaining management checks are done (for example, any required checks on message content), and the message is locked into the queue. Statistical logging is done at this point.

## 3.5 Channels

The term "channel" is used in PP to describe a number of somewhat different components. In essence, each channel takes a message as input, and then provides a different message as output. A channel may put a message into the queue, remove a message from the queue, or transform a message within the queue. Channels which are controlled by the QMGR access the queue through a library. They are trusted processes, and will update the queue. A channel will operate entirely under the direction of the QMGR, and no intelligence is involved. There are several types of channel, which are now described.

### 3.5.1 Outbound Protocol Channels

This basic type of channel will take a message from the queue and transfer it using a message transfer protocol. The outbound protocol channels supported by PP are:

- X.400/P1 (1984)
- X.400/P1 (1988)
- JNT Mail

- SMTP
- UUCP
- DEC Mail 11

Interestingly, the implementation of the X.400 protocol is not really a major problem. The use of the PEPY ASN.1 compiler from the ISODE package has made the mapping of the PP message transfer services onto OSI a relatively mechanical operation [Ros90a, OR88].

### 3.5.2 Other Outbound Channels

An outbound channel is always the last applied to a recipient, and so will cause the message to leave the queue (for that recipient). This does not include handling of delivery notifications, which will happen after the outbound channel is run. There are a number of outbound channels, which are not protocol channels. The first is local delivery, where the message is simply delivered into a local file. PP supports two styles of local delivery:

1. Delivery into a UNIX-style text mailbox.
2. Delivery into a UNIX directory-structured message, equivalent to the PP queue model. This is a flexible format, which has proved very useful for prototyping multimedia user agents.

Local delivery supports delivery time processing based on the delivery parameters and contents of the message. This allows for the user to file messages and to make private actions such as holiday notification or user alert in an X Window System alert program.

An outbound channel is also used to support distribution lists. The destination, in terms of the incoming message, will be the list. The list channel will expand the list, perform any necessary management checks (e.g., permission to send to the list), and resubmit the message as a new message. This means that lists will be provided at the P2 level, rather than at the P1 level. For PP, the major consideration is the ability to support distribution lists for RFC 822 and X.400(1984) systems in a protocol independent manner. The X.400(1988) (protocol dependent) list mechanisms will be fully supported in future releases of PP. In practice, the main difference is whether or not the MTS identifier is preserved across list expansion.

There is also an outbound channel to support the RFC 1148 mapping of delivery notifications onto text messages. PP will map all errors onto delivery notifications; therefore this channel is a critical component, because RFC 822 based systems do not support delivery notifications as protocol elements.

Use is made of appropriate Nameservers and Directories. The SMTP channel uses the BIND nameserver [TPRZ84]. The distribution list channel utilises the OSI directory service by use of the QUIPU DUA API. Further use of the OSI directory is planned.

There is a special channel to deliver messages via G3 fax. This can be seen as a PP-specific implementation of a G3 fax access unit. This is a very useful component for operational services.

### 3.5.3 Inbound Channels

Inbound channels perform the opposite to outbound channels. For each of the protocols supported, there is a channel which will act as a server for the protocol. When an inbound message is received, the channel will invoke Submit. The channel will then pass messages into Submit.

It is also possible for a channel to act as both inbound and outbound. This is necessary to support two-way alternate mode reliable transfer for X.400, or to support P3/P7 style message retrieval which is user agent initiated. In this case, the channel will start as an inbound channel, typically by being invoked as a protocol server. Then it will connect to the QMGR using ROS. The QMGR can choose to accept or reject the association. If it accepts the association, the QMGR will take control and then the channel will behave as an outbound channel. In terms of the QMGR, the use of ROS makes this control model straightforward to provide.

### 3.5.4 Message Reformatting and Protocol Conversion

The flexible handling of reformatting is one of the most important components of PP. This is achieved by reformatting channels which map from one message form into another. As discussed, Submit will calculate a sequence of reformatting channels for each recipient in order to provide the correct conversions. Internally, PP represents different body part and header formats as strings (e.g., "ia5" or "jnt-mail"). Channels will support a set of formats, represented by these strings. The channel may choose to map these into protocol specific encodings (e.g., MTS encoded information types). This approach allows for complex mappings to be calculated and for general extension.

In terms of the overall queue structure, a reformatting channel will take the message directory of a given name, and then create a parallel directory with the new, reformatted message in it. The new directory will have the name of the old one, with the name of the formatting channel appended (e.g., when channel "bitmap2fax" is applied to message directory *base*, a directory *base.bitmap2fax* is created). This will ensure uniqueness when a message undergoes several complex sequences of transformations for different recipients, and will optimise reformatting for multiple recipients.

There are two basic types of reformatting: those which preserve the directory structure, and those which do not. The channels which change directory structure are typically single processes specifically designed for the transformation in question. Channels in PP which fall into this category are:

- Mapping from a flat (i.e., ASN.1 encoded) P2 message into a PP directory hierarchy.
- The reverse of the previous mapping.
- Mapping from a directory hierarchy into an RFC 822 message, according to RFC 934 [RS85].

Many other reformatting channels preserve the directory hierarchy, and simply map from one body part syntax to another. These channels are supported by use of a generic reformatting channel which will drive a simple filter to perform the mapping. Body parts which are not affected by the filter are simply linked across, which avoids unnecessary copying of data. This will enable a wide range of body part types to be supported independently of the core PP code.

Protocol Conversion is an important form of reformatting. In terms of the PP model, protocol conversion channels are no different from other reformatting channels. PP will support RFC 1148 reformatting between X.400 and RFC 822, and also reformatting between variants of RFC 822. X.400 1988 to 1984 downgrading is also supported with a mapping from content type 22 to content type 2 (P2 downgrading).

### 3.5.5 Housekeeping Channels

There are a number of channels which are used for housekeeping operations on the queue. These functions are:

- Removing messages which have been fully processed.
- Tidying up "orphan" entries in the queue.
- Loading the queue from disk.

## 3.6 Robustness Issues

The manner in which delivery notifications are handled is of interest. Delivery notifications are stored with the message, as described above. The queue interface library allows any channel to add a delivery notification. Thus, if a processing error occurs, the channel detecting the error will update the queue and create an appropriate delivery notification. At a later stage, the QMGR can invoke processing of delivery notifications through a channel appropriate for the message originator.

When return of content is requested as a service, this is achieved by use of protocol. It was originally intended that the QMGR may ask for delivery acknowledgement and hold the message locally, rather than asking for return of content as a remote service, and this approach may still be implemented. When the appropriate delivery notification returns, Submit will determine (from the QMGR) which message to associate it with, so that a given recipient can be marked as "delivered and confirmed." This approach seemed a useful way to provide the return of content service (which is particularly important for protocol conversion) in the light of many X.400 services which do not provide it as a remote service. There are real problems associated to guarantee the routing the delivery report back to the MTA which holds it. With this approach is the option to specify "reliable delivery," where PP will specify positive delivery notification, and not remove the message from the queue until it arrives, which may prove to be a valuable user service.

PP goes to some length to only take responsibility for messages when it can do so reliably. The default PP approach is to only accept a message where it can robustly deliver a delivery report back. This means that there will be strict checking of the return address. Some system administrators find this awkward, but it has definite benefits in terms of the overall quality of service.

## 3.7 Queue Control

The QMGR (queue manager) is a single process which controls the scheduling of PP. Experience has shown that disk based queues cause serious performance problems due to the overhead of reading a large queue, typically stored in a UNIX directory. Therefore, the QMGR is memory based, and *never* accesses the queue on disk. The QMGR accesses the external world by use of a protocol based on ROS (OSI Remote Operations service), which supports a wide range of functionality [ISO88]. This use of ROS means that the QMGR does not even have to be resident on the same machine as the queue, and one QMGR could manage several queues. Channels which are invoked by the QMGR are initialised by establishing an OSI association from the QMGR to the channel. The first operation a QMGR must apply is to access a process which will read the queue. This operation is used at intervals to ensure that the QMGR's list reflects the *real queue on the disk*. It may then start channels by establishing associations, and sending commands to deliver messages to explicit recipients. As the QMGR does no processing of messages, it should be fast and able to control many channels.

The queue message control files are read into primary memory, and ordered into a linked structure with complex cross-links sorting the queue in several fashions. The queue can then be scheduled on the basis of many criteria, including:

- Maintaining a connection with a remote MTA (this can be awkward with a disk-based queue).
- Keeping a channel association open.
- Processing high priority messages rapidly.
- Handling timeouts/connection failures to remote MTAs.

The QMGR also allows for a number of useful management aspects. It will control queue maintenance, and send off warning and timeout messages, which is a valuable function not provided by X.400. In addition there are operations to monitor and control the queue at various levels:

- Single message.
- An MTA/Channel pair.
- A whole channel.
- The entire queue.

The manager or user can read selected information about progress. Filters may also be applied, so that the user can ask "Tell me about all of my messages". The manager can turn processing on or off at any level, and modify the contents of per message and per host caches. There is almost certainly scope for cooperating QMGRs to optimise processing in a local environment (e.g., by sharing information on MTA failures). The manager may also choose to force immediate processing of specific messages.

The QMGR also controls cleaning of the queue. Special channels will be invoked to generate warning messages, and to generate delivery notifications on message timeout. A special channel is used to delete messages which do not require further processing.

## 3.8 Management

A good deal of attention has been paid to management features in PP. The intention is to provide a system which is robust and manageable for large volumes of traffic. A key component of PP Management is the MTA console which uses X Window System, illustrated in Figure 3.4.

The full functionality of the QMGR protocols will be used by an MTA Console process. The MTA Console uses the QMGR access protocol to determine and control the state of the queue. In its default mode it provides a permanent display of the status of the MTA which is refreshed at appropriate intervals. This is oriented towards a colour display, so that error states can be indicated by a change from green to yellow to red. There are also load charts to give an indication of the overall load on the MTA, by a number of different metrics. The MTA Console has a control mode where it can be used to examine the status of individual messages, and to give hints to the QMGR as to how it should process the message.

There is a complex scheme of authorisation. This allows for the following services:

- Specification of an overall policy based on channel pairs. MTAs can be grouped on channels to allow for specific types of routing policy. This allows for the following options: open flow; no flow; positive authorisation; negative authorisation. This can lead to the message being rejected or to sending of a warning message.

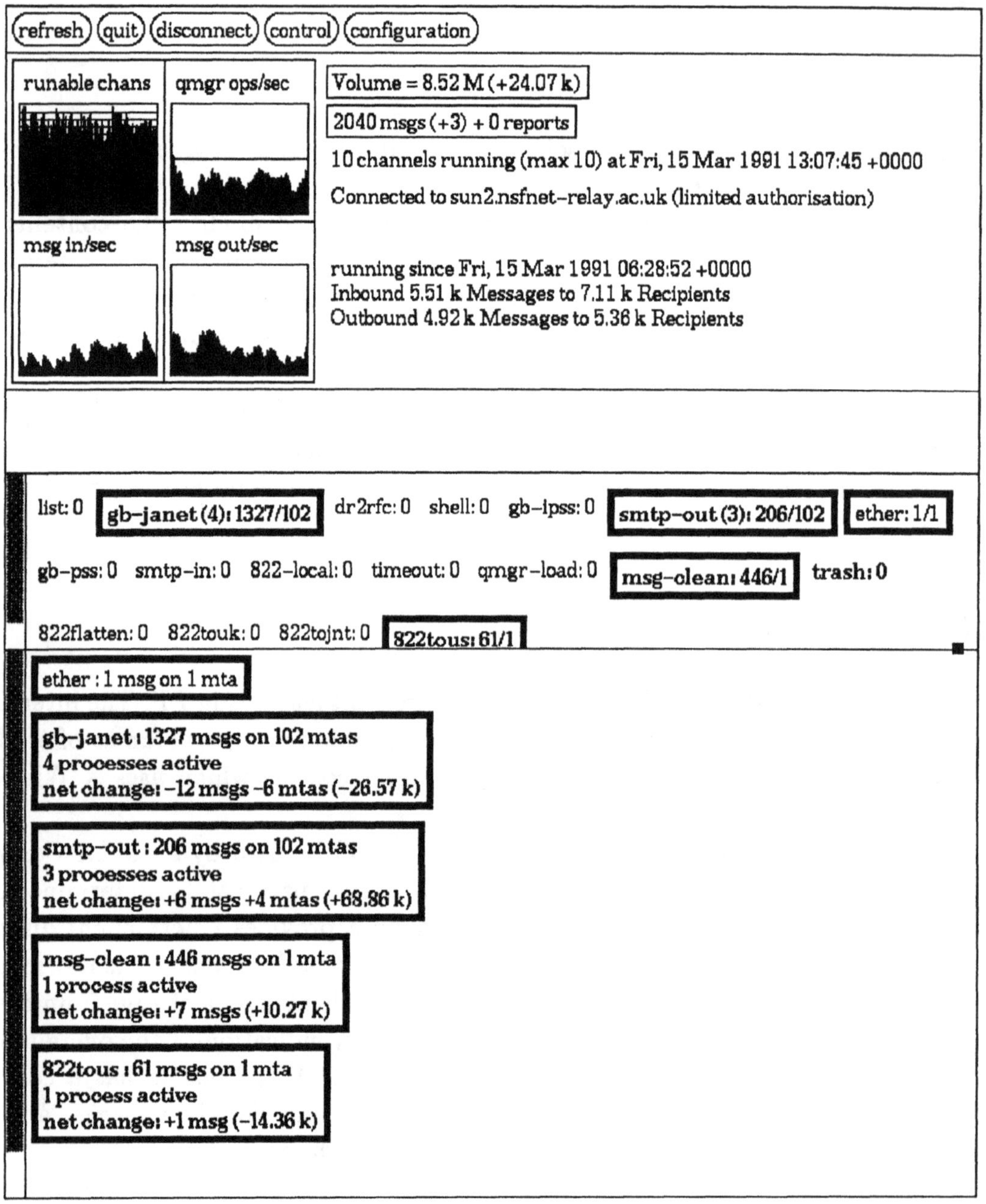


Figure 3.4: MTA Console

- Authorisation on the basis of identified user.
- Authorisation on the basis of (charged) MTA.
- Control of size of message, and permitted encoded information types.

This information is logged in a standard format. These logs, in conjunction with the authorisation tables, give sufficient information to generate bills and other administrative information. In addition to the basic flow information, statistical information is logged on delivery report codes and on delays. These can be processed to generate information on the performance of the MTA.

## 3.9 Submission Time Checking

The per-address checking introduced in Section 3.4 is now described in more detail. It can only be described at this stage, as it needs an overall view of PP to be understood. Currently PP uses table based address handling, with access optimised by the use of hashed lookup. In due course, this will be replaced by the OSI directory.

The first step is to determine a set of MTAs which are suitable as a next hop. This is is done by a calculation which is specific to the address type. For X.400, the "or" table is used, and for RFC 822, the "domain" table. Both of these tables represent a tree hierarchy. The functionality of this approach is described in more detail in [Kil87]. Alternative values are resolved into a "normalized" form. A set of possible MTAs are identified. For some of these MTAs, a channel is also identified. For example, domain lookup will often identfy a defaults an SMTP based channel. If no MTAs are determined directly, an RFC 1148 mapping is attempted to see if routing can be done for the other type of address (i.e., if an X.400 address is supplied it is mapped to RFC 822 and checked in that format or vice versa).

An MTA can support a number of local address spaces, perhaps associated with separate organisations being supported by the MTA. Each local address space is coherent between RFC 822 and X.400. For each local address space, there is an "alias" table which does two things:

1. Specifies alternative values (synonyms), which allow for a local "normalization" of addresses, possibly to nonlocal values.
2. Provides a redirect function, which retains the address in its original form, but redirects an MTS recipient to a new address.

When a local user is identified, this is looked up in the "user" table. This local space may be supported by several MTAs. If a user can be reached by only a subset of the MTAs, this is indicated here. If the message has to be delivered to an MTA other than the current one, then this MTA is selected. A user may have several associated channels. A typical use for this is to have one channel for simple text-only messages and another for messages with other encoded information types, which enables an easy transition to use of a multimedia user agent.

If there are MTAs selected without channels, then the "channel" table is used to select one or more channels. This approach allows MTAs which support two protocols to transfer by whichever protocol avoids protocol conversion. This is a very desirable feature in a multi-protocol environment. It will allow for smooth introduction of X.400.

At the end of this initial routing, there will be a set of channel/MTA pairs identified for the address. Then "format calculations" are made. If any changes are needed, the first step is always to explode the message into the generic internal format, and the last step is to flatten the message into the appropriate protocol specific output format. Format calculation is done by reference to channels which map between pairs of body part types. When Submit is initialised, the mappings of these channels are loaded into a matrix, which facilitates the calculation of multistep conversions. Protocol conversion is done in an analogous manner, with mappings between the headers of messages. Each conversion has an associated cost. The set of channel/MTA pairs will now be ordered by overall conversion cost. This will allow the route to be chosen which minimises the amount of transformation of the message. Finally, the authorisation checks are applied, and the first channel/MTA pair which passes the authorisation checks will be used.

## 3.10 Implementation Issues

There are a few aspects of the implementation which are worthy of specific note. The first is the use of the ISODE package [Ros90a]. This has provided the underlying OSI required for X.400, and the QMGR ROS. The PEPY tool has been used to automatically generate the X.400 ASN.1, and the ROSY and POSY tools have been used to automate the QMGR protocols.

The whole PP system uses a flexible runtime tailoring system, which is used to set various parameters which may vary across a site. In particular:

- Protocol and formatting channel definitions.
- Addressing tables.
- Definitions of encoded information types.

This allows for very rapid extension to add in new networks or reformatting.

Extensive use is made of logging, which can be tailored to a wide range of levels. Besides basic logs for operator, statistics, and debugging, it is also possible to select logs for specific channels or specific messages.

## 3.11 Conformance

The only non-OSI protocol to have a conformance specification is SMTP, which is defined in the host requirements [Bra89]. The PP SMTP is believed to conform to this, although there is no test suite.

PP supports P1(1984). This is a full implementation. It has not been conformance tested, or matched against any of the standard profiles. It is believed that there are no major conformance problems. It is expected to analyze profile conformance in detail during 1991, and that PP will be made to conform to the key European and U.S. profiles before this book is published.

PP supports the core of P1(1988) in both normal and X.410 mode. There are no conformance tests available. All elements of the protocol are handled, but not all of the associated semantics. There is currently no support for:

- Security services.
- Physical delivery (postal service interworking).
- Some aspects of directory usage.

## 3.12 Deployment and Interoperability

PP was first deployed at CeBIT Fair in Hannover in March 1989. Its first major service operation has been to provide X.400 gatewaying services for the UK Academic Community. These services are operated at the University of London Computer Centre. In providing these services, the PP system has interworked with about 40 other different implementations of P1(1984). There have been no major problems in achieving this, although there is some special code to deal with bugs in other X.400 implementations. PP is being taken by sites around the world, particularly for use as a gateway or conversion service.

The 1988 protocols are newer, and the implementation has not been used so extensively. P1(1988) messages have been exchanged with two other implementations, and these are believed to be amongst the earliest uses of this protocol. There has been much interest in PP from the commercial world, and some manufacturers will be using PP as a product base.

## 3.13 Expected Evolution

The major ongoing work on PP is to improve the system in the light of operational experience, and this is expected to lead to the following new components:

- Support for message store protocols, and in particular P7 [MHS88b]. The design for this system is described in [Kil91b]. This provides a general purpose implementation of the message store and a number of private extensions which allow storage of objects other than messages which are called Message-Like Objects (MLO). The PP message store Defines a C API, which can be used by implementors of user agents.
- Development of a number of advanced user agents, especially those with support for multimedia capability, will be done in association with PP, although they will not be a direct part of PP.

- Extensions to the QMGR, to give more sophisticated scheduling. Possibilities include:
  - Reducing processing effort when the CPU load average increases.
  - Scheduling to optimise PTT MHS tariffs.
- Fuller use of OSI directory services will lead to all of PP's tables being replaced in a backwards compatible manner. This will be for local services and for remote services such as routing.
- PP has a lot of management features. Its deployment has led to the demand for further features. In particular, more control is needed from the console in order to modify the queue (e.g., deletion or redirects). There is also a need for cooperative management of a set of MTAs.
- There is much interest in secure messaging, and it is hoped to add a number of the X.400 security features into PP.

## 3.14 Analysis of Design Choices

A fundamental issue is the choice of IPC (interprocess communication) for PP. PP uses a local text-based protocol for submission, and ROS for everything else. This difference is largely for historical reasons. Use of one protocol for the IPC would probably have been cleaner. The use of ROS for the management access has been highly beneficial, due to the ability to monitor MTAs remotely. Functionally, the use of ROS has been a definite success. In general, the ROS-based IPC has a quite high overhead, although we are currently doing extensive work to tune the performance. If it can be tuned sufficiently well, it is probably the best choice for all the IPC. If not, a simpler mechanism would be preferable, perhaps mapping onto the OSI transport service for remote access.

For a number of reasons, it was decided not to use a standard protocol, such as P3, for message submission. The arguments for doing this were:

- Migration becomes much easier when this key internal protocol is a superset of all supported external protocols.
- For user agents and some protocols, it is important to perform address checking prior to transferring the content of the message. P3 does not support this, which is a major deficiency.
- Submit supports both the message transfer abstract service and the MTA abstract service, whereas P3 only supports the former, and a single unified protocol seems desirable.

We believe that experience bears out the validity of these arguments. Some of the other design choices of particular interest are:

### 3.14.1 Protocol Independence

There is clearly a big demand for this. We believe that many sites are choosing PP instead of the many existing X.400 systems precisely for this reason. Most sites wish to operate a mail service, and are not particularly concerned about protocols.

### 3.14.2 Process Modularity

PP has a large number of processes, some of which are quite large (over one MByte). This modularity has been very useful to extend PP. The extensibility is worth the performance cost in many cases.

### 3.14.3 QMGR

The single Queue Manager is a potential bottleneck, but analysis suggests that it will scale to the levels of traffic envisaged, and that it will not be the throughput limit. The unified management view provided by the QMGR has been very important.

### 3.14.4 The Queue Format

The text-based address file has proved its utility in debugging operational problems, although the change away from the protocol representation can sometimes be awkward. The UNIX directory structure of the message has been viewed by some as prohibitively extravagant. However, it has enabled format conversion to be introduced in a flexible and independent manner. I believe that the benefits well justify the cost.

### 3.14.5 Formatting and Conversion approach

The formatting approach has yet to be proven for body part conversion, although it has proven very useful for dealing with protocol conversion. The management aspects of dealing with a very large number of formats may be prohibitive.

### 3.14.6 Management Features

The management features have been a real success. Even more are needed. The MTA Console has been enthusiastically received.

### 3.14.7 Tailoring

The tailoring approach is general and flexible. It is too complex for handling simple cases, and should have a mechanism to deal better with defaults. When suitable skeleton configurations have been provided, the system has been installed without undue difficulty. The improvements in this area need to be tied in with general improvement and automation of the installation procedures.

### 3.14.8 Tables

The modular approach to the PP tables has given a lot of power. However, the configuration has been complex, particularly for simple sites. The transition to use of directory should help this substantially.

### 3.14.9 Overall Performance

Current tuning work on PP has brought it to a level where it can handle up to 50 000 messages per day on a medium sized server. This is about one message in two seconds. We believe that we can increase this to about a million messages per day, with the performance limitation being the filestore on the server. Given that a message will usually remain in the queue for several seconds, this requires PP to operate about a hundred channels simultaneously.

## 3.15 Conclusions

The PP system has been effectively deployed in many places. It is being used to replace existing services. Many managers are finding that the functionality and robustness of PP justify the effort of installing and configuring this large piece of software. It seems likely that PP will be used in many of the research community's major mail gateways around the world.

# Bibliography


[All83] E. Allman. SENDMAIL — an internetwork mail router, 1983.

[BK91] P. Barker and S.E. Kille. The COSINE and Internet X.500 schema, March 1991.

[Bra89] R. Braden. Requirements for internet hosts — application and support. Request for Comments 1123, DDN Network Information Center, SRI International, October 1989.

[CCI88a] The Directory — authentication framework, December 1988. CCITT Recommendation X.509.

[CCI88b] The Directory — overview of concepts, models and services, December 1988. CCITT X.500 Series Recommendations.

[CHI+87] R.H. Cole, C.S. Hall, C. I'Anson, D. Rush, and J. Walker. Mobile Access to secure interpersonal messaging. In *Conference on Open Systems*. ONLINE, April 1987.

[Chi89] P. Chilton. *Introducing X.400*. NCC Publications, 1989. ISBN 0-85012-692-4.

[Cra89] J.A.I. Craigie. UK academic community directory service pilot project. *Computer Networks and ISDN Systems*, 17:305–310, 1989.

[Cro82] D.H. Crocker. Standard of the format of ARPA internet text messages. Request for Comments 822, DDN Network Information Center, SRI International, August 1982.

[Goo91] D. Goodman. COSINE/X.500: an international pilot directory. In *The Electronic Directories Conference*. ONLINE, April 1991.

[ISO87] ISO/CCITT. Specification of abstract syntax notation one (ASN.1), 1987.

[ISO88] Remote operations: Model, notation and service definition, December 1988. ISO/CCITT.

[KB85] S.E. Kille and D.H. Brink. A model of message flow control. *Computer Communication Review*, pages 40–48, October 1985.

[Kil84] S.E. Kille. JNT mail protocol (revision 1.0). Technical report, Joint Network Team, Rutherford Appleton Laboratory, March 1984.

[Kil85] S.E. Kille. Mapping the global naming tree onto a relational database. In *2nd International Symposium on Computer Message Systems, Washington*. North Holland Publishing, September 1985.

[Kil86a] S.E. Kille. Gatewaying between X.400 and other message protocols. In *Conference on Electronic Messaging Systems*, pages 239–248. ONLINE, August 1986.

[Kil86b] S.E. Kille. Mapping between X.400 and RFC 822. Request for Comments 987, DDN Network Information Center, SRI International, June 1986. Also available as UCL Technical Report 120 and as MailGroup Note 19.

[Kil87] S.E. Kille. MHS use of directory service for routing. In *IFIP 6.5 Conference on Message Handling, Munich*, pages 157–164. North Holland Publishing, April 1987.

[Kil90a] S.E. Kille. Management in QUIPU. Research Note RN/90/88, Department of Computer Science, University College London, December 1990.

[Kil90b] S.E. Kille. Mapping between X.400(1988) / ISO 10021 and RFC 822. Request for Comments 1148, DDN Network Information Center, SRI International, March 1990. Also available as MailGroup Note 23.

[Kil90c] S.E. Kille. Using the OSI directory to achieve user friendly naming. Research Note RN/90/29, Department of Computer Science, University College London, February 1990.

[Kil91a] S.E. Kille. Piloting directory services: A transition to full service. In *The Electronic Directories Conference*. ONLINE, April 1991.

[Kil91b] S.E. Kille. PPMS — The PP message store: Overall design. Research Note RN/91/5, Department of Computer Science, University College London, February 1991.

[Kin84] D.P. Kingston. MMDFII: A technical review. In *Usenix Conference*, Salt Lake City, August 1984.

[KK87] G.J. Knight and P.T. Kirstein. Project INCA — an OSI approach to office communications. In *Proc. OSI 87 Conference*. ONLINE, April 1987.

[KLK87] T. Knowles, J. Larmouth, and K.G. Knightson. *Standards for Open Systems Interconnection.* Blackwell Scientific Press, Oxford, 1987. ISBN 0-07-035119-8.

[Man89] C. Manros. *The X.400 Blue Book Companion.* Technology Appraisals, 1989. ISBN 1-871802-00-8.

[MHS84] Recommendations X.400, October 1984. CCITT SG 5/VII, Message Handling Systems: System Model - Service Elements.

[MHS88a] CCITT recommendations X.400 / ISO 10021, April 1988. CCITT SG 5/VII / ISO/IEC JTC1, Message Handling: System and Service Overview.

[MHS88b] CCITT recommendations X.413/ ISO nnnn-1, November 1988. CCITT SG 5/VII, Message Handling Systems: Message Store: Abstract Service Definition.

[Moc84] P.V. Mockapetris. A domain nameserver scheme. In *IFIP WG 6.5 Conference, Nottingham.* North Holland Publishing, May 1984.

[OR88] J.P. Onions and M.T. Rose. The applications cookbook. In *IFIP WG 6.5 Conference on Message Handling Systems and Distributed Applications.* North Holland Publishing, September 1988.

[Pos82] J.B. Postel. Simple Mail Transfer Protocol. Request for Comments 821, DDN Network Information Center, SRI International, August 1982.

[Pre85] D.L. Presotto. Upas — a simpler approach to network mail. In *Usenix Proceedings*, 1985.

[Qua90] J.S. Quarterman. *The Matrix: Computer Networks and Conferencing Systems Worldwide.* Digital Press, 1990. ISBN 1-55558-033-5.

[RC86] M.T. Rose and D.E. Cass. OSI transport services on top of TCP. *Computer Networks and ISDN Systems*, 12(3), 1986.

[RC87] Marshall T. Rose and Dwight E. Cass. ISO Transport Services on top of the TCP. Request for Comments 1006, DDN Network Information Center, SRI International, May 1987.

[Ros89] M.T. Rose. *The Open Book: A Practical Perspective on Open Systems Interconnection.* Prentice Hall Series in Innovative Computing. Prentice-Hall, Englewood Cliffs, New Jersey, 1989. ISBN 0–13–643016–3.

[Ros90a] M.T. Rose. The ISO development environment: User's manual (version 6.0), January 1990.

[Ros90b] M.T. Rose. PSI/NYSERNet White Pages Pilot Project: Status Report. Technical Report 90–09–10–1, Peformance Systems International, Inc., September 1990.

[Ros91] M.T. Rose. *The Little Black Book: Mail-bonding with OSI Directory Services.* Prentice Hall Series in Innovative Computing. Prentice-Hall, Englewood Cliffs, New Jersey, 1991. ISBN 0–13–683210–5.

[RS85] M.T. Rose and E.A. Stefferud. Proposed standard for message encapsulation. Request for Comments 934, DDN Network Information Center, SRI International, January 1985.

[TPRZ84] D.B. Terry, M. Painter, D.W. Riggle, and S. Zhou. The Berkeley internet name domain server. In *Usenix, Salt Lake City*, August 1984.

[Whi84] J.E. White. A user-friendly naming convention for use in communication networks. In *IFIP WG 6.5 Working Conference, Nottingham.* North Holland Publishing, May 1984.

[XDS90] X/Open directory services API specificaction (version 1.0), 1990. X.400 API Association and X/Open Company Limited.

# Part II

# QUIPU Manual: Introduction

# The ISO Development Environment: User's Manual

## *Volume 5: QUIPU*


Colin J. Robbins
X-Tel Services Ltd

Stephen E. Kille
Department of Computer Science
University College London

# Preface

The software described herein has been developed as a research tool and represents an effort to promote the use of the International Organisation for Standardisation (ISO) interpretation of open systems interconnection (OSI), particularly in the Internet and RARE research communities.

## Notice, Disclaimer, and Conditions of Use



In particular, the Northrop Corporation provided the initial sponsorship for the ISODE and the Wollongong Group, Inc., also supported this effort. The ISODE receives partial support from the U.S. Defense Advanced Research Projects Agency and the Rome Air Development Center of the U.S. Air Force Systems Command under contract number F30602–88–C–0016 to NYSERNet Inc.

# Revision Information

The manual contained in Parts II–VII of this book is a pre-release of version 7.0 of QUIPU. No changes are expected. Any changes will be clearly documented in the release.

# Release Information

If you would like a copy of the release described in this document, there are expected to be several avenues available:

- NORTH AMERICA
  For mailings in NORTH AMERICA, send a cheque for 375 U.S. Dollars to:

  | | |
  |---|---|
  | Postal address: | University of Pennsylvania<br>Department of Computer and Information Science<br>Moore School<br>Attn: David J. Farber (ISODE Distribution)<br>200 South 33rd Street<br>Philadelphia, PA 19104-6314<br>U.S.A. |
  | Telephone: | +1 215 898 8560 |

  Specify one:

  1. 1600bpi 1/2–inch tape, or
  2. Sun 1/4–inch cartridge tape.

  The tape will be written in *tar* format and returned with a documentation set. Do not send tapes or envelopes. Documentation only is the same price.

- EUROPE
  For mailings in EUROPE, send a cheque or bankers draft and a purchase order for 200 Pounds Sterling to:

  | | |
  |---|---|
  | Postal address: | Department of Computer Science<br>Attn: Natalie May/Dawn Bailey<br>University College London<br>Gower Street<br>London, WC1E 6BT<br>UK |

  For information only:

  | | |
  |---|---|
  | Telephone: | +44 71 380 7214 |
  | Fax: | +44 71 387 1397 |
  | Telex: | 28722 |
  | Internet: | `natalie@cs.ucl.ac.uk`<br>`dawn@cs.ucl.ac.uk` |

  Specify one:

  1. 1600bpi 1/2–inch tape, or

2. Sun 1/4–inch cartridge tape.

The tape will be written in *tar* format and returned with a documentation set. Do not send tapes or envelopes. Documentation only is the same price.

- EUROPE (tape only)
  Tapes without hardcopy documentation can be obtained via the European UNIX[1] user group (EUUG). The ISODE 7.0 distribution is called EUUGD14.

| | |
|---|---|
| Postal address: | EUUG Distributions<br>c/o Frank Kuiper<br>Centrum voor Wiskunde en Informatica<br>Kruislann 413<br>1098 SJ Amsterdam<br>The Netherlands |
| For information only: | |
| Telephone: | +31 20 5924056<br>(or +31 20 5929333) |
| Telex: | 12571 mactr nl |
| Telefax: | +31 20 5924199 |
| Internet: | `euug-tapes@cwi.nl` |

Specify one:

1. 1600bpi 1/2–inch tape: 130 Dutch Guilders.
2. 800bpi 1/2–inch tape: 130 Dutch Guilders.
3. Sun 1/4–inch cartridge tape (QIC-24 format): 190 Dutch Guilders.
4. 1600 1/2–inch tape (QIC-11 format): 190 Dutch Guilders.

If you require DHL this is possible and will be billed through. Note that if you are not a member of EUUG, then there is an additional handling fee of 300 Dutch Guilders (please enclose a copy of your membership or contribution payment form when ordering). Do not send money, cheques, tapes or envelopes, you will be invoiced.

- PACIFIC RIM
  For mailings in the Pacific Rim, send a cheque for 250 dollars Australian to:

| | |
|---|---|
| Postal address: | CSIRO DIT<br>Attn: Andrew Waugh (ISODE Distribution)<br>55 Barry Street<br>Carlton, 3053<br>Australia |

[1]UNIX is a trademark of AT&T Bell Laboratories.

For information only:

Telephone: +61 3 347 8644
Fax: +61 3 347 8987
Internet: ajw@ditmela.oz.au

Specify one:

1. 1600/3200/6250bpi 1/2-inch tape, or
2. Sun 1/4-inch cartridge tape in either QIC-11 or QIC-24 format.

The tape will be written in *tar* format and returned with a documentation set. Do not send tapes or envelopes. Documentation only is the same price.

- Internet
  If you can FTP to the Internet, you can use anonymous FTP to the host `uu.psi.com` `[136.161.128.3]` to retrieve `isode-7.tar.Z` in BINARY mode from the `isode/` directory. This file is the *tar* image after being run through the compress program and is approximately 4.5MB in size.

- NIFTP
  If you run NIFTP over the public X.25 or over JANET, and are registered in the NRS at Salford, you can use NIFTP with username "guest" and your own name as password, to access `UK.AC.UCL.CS` to retrieve the file `<SRC>isode-7.tar`. This is a 14MB *tar* image. The file `<SRC>isode-7.tar.Z` is the *tar* image after being run through the compress program (4.5MB).

- FTAM on the JANET or PSS
  The source code is available by FTAM at the University College London over X.25 using JANET (DTE `00000511160013`) or PSS (DTE `23421920030013`) with TSEL `259` (ASCII encoding). Use the "anon" user-identity and retrieve the file `<SRC>isode-7.tar`. This is a 14MB *tar* image. The file `<SRC>isode-7.tar.Z` is the *tar* image after being run through the compress program (4.5MB).

- FTAM on the Internet
  The source code is available by FTAM over the Internet at host `osi.nyser.net` `[192.33.4.10]` (TCP port 102 selects the OSI transport service) with TSEL 259 (numeric encoding). Use the "anon" user-identity, supply any password, and retrieve `isode-7.tar.Z` from the `isode/` directory. This file is the *tar* image after being run through the compress program and is approximately 4.5MB in size.

For distributions via FTAM, the file service is provided by the FTAM implementation in ISODE 5.0 or later (IS FTAM).

For distributions via either FTAM or FTP, there is an additional file available for retrieval, called `isode-ps.tar.Z` which is a compressed *tar* image (7MB) containing the entire documentation set in PostScript format.

## Discussion Groups

The Internet discussion group `ISODE@NIC.DDN.MIL` is used as a forum to discuss ISODE. Contact the Internet mailbox `ISODE-Request@NIC.DDN.MIL` to be asked to be added to this list.

# Acknowledgements

Many people have made comments about and contributions to the ISODE which have been most helpful. The following list is by no means complete:

The first three releases of the ISODE were developed at the Northrop Research and Technology Center, and the first version of this manual is referenced as NRTC Technical Paper #702. The initial work was supported in part by Northrop's Independent Research and Development program.

The Wollongong Group supported ISODE for its 4.0 and 5.0 release. They deserve much credit for that. Furthermore, they contributed an implementation of RFC1085, a lightweight presentation protocol for TCP/IP-based internets.

The ISODE is currently supported by Performance Systems International, Inc. and NYSERNet, Inc. It should be noted that PSI/NYSERNet support for the ISODE represents a substantial increase in commitment. That is, the ISODE is now a funded project, whereas before ISODE was always an after-hours activity. The NYSERNet effort is partially supported by the U.S. Defense Advanced Research Projects Agency and the Rome Air Development Center of the U.S. Air Force Systems Command under contract number F30602–88–C–0016 to NYSERNet Inc.

Christopher W. Moore of the Wollongong Group has provided much help with ISODE in terms of both policy and implementational matters. He also performed Directory interoperability testing against a different implementation of the OSI Directory.

Dwight E. Cass of the Northrop Research and Technology Center was one of the original architects of *The ISO Development Environment*. His work was critical for the original proof of concept and should not be forgotten. John L. Romine also of the Northrop Research and Technology Center provided many fine comments concerning the presentation of the material herein. This resulted in a much more readable manuscript. Stephen H. Willson, also of the Northrop Research and Technology Center, provided some help in verifying the operation of the software on a system running the AT&T variant of UNIX.

The *librosap* (3n) library was heavily influenced by an earlier native-TCP version written by George Michaelson, formerly of University College London, in the United Kingdom. Stephen E. Kille, of University College London, provided valuable feedback on the *pepy* (1) utility. In addition, both Steve and George provided us with some good comments concerning the *libpsap* (3) library. Steve is also the conceptual architect for the addressing scheme used in the software, and he modified the *librosap* (3n) library to support half-duplex mode when providing ECMA ROS service. George contributed the CAMTEC X.25 interface. Simon Walton, also of University College London, has been very helpful in providing constant feedback on the ISODE during beta-testing.

The INCA project donated the QUIPU Directory implementation to the ISODE. Stephen E. Kille, Colin J. Robbins, and Alan Turland, at the time all of University College London, are the three principals who developed the 6.0 version of the directory software. In addition, Steve Titcombe, also of UCL spent considerable time on the DIrectory SHell (DISH), and Mike Roe formerly of UCL, put a large amount of effort into the security requirements of QUIPU. Development of the current version of QUIPU has been coordinated by Colin J. Robbins now of X-Tel Services Ltd, and designed by Stephen E. Kille.

The UCL work has been partially supported by the commission of the EEC under its ESPRIT program, as a stage in the promotion of OSI standards. Their support has been vital to the UCL activity. In addition, QUIPU is also funded by the UK Joint Network Team (JNT).

Julian P. Onions, of X-Tel Services Ltd is the current *pepy*(1) guru, having brainstormed and implemented the encoding functionality along with Stephen E. Easterbrook formerly of University College London. Julian also contributed the UBC X.25 interface along with the TCP/X.25 TP0 bridge, and has also contributed greatly to *posy*(1). Julian's latest contribution has been a *transport service bridge*. This is used to masterfully solve interworking problems between different OSI stacks (TP0/X.25, TP4/CLNP, RFC1006/TCP, and so on).

John Pavel and Godfrey Cowin of the Department of Trade and Industry/ National Physical Laboratory in the United Kingdom both contributed significant comments during beta-testing. In particular, John gave us a lot of feedback on *pepy*(1) and on the early FTAM DIS implementation. John also contributed the SunLink X.25 interface.

Keith Ruttle of CAMTEC Electronics Limited in the United Kingdom contributed both the driver for the new CAMTEC X.25 interface and the CAMTEC CONS interface (X.25 over 802 networks). This latter driver was later removed from the distribution for lack of use.

In addition, Andrew Worsley of the Department of Computer Science at the University of Melbourne in Australia pointed out several problems with the FTAM DIS implementation. He also developed a replacement for *pepy* and *posy* called *pepsy*. After moving to University College London, he improved this system and integrated into the ISODE.

Olivier Dubous of BIM sa in Belgium contributed some fixes to concurrency control in the FTAM initiator to allow better interworking with the VMS[2] implementation of the filestore. He also suggested some changes to allow interworking with the FTAM T1 and A/111 profiles.

Olli Finni of Nokia Telecommunications provided several fixes found when testing interoperability with the TOSI implementation of FTAM.

Mark R. Horton of AT&T Bell Laboratories also provided some help in verifying the operation of the software on a 3B2 system running UNIX System V release 2. In addition, Greg Lavender of NetWorks One, under contract to the U.S. Navy Regional Data Automation Center (NARDAC), provided modifications to allow the software to run on a generic port of UNIX System V release 3.

[2]VMS is a trademark of Digital Equipment Corporation.

Steve D. Miller of the University of Maryland provided several fixes to make the software run better on the ULTRIX[3] variant of UNIX.

Jem Taylor of the Computer Science Department at the University of Glasgow provided some comments on the documentation.

Hans-Werner Braun of the University of Michigan provided the inspiration for the initial part of Section 4.2.

A previous release of the software contained an ISO TP4/CLNP package derived from a public-domain implementation developed by the National Institute of Standards and Technology (then called the National Bureau of Standards). The purpose of including the NIST package (and associated support) was to give an example of how one would interface the code to a "generic" TP4 implementation. As the software has now been interfaced to various native TP4 implementations, the NIST package is no longer present in the distribution.

John A. Scott of the MITRE Corporation contributed the SunLink OSI interface for TP4. He also wrote the FTAM/FTP gateway which the MITRE Corporation has generously donated to this package.

Philip B. Jelfs of the Wollongong Group upgraded the FTAM/FTP gateway to the "IS-level" (International Standard) FTAM.

Rick Wilder and Don Chirieleison of the MITRE Corporation contributed the VT implementation which the MITRE Corporation has generously donated to this package.

Jacob Rekhter of the T. J. Watson Research Center, IBM Corporation, provided some suggestions as to how the system should be ported to the IBM RT/PC running either AIX or 4.3BSD. He also fixed the incompatibilities of the FTAM/FTP gateway when running on 4.3BSD systems.

Ashar Aziz and Peter Vanderbilt, both of of Sun Microsystems Inc., provided some very useful information on modifying the SunLink OSI interface for TP4.

Later on, elements of the SunNet 7.0 Development Team (Hemma Prafullchandra, Raj Srinivasan, Daniel Weller, and Erik Nordmark) made numerous enhancements and fixes to the system.

John Brezak of Apollo Computer, Incorporated ported the ISODE to the Apollo workstation. Don Preuss, also of Apollo, contributed several enhancements and minor fixes.

Ole-Jorgen Jacobsen of Advanced Computing Environments provided some suggestions on the presentation of the material herein.

Nandor Horvath of the Computer and Automation Institute of the Hungarian Academy of Sciences while a guest researcher at the DFN/GMD in Darmstadt, FRG, provided several fixes to the FTAM implementation and documentation.

George Pavlou and Graham Knight of University College London contributed some management instrumentation to the *libtsap*(3n) library.

---

[3] ULTRIX is a trademark of Digital Equipment Corporation.

Juha Heinänen of Tampere University of Technology provided many valuable comments and fixes on the ISODE.

Paul Keogh of the Nixdorf Research and Development Center, in Dublin, Ireland, provided some fixes to the FTAM implementation.

Oliver Wenzel of GMD Berlin contributed the RFA system.

L. McLoughlin of Imperial College contributed Kerberos support for the FTAM responder.

Kevin E. Jordan of CDC provided many enhancements to the G3FAX library.

John A. Reinart of Cray Research contributed many performance enhancements.

Ed Pring of the T. J. Watson Research Center, IBM Corporation, provided several fixes to the SMUX implementation in ISODE's SNMP agent.

Finally, James Gosling, author of the superb Emacs screen editor for UNIX, and Leslie Lamport, author of the excellent LaTeX document preparation system both deserve much praise for such winning software. Of course, the whole crew at U.C. Berkeley also deserves tremendous praise for their wonderful work on their variant of UNIX.

Marshall T. Rose
Mountain View, California

# Chapter 4

# Overview

This document describes a non-proprietary implementation of some of the protocols defined by the International Organisation for Standardisation and International Electrotechnical Commission (ISO/IEC), the International Telegraph and Telephone Consultative Committee (CCITT), and the European Computer Manufacturer Association (ECMA).[1]

The purpose of making this software openly available is to accelerate the process of the development of applications in the OSI protocol suite. Experience indicates that the development of application level protocols takes as long as or significantly longer than the lower level protocols. By producing a non-proprietary implementation of the OSI protocol stack, it is hoped that researchers in the academic, public, and commercial arenas may begin working on applications immediately. Another motivation for this work is to foster the development of OSI protocols both in the European RARE and the U.S. Internet communities. The Internet community is widely known as having pioneered computer-communications since the early 1970's. This community is rich in knowledge in the field, but currently is not actively experimenting with the OSI protocols. By producing an openly available implementation, it is hoped that the OSI protocols will become quickly widespread in the Internet, and that a productive (and *painless*) transition in the defense data network (DDN) might be promoted. The RARE community is the set of corresponding European academic and research organizations. While they do not have the same long implementation experience as the Internet community, they have a deep commitment to international standards. It is intended that this release gives vital early access to prototype facilities.

[1]In the interests of brevity, unless otherwise noted, the term "OSI" is used to denote these parallel protocol suites.

## 4.1 Fanatics Need Not Read Further

This software can support several different network services below the transport service access point (TSAP). One of these network services is the DoD transmission control protocol (TCP)[JPost81].[2] This permits the development of the higher level protocols in a robust and mature internet environment, while providing us the luxury of not having to recode anything when moving to a network where the OSI transport protocol (TP) is used to provide the TSAP. However, the software also operates over pure OSI lower levels of software. It is mainly used in that fashion — outside of the United States.

Of course, there will always be "zealots of the pure faith" making claims to the effect that:

> *TCP/IP is dead! Any work involving TCP/IP simply dilutes the momentum of OSI.*

or, from the opposite end of the spectrum, that

> *The OSI protocols will never work!*

Both of these statements, from diametrically opposing protocol camps are, of course, completely unfounded and largely inflammatory. TCP/IP is here, works well, and enjoys a tremendous base of support. OSI is coming, and will work well, and when it eventually comes of age, it will enjoy an even larger base of support.

The role of ISODE, in this maelstrom that generates much heat and little light, is to provide a useful transition path between the two protocol suites in which complementary efforts can occur. The ISODE approach is to use the strengths of both the DDN and OSI protocol suites in a cooperative and positive manner. For a more detailed exposition of these ideas, kindly refer to [MRose90c] or the earlier work [MRose86].

## 4.2 The Name of the Game

The name of the software is the ISODE. The official pronunciation of the ISODE, takes four syllables: *I-SO-D-E*. This choice is mandated by fiat, not by usage, in order to avoid undue confusion.

Please, as a courtesy, do not spell ISODE any other way. For example, terms such as ISO/DE or ISO-DE do not refer to the software! Similarly, do not try to spell out ISODE in such a way as to imply an affiliation with the International Organization for Standardization. There is no such relationship. The *ISO* in ISODE is not an acronym for this organization. In fact, the *ISO* in ISODE doesn't really meaning anything at all. It just has a catchy two syllable sound.

[2] Although the TCP corresponds most closely to offering a transport service in the OSI model, the TCP is used as a connection-oriented network protocol (i.e., as coservice to X.25).

## 4.3 Operating Environments

This release is coded entirely in the *C* programming language[BKern78], and is known to run under the following operating systems (without any kernel modifications):

**Berkeley UNIX** The software should run on any faithful port of 4.2BSD, 4.3BSD, or 4.4BSD UNIX. Sites have reported the software running: on the Sun-3 workstation running Sun UNIX 4.2 release 3.2 and later; on the Sun Microsystems workstation (Sun-3, Sun-4, and Sun-386i) running SunOS release 4.0 and later; on the VAXstation[3] running ULTRIX, on the Integrated Solutions workstation; and on the RT/PC running 4.3BSD.[4] In addition to using the native TCP facilities of Berkeley UNIX, the software has also be interfaced to versions 4.0 through 6.0 of the SunLink X.25 and OSI packages (although Sun may have to supply you with some modified `sgtty` and `ioctl` include files if you are using an earlier version of SunLink X.25). The optional SunLink Communications Processor running DCP 3.0 software has also been tested with the software.

**AT&T UNIX** The software should run on any faithful port of SVR2 UNIX or SVR3 UNIX. One of the systems tested was running with an Excelan EXOS[5] 8044 TCP/IP card. The Excelan package implements the networking semantics of the 4.1aBSD UNIX kernel. As a consequence, the software should run on any faithful port of 4.1aBSD UNIX, with only a minor amount of difficultly. As of this writing, however, this speculation has not been verified. The particular system used was a Silicon Graphics IRIS workstation.[6]

Another system was running the WIN TCP/IP networking package. The WIN package implements the networking semantics of the 4.2BSD UNIX kernel. The particular system used was a 3B2 running System V release 2.0.4, with WIN/3B2 version 1.0.

Another system was also running the WIN TCP/IP networking package but under System V release 3.0. The WIN package on SVR3 systems emulates the networking semantics of the 4.2BSD UNIX kernel but uses STREAMS and TLI to do so.

---

[3]VAXstation is a trademark of Digital Equipment Corporation.

[4]Do not however, attempt to compile the software with the SunPro *make* program! It is not, contrary to any claims, compatible with the standard *make* facility. Furthermore, note that if you are running a version of SunOS 4.0 prior to release 4.0.3, then you may need to use the *make* program found in */usr/old/*, if the standard *make* you are using is the SunPro *make*. In this case, you will need to put the old, standard *make* in */usr/bin/*, and you can keep the SunPro *make* in */bin/*.

[5]EXOS is a trademark of Excelan, Incorporated.

[6]This test was made with an earlier release of this software, and access to an SGI workstation was not available when the current version of the software tested. However, the networking interface is still believed to be correct for the Excelan package.

**AIX** The software should run on the IBM AIX Operating System which is a UNIX-based derivative of AT&T's System V. The particular system used was a RT/PC system running version 2.1.2 of AIX.

**HP-UX** The software should run on HP's UNIX-like operating system, HP-UX. The particular system used was an Indigo 9000/840 system running version A.B1.01 of HP-UX. The system was also reported to have run on an HP 9000/350 system under version 6.2 of HP-UX.

**ROS** The software should run on the Ridge Operating system, ROS. The particular system used was a Ridge-32 running version 3.4.1 of ROS.

**Pyramid OsX** The software should run on a Pyramid computer running OsX. The particular system used was a Pyramid 98xe running version 4.0 of OsX.

Since a Berkeley UNIX system is the primary development platform for ISODE, this documentation is somewhat slanted toward that environment.

## 4.4 Organisation of the Release

A strict layering approach has been taken in the organisation of the release. The documentation mimics this relationship approximately: the first two volumes describe, in top-down fashion, the services available at each layer along with the databases used by those services; the third volume describes some applications built using these facilities; the fourth volume describes a facility for building applications based on a programming language, rather that network-based, model; and, the fifth volume describes a complete implementation of the OSI directory.

In *Volume One*, the "raw" facilities available to applications are described, namely four libraries:

- The *libacsap* (3n) library, which implements the OSI association control service (ACS).
- The *librosap* (3n) library, which implements different styles of the OSI remote operations service (ROS).
- The *librtsap* (3n) library, which implements the OSI reliable transfer service (RTS). and,
- The *libpsap* (3) library, which implements the OSI abstract syntax and transfer mechanisms.

In *Volume Two*, the services upon which the application facilities are built are described, namely three libraries:

- The *libpsap2* (3n) library, which implements the OSI presentation service.
- The *libssap* (3n) library, which implements the OSI session service. and,

- The *libtsap* (3n) library, which implements an OSI transport service access point.

In addition, there is a replacement for the *libpsap2*(3n) library called the *libpsap2-lpp*(3n) library. This implements the lightweight presentation protocol for TCP/IP-based internets as specified in RFC-1085.

In addition, *Volume Two* contains information on how to configure the ISODE for your network.

In *Volume Three*, some application programs written using this release are described, including:

- An implementation of the ISO FTAM which runs on Berkeley or AT&T UNIX. FTAM (file transfer, access and management), is the OSI file service. The implementation provided is fairly complete in the context of the particular file services it offers. It is a minimal implementation inasmuch as it offers only four core services: transfer of text files, transfer of binary files, directory listings, and file management.

- An implementation of an FTAM/FTP gateway, which runs on Berkeley UNIX.

- An implementation of the ISO VT which runs on Berkeley UNIX. VT (Virtual Terminal) is the OSI terminal service. The implementation consists of a basic class, TELNET profile implementation.

- An implementation of the "little services" often used for debugging and amusement.

- An implementation of a simple image database service.

In *Volume Four*, a "cooked" interface for applications using remote operations is described, which consists of three programs and a library:

- The *rosy* (1) compiler, which is a stub-generator for specifications of remote operations.

- The *posy* (1) compiler, which is a structure-generator for ASN.1 specifications.

- The *pepy* (1) compiler, which reads a specification for an application and produces a program fragment that builds or recognises the data structures (APDUs in OSI argot) which are communicated by that application.

- The *librosy*(3n) library, which is a library for applications using this distributed applications paradigm.

In *Volume Five*, the QUIPU directory is described, which currently consists of several programs and a library:

- The *quipu*(8c) program, which is a directory system agent (DSA);

- The *dish*(1c) family of programs, which are a set of directory shell commands; and,

- The *libdsap*(3n) library, which is a library for applications using the directory.

## 4.5 A Note on This Implementation

Although the implementation described herein might form the basis for a production environment in the near future, this release is not represented as "production software".

However, throughout the development of the software, every effort has been made to employ good software practices which result in efficient code. In particular, the current implementation avoids excessive copying of bytes as data moves between layers. Some rough initial timings of echo and sink entities at the transport and session layers indicate data transfer rates quite competitive with a raw TCP socket (most differences were lost in the noise). The work involved to achieve this efficiency was not demanding.

Additional work was required so that programs utilising the *libpsap*(3) library could enjoy this level of performance. Although data transfer rates at the reliable transfer and remote operations layers are not as good as raw TCP, they are still quite impressive (on the average, the use of a ROS interface (over presentation, session, and ultimately the TCP) is only 20% slower than a raw TCP interface).

## 4.6 Changes Since the Last Release

A brief summary of the major changes between v. 6.0 and v. 7.0 are now presented. These are the user-visible changes only; changes of a strictly internal nature are not discussed.

- A new program, *pepsy*, has been developed to replace both *pepy* and *posy*. It is described in *Volume Four*.
- The *dsabuild* program has been removed, in favor of some shell scripts.
- The "higher performance nameservice" has been discontinued in favor of a "user-friendly nameservice". As such, the syntax of the `str2aei` routine has changed. This routine will soon be deprecated, so get in the habit of using the new `str2aeinfo` routine discussed in the ISODE Manual.
- The `na_type` and `na_subnet` fields of the network address structure described in the ISODE Manual have been renamed. For compatibility, macros are provided. These macros will be removed after this release.
- The stub directory facility is now deprecated in favor of an OSI directory based approach. As a result, the *aetbuild* program has been removed.

As a rule, the upgrade procedure is a two-step process: first, attempt to compile your code, keeping in mind the changes summary relevant to the code; and, second, once the code successfully compiles, run the code through *lint* (1) with the supplied lint libraries.

Although every attempt has been made to avoid making changes which would affect previously coded applications, in some cases incompatible changes were required in order to achieve a better overall structure.

# Chapter 5

# Overview of QUIPU

## 5.1 Summary

QUIPU is a Public Domain implementation of the OSI directory as specified in CCITT X.500 Recommendations / ISO 9594 for directory services [ISO88, CCITT88]. It is intended to provide an environment for experimentation and for early pilots using standardised directory services. QUIPU is currently aligned to the ISO IS. QUIPU is also aligned to the NIST directory Implementors Guide Version 1, with the following exceptions:

- QUIPU does not enforce the bounds constraints on attributes, filters or APDU size.
- T.61 string formatting characters are not rejected.
- If a DN is supplied with no password in an unprotected simple bind, QUIPU does not always check to see if the DN exists. If the DSA connected to can say authoritatively the DN does not exist, the association is rejected. However, if a chain operation is required to check the DN, the bind is allowed.
- When comparing attributes of UTCtime syntax, if the seconds field is omitted, QUIPU does not perform the match correctly (i.e., the seconds field in the attribute values should be ignored, but is not).
- QUIPU always supplies the optional chaining argument "originator" even if the CommonArgument "requestor" is used.
- QUIPU always supplies the optional chaining argument "target" even if the base object in the DAP arguments is the same.
- The object class "without an assigned object identifier" is not recognised unless the "alias" object class is also present.
- Non Specific Subordinate References are never followed by a QUIPU DSA, but they are passed on correctly to the client if generated.

- The "entryOnly" chaining argument introduced by the DIG is recognised, but never set by a QUIPU DSA.[1]

QUIPU is intended to provide an environment for early experimentation with standardized directory services. It is used by the ISODE for identification of the location of OSI applications (including QUIPU) and for provision of white and yellow page services. The directory abstract service and DSA abstract service defined in [CCITT88, ISO88] and their associated protocols are supported.

Major aspects of the QUIPU implementation are:

- Use of memory structures to provide fast access.
- Activity scheduling within the DSA to allow for multiple accesses.
- General and flexible searching capabilities.
- Extensions to provide access control.
- External schema management.
- Use of the directory to control distributed operations.

The current implementation provides a DSA, and a procedural interface to the directory abstract service, which will enable other applications to use the directory. There is also a directory shell interface — DISH. This provides full access to the directory abstract service, using the procedural interface. standard distributed operations are used with both referrals and chaining (using the directory system protocol) provided.

A full discussion of the design issues relating to QUIPU can be found in [SKill89b].

## 5.2 Pronouncing QUIPU

The name of the INCA directory is QUIPU. The official pronunciation of QUIPU takes two syllables: *kwip-ooo.*

## 5.3 Why QUIPU

QUIPU was originally developed as a part of the INCA project. The Incas of Peru did not have writing. Instead, they stored information on strings, carefully knotted in a specific manner and with coloured thread, and attached to a larger rope. These devices were known as *Quipus.* The encoding was obscure, and could only be read by selected trained people: the *Quipucamayocs.* The Quipu was a key component of Inca society, as it contained information about property and locations throughout the extensive Inca empire.

[1] It is generated if the COMPAT_6_0 compile option is removed — See Section 16.1.

# 5.4 Objectives

## 5.4.1 General Aims

QUIPU has a number of general aims:

- To produce an implementation which follows the emerging OSI directory standards.
- Flexibility to enable the system to be used for experimentation and research into problems relating to directory service.
- Investigation of distribution and replication.
- Pilot experimental usage.

## 5.4.2 Technical Goals

The major goals of the QUIPU directory service are:

- Full support of the directory access protocol, directory system protocol, and distributed operations, as defined in [CCITT88].
- Support of the majority of the service elements specified in [CCITT88].
- Ability for interworking with other directory implementations, including use of referrals and chaining.
- Very full searching and matching capabilities, beyond the minimum required by [CCITT88].

The following are not goals:

- In practice, the memory based approach has led to a quite fast lookup and searching.
- The ability to handle very large volumes of data (e.g., greater than 100 MB or 1 Million entries per DSA) is not a requirement.
- Substantial data robustness is not required: there is no need to employ complex data backup techniques.
- Use (as opposed to provision) of authentication services.

# 5.5 Roadmap

This manual is split into six parts in this book. You are reading Part II, which is a general introduction. Part III describes a set of user interfaces (DUAs) developed as part of QUIPU. Part IV, an administrators guide, describes how to set up both the DUAs introduced in Part III, and how to install and manage a QUIPU directory system agent (DSA). Part V is a programmers guide which discusses a procedural interface to the directory for those of you who want to write your own DUAs. Part

VI is a discussion of some of the design issues not already covered elsewhere; this is essentially included for those of you who are interested in the DSA implementation. Finally, Part VII contains appendices.

## 5.6 QUIPU Support Address

If you have any problem installing QUIPU, following the documentation or any other QUIPU-related problems, then there are two discussion lists.

Comments concerning the operation of QUIPU should be addressed to the QUIPU support address:

| | |
|---|---|
| Internet Mailbox: | `quipu-support@cs.ucl.ac.uk` |
| Janet Mailbox: | `quipu-support@uk.ac.ucl.cs` |
| X.400 Mailbox: | `surname = quipu-support` |
| | `ou = cs` |
| | `Org = UCL` |
| | `PRMD = UK.AC` |
| | `ADMD = Gold 400` |
| | `C = GB` |

Or, you could look up the mailbox attribute of

```
c=GB
o=University College London
ou=Computer Science
cn=QUIPU-Support
```

in the directory.

There is also a discussion list for a general discussion of topics related to QUIPU; the address is as above, but with "quipu-support" replaced by just "quipu" (e.g., quipu@cs.ucl.ac.uk). We suggest that everybody who is intending to run QUIPU should be on this list, as this will be used to keep you informed of what is happening. Details of updates will also be sent to this list.

If you would like to be added to the quipu discussion list, send a message to "quipu-request" (e.g., quipu-request@cs.ucl.ac.uk).

## 5.7 Acknowledgements

QUIPU was developed at the Department of Computer Science at University College London, under the ægis of the INCA (Integrated Network Communication Architecture) project, which is project 395 of ESPRIT (European Strategic Programme for Research into Information Technology). The partners of INCA (GEC plc, Olivetti, Nixdorf AG, and Modcomp GmbH) are acknowledged for releasing this software into the public domain.

Continued funding of QUIPU as openly available software is provided by the Joint Network Team (JNT).

QUIPU 6.0 was implemented primarily by Colin Robbins and Alan Turland, with considerable help from Marshall Rose of Performance Systems International. Mike Roe implemented the authentication code, and the T.61 string handling code.

After QUIPU 6.0, the core development has been from Colin Robbins. Tim Howes of University of Michigan has kindly donated the very valuable "TURBO" options to QUIPU. Alan Turland has added the asynchronous DUA interface.

Chris Moore of the Wollongong Group helped considerably in the early development of QUIPU, and integration with ISODE. Simon Walton of University College London, also provided much help in integrating the software with ISODE.

Steve Titcombe of University College London did much of the early work on DISH, and is now working on the management tools.

Paul Sharpe, of GEC Hirst Research Laboratories put considerable effort into the early development of SD. This work was continued at Brunel University by Andrew Findlay, Damanjit Mahl, and Stefan Nahajski who have also developed the POD and XD interfaces.

Paul Barker of University College London has designed and developed the "dsc" DUA interface, the DSA log processing scripts and has provided very valuable feedback throughout the project.

Whilst at UCL on secondment from CSIRO, Andrew Worsley put considerable effort into enhancing Pepsy to provide all the extra features the QUIPU needed to be able utilise the tool.

George Michaelson of the University of Queensland, Julian P. Onions of X-Tel Services Ltd, Andrew Findlay of Brunel University, Gier Pederson from the University of Oslo, Petri Jokela of Telecom in Finland, Juha Heinanen of the Tampere University of Technology, Peter Yee from NASA and Piete Brooks of Cambridge University, have all run various test versions of the system, and provided much useful feedback.

Kevin Jordan from The Control Data Corporation has given the G3 fax handling code a much needed overhaul.

# Part III

# QUIPU Manual: User's Guide

# Chapter 6

# The OSI Directory

This chapter is designed as a quick introduction to the model of X.500 directories, to provide the reader with sufficient information to be able to understand the following chapters.

## 6.1 The Model

The OSI directory is intended to support human user querying, allowing users to find, *inter alia*, telephone and address information of organisations and other users.

It is also intended to support electronic communication such as message handling systems and file transfer. The directory provides name to address mapping to support, for example, OSI presentation address look-ups. Message handling systems will be provided with support for user-friendly naming, security and distribution lists.

In essence the directory is a database with certain key characteristics.

- The directory is intended to be very large and highly distributed. It is anticipated that the directory will be distributed largely on an organisational basis.
- The directory is hierarchically structured, the entries being arranged in the form of a tree called the directory information tree (DIT). An example DIT is shown in Figure 6.1. Entries near the root of the tree will usually represent objects such as countries (e.g., "GB") and organisations (e.g., "University College London"), entries at or near the leaves of the tree will represent people (e.g., "Colin Robbins"), equipment or application processes.
- Read and search operations will dominate over modification operations.
- Temporary inconsistencies in the data are acceptable. This greatly facilitates the replication of data in the directory by obviating concerns about record locking and atomic operations.

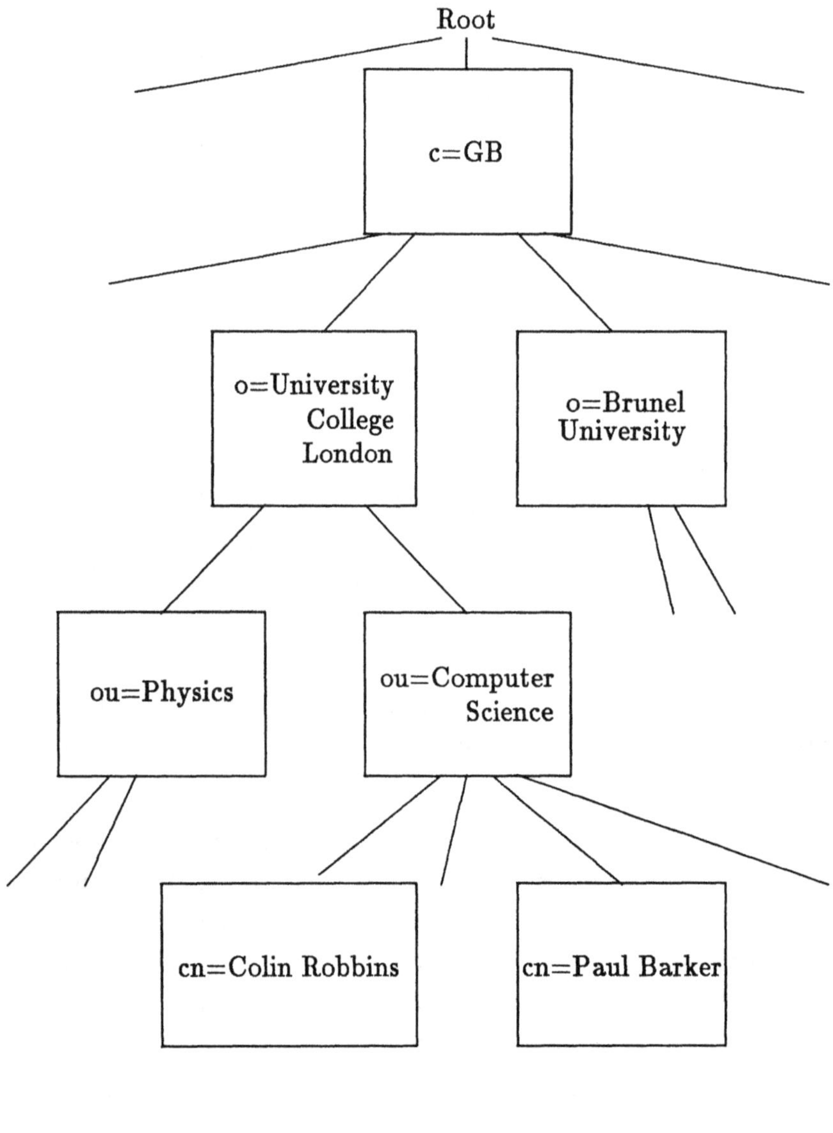


Figure 6.1: Example DIT

## 6.2 Information Representation

There are various structures needed to represent the data required in the directory database. These are described briefly below.

### 6.2.1 Object Identifiers

An important part of the OSI world is the object identifier (OID).

An OID is a hierarchy of numbers used uniquely to describe various objects within the OSI world: for example, "1.0.8571.1.1" describes the FTAM protocol; "0.9.2342.19200300.99.1" defines a QUIPU attribute type. The strings of numbers look "horrible" and can be difficult to remember. As such, QUIPU provides a mapping from OIDs to "strings", so that easy to remember strings can be used in place of the numeric OIDs, for example "iso ftam" or "quipuAttributeType".

The mappings are defined in a set of oidtables which are discussed in Section 18.11.

### 6.2.2 Attributes

The directory holds information about various entities, such as a person or an organisation. The information is held in an information object, typically referred to as an *entry*. An entry consists of a set of one of more attributes (see Figure 6.2).

An attribute is represented by an attribute type and a set of attribute values. An attribute with a single value is represented as follows:-

<attribute type> "=" <attribute value>

The attribute type can either be a string (which must be in the attribute oidtable — see Section 18.11) or the OID in a dotted decimal format.

Each attribute value is represented by a string, the format of the attribute value depends upon the syntax defined in the oidtables, but in general will be a string.

So

```
roomNumber = G24
2.5.4.20   = 453-5674
commonName = Colin Robbins & Colin John Robbins
photo      = {ASN} 0308207b4001488001fd...
```

is an example of an entry, with 4 attributes. The "commonName" attribute is multivalued, with the two values separated by the "&" symbol. Notice how the "photo" attribute does not have a specific string format, so a hexadecimal "ASN.1" representation is used. "2.5.4.20" is an object identifier represented in numeric form.

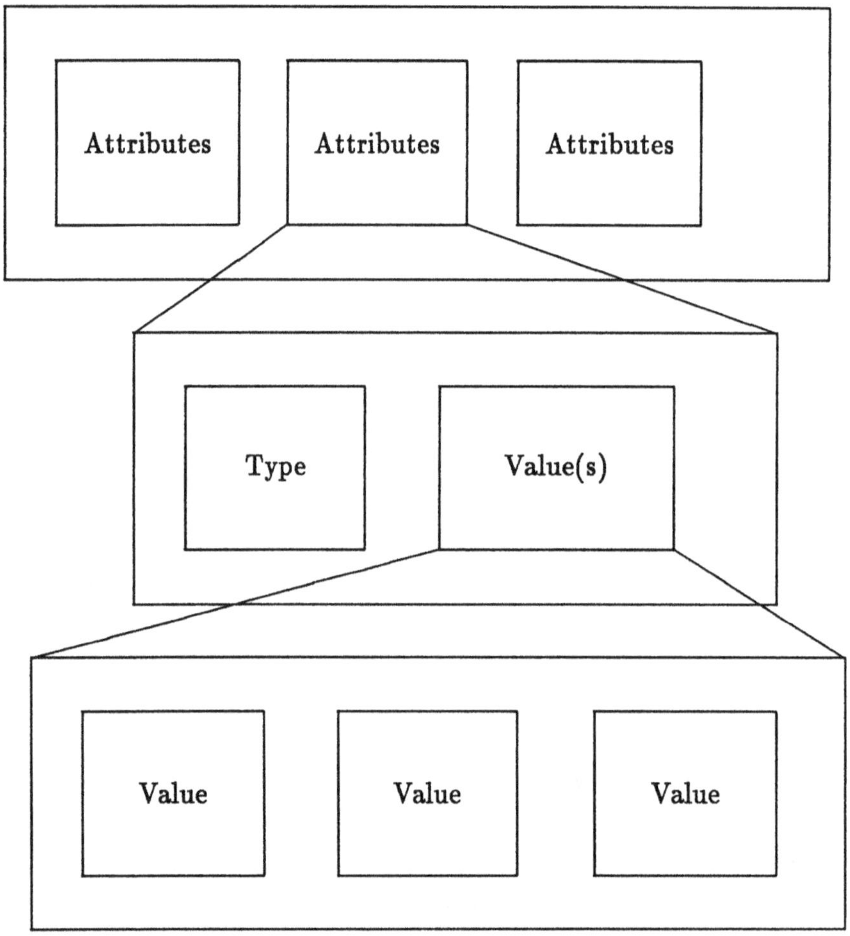


Figure 6.2: Structure of an Entry

### 6.2.3 Names

Within an entry, some attributes (generally one) have special importance, and are called distinguished attributes. The collection of these attributes form the relative distinguished name (RDN).

An RDN is usually represented by a single valued attribute, thus

```
commonName = Alan Turland
organization = University College London
```

are valid RDNs.

An RDN made up of multiple distinguished attributes uses the % symbol to separate the values, for example

```
userid = quipu % commonName = Colin Robbins
```

A distinguished name (DN) is the sequence of RDNs that uniquely define a node in the directory information tree (DIT). These are represented as follows:-

RDN [ "@" RDN ...]

So

```
countryName = GB @ organization = University College London
```

is an example of a valid DN.

In some cases an RDN or DN is specified relative to a node other than the root in the DIT. To be unambiguous a DN may be rooted using a leading "@", for example

```
@ countryName = GB @ organization = University College London
```

## 6.3 Directory User Agent

The directory user agent (DUA) is the entity you as a user will connect to when you interact with the directory service. It will help you formulate your queries, wrap them up in the required protocol, pass them to the directory, and then show you the results obtained.

The X.500 standard defines only the protocol the DUA should use when talking to the directory, and as such DUAs come in many varieties, but the basic concepts are the same.

A DUA talks to the directory using the directory access protocol (DAP).

The following chapters of this part of the manual describe several such DUA interfaces available in the ISODE. It is left to system managers to decide which form of interface is appropriate at your site, and which to install. There now follows a brief description of each interface:

**dish:** The directory shell
This interface give a user full access to the DAP, and as such may be complex for novice users.

**sid:** Steve's Interface to DISH
A set of scripts that make DISH usable for novice users.

**dsc:** Directory SCript
A shell script using DISH aimed at novice users.

**fred:** FRont End to Dish
Fred provides a white pages user interface, which hides most of the complexity of the OSI directory.

**pod:** Popup directory
A DUA for the X Window System[1].

**xd:** X directory
Another DUA for the X Window System.

**sd:** Screen directory
A curses-based DUA.

**ufn:** User Friendly Name
A very simple example interface that takes a UFN and returns a distinguished name [SKill90].

## 6.4 Directory System Agent

The directory system agent (DSA) is the entity that generates the results to requests from a DUA. It may handle the request itself, ask another DSA (using the directory system protocol), or advise the DUA to contact another DSA (see Figure 6.3). This part of the directory is discussed more in Parts IV and VI of this manual. Here we shall concentrate on the DUA.

---

[1]The X Window System is a trademark of the Massachusettes Institute of Technology

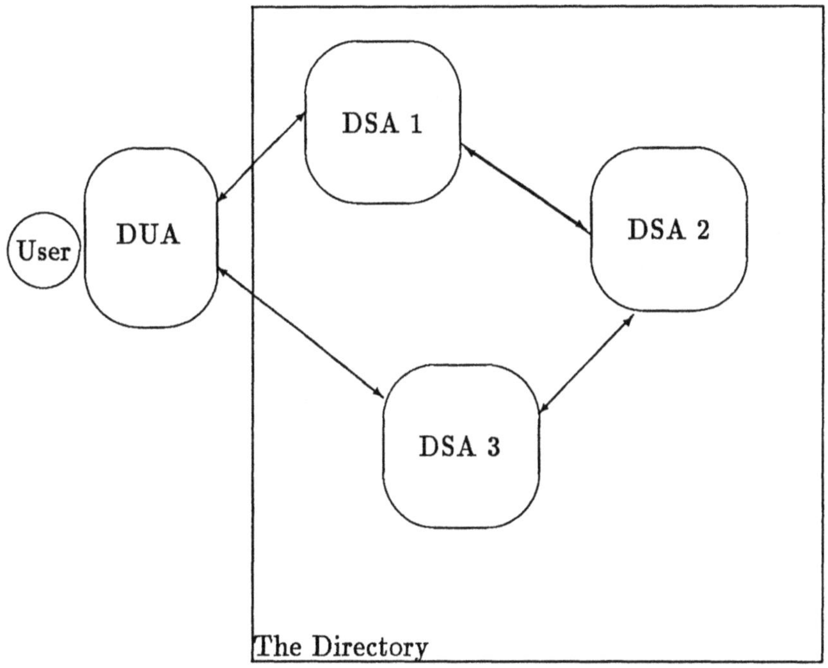


Figure 6.3: DUA/DSA Interaction

# Chapter 7

# DISH

This chapter describes DISH, a directory shell interface to the directory. It provides an interface to the directory in an similar manner to the way that MH provides an interface to a message handling systems. As with MH, DISH can either be invoked as a single process with the full repertoire of commands built in, or it can be invoked by individual shell commands. This latter style allows DISH to be used with others tools to provide very flexible access to the directory.

DISH provides a very powerful interface onto the directory and gives a user access to the full directory access protocol(DAP). The price of such comprehensiveness is complexity. DISH has a large number of flags, and both the syntax and volume of typing required can seem forbidding to the novice user. One compromise solution is to use DISH to build interfaces which are easier to use and more intuitive, for example SID and DSC (see Chapters 8 and 9).

To run DISH in interactive mode invoke *dish*(1c), then issue any of the commands described in Section 7.1. This mode of operation is especially useful for novice users. The process of connecting to the directory — binding — takes place automatically when the program is invoked, and an unbind is issued when you quit.

The arguments to *dish*(1c) are the same as for bind (see Section 7.1.13), with the addition of a "-pipe" flag which is used to start DISH in "shell" mode (see Section 7.7) (Note: "dish -pipe &" has the same effect as the shell command "bind").

## 7.1 Commands

Each of the DISH commands described in this section has a large number of valid flags. The full names of the flags are given below; however, the shortest unique name is sufficient to select the flag. Similarly, when DISH is used interactively the shortest unique name is taken for the command name (e.g., "l" for "list"). There is an exception in that "sh" is interpreted as "showentry", "shown" must be typed for "showname".

The additional flag `-help` can be specified with every command to get limited runtime help.

### 7.1.1 Moveto

With nearly every command it is possible to supply the distinguished name of the object you want to reference. In the syntax used to describe the DISH commands this is represented by

```
<object>.
```

An initial '`@`' in an object description specifies that the name is relative to the root of the directory information tree (DIT), otherwise the name is taken as being relative to the current position in the DIT. The special name component ".." is used to mean "one position up" from the current position. Some examples of valid names and their interpretation relative to how a distinguished name is built up are shown below by the following sequence of names:

**`@c=GB@o=University College London@ou=Computer Science:`**
The specified object is
"c= GB @ o= University College London @ ou= Computer Science".

**`cn=Colin Robbins:`** describes the object cn=Colin Robbins relative to the current position ("c= GB @ o= University College London @ ou= Computer Science @ cn= Colin Robbins"). Spaces in a name will be seen as the start of a separate argument by the shell, so the name must be quoted.

**`..@cn=Steve Titcombe:`** describes the entry cn=Steve Titcombe at the same level in the DIT as the current position ("c= GB @ o= University College London @ ou= Computer Science @ cn= Steve Titcombe").

Objects can also be expressed in the form of sequence numbers and nicknames. See Sections 7.2 and 7.4.1.

When you specify an object, the current position in the DIT is not changed. To change the current position you should use the command

```
moveto [-[no]pwd] [-[no]check] <position>
```

The `-pwd` flag tells moveto to print the current position in the DIT. The `-nocheck` flag tells moveto NOT to check the entry exists, normally, moveto will invoke `read` to check that the named entry exists.

The current position can also be changed with the `-move` flag to showentry and list commands (see Sections 7.1.3 and 7.1.2).

### 7.1.2 Showentry

```
showentry [<object>] [-[no]cache] [-[no]name]
          [-[no]move]
          [<any of the read arguments>]
          [<any of the fred arguments>]
```

Showentry will display some or all of the attributes of the specified entry. A combination of the read argument flags and your */.quipurc* file described later in the chapter are used to define which attributes to show.

The **-noname** option tells showentry to show the distinguished name of the current entry as well as the attributes.

**-cache** is used to tell showentry to use cached information only — do not issue a read operation. This is used to see what the DUA has cached, and then get information when the local DSA is unavailable.

**-nocache** is used to enforce a directory read. This is used to update the cache directly.

**-move** is used to tell DISH to change the current position in the DIT to the object specified as well as showing the requested attributes.

See Section 7.1.4 for a discussion of the flags for FRED.

#### read flags

These flags are used by showentry (1), showname (1) and search (1).

```
[-[no]types <attribute-type> *] [-[no]all]
[-[no]value] [-[no]show]
[-[no]key] [-edb]
[-proc <syntax> <process>]
```

The **all** flag request that all attributes are read (default).

The **value** flag reads the attribute value, which is the default, the inverse is to read the attribute types only.

The **novalue** flag says print the attribute types only.

The **show** flag is used to make DISH show the requested attributes (this is the default for read, but not for search).

The **key** flag determines whether the key (attribute type) will be shown along with the attribute value.

The **edb** flag requests that the data is displayed in "EDB" format, that is, a format which can be used in QUIPU data files. This is not such a nice format to present users, but is easier to manage in shell scripts.

The **type** flag requests that only the supplied attributes are read from the DSA; the inverse of this **-notype** does not prevent the attributes being read (as there is no easy mechanism to perform this within X.500), but it does stop them being shown.

The **proc** flag is used to instruct the display routines to use an external process to display the attribute. For example if you have a process that displays presentation elements representing "OID's" in a particular way, then you can use

```
showentry -proc OID /usr/bin/oid_display_process.
```

All OIDs will then be displayed using "/usr/bin/oid_display_process". The process should read the presentation element from the standard input, and place any textual results on the standard output.

### 7.1.3 List

```
list [<object>] [-nocache] [-noshow] [-[no]move]
```

This function displays the relative distinguished names of the children below your current position in the DIT. Typically, if there are a large number of children, you will not be able to list them all, as a "sizelimit" will prevent you. For example

```
DISH -> list
1    commonName=Camayoc
2    commonName=Colin Robbins
3    commonName=Jess
4    commonName=Julian Onions
5    commonName=lancaster
6    commonName=PP Support
7    commonName=QUIPU Support
8    commonName=Tony Roadknight
9    commonName=Hugh Smith
10   commonName=Peter Cowen
(Limit problem)
DISH ->
```

shows a size limit of 10. Using the `-sizelimit` service control you can often increase this limit up to some administrative limit (typically 100) set by the DSA you are connected to.

`-nocache` tells list to reread the directory — do not use cached information.

`-noshow` tells list not to display the names found, but still construct sequences (see Section 7.2).

`-move` is used to tell DISH to change the current position in the DIT to the object specified.

### 7.1.4 Search

```
search  [[-object] <object>]
        [-baseobject] [-singlelevel] [-subtree]
        [[-filter] <filter>]
        [-[no]relative] [-[no]searchaliases]
        [-[no]partial] [-hitone]
        [<any of the read arguments>]
        [-fred [-expand] [-full] [-summary]
               [-nofredseq] [-subdisplay]]
```

Search the DIT, starting at the object specified, for entries that match the given filter. When an entry is found to match the filter, only distinguished name is printed unless a '`-show`' option is specified, when the attributes are displayed as well.

If no filter is specified, a default filter (which matches any object in the DIT) is used. This operation has a similar effect to a list operation, but attributes can be shown at the same time.

If no flags are given to a search command, then only one parameter is allowed. This is taken to be the filter and NOT the base object as in ALL the other commands. The flags `-filter` and `-object` are supplied to allow the user to specify if both a filter and base object are required. (NOTE only one need be flagged.) For example, the following are all valid search commands:

```
search
search <filter>
search -filter <filter>
search -object <object>
search -filter <filter> -object <object>
search <filter> -object <object>
search -filter <filter> <object>
```

whereas

```
search <object>           (interpreted as a filter !)
search <filter> <object>
```

are not valid.

The three flags `-baseobject`, `-singlelevel`, and `-subtree`are mutually exclusive. They are used to control the depth of the search operation. The `-baseobject` option searches only the specified object. The `-singlelevel`option specifies all siblings of the specified object should be searched. The flag `-subtree`searches all the levels below and including the current position recursively. The default is `-singlelevel`.

For example:

| Class | Characters |
|---|---|
| 1 | BFPV |
| 2 | SCGJKQXZ |
| 3 | DT |
| 4 | L |
| 5 | MN |
| 6 | R |
| 0 | all others (ignored) |

Figure 7.1: Soundex Character Classes

```
search -object
   "@c=GB@o=University College London@ou=Computer Science"
   -subtree -filter "cn=colin robbins" -type telephoneNumber
   -show
```

will search the DIT subtree below "c=GB @ o=University College London @ ou=Computer Science" for an exact match of "colin robbins", and then call showentry to display the *telephoneNumber* attribute.

The `-norelative` flag is used to tell `showname` to print the full distinguished name of the results; otherwise, the name relative to the current position is printed.

The `-[no]searchaliases` flag directs the search as to whether aliases encountered in the search should be dereferenced and thus searched. This is different to the `-[dont]dereferencealias` service control which defines what happens to aliases found when locating the base object of the search, whilst the `-[no]searchaliases` controls aliases encountered in the siblings of base search object. The default is "`-dereferencealias -nosearchaliases`".

The `-hitone` flag is used to tell DISH to consider it an error if the search returns more than one entry. This is particularly useful when using DISH from shell scripts (see Section 7.7).

From time to time, search will not be able to do the entire search, and will return partial results; the `-nopartial` directs DISH not to print the partial result information. To see the full set of partial results, both `-partial` and `-show` are needed; otherwise only a summary is printed. Unlike referral errors, DISH does not follow these partial references.

### More on Matching

When searching for an exact match ("="), the "*" character is used as a wildcard, and a substring match takes place (unless only a "*" is specified, when a *presence* match is used; hence any entry containing that attribute will be matched). For example, "`Colin*`" will match any attribute value starting with the string "`Colin`" and "`*Robbins`" any attribute value ending in the string "`Robbins`". When constructing a substring filter, it should be noted that a QUIPU DSA can resolve searches of the form `string*` significantly faster than searches of the `*string*` or `*string` form.

Remember that a large number of the standard attributes match case independently; for example "x-tel" will match "X-Tel".

As well as an exact equality match, the following types of match can be specified:

| | |
|---|---|
| `~=` | `Approximately equals.` |
| `>=` | `Greater than or equal.` |
| `<=` | `Less than or equal.` |

The Approximate match method used is DSA dependent. A QUIPU DSA uses a soundex based algorithm. This works by grouping similar-sounding characters into classes. The classes and their corresponding characters are shown in Figure 7.1. The first character of a word is always used as the first character of its corresponding soundex code. Adjacent similar characters are ignored. Thus, the word "Robbins" has soundex code "R152". Since the word "Robens" also has soundex code "R152", these two words are approximately equal. To match multiple words each of the target words must appear in order in the string to which it is being compared. There may, however, be other items in between the words matched. For example: "Tim Howes" would match "Timothy Alan Howes" since "Tim" matches "Timothy," "Howes" matches "Howes," and the matched words are in the proper order.

Filter items can be linked with *and* "`&`", or *or* "`|`". Brackets "`( )`" should be used to enforce the Boolean ordering of the expressions, otherwise the evaluation is left to right. A *not* "`!`" can be used to specify the Boolean *not* operator.

If a filter does not have a type specified, e.g., "-filter steve", then an approximate match for the specified common name is assumed (in this case "-filter cn~=steve" is assumed).

A more complex example of a filter that searches for anybody whose is a member of staff or a student, who has a "drink" attribute, whose name approximately matches "steve", but whose surname is not "Kille":-

```
cn~=steve & (userClass = staff | userClass = student) &
            (! surname = Kille) & drink = *
```

A list of all the attributes that can be used to search for an entry is given in Chapter 14, together with a description of the type matching allowed.

### fred flags

These flags are used by FRED, and are activated when the `-fred` flag is given.

The **-expand** flag indicates that any matched entry should be displayed in full followed by children entries.

The `-full` flag indicates that if more than one entry is matched on a search, then all entries should be displayed in full.

The `-summary` flag indicates that a one-line display should be used for the entry.

The `-subdisplay` flag indicates that a one-line display should be used for the entry, followed by the entry's children.

The `-nofredseq` flag indicates that the entry (and children) should not be added to the current sequence.

The `-fredlist` flag indicates that any attributes containing DNs should be flagged when using the DA service.

### 7.1.5 Add Entry

```
add [<object>] [-draft <draft> [-noedit]] [-template <draft>]
    [-newdraft] [-objectclass <objectclass>]
```

Add is used to add entries to the DIT. This invokes editentry on the draft entry. If there is not a draft entry specified, a draft entry of the specified objectclass (default — thornperson & quipuObject) is created. The default draft file is *.dishdraft* in your home directory, this can be altered with the `-draft` option.

When editing has finished, an add operation is sent to the directory (the `-noedit` flag following a `-draft` stops the editor being invoked).

`-newdraft` causes the current draft to be overwritten with a new template of the appropriate objectclass.

`-template` is used to specify a template that should be used during editing.

On successful completion of the add, the draft entry is renamed with a suffix of ".old".

### 7.1.6 Editentry

```
editentry <draft>
```

This option is only available from the shell, and not from the DISH program. It is generally not invoked directly by a user, but by the other DISH commands.

editentry invokes an editor (as defined by the users $EDITOR environment variable) on the current draft entry. In a future release it is hoped to have an editor that knows about the syntax of an entry, and thus ensures that the entry you have supplied is syntactically correct.

### 7.1.7 Delete Entry

```
delete [<object>]
```

The specified entry is removed from the DIT (remember that X.500 only allows leaf entries to be deleted).

### 7.1.8 Modify Entry

```
modify [<object>] [-draft <draft> [-noedit]] [-newdraft]
        [-add <attribute type>=<attribute value>]
        [-remove <attribute type>=<attribute value>]
        [<any of the showentry arguments>]
```

Modify is used to modify existing entries in the DIT, and has two modes of operation. The first is used to modify specific attributes and uses the -add and -remove flags to add and remove single attributes and values. Many of these can be strung together in the same command, e.g.,

```
modify -add "description=new attribute" -remove "drink=Chocolate".
```

The second method is used for altering many attributes at the same time. Initially "showentry -all -edb -nocache" is used to get the current DIT entry, and place a copy of it in your .dishdraft file. If the -draft option is specified then the given file is used. After editing, any changes to the entry are sent to the directory (the -noedit flag following a -draft stops the editor being invoked).

The draft file is handled in the same way as with add, except that when a new draft is created, the current values of the attributes are read from the directory.

### 7.1.9 ModifyRDN

```
modifyrdn [<object>] -name <newrdn> [-[no]delete]
```

This is used to modify the RDN of an entry. The RDN cannot be changed using the modify operation (remember, as with delete X.500 only allows this operation on leaf nodes).

The -nodelete flag is used to prevent the old RDN being removed as an attribute of the entry.

### 7.1.10 Showname

```
showname [<object>] [-[no]compact] [-[no]cache] [-[no]ufn]
          [<any of the read arguments>]
```

A name can be printed either in compact form (as seen in EDB or dishdraft files), just showing the distinguished name, in a UFN format (default), or by showing the distinguished attributes one per line.

### 7.1.11 Compare

```
compare [<object>] -attribute <attribute> [-[no]print]
```

For example

```
compare userclass=student
```

This command has a return value of true or false (1 or 0).

If '-print' is specified the strings "TRUE" or "FALSE" are printed.

### 7.1.12 Squid

```
squid [-sequence [<name>]]
      [-alias <object>] [-version]
      [-user] [-syntax]
      [-fred]
```

The command *squid* (status QUIPU DISH) with no parameters will inform you of the current status of your DISH process for example:

```
Connected to Armadillo at Internet=128.40.16.220+2005
Current position: @c=GB@o=Nottingham University
User name: @c=GB@o=University College London@
           ou=Computer Science@cn=Colin Robbins
Current sequence 'default'
```

`-sequence` makes squid print the specified sequence. Sequences are described in Section 7.2.

`-alias` adds the given DN to the current sequence.

`-version` prints the version number of the DISH process and associated ISODE and DSAP libraries.

`-user` prints the DN you are bound as.

`-syntax` prints the directory syntaxes known to DISH.

`-fred` must be the first argument if supplied. It causes any Distinguished names printed by the command to be shown using the user-friendly naming notation rather than the DN notation.

### 7.1.13 Bind

```
bind [-noconnect] [[-user] [<username>]]
     [-password [<password>]] [-[no]refer]
     [-call <dsaname>]
     [-simple] [-protected] [-strong] [-noauthentication]
```

This is used to (re)connect to the directory. This is not normally required, as each command will bind as necessary, but allows advanced users to contact specified DSAs and change their username.

`-noconnect` is used to start DISH (and cache) without connection to a directory.

`-[no]refer` is used to tell DISH whether to automatically follow referrals issued by the DSA, by default they are followed.

To connect to the directory you need to be authenticated. There are four flags to control the level of authentication DISH attempts to use. The lowest level of authentication is "anonymous", which is used when you do not supply a distinguished name. A DSA may respond with "inappropriate authentication" which means you should use a higher level of authentication. The next level of authentication is achieved by supplying a Distinguished Name only, with no password. The `-noauthentication` is used to tell DISH not to prompt for a password. The next levels are "simple" and "protected simple" authentication which use the `-simple` and `-protected` flags respectively. These present a textual password to the directory which the directory the uses to authenticate you. Using `-simple` the password is sent across the network "in the clear," whereas `-protected` encrypts it; thus you are advised to used `-protected` if your directory supports it.

The `-strong` flag tells DISH to send strong authentication credentials to the directory. This is not fully implemented in this version of QUIPU.

To connect to the DSA using "simple" or "protected" authentication, you must supply a distinguished name (`-user`) and password (`-password`). This, however, reveals your password to anybody who is looking at your terminal but is useful for issuing bind operations from a shell script. To prevent this, you need to place the password in your UNIX protected *.quipurc* (see Section 7.4.1). Alternatively, if you do not supply a password, you will be prompted for one (with echoing turned off).

### 7.1.14 Unbind

```
unbind [-noquit]
```

This is used to break the connection to a DSA. If `-noquit` is specified, the DISH process does not die (This is used to maintain the cache.)

To be "friendly" to other users, you should unbind when you have finished using the directory — put an unbind in your *.logout* file if you use DISH from the shell.

### 7.1.15 FRED

```
fred [-display <name>]
     [-dm2dn [-list] [-phone] [-photo] <domain-or-mailbox>]
     [-expand [-full] <DN>]
     [-ufn [-list,] [-mailbox,] [-phone,]
           [-photo,] [-options %x,] <name...>]
     [-ufnrc <list...>]
```

This is used by the FRED program to provide some functions which would otherwise require complicated interactions between FRED and DISH.

`-display` is used to set the address of an X Window display.

`-dm2dn` is used to map a domain name from the DNS or a mailbox into a distinguished name in the directory. The `-list` suboption returns a list of possible matches, `-phone` returns the phone number attribute of the matched entry, and `-photo` returns the photo attribute of the matched entry.

`-expand` is used to see if a node has children.

`-ufn` is used to perform a user-friendly naming match. The `-list` suboption returns a list of possible matches, `-mailbox` returns the mailbox attribute of the matched entry, `-phone` returns the phone number attribute of the matched entry, `-photo` returns the photo attribute of the matched entry, and `-options` is used to customise the behavior of the matching algorithm.

`-ufnrc` is used to set the search list for user-friendly naming.

## 7.2 Sequences

Results returned by *search* and *list* operations may be long, and for this reason have a reference number printed beside them. The reference number can be used as the "object" in any of the calls to the directory. Thus

```
showentry 6
```

shows the entry labelled with the sequence number 6 by a previous *search* or *list* operation.

When you come into DISH by default, the resultant numbers of list and search operations are added to a sequence called "default".

Two flags

```
[-sequence <name>] [-nosequence]
```

are used to control sequences. The `-nosequence`flag is use to completely remove the concept of sequences (so no numbers are printed by list or search).

To get a different sequence (hence renumber from 1 again), you can change this to mysequence with a

```
-sequence mysequence
```

flag.

The special keyword `reset`is used to reset the current sequence, thus causing future operations to be renumbered from 1. This is different to setting a new sequence, as the old sequence values are removed.

Occasionally you will want to search an entry defined in one sequence, putting the results in another. For this purpose the special token "result" is recognised, thus

```
search 4 -sequence xxx -sequence result yyy
```

will search entry 4 as defined by sequence "xxx", but place the results in sequence "yyy".

## 7.3 Service Controls

All the commands described in Sections 7.1.2 through 7.1.11 have additional flags to control the type of service provided. The advice to a novice user is let these flags take their default values.

The flags recognised are listed below:-

`-(no)preferchain`: Advise the DSA (not) to chain the operation if required — The DSA **IS** allowed to ignore the advice!

`-(no)chaining`: (Prohibit) Allow the use of chaining.

`-(dont)usecopy`: (Prohibit) Allow the use of a cached or slave copy of the data. Note that this refers to data cached in the DSA; there are separate flags (already described) for data cached in the DUA.

`-(dont)dereferencealias`: (Do not) dereference aliases if found in the path of a query.

`-low`: Flag the query as low priority.

`-medium`: Flag the query as medium (default) priority.

`-high`: Flag the query as high priority.

`-timelimit` *n*: Set the time limit to *n* seconds.

`-notimelimit`: Do not specify a time limit.

`-sizelimit` *n*: Set the size limit to *n* entries.

`-nosizelimit`: Do not specify a size limit.

`-(no)localscope`: (Do not) limit operation to local scope.

`-(no)refer`: (Do not) automatically follow referrals issued by the DSA.

`-strong`: Ask the DSA to use strong authentication when sending the results.

## 7.4 Tailoring

There are two levels of tailoring that control the operation of the DISH DUA. First of all there is the system wide tailor file *dsaptailor* (found in the ISODE ETCDIR directory, usually */usr/etc/*), and then users private tailor file *.quipurc*.

The file *dsaptailor* is described in Section 17.2.

### 7.4.1 .quipurc

The file *.quipurc* is read by `dish` on startup, and has the following format:-

```
flag: value
```

The following flags are currently recognised:-

`username`: The name of the user to be used when binding.

`password`: The password to use when binding. For this reason care should be taken to ensure you .quipurc file is not publicly readable.

`cache_time`: How long to keep the DISH process alive after unbinding (specified in minutes).

`connect_time`: How long to keep a connection open, if there is no activity (specified in minutes).

`service`: A list of default service control flags (as defined in Section 7.3).

`sequence`: Add the supplied DN parameter to the default sequence.

`dsap`: This can be followed by one of the dsaptailor options described in Section 17.2.

`isode`: This can be followed by one of the ISODE tailor options described in Volume 1 of the ISODE manual.

`notype`: The argument is expected to be an attribute type. This attribute will not be displayed by showentry by default.

`type`: The only valid argument for this entry is "unknown," and says that unknown attributes should be shown; by default, they are not shown.

`certificate`: Used for strong authentication.

`secret_key`: Used for strong authentication.

`<dish command>`: A list of default flags to be used when "command" is used. For example:

```
showname: -compact
```

says that **showname** should always be invoked with the **-compact** flag set.

**<nickname>**: A nickname entry, for example

```
cjr: "c=GB@o=X-Tel Services Ltd@cn=Colin Robbins"
```

This can then be used in distinguished name arguments, for example

```
showentry cjr
```

will show the entry for "Colin Robbins".

## 7.5 Remote Management of the DSA

```
dsacontrol [-[un]lock <entry>] [-dump <directory>]
           [-tailor <string>] [-abort]
           [-restart] [-info] [-refresh <entry>]
           [-resync <entry>] [-slave [<entry>]]
```

If the *dish* program is bound to the DSA as the directory manager (See Section 7.1.13 on binding), then it may be used (primitively) to manage the DSA. This feature is discussed in [SKill89b] and Section 18.3.1 of this manual.

**(un)lock** used to (un)lock subtrees of the DIT held locally. This (allows) prevents users to modify the DIT.

**dump** causes a copy of the local DIT to be dumped into the specified directory. Note that when the DSA dumps its in-core database, it does so relative to the possibly remote UNIX directory from which the DSA was started, not the directory that *dish* (1c) was invoked in. So it is best to specify path names in full to ensure the database is dumped where you expect it to be.

**tailor** is used to pass tailor command to a running DSA. The format of "string" is the same as a line in the *quiputailor* file. For example:-

```
dsacontrol -tailor "dsaplog level=all"
```

will turn the DSA logging on full.

**refresh** tells the DSA to reread subtree "entry" from disk. As with all dsacontrol commands, entry must be the full DN of the target entry, the DISH concept of current position is not used. Also, if relating to a disk operation, the CASE of the DN must be correct as well.

**resync** tells the DSA to re-write the subtree entry to disk.

**slave** tell the DSA to update its SLAVE EDB files. The keyword root is used to identify the root EDB file. The keyword shadow is used to tell the DSA to update any entries it has shadow copies of. See Section 18.10 for details.

`abort` tells the DSA to stop. `restart` tells the DSA to stop, then restart.

`info` asks the DSA to return some statistics about its database.

The error messages returned from a DSA are somewhat obscure when using dsacontrol. There are four things DISH may report:

1. `DONE`: the operation has been successfully completed;
2. `Scheduled`: the operation has been scheduled, and will be completed as soon as possible;
3. `Access rights insufficient`: you are not bound as the DSA manager;
4. `Unwilling to perform`: the DSA was unable to perform the task, this generally means the argument to dsacontrol was wrong.

## 7.6 Caching in the DUA

All results returned from read and list operations are cached in memory in the DUAs. The cache is then used if possible to answer queries. The cache is kept for *cache_time* minutes as specified in the *tailor* files.

Disk caching has not been implemented yet, but it is intended to extend the in-core caching, so that the cached data can be written to disk. When the DUAs start up, the user will have the option to read this cache. Similar support for private data may be provided.

## 7.7 Running DISH from the Shell

Each of the DISH commands mentioned in this chapter to 7.5 can be applied directly to the shell, without having to first invoke *dish*. This has the advantage that the result can be piped through programs like *more* thus giving the users flexibility in how they view the data.

Chapter 16 describes how to install this extra feature of DISH.

Each time a new shell is invoked and a DISH command entered, a new DISH will be invoked. This is sometimes not required. To prevent this from happening an environment variable DISHPROC can be set, and should be the TCP address to use for communication, for example:

```
127.0.0.1 12345
```

where 127.0.0.1 is the IP address, and 12345 is the TCP port. The two example scripts show how the TCP port may be generated if required under `sh`. For `csh` you might use

```
if (${?DISHPROC} == 0) then
        setenv DISHPROC "127.0.0.1 `expr $$ + 10000`"
endif
```

### 7.7.1 DISHinit

A program called *dishinit* can be use to bind to the directory as the manager, read certain information and create a default `.quipurc` file for a specified user. This is a useful utility for new databases. If the `dsaptailor` variable `dishinit` is set to on, dishinit will be invoked by `dish` whenever is can not find a .quipurc file.

`dishinit` needs three parameters to be set in order to bind as the manage, and search the local subtree. These parameters are defined at the top of the dishinit script and are:

**manager** The DN of the manager of the local DSA.

**password** The manager's password (the script should be protected with UNIX file protection).

**position** The DN of the local sub-set of the DIT. This is where the entries for users will be looked for.

### 7.7.2 Example Scripts

Two example scripts have been supplied as part of ISODE, and can be found in the *others/quipu/uips/dish* directory.

**dsaping** Contacts all the DSAs at a given level in the DIT, and gathers some statistics.

**dsalist** Produces a list of all the known DSAs in the DIT.

### 7.7.3 Files

When the multiple command version of DISH is compiled on a machine that does not support sockets, name pipes are used to communicate with the a background process.

The file /tmp/dish<pid> is used by DISH to write results to the calling processes, where the pid is the process id of the calling process.

The file /tmp/dish–<tty>–<uid> is used by calling process to send commands to DISH, where *tty* is the users terminal number, and *uid* their user id.

# Chapter 8

# SID

SID (Steve's interface to DISH) is a directory user agent, designed to be incredibly easy to use. It is implemented as a simple set of scripts to the DISH DUA.

There are a lot of flags to DISH. This can make it awkward to use, and in general shows too much directory-specific information. Fred has a centralised view of the world, and does not give the advantages of a shell based interface.

SID is a simple approach of giving appropriate aliases to access DISH commands. It is targetted for searching for people and organisations. It may be useful "as is" to others, and also give an indication as to how DISH may be used.

## 8.1 Quickstart

**WARNING** Before you start to try SID, you must have the variable DISHPROC set in your environment. The mechanism suggested in Section 8.6 is a good way to achieve this. To experiment, csh users can type the incantation:

```
% setenv DISHPROC "127.0.0.1 `expr $$ + 1000`"
```

To find users within your Organisation is very easy. The default setup is optimised for your particular Organisational Unit. Simply use the command **psearch** with a single argument to identify the user looked for. This will identify all users with this key as a substring. For example:

```
% psearch steve
countryName=GB
organisation=University College London
department=Computer Science

1   cn=Steve Kille
telephoneNumber     - +44-1-380-7294 (work)
telephoneNumber     - 01-350-2888 (home)
```

```
2    cn=Stephen Titcombe
telephoneNumber    - +44-1-387-7050 x 3674/5
telephoneNumber    - Term = 01-388-4741
3    cn=Stephen Sackin
4    cn=Steve Wilbur
telephoneNumber    - +44-1-380-7287
5    cn=Stephen Usher
telephoneNumber    - +44-1-387-7050 x 3674/5
6    cn=Kevin Steptoe
7    cn=Tomasz Stepniak
8    cn=Stefan Penter
telephoneNumber    - +44-1-387-7050 x 3674/5
9    cn=Stephania Loizidou
10   cn=Steve Hodges
telephoneNumber    - +44-1-387-7050 x 3674/5
11   cn=Steve Davey
telephoneNumber    - +44-1-387-7050 x 7280 or 7289
12   cn=Steve Chan
telephoneNumber    - +44-1-387-7050 x 3674/5
13   cn=Steven Britton
telephoneNumber    - +44-1-387-7050 x 3715
14   cn=Stephen Beckles
telephoneNumber    - +44-1-387-7050 x 3674/5
15   cn=Steven Bacall
telephoneNumber    - +44-1-387-7050 x 3674/5
telephoneNumber    - dd 01-387-6978 (Campbell House)
```

Each match will have an associated number. To show a given entry, just use the command **showentry**, with the number identifying the entry as the single argument. For example, to show entry 1 (Steve Kille):

```
% showentry 1
c=GB@o=University College London@ou=Computer Science@cn=Steve Kille
Address             - 35 Elspeth Road
                      London
                      SW11 1DW
userClass - csresstaff
photo - (See X window, pid 598)
roomNumber          - G24
favouriteDrink      - Pinta - Brakspears
info                - Directory worker
rfc822Mailbox       - S.Kille@cs.ucl.ac.uk
textEncodedORaddress - /Pn=Stephen.Kille/Ou=cs/O=ucl/ \
                      Prmd=uk.ac/admd=gold 400/c=gb/
userid              - steve
telephoneNumber     - +44-1-380-7294 (work)
telephoneNumber     - 01-350-2888 (home)
description         - New Description
```

```
surname            - Kille
name               - Steve E. Kille
name               - Stephen Kille
name               - Steve Kille
```

If you are running the X Window system, a picture will be displayed if it is present.

If you wish to search all of your Organisation, simply give a second argument to **psearch**. For example, to search UCL give "ucl" as shown:

```
% psearch baker ucl
Searching for People matching "baker" under:
countryName=GB
organisation=University College London

4   ou=French Lang and Lit@cn=F Baker
telephoneNumber  - 3077
5   ou=Economics@cn=V Bashkar
telephoneNumber  - 2286
6   ou=Biochemistry@cn=J Basra
telephoneNumber  - 2185
7   ou=Bartlett School@cn=H Bowker
telephoneNumber  - 7453
8   ou=Anatomy and Embryol@cn=D Becker
telephoneNumber  - 3293
9   ou=Computer Science@cn=Malcolm Booker
telephoneNumber  - +44-1-387-7050 x 3645
10  ou=Computer Science@cn=Imtiaz Bashir
telephoneNumber  - +44-1-387-7050 x 7304
11  ou=Computer Science@cn=Benjamin Bacarisse
telephoneNumber  - +44-1-380-7212 (work)
telephoneNumber  - 01 987 2746 (home)
12  ou=Surgery@cn=L Baker
telephoneNumber  - 82-5255
13  ou=History Of Art@cn=B A Boucher
telephoneNumber  - 7210
14  ou=Geological Sciences@cn=J R Baker
telephoneNumber  - 2382
15  ou=Secretary's Office@cn=I H Baker
telephoneNumber  - 3000
```

## 8.2 Example Usage

A typical sequence to find someone outside your organisation is now shown:

```
% osearch nott
Searching in country "gb" for Organisations matching "nott"
1    o=Nottingham University
telephoneNumber  - +44-0602-484848x2862
2    o=NPL
3    o=JNT
telephoneNumber  - +44-0235-445724
% psearch smith 1
Searching for People matching "smith" under:
countryName=GB
organisation=Nottingham University

4    ou=Computer Science@cn=Hugh Smith
telephoneNumber  - extn 2862 (Departmental Secretary)
% showentry 4
c=GB@o=Nottingham University@ou=Computer Science@cn=Hugh Smith
photo            - (See X window, pid 1076)
telephoneNumber  - extn 2862 (Departmental Secretary)
description      - lecturer
surname          - Smith
name             - Hugh.Smith
name             - Hugh Smith
```

## 8.3 Use of Nicknames

It is convenient to have nicknames (private aliases) set up for commonly accessed parts of the directory information tree. These can be set up in the QUIPU profile (see Section 8.6), which sets up the nickname 'us'. Two nicknames used in the examples are:

**ucl:** Country GB; Organsisation University College London.

**cs:** Country GB; Organsisation University College London; Organisational Unit Computer Science.

Aliases may be used as an alternative to sequence numbers.

## 8.4 SID Commands

The initial SID commands are:

**osearch:** (Organisation Search) Search for an organisation. The first argument is the organisation being searched for. For example:

```
% osearch nott
```

This searches for any organisations approximating to this string, or containing it as a substring.

The second (optional) argument is the two letter country code (e.g., GB, US, ES, etc.). Use **clist** to find these codes. The default country is the previous one searched. Example:

```
% osearch psi us
```

**psearch:** (Person Search) Search for a person. The first argument is a key to identify the person. Approximate and substring matches are made. There are two ways of using psearch.

1. Search an identified organisation, using the second argument to osearch. Example where the organisation is identified by a nickname:

   ```
   % psearch kirstein ucl
   ```

   Example where the organisation is identified by a sequence number,returned by a previous osearch command.

   ```
   % psearch steve 29
   ```

2. Move explicitly to an organistion, and then use psearch with only one argument. This is useful when repeated searches will be made from one point. Example:

   ```
   % moveto  ucl
   % psearch kirstein
   ```

**clist:** (Country List) Used to give a list of countries, with friendly descriptions, as well as the two-letter code.

**ousearch:** (Organisational Unit Search) Search for an OU. Analogous to psearch. This is appropriate for use where organisations are large, and a full search takes too long.

**dlist:** (directory List) This uses the search command to provide a listing of directory information, without a clutter of wild South American animals.

## 8.5 Standard DISH Commands

The following DISH commands are useful "as is" for normal users, and are considered to be a part of SID.

**showentry:** Show an entry. The single argument is typically the numeric key returned by a search. This will be used a lot, and it is likely to be worthwhile setting up an alias. The author uses ds (directory show). Example, using a sequence number returned by a search:

```
% showentry 36
```

**moveto:** Move to a defined location. Example of moving to a nickname defined location:

```
% moveto ucl
```

**modify:** To modify your own entry, this command is used with the single argument "me". For example:

```
% modify me
```

## 8.6 QUIPU Profile

This is a suggested template for ".quipurc", note that this is very similar to the default file installed by *dishinit* described in Section 7.7.1.

```
username:c=GB@o=University College London@
    ou=Computer Science@cn=Steve Kille
me:c=GB@o=University College London@
    ou=Computer Science@cn=Steve Kille
password:steve

position: @c=GB@o=University College London@ou=Computer Science
notype: acl
notype: treestructure
notype: masterdsa
notype: slavedsa
notype: objectclass
notype: lastmodifiedby
notype: lastmodifiedtime
notype: userpassword
cache_time: 30
connect_time: 2

us: c=us
moveto: -pwd
showentry: -name
```

You must set the environment variable DISHPROC. This can be done by the following in the *.login* file (csh):

```
if (${?DISHPROC} == 0) then
        setenv DISHPROC "127.0.0.1 `expr $$ + 1000`"
endif
```

# Chapter 9

# DSC

'*dsc*' (which might stand for directory script) is a directory user interface originally written as UCL's public access user interface at University College London. It is primarily aimed at the novice user, although the user is allowed to select a more advanced interface, sd, if the user feels confident about using the directory. The simple interface is restricted to looking up email addresses and telephone numbers for people. In order to keep the number of questions the user is asked to a minimum, the interface currently only searches within a single country. Clearly the interface could be changed to allow a wider scope of querying.

The interface is written as a *dish* script. It is regretted that the interface only runs on Bourne-style shells, which support functions. An enhanced version of dsc written in *C* is currently under development.

## 9.1 Starting Up

On invoking the interface, a preamble is displayed showing the user the form of the questions which they will be asked to enter. The user is then asked to select a style of interface thus:

```
easy or advanced interface? (e/a):
```

where the default is 'easy'. See the Chapter 10 on *sd* for a description of the "advanced" interface.

## 9.2 A Simple Local Search

The user is now asked the following series of questions:

```
Enter the person's name (or "?" for help, "q" to quit):
Enter department ("Return" to search all depts, * to list depts):
Enter site ("Return" for local site, * to list all sites):
```

A local query for people called Barker would be specified thus:

```
Enter the person's name (or "?" for help, "q" to quit): barker
Enter department ("Return" to search all depts, * to list depts):
Enter site ("Return" for local site, * to list all sites):
```

The results would be displayed thus:

```
name:           T Barker
department:     Finance Division
phone:          2553

name:           Paul Barker
department:     Computer Science
phone:          7366
email:          P.Barker@uk.ac.ucl.cs
```

## 9.3 Searching Further Afield

Substring matching is used to simplify the specification of queries. Searching can be done on up to five organisations from one query. This limit was arbitrarily chosen to curtail expansive searching. The behaviour of the interface can be seen from the following query and set of results:

```
Enter the person's name (or "?" for help, "q" to quit): smith
Enter department ("Return" to search all depts, * to list depts): comp
Enter site ("Return" for UCL, * to list all sites): ford

Searching site: Salford University Business Services Ltd...
No such department
Searching site: Salford University...
No such department
Searching site: Rutherford Appleton Laboratory...
No such department
Searching site: Bradford University...
  Searching dept: Computer Science...
  Searching dept: Computer Centre...
Searching site: Oxford University...
  Searching dept: Computing Service...

name:           Margaret Smith
department:     Computing Service
phone:          0865-...
organisation:   Oxford University

name:           Prof R A J Ord-Smith
department:     Computer Centre
phone:          0274 ...
email:          R.A.J.Ord-Smith@bradford.ac.uk
organisation:   Bradford University
```

## 9.4 The Appearance of the Results

Telephone numbers may be configured to appear as local extensions if appropriate, or the country code ommitted if within the same country. Electronic mail addresses are by default in rfc822 domain order, but may be configured to U.K. grey-book order.

If more than 20 entries are returned, the results are given in a condensed format:

```
N Jones         2510          UCL Union
A Jones         82-9802       Surgery
T Jones         7077          Student Residences Office
T Jones         2338          Slade School of Fine Art
D Jones         82-5279       Physiology
C L Jones       7139          Physics and Astronomy
G O Jones       3468          Physics and Astronomy
P S Jones       3483          Physics and Astronomy
...
```

## 9.5 Quitting

Type 'q' at the prompt for a person's name.

# Chapter 10

# SD

SD is a simple directory user agent for X.500 directory services developed from the WIDGET (window interface developed at GEC Hirst) interface. It is included only as an example of an X.500 interface, and how to use the procedural interface, it is not considered to be fully developed.

SD supports the following directory operations:-

- read
- list
- search

SD is limited in it's flexibility and does not allow modification of entries. If you want to use the full power of X.500 you should use the DISH interface described in Chapter 7.

SD is curses based, and splits the users screen up into a number of small areas called "widgets". Each widget is used to enter information.

## 10.1 Types of Widget

There are various types of "widget" used by the SD program, these are described in the following sections.

Each widget (except label widgets) have an identification "letter" associated with them, this is indicated by the left most character in the widget, for example, the widget below is identified by the letter "b".

```
h help
```

### 10.1.1 Label Widgets

Label widgets are used to simply write information to the screen, they do not accept any form of input.

### 10.1.2 Command Widgets

A command widget is used to make the program take some kind of action, such as send a *list* operation to the directory, or to change the set of widgets displayed.

To issue the command type the letter indicated in the widget.

### 10.1.3 Dialog Widgets

Dialog widgets are used to get information from the user. To use a dialog widget, press the letter associated with the widget. Any further input from the keyboard will be entered into the widget, a "return" character is used to end the input.

### 10.1.4 Toggle Widgets

Toggle widgets are used to select one of a set of pre-determined values. Simply enter the widget letter, and the value will change the next value in the circular list.

## 10.2 Using SD

The SD interface is invoked with the *sd* command. Help is given at any stage by typing '?', type 'q' to quit.

### 10.2.1 Main Options

The "main options" set of widgets, presents the users with *quit, help, list, widen, history, search for* and *goto* commands.

The *search area* label widget informs the user of the currently visited directory entry. All directory operations are performed relative to the current *search area.*

### 10.2.2 List

The *list* operation causes SD to list a limited number of entries below the *search area.* The results are displayed in an enumerated list.

### 10.2.3 Search For

The *search for* command requires the user to enter a *search value* after invocation. The *search value* can be a single filter item or a value based on the current search type, displayed in the *type* label widget. In general a value based on the current type is used. For example if the current type is "Person" a suitable value might be "findlay" or "nahajski", or if the current type is "Department" then a suitable value might be "Computer Centre".

The attribute type is selected with the *type* toggle widget.

Any entries that match the given information are displayed in an enumerated list. If a single match is made then the contents of that entry are displayed and it also becomes the current *search area*, assuming that it is a non-leaf entry.

### 10.2.4 Go To Number

The *go to number* operation allows the user to visit and read a listed entry (lists can be displayed as a result of *list* or *search* operations. To visit and view a listed entry, simply type in the number of the entry directly.

### 10.2.5 Scrolling Lists

In order to simplify viewing of long lists of entry names a simple scrollbar feature is provided.

The scrollbar is displayed on the left side of the viewing area. The entries currently being viewed are represented by the block of "*" characters, the length of the complete scrollbar represents the length of the entire list.

To scroll downwards press the "[" key, to scroll upwards press the "]" key.

### 10.2.6 Help

The *help* command invokes a set of command widgets. Each command will bring up help text concerning the specified topic, e.g., the *search for* operation.

## 10.3 Configuration of SD

SD can be configured on a system-wide or per-user basis. SD installs system default files into a directory called *sd/duaconfig/* under ISODE"'s ETCDIR.

Per-user configuration files other than *.duarc*, must be held under a directory *.duaconfig/* contained in a user's home directory.

The SD configuration files are:

```
<CONFIGDIR>/readTypes,
<CONFIGDIR>/duaconfig/filterTypes/Type_*,
<CONFIGDIR>/duaconfig/typeDefaults.
```

### 10.3.1 The .duarc file

The *.duarc* file is analogous to the *.quipurc* file for DISH (see Section 7.4.1), though less extensive in the number and flexibility of options provided. It has the following format:-

```
flag: value
```

The following flags are currently recognised:-

**username:** The name of the user to bind as.

**password:** The password to use when binding. For this reason care should be taken to ensure your *.duarc* file is not publicly readable.

**service:** A list of default service control flags (as defined in Section 7.3).

**dsap:** This can be followed by one of the dsaptailor options described in Section 17.2.

**isode:** This can be followed by one of the ISODE tailor options described in Volume 1 of the ISODE manual.

**history:** This can be followed by a number that specifies the number of entry names to be maintained in the history buffer.

**prefergreybook:** For those who prefer grey book mail address format. This takes values of TRUE or FALSE.

### 10.3.2 The readTypes file

The file *readTypes* contains a list of attributes that are to be read for entry display. The format of this file is;

```
"quotedAttributeName" numericOid
```

an example line then being

```
"photo"          0.9.2342.19200300.100.1.7
```

This format was chosen as it is the same format as the output from the OIDDUMP utility provided with ISODE.

### 10.3.3 The filterTypes files

SD searches are based upon a complex filter, e.g. the default filter for the type *Person* is:-

```
objectClass=person AND (cn~=* OR sn~=* OR title~=*)
```

Where represents a value supplied at search time.

The directory *filterTypes/* contains a set of files, each with a prefix *Type_*, describing the set of such abstract types used in SD. The set of contained files may be edited or added to.

The syntax used in these files is shown in the example below:-

```
<filter_type> ::= <filter_name> <filter>
<name> ::= "name:" <asciistring>
<filter> ::= <filter_item> | <assertion>
<assertion> ::= "(" <filt_type> <filter> <filter> <filter_list> ")"
<filter_list> ::= <filter> <filter_list> | <filter> | NULL
<filter> ::= <filter_item> | <assertion>
<filter_item> ::= "(" NUMERIC_OID <match_type> <value> ")"
<filt_type> ::= "&" | "|"
<match_type> ::= "=" | "~=" | "%="
<value> ::= "*" | STRING
<comment> ::= "#" STRING
```

Where the symbol " =" represents approximate match, "The "*" character for value represents a value supplied at search time.

As an example, the file representing the default type *Person* is:-

```
#Composition of type Person
name:"Person"
( & (2.5.4.0="2.5.6.6") # objectClass = person
    ( | (2.5.4.3~=*) # cn (common name)
(2.5.4.4~=*) # sn (surname)
(2.5.4.12~=*))) # title
```

### 10.3.4 The typeDefaults file

The *typeDefaults* file defines the relationships between each of the type defined in the *filterTypes* directory. This is best described by the following example line from the provided *typeDefaults* file.

```
2.5.4.10:Person, Place, Department: Person
```

The first field defines the type of entry to which this line applies, the OID shown here is the one for *organizationName*. The second field lists the SD search types which are available when visiting an entry of the specified type. So this line specifies that the types *Person*, *Place* and *Department* are available when visiting an entry of type *organizationName*. The third field defines the default search type to be used when visiting an entry of the specified type.

# Chapter 11

# FRED

*FRED* is a DUA optimised for White Pages queries; it is actually implemented as an interface to *dish*, hence the name FRED — font end to DISH.

## 11.1 Giving Commands to FRED

After invoking FRED, you are prompted with `fred>` indicating that FRED is ready.

If FRED is invoked interactively, it will look for a file in your home directory called *.fredrc*. It will execute the commands contained in this file just as if you had typed them directly to FRED. Following this, you are given the `fred>` prompt.

## 11.2 Let Your Fingers Do the Walking

Although FRED has several commands, the most interesting command is `whois`, which performs a white pages query.

Let's begin with some simple examples and introduce the other commands along the way. If you already know the handle of the person you are interested in finding out about, just give the handle:

```
fred> whois @c=US@cn=Manager
Manager (1)

Handle:          @c=US@cn=Manager
```

### 11.2.1 The Alias Command

Since handles are long strings, FRED will automatically maintain a list of aliases of the entries you have seen in the current session. The alias is always a number. When an entry is displayed, it appears on the first line in parenthesis after the name of the object. In the example above, the alias is `1`.

To find out what aliases are currently defined, use the `alias` command:

```
fred> alias
1     @c=US@cn=Manager
```

Thus, the previous `whois` command could have been shortened to simply:

```
fred> whois !1
Manager (1)

Handle:          @c=US@cn=Manager
```

Each time you invoke FRED, its list of aliases is empty. If there are few handles which you use often, you might wish to define them in your *.fredrc* file, e.g.,

```
alias "@c=US@o=DMD@cn=Manager"
```

Of course, the ordering of aliases is important. FRED will start numbering from 1 starting with the first `alias` command.

### 11.2.2 Back to Searching

Suppose however, that you don't know the handle for the person. In this case, you need to specify some search parameters. Logically, the first step is to ascertain the organization which the person is likely to be associated with, e.g., "Performance Systems International". This is done as:

```
fred> whois organization psi
Performance Systems International (1)  +1 800-836-0400 (Operations)
     aka: PSI

PSI Inc.
  Reston International Center
  11800 Sunrise Valley Drive
  Suite 1100
  Reston, VA 22091
  US

PSI Inc.
  5201 Great American Parkway
  Suite 3106
  Santa Clara, CA 95054
  US

PSI Inc.
  165 Jordan Road
  Troy, NY 12180
```

```
  US

Telephone: +1 800-836-0400 (Operations)
           +1 800-82PSI82 (Sales)
           +1 703-620-6651 (Corporate/Reston Office)
           +1 518-283-8860 (Troy Office)
           +1 408-562-6222 (Santa Clara Office)
FAX:       +1 703-620-4586
           +1 518-283-8904
           +1 408-562-6223

value-added provider of networking services

Locality:    Reston, Virginia

Name:      Performance Systems International, US (1)
Modified: Mon Jul 30 05:18:24 1990
      by: Manager, Performance Systems International,
            US (2)
```

Second, to search for a particular person, you might use:

```
fred> whois rose -area 2
Marshall Rose (3)      mrose@psi.com
     aka: mtr
     aka: Marshall T. Rose

Principal Scientist
PSI, Inc.
  POB 391776
  Mountain View, CA 94039
  US

PSI, Inc.
  5201 Great American Parkway
  Suite 3106
  Santa Clara, CA 95054
  US

Telephone: +1 415-961-3380
           +1 408-562-6222 x6221
FAX:       +1 415-961-3282
           +1 408-562-6223

Mailbox information:
  internet: mrose@psi.com
```

```
  internet: mrose@cheetah.ca.psi.com

Principal Implementor of the ISO Development Environment

Beleaguered Manager of the PSI White Pages Pilot Project

A savvyNerd according to noSauce

Locality:     Santa Clara, California

Drinks:         Iced Tea (and lots of it...)

Name:       Marshall Rose, Mountain View,
              Research and Development,
              Performance Systems International,
              US (3)
Modified: Mon Sep 24 14:43:36 1990
      by: Manager, US (5)
```

Note the use of the alias 2. The command could also have been:

```
fred> whois rose -area "@c=US@o=Performance Systems..."
   ...
```

Double-quotes are used so that the DN appears as a single token to FRED.

Of course, this two-step process, whilst logical, is tedious. Thus, you can combine them like this:

```
fred> whois rose -org psi
   ...
```

which says to look for any organisations with "psi" in its name. Then, for each one, look for something called "rose".

### 11.2.3 The Area Command

Suppose you want information on several persons belonging to an organization. You can use the area command, by itself, to tell FRED where to search for subsequent commands. For example,

```
fred> area "@c=US@o=Performance Systems International"
```

or simply

```
fred> area 2
```

Both tell FRED the default area used by the `whois` command. Of course, you can still use the '`-area`' area with the `whois` command to override the default area. Thus,

```
fred> whois alan -area "@c=US@o=Columbia University"
```

will do what you expect.

If you use the area command without any arguments, FRED will tell you what its default area is:

```
fred> area
@c=US@o=Yoyodyne
```

This indicates the default area for all commands, *including* any subsequent area commands. Thus, issuing

```
fred> area @c=US@o=Yoyodyne
@c=US@o=Yoyodyne

fred> area ou=Research
@c=US@o=Yoyodyne@ou=Research
```

is equivalent to

```
fred> area @c=US@o=Yoyodyne@ou=Research
@c=US@o=Yoyodyne@ou=Research
```

because a leading "@"-sign was not used before ou=Research.

As you might expect, there is a special string ".." which may be used to move up one level:

```
fred> area ..
@c=US@o=Yoyodyne
```

Combinations are possible as well, such as

```
fred> area ..@"o=Performance Systems International"
@c=US@o=Performance Systems International
```

which moves up a level and then down to
o=Performance Systems International

### 11.2.4 Getting Help

For a brief summary of FRED commands, type:

```
fred> help ?
```

This will list the commands that FRED knows about along with a one-line summary of their function.

For help on a particular command, type the name of the command followed by '-help', e.g.,

```
fred> alias -help
```

If you need more help, try

```
fred> manual
```

which is the same as

```
% man fred
```

from the shell.

### 11.2.5 Quitting

To terminate FRED, simply use:

```
fred> quit
```

## 11.3 Advanced Usage

This chapter has given a very brief overview of the basic FRED commands. For full details you should consult [MRose90a], which tells you how to make more complex search requests, edit your own entry, and how to use FRED to compose mail addresses using the MH mail system.

# Chapter 12

# POD

POD is a directory user agent developed for the X Window System version 11 release 4, using the Athena widget set. It is intended to be an interface for the "naive" user. If you want to use the full power of X.500 you should use the DISH interface described in Chapter 7 of this manual.

## 12.1 Types of Widget

POD makes use of various simple on-screen devices called widgets. The most important of these are described in the following sections.

### 12.1.1 Buttons

A button is a rectangular screen area which when selected will activate some specific function. A button is selected by pointing at it with the cursor and then clicking with the first mouse button.

Most buttons contain a label and sometimes graphics which denote the button's function. In addition POD buttons are denoted by a change to a pointing hand cursor or by a border becoming highlighted.

A button box is simply a collection of buttons.

### 12.1.2 Dialogue Boxes

A dialogue box is a means of supplying textual information to an application, and can be thought of as a miniature text editor. The dialogue boxes used in POD follow the command structure of the EMACS editor.

Dialogue boxes, like most others widgets, only become active (or have the input focus) when pointed at by the cursor.

### 12.1.3 Menus

A menu is a vertically arranged collection of buttons that appears on selection of a menu button.

## 12.2 Using POD

POD is invoked with the following command:

```
pod [-t <tailor file>] [-T <oidtable>]
    [-c <dsa address>] [-u <quoted username>] [-p <password>]
```

-t is used to tell POD which *tailor* file to use in place of the default system dsaptailor file.

-T is used to force POD to use an alternative oidtable.

-c is used to bind to a DSA other than the local default.

-u is used to bind as a specific user.

-p is used to bind against the given password.

POD is made up of a number of separate windows, described in the following sections.

### 12.2.1 The Main Window

POD's main window is comprised of three sections: a current position display, a search input box and a button box. Each of these is described below.

#### Current Directory Position

All operations are performed relative to a base directory entry. The name of this entry is displayed in the main window under the title "Current Directory Position."

Parts of the displayed entry name can be selected in order to move to other positions in the directory.

#### Searching for Entries

The search input area contains a dialogue box and a menu button.

The dialogue box is used to enter a value describing an entry to be searched for; for example if searching for the entry for "Damanjit Mahl" a suitable value would be "D Mahl."

The menu button specifies the type of entry being searched for (the search type); in the above example this would be "Person." The search type can be changed by pulling down the menu attached to the type button and selecting from the contained list of types.

Searches are activated by clicking on the "Search" button or by pressing the Return key.

#### Main Functions

The buttons displayed in POD's main window are:

**Quit:** Quit from POD.

**Help:** Invoke interactive help.

**Search:** Search for specified entry.

**List:** List entries under current position.

**History:** - Display history of visited entries.

### 12.2.2 The List Window

A *list* window displays a list of named directory entries, which can be returned as a result of list, search or history operations. It comprises a pair of buttons, a list display and two message bars.

The upper message bar contains the information regarding the source of the displayed list, e.g., "Result of List under Brunel University." The lower message bar contains errors and constraint messages.

#### List Display

To move to or read a listed entry simply click on that entry's name. Non-leaf entries cause a move and read, whereas leaf entries only cause a read.

#### Close and Keep Buttons

The *close* button can be used to close the *list* window. Note that this does not iconify the window but rather deletes it and all contained information.

The *keep* button can be used to make the information contained in the *list* window semi-permanent. In the default case, results from ensuing list/search operations overwrite any unkept list windows, thereby limiting the number of windows containing temporary information to one. If the *keep* button is selected, displayed information becomes semi-permanent, and is only removed if the *close* button is selected. The text in a *keep* button changes from Keep to Kept upon selection, in order to distinguish from list windows containing transient data.

The *list* window that displays the session history does not have a *keep* button.

### 12.2.3 The Read Window

The *read* window displays selected parts of a directory entry. It is comprised of a message bar, a button box and a *text* window.

The message bar displays the entry's name. If selected this bar places the complete distinguished name of an entry into the primary X cut buffer. Ordinarily this is of little use, though it can help when modifying attributes that require a distinguished name as a value.

The *text* window displays the body of the entry, which currently contains textual information and may contain a (single) fax image stored in the photo attribute.

It is possible to cut text from the *text* window.

The *close* and *keep* buttons perform a similar function to those described above for the *list* window.

The *modify* button activates a window containing facilities to modify the entry being read.

### 12.2.4 The Modify Window

The *modify* window allows the user to modify the attributes of an entry. Each attribute value displayed in the *text* window is contained in its own dialogue box. Pointing to a dialogue box will allow editing of the contained value.

Each value has an associated menu button (denoted by the menu icon) which allows various operations on a particular value, e.g., delete value, undo changes, etc. In addition each attribute label, e.g., "commonName", is itself a menu button and allows various operations on all values associated with that attribute, e.g., delete all values, undo all changes to this attribute, add a new value field. Undo operations only undo all changes since the last successful modify operation or else return all affected values to their original states.

The *close* and *keep* buttons behave consistently with those described for the *read* and *list* windows.

The *modify* button attempts to make the modification entered into the *text* window. A message reporting the success (or otherwise) of a modification request is displayed in the lower right *message* window.

### 12.2.5 Error and Message Popups

From time to time, during or after directory operations, POD will provide error or status reports in a popup that appears in the top left corner of the screen. Errors sometime require the user to click on the *error* window before normal operation can resume.

## 12.3 Configuration of POD

POD can be configured on a system-wide or per-user basis. POD installs system default files into a directory called *xd/duaconfig/* under ISODE's ETCDIR.

Per-user configuration files other than *.podrc*, must be held under a directory *.duaconfig/* contained in a user's home directory.

The POD configuration files are

```
<CONFIGDIR>/readTypes,
<CONFIGDIR>/duaconfig/friendlyNames,
<CONFIGDIR>/duaconfig/filterTypes/Type_*,
<CONFIGDIR>/duaconfig/typeDefaults.
```

### 12.3.1 The .podrc File

The *.podrc* file is analogous to the *.quipurc* file for DISH (see Section 7.4.1), though less extensive in the number and flexibility of options provided. It has the following format:

```
flag: value
```

The following flags are currently recognised:

**username:** The name of the user to bind as.

**password:** The password to use when binding. For this reason care should be taken to ensure your *.podrc* file is not publicly readable.

**service:** A list of default service control flags (as defined in Section 7.3).

**dsap:** This can be followed by one of the dsaptailor options described in Section 17.2.

**isode:** This can be followed by one of the ISODE tailor options described in Volume 1 of the ISODE manual.

**history:** This can be followed by a number that specifies the number of entry names to be maintained in the history buffer.

**prefergreybook:** For those who prefer grey book mail address format. This takes values of TRUE or FALSE.

**readnonleaf:** This tells POD whether or not to read non-leaf entries. Values are TRUE or FALSE.

### 12.3.2 The readTypes File

The file *readTypes* contains a list of attributes that are to be read for entry display. The format of this file is;

```
"quotedAttributeName" numericOid
```

an example line then being

```
"photo"                 0.9.2342.19200300.100.1.7
```

This format was chosen as it is the same format as the output from the OID-DUMP utility provided with ISODE.

### 12.3.3 The friendlyNames File

This file maps attribute names onto user-friendly names, for use in displaying the 'Current Directory Position.' The current defaults map the names onto empty strings so that the bare values are shown, e.g.:

```
The World
GB
Brunel University
```

The format of the file is

```
attribute list : friendly name
```

where an attribute list can be one or more comma-separated attribute names.

### 12.3.4 The filterTypes Files

POD searches are based upon a complex filter; e.g., the default filter for the type *Person* is

```
objectClass=person AND (cn~=* OR sn~=* OR title~=*)
```

Where "*" represents a value supplied at search time.

The directory *filterTypes/* contains a set of files, each with a prefix *Type_*, describing the set of such abstract types used in POD. The set of contained files may be edited or added to.

The syntax used in these files is shown in the example below:

```
<filter_type> ::= <filter_name> <filter>
<name> ::= "name:" <asciistring>
<filter> ::= <filter_item> | <assertion>
<assertion> ::= "(" <filt_type> <filter> <filter>
                 <filter_list> ")"
<filter_list> ::= <filter> <filter_list> | <filter> | NULL
<filter> ::= <filter_item> | <assertion>
<filter_item> ::= "(" NUMERIC_OID <match_type> <value> ")"
<filt_type> ::= "&" | "|"
<match_type> ::= "=" | "~=" | "%="
<value> ::= "*" | STRING
<comment> ::= "#" STRING
```

Where the symbol “ =” represents approximate match, “%=” represents substring match and “=” represents exact match. The “*” character for value represents a value supplied at search time.

As an example, the file representing the default type ‘Person’ is:

```
#Composition of type Person
name:"Person"
( & (2.5.4.0="2.5.6.6") # objectClass = person
    ( | (2.5.4.3~=*) # cn (common name)
(2.5.4.4~=*) # sn (surname)
(2.5.4.12~=*))) # title
```

### 12.3.5 The typeDefaults File

The *typeDefaults* file defines the relationships between each of the type defined in the *filterTypes* directory. This is best described by the following example line from the provided *typeDefaults* file:

```
2.5.4.10:Person, Place, Department: Person
```

The first field defines the type of entry to which this line applies, the OID shown here is the one for *organizationName*. The second field lists the POD search types which are available when visiting an entry of the specified type. So this line specifies that the types *Person*, *Place* and *Department* are available when visiting an entry of type *organizationName*. The third field defines the default search type to be used when visiting an entry of the specified type.

# Chapter 13

# Xd

Xd is a Directory User Agent (DUA) for the X Window System which provides access to the OSI X.500 Directory. It was developed (along with Xdsm, and an early version of POD) as a prototype DUA to stimulate feedback for the design of full DUAs for X and Microsoft Windows.

## 13.1 Starting Xd

Xd accepts the usual command line parameters for X applications. These are described in the online manual pages ( X(1) ). Xd also recognises the following options which relate to the QUIPU directory services:

```
-t tailor file
-c dsa name
-T oid table
-D directory
```

If Xd has not been installed, it is necessary to load the X resources file into the server. The following command in the Xd directory should achieve this:

*xrdb –merge Xd.ad*

If you change any of the resources in the *Xd.ad* file, you will need to load them into the server again. The –load option to xrdb overwrites all resources already in the server, but may be useful when a resource is to be removed. *xrdb –query* lists the current contents of the server's resource database.

## 13.2 The Components of Xd

The components which make up Xd are described below:

**Quit:** Exits Xd

**Help:** Pressing the *help* button invokes a popup window comprising a *quit* button and a help text window. The help displayed in the text window is dependent on the position of the mouse. So entering the *type* button area will display a help page describing the Type button function. Entering the *help* button restores the *general help* page, and pressing *help* restores the popup to its position just above the *help* button. The *quit* button on the *help* popup removes the popup. The *help* popup does not stop other Xd buttons operating.

**Search Area:** The search area shows the current directory position. This is the base position from which lists and searches are performed.

**Search For:** This shows the current string being searched for. All keyboard input is focused on this widget. It accepts most EMACS-like commands for line editing, and carriage return starts a search.

**Type:** The Type area has a button which invokes a menu of possible search types, and a text area showing the current search type. The search type specifies a search filter which will be used for searches. When the current directory position is changed, default search type and search type options are set. The filters and defaults are configurable. This is described in the manual entry for POD.

**Read Area:** All directory reads, and any errors, are displayed in this text widget. Photographs can be displayed automatically using Xphoto, and can be destroyed by clicking on the photograph.

**Search/List Buttons:** The search and list buttons should be quite obvious. Search performs a search using the string and type specified. List shows the children of the current position.

**Widen:** Widen makes the current position one stage less specific.

**Look back:** The look back button invokes a popup with a list of the last ten places selected from the list area. Clicking on an item in the list, makes that the new current position. The popup is only large enough to contain the longest directory position currently in the list. If a place is added to the list whilst it is still popped up, the popup does not resize.

**List Area:** The final area in Xd is the list area. This is used to display the results of lists and searches. Selecting an item from the list area causes Xd to try and read the entry and make the entry the current position. Making a leaf entry the current position is meaningless, as it will have no children and lists or searches will be pointless. Such is life!

## 13.3 Driving Xd

To "press" a button, move the cursor (that funny hand shape) and click (press and release) button one (usually the left hand button) on the mouse. To select an item from a list, point the cursor at the item you want to select and click button one on the mouse.

To scroll a read or list area, move the cursor into the scrollbar and press button two on the mouse. Now move the mouse up and down or left and right until the required screen area is displayed. Now release the mouse button. The thick horizontal lines with the black squares at one end allow the relative sizes of the bounded areas to be changed. Grab the line by pressing a mouse button on the black box (handle), move the mouse, then release the button.

## 13.4 Configuration

The configuration of search filters was mentioned earlier in the context of the Type button and menu. This configuration is common between POD and Xd. A directory called duaconfig (under *Xd/Xd* in the source tree) contains example configuration files. A description of these configuration files is given in the Chapter on POD (Chapter 12). Note however that there are a few differences.

- The *friendlyNames* file is POD specific.
- Xd uses *.quipurc* not *.podrc*.
- Xd only recognises username, password, isode, dsap and service fields of *.quipurc*

# Chapter 14

# Attribute Syntaxes

All attributes recognised by QUIPU have an associated "string" representation which is used to store the data in the DSA. This chapter describes all the currently recognised syntaxes.

For most of the syntaxes, a BNF description is given, using the following base description:

```
<a> ::= any of the 52 upper and lower case IA5 letters
<d> ::= any IA5 digit 0-9
<k> ::= any of the 52 upper and lower case IA5 letters,
              IA5 digits, and "-" (hyphen)
<p> ::= any IA5 character in ASN.1 PrintableSting
<CRLF> ::= IA5 Newline
<letterstring> ::= <a> | <a> <letterstring>
<numericstring> ::= <d> | <d> <numericstring>
<keystring> ::= <k> | <k> <keystring>
<printablestring> ::= <p> | <p> <printablestring>
```

The BNF description of attributes can be found in Appendix B, but this does not repeat the BNF used for syntaxes given below.

## 14.1 Standard Syntaxes

This section describes the Attribute Syntaxes defined by X.500.

There are many attributes that are represented by a sequence of printable characters. There are various ways in which the contents of the string is restricted, each is represented by a different syntax, which are described below.

### 14.1.1 PrintableString

| Standard Attributes | QUIPU Attributes |
|---|---|
| serialNumber | execVector |

The printable string characters are:

A through Z
a through z
0 through 9
' (apostrophe)
( (left parenthesis)
) (right parenthesis)
+ (plus-sign)
, (comma)
- (hyphen)
. (period)
/ (solidus)
: (colon)
? (question-mark)
space

The value can be any character listed above, with matching as for CaseExactString.

When matching, multiple white spaces and tabs are treated as a single space character.

Approximate matching is supported for this syntax.

The only standard attribute of this type is `serialNumber`, this is used in the `device` objectClass, and represents the serial number of the device. QUIPU defines an `execVector` attribute which is used by the *iaed* program as the vector to pass to a program when starting it.

### 14.1.2 CaseExactString

No attributes currently use this syntax. Matching is as for PrintableString.

The value for this syntax can be one of two types, either a printable string, or a T.61 string represented as follows:

```
<StringValue> ::= "{T.61}" <T61String> | <printablestring>
<T61String>   ::= Any character defined to be in T.61 String.
```

If a T.61 string is used, where possible the character is displayed using the equivalent ASCII character. Characters in T.61 string that can not be represented by an equivalent ASCII character are quoted, using "\xx" where "xx" is the hexadecimal value of the character.

However, if your terminal has the ability to display characters using an ISO 8859-1 font (for example some of the X Window System fonts) then a large number of the T.61 characters can be displayed (and so are not quoted in hex!). You will need to tell the DUA that you have the ability to display the ISO 8859-1 characters. This can be achieved in one of three ways:

| Hex code | Description | Character |
|---|---|---|
| c1 | grave accent | ò |
| c2 | acute accent | ó |
| c3 | circumflex | ô |
| c4 | tilde | õ |
| c5 | macron | ō |
| c7 | single dot | ȯ |
| ca | ring | å |
| cb | cedilla | ç |
| cc | underscore | o̲ |
| cd | umlaut | ö |
| cf | caron | ǒ |
| a1 | inverted exclamation mark | ¡ |
| a3 | pound sign | £ |
| a4 | dollar sign | $ |
| a6 | hash | # |
| a7 | paragraph sign | § |
| ab | left quotation mark | « |
| b0 | ring | å |
| b1 | plus/minus | ± |
| b5 | greek letter mu | $\mu$ |
| b6 | pilcrow | ¶ |
| b8 | division sign | ÷ |
| bb | right quotation mark | » |
| bc | quarter sign | $\frac{1}{4}$ |
| bd | half sign | $\frac{1}{2}$ |
| be | three-quarters sign | $\frac{3}{4}$ |
| bf | inverted question mark | ¿ |
| e0 | greek letter omega | Ω |
| e1 | AE | Æ |
| e8 | L stroke | Ł |
| e9 | O stroke | Ø |
| ea | OE | Œ |

Table 14.1: T.61 Character Codes

- In the system-wide dsaptailor file, you can add

```
ch_set ISO8859
```

or

- in your .quipurc file you can add

```
dsap: ch_set ISO8859
```

However not all the DUA interfaces read this files (DISH does!) or

- set the environment variable CH_SET to "ISO8859", e.g., using "csh"

```
setenv CH_SET ISO8859
```

To enter T.61 characters is a little more tricky. In T.61 accented characters are represented by two octets, the first indicating the accent and the second the base character to be accented. Note that some combinations of accent and character do not have an equivalent in ISO 8859-1, and hence cannot be displayed on an ISO 8859-1 device. Table 14.1 shows some of the characters that can be represented, for the accented characters only the first octect is shown, the second octect can typically be any character, "o" is used in most of the examples.

For instance, to enter the T.61 string "Galápagos Penguin," you should use

```
{T.61}Gal\c2apagos Penguin
```

The acute accent is represented by the "\c2" and appears over the following character — "a" in this case.

### 14.1.3 CaseIgnoreString

| Standard Attributes |
|---|
| knowledgeInformation |
| commonName |
| surname |
| localityName |
| stateOrProvinceName |
| streetAddress |
| organizationName |
| organizationalUnitName |
| title |
| description |
| businessCategory |
| postalCode |
| postOfficeBox |
| physicalDeliveryOfficeName |

| RARE Attributes |
|---|
| userid |
| textEncodedORaddress |
| info |
| favouriteDrink |
| roomNumber |
| userClass |
| host |
| documentIdentifier |
| documentTitle |
| documentVersion |
| documentLocation |
| durName |
| wkdName |
| protocolProfile |
| objectID |
| friendlyCountryName |

The syntax is the same as CaseExactString, except that when matching 'characters that differ only in their case are considered identical.'

Approximate matching is supported for this syntax.

The use of some of the attributes is now described, the more obvious ones are omitted.

**knowledgeInformation:** A description of knowledge mastered by a DSA.

**localityName:** Used to identify the geographical area or locality in which the object is physically located e.g.,

```
London
```

**stateOrProvinceName:** describes the state in which the `locality` is found; e.g.,

```
New York
```

**title:** An objects job title, e.g.,

```
Technical Manager
```

**businessCategory:** describes the business of the object, e.g.,

```
networking
```

This is used to find people sharing the same occupation.

**physicalDeliveryOfficeName:** describes the geographical location of the physical delivery office which services the postal address of this object; e.g.,

```
Troy
```

**friendlyCountryName:** A "nice" name for countries, as opposed to the two letter codes enforced by use of `CountryName`, for example

```
Great Britain
```

### 14.1.4 CaseIgnoreList

No standard attributes currently use this syntax.

The CaseIgnoreList syntax consists of a sequence of CaseIgnoreString values as shown by the BNF below.

```
list = <list_component> | <list_component> "$" <list>
list_component = [ "{T61}" ] <string>
```

When the list is displayed to a user, the "$" is replaced with a newline. Ordering is preserved. For example, the entry in an EDB file

```
caseIgnoreAttribute= this is a $ multi line $\
attribute definition
```

would be shown to a user as

```
caseIgnoreAttribute= this is a
                     multi line
                     attribute definition
```

QUIPU only allows equality matching for this syntax.

### 14.1.5 CountryString

| Standard Attributes |
| --- |
| countryName |

This syntax is treated as a PrintableString, with matching rules as for CaseIgnore-String, and the restriction that the string must be one of the codes defined by ISO 3166.

### 14.1.6 IA5String

| QUIPU Attributes |
| --- |
| control |
| quipuVersion |

| RARE Attributes |
| --- |
| aRecord |
| mDRecord |
| mXRecord |
| nSRecord |
| sOARecord |
| cNAMERecord |

This syntax is handled as PrintableString, except a wider range of characters are recognised (i.e., any character in IA5 string, characters such as NewLine are quoted using the same mechanism as described for T.61 string in Section 14.1.2), with matching rules as for CaseExactString.

### 14.1.7 VisibleString

| RARE Attributes |
| --- |
| nRSSystemDescription |

This is currently treated as an ASN.1 attribute (see Section 14.6).

### 14.1.8 OctetString

No attributes use this syntax directly.

Characters that cannot be printed as an ASCII are represented using the quoting mechanism described in Section 14.1.2.

### 14.1.9 NumericString

| Standard Attributes |
|---|
| x121Address<br>internationaliSDNNumber |

The value is simply a numeric string (digits 0 through 9 only)

```
<NumericValue> ::= <numericstring>
```

The two attributes are used thus:

**x121Address:** defines the X.121 Address of an object as defined by the CCITT Recommendation X.121.

**internationaliSDNNumber:** An International ISDN Number as defined by CCITT Recommendation E.164.

### 14.1.10 DestinationString

| Standard Attributes |
|---|
| destinationIndicator |

Behaves as a `<printablestring>`, with CaseIgnoreString matching rules.

The only attribute of the type `destinationIndicator` is used to define the addressee as required by the Public Telegram Service.

### 14.1.11 TelephoneNumber

| Standard Attributes |
|---|
| telephoneNumber |

| RARE Attributes |
|---|
| homePhone |

| PSI Attributes |
|---|
| mobileTelephoneNumber<br>pagerTelephoneNumber |

The value should be a string describing the phone number of the object using the international notation; e.g.,

```
+1 518-283-8860
```

or

```
+1 518-283-8860 x1234
```

In general, the syntax is:

```
"+" <country code> <national number> [ "x" <extension> ]
```

Matching is as defined for CaseExactString, except that all space and "–" characters are skipped during the comparison.

### 14.1.12 PostalAddress

| Standard Attributes |
|---|
| postalAddress |
| registeredAddress |
| homePostalAddress |

```
<PostalAddressValue> ::= <address_component> |
                         <address_component> "$" <address>
<address_component> = <StringValue>
```

For example `UCL $ Gower Street $ London`. You are limited to a maximum of 6 <address_component>'s, each with a maximum of 30 characters. (Note each <address_component> can include T.61 strings; see Section 14.1.2 for details of this).

Please note: substring matching is not supported by QUIPU for this syntax.

### 14.1.13 DN

| Standard Attributes |
|---|
| aliasedObjectName |
| member |
| owner |
| roleOccupant |
| seeAlso |

| QUIPU Attributes |
|---|
| masterDSA |
| slaveDSA |
| relayDSA |

| MHS Attributes |
|---|
| mhsMessageStoreName |

| RARE Attributes |
|---|
| manager |
| documentAuthor |
| secretary |
| lastModifiedBy |
| associatedName |

```
<DNValue> ::= <name>
```

Distinguished names are discussed in Section 6.2.3, the BNF is repeated for completeness:

```
<DNValue> ::= <rdn> | <rdn> "@" <DNValue>
<rdn> ::= <attribute> | <attribute> "%" <rdn>
```

The DNs held by the attribute have the following meanings:-

**aliasedObjectName:** The name of an aliased object.

**member:** Specifies a member of a `groupOfNames`.

**owner:** The name of the person responsible for the associated object.

**roleOccupant:** The person who fills an organisational role.

**seeAlso:** Other objects that may be of interest.

**masterDSA:** The DSA holding the master EDB file.

**slaveDSA:** DSAs holding slave EDB files.

**relayDSA:** A DSA to relay operations to if your DSA is not connected to a needed network community. Section 18.2.3 describes this in more detail.

**manager:** The manager of a DSA.

**documentAuthor:** Author of a document.

**secretary:** The name of a personal Secretary.

**lastModifiedBy:** The object that last modified the referenced object.

**associatedName:** The DN associated with a DNS domain.

### 14.1.14 OID

| Standard Attributes |
|---|
| supportedApplicationContext |

| MHS Attributes |
|---|
| mhsDeliverableContentTypes |
| mhsDeliverableEits |
| mhsSupportedAutomaticActions |
| mhsSupportedContentTypes |
| mhsSupportedOptionalAttributes |

```
<OIDValue> ::= <oid>
```

All the syntaxes in this section are represented by OIDs as follows:

```
<oid> ::= <keystring> "." <numericoid> |
          <keystring> |
          <numericoid>
<numericoid> ::= <numericstring> |
                 <numericstring> "." <numericoid>
```

For example `2.3.4.2` or `attribute.6`.

In general, the value will be a string using oidtable mappings.

### 14.1.15 ObjectClass

| Standard Attributes |
| --- |
| objectClass |

Although essentially an OID, a separate syntax is provided as an OID has additional semantics when used as an object class.

### 14.1.16 TelexNumber

| Standard Attributes |
| --- |
| telexNumber |

```
<TelexNumberValue> ::= <printablestring> "$" <printablestring>
                       "$" <printablestring>
```

This is used to represent `number $ country $ answerback`, for example `007 28722 $ G $ UCLPHYS`.

### 14.1.17 TeletexTerminalIdentifier

| Standard Attributes |
| --- |
| teletexTerminalIdentifier |

```
<TeletexTerminalIdentifierValue> ::= <printablestring>
           "$" <optstr> "$"  <optstr> "$" <optstr>
           "$" <optstr> "$" <optstr>
<optstr> ::= <printablestring> | (null)
```

Used to represent

```
terminal $ graphic $ control $ page $ misc $ private
```

### 14.1.18 FacsimileTelephoneNumber

| Standard Attributes |
| --- |
| facsimileTelephoneNumber |

```
<FacsimileTelephoneNumberValue> ::= <printablestring>
                                    [ "$" <faxparameters> ]
<faxparameters> ::= <faxparm> | <faxparm>
                    "$" <faxparameters>
<faxparm> ::= "twoDimensional" | "fineResolution" |
           "unlimitedLength" | "b4Length" |
           "a3Width" | "b4Width" | "uncompressed"
```

For example `+44 602 123-4567 $ twoDimensional`

### 14.1.19 DeliveryMethod

| Standard Attributes |
|---|
| preferredDeliveryMethod |

| MHS Attributes |
|---|
| mhsPreferredDeliveryMethods |

```
<DeliveryValue> = <pdm_component> | <pdm_component> "$" <pdm>
pdm_component = "any" | "mhs" | "physical" | "telex" |
                "teletex" | "g3fax" | "g4fax" | "ia5" |
                "videotex" | "telephone"
```

For example `mhs $ telephone`.

### 14.1.20 PresentationAddress

| Standard Attributes |
|---|
| presentationAddress |

For more details see Volume 1 of the ISODE manual and [SKill89a].

### 14.1.21 Password

| Standard Attributes |
|---|
| userPassword |

See Section 15.1 for a discussion of this attribute.

### 14.1.22 Certificate

| Standard Attributes |
|---|
| userCertificate |
| cACertificate |

```
<CertificateValue> ::= <Algorithm> "#" <EncryptedValue> "#"
          <Issuer> "#" <Subject> "#" <Algorithm> "#"
          <ProtocolVersion> "#" <Serial> "#" <Validity> "#"
          <Algorithm> "#" <EncryptedValue>

<Algorithm> ::= <OID> "#" <AlgorithmParameters>
<AlgorithmParameters> ::= | <IntegerValue> |
                            "{ASN}" <HexString>
<Issuer> ::= <DN>
<Subject> ::= <DN>
<ProtocolVersion> ::= <IntegerValue>
<Serial> ::= <IntegerValue>
<Validity> ::= <UTCTime> "#" <UTCTime>
<EncryptedValue> ::= <HexString> | <HexString> "-" <Digit>
```

### 14.1.23 CertificatePair

| Standard Attributes |
|---|
| crossCertificatePair |

```
<CertificatePairValue> ::= [<CertificateValue>] "|"
                           [<CertificateValue>]
```

At least one certificate should be present, although QUIPU will not enforce this.

### 14.1.24 CertificateList

| Standard Attributes |
|---|
| authorityRevocationList |
| certificateRevocationList |

```
<CertificateListValue> ::= <AlgorithmValue> "#" <Issuer> "#"
                  <AlgorithmValue> "#" <EncryptedValue> "#"
                  <UTCTime> ["#" <RevokedCertificates>]

<RevokedCertificates> ::= <AlgorithmValue> "#"
                  <EncryptedValue>
                  [ "#" *(<RevokedCertificate> "#") ]

<RevokedCertificate> ::= <Subject> "#" <AlgorithmValue> "#"
                  <SerialNumber> "#" <UTCTime>
```

### 14.1.25 Guide

| Standard Attributes |
|---|
| searchGuide |

```
<GuideValue>    ::= [<objectClass> "#"] <Criteria>
<Criteria>      ::= <CriteriaItem> | <CriteriaSet> |
                    "!" <Criteria>
<CrtieriaSet>   ::= ["("] Criteria "@" CriteriaSet [")"] |
                    ["("] Criteria "|" CriteriaSet [")"]
<CriteriaItem>  ::= ["("] <attributetype> "$" <matchType> [")"]
<matchType>     ::= "EQ" | "SUBSTR" | "GE" | "LE" | "APPROX"
```

Note the use of @ for 'and', as the & symbol has other meaning here.
Some examples of Search Guide are:

```
Person # commonName $ APPROX
( organization $ EQ ) @ (commonName $ SUBSTR)
( organization $ EQ ) @ ((commonName $ SUBSTR) | \
                         (commonName $ EQ))
```

### 14.1.26 UTCTime

| Standard Attributes |
|---|
| lastModifiedTime |

```
<UTCTimeValue> ::= <printablestring>
```

The string should be formatted using the template yymmddhhmmssz where yy represents the year; mm represents the month; dd represents the day; hh represents hours; mm represents minutes; ss represents seconds; z represents the timezone.

For example the string 890602093221Z is used to represent 09:32:21 at GMT, on June 2nd, 1989.

### 14.1.27 Boolean

No attributes use this syntax.

```
<BooleanValue> ::= <boolean>
<boolean>      ::= "TRUE" | "FALSE"
```

### 14.1.28 Integer

| MHS Attributes |
|---|
| mhsDeliverableContentLength |

```
<IntegerValue> ::= <d>
```

### 14.1.29 AccessPoint

| QUIPU Attributes |
|---|
| subordinateReference<br>crossReference<br>nonSpecificSubordinateReference |

```
<AccessPointValue> ::= <DN> "#" <PresentationAddress>
```

These attribute are used to give references to Non-QUIPU DSAs and are discussed in Section 18.6.

## 14.2 QUIPU Attribute Syntaxes

### 14.2.1 ACL

| QUIPU Attributes |
|---|
| accessControlList |

```
<aclvalue> ::= <aclwho> "#" <aclwhat> "#" <acltype> ["#"]
<aclwho> ::= "self" | "others" | "group #" <namelist> |
"prefix #" <namelist>
<aclwhat> ::= "none" | "detect" | "compare" |
                     "read" | "add" | "write"
<acltype> ::= "child" | "entry" | "default" |
                     "attributes #" <oidlist>
<oidlist> ::= <oid> | <oidlist> "$" <oid>
```

The use of ACL is discussed in Section 15.2.

### 14.2.2 Schema

| QUIPU Attributes |
|---|
| treeStructure |

Schema is currently represented by a single OID, and discussed fully in Section 18.7.

### 14.2.3 ProtectedPassword

| QUIPU Attributes |
|---|
| protectedPassword |

```
<ProtectedPasswordValue> ::= <StringValue>
```

The password encryption mechanism is encapsulated within the matching rules for this attribute; two values are "equal" if they are identically equal or if one is an encrypted representation of the other.

Note that "equals" is not transitive for this attribute: If $a = b$ and $b = c$, testing $a = c$ may give "incomparable" rather than "true" as the result. The reason for this is that in some circumstances properly testing this attribute for equality would consume an unacceptable amount of time. The security of the encryption mechanism depends on this!

### 14.2.4 SecurityPolicy

| QUIPU Attributes |
|---|
| entrySecurityPolicy<br>dsaDefaultSecurityPolicy<br>dsaPermittedSecurityPolicy |

This attribute is currently handled as "ASN.1", see Section 14.6.

### 14.2.5 EdbInfo

| QUIPU Attributes |
|---|
| eDBinfo |

```
<EdbInfoValue> ::= <name> "#" <name> "#" <namelist> ["#"]
```

This attribute is discussed in Section 18.10.

### 14.2.6 InheritedAttribute

| QUIPU Attributes |
|---|
| InheritedAttribute |

```
<InheritedAttributeValue> ::= [ <oid> "$" ]
                              [ "always" <InheritedList> ]
                              [ "default" <InheritedList> ]
<InheritedList> ::= "(" NEWLINE <AttributeSequence> NEWLINE ")"
```

This attribute is discussed in Section 18.7.5.

## 14.3 RARE Attribute Syntaxes

These syntaxes are also described in [SKill89c].

### 14.3.1 Mailbox

| RARE Attributes |
|---|
| otherMailbox |

```
<MailboxValue> ::= <printablestring> "$" <IA5String>
```

For example `internet $ quipu-support@cs.ucl.ac.uk`.

### 14.3.2 CaseIgnoreIA5String

| RARE Attributes |
|---|
| rfc822Mailbox |
| domainComponent |
| nRSTextualDescription |
| associatedDomain |

These attributes are handled as IA5Strings, but use the matching rules for the CaseIgnoreString syntax.

### 14.3.3 Photo

| RARE Attributes |
|---|
| photo |

Photos are a special case of "ASN.1" (see Section 14.6), but the output format is different. Your attention is drawn to Section 18.7.4 which discusses storing large attributes in a separate file.

With this version of QUIPU, the attribute should be encoded as a bitstring, in a two-dimensional G3FacsimilePage encoding (as per recommendation T.4). However, in the future this will migrate to an X.400 bodypart, containing a G3FacsimilePage, with the advantage this can then be one- or two-dimensional. The current photo decoders will recognise the new format.

### 14.3.4 Audio

| RARE Attributes |
|---|
| audio |

The data is in the form of a u-law encoded sound file. If you have a Sun Microsystems Sun 4 workstation, the demonstration 'play' utility can be used to play the attributes. (A modified version of 'play' that ignores the file header is better — such as that made available by J. Michael Bauer of the University of Calgary. QUIPU-support can supply details if required.)

This is an interim demonstration attribute; the format is temporary and may be replaced when a suitable standard audio encoding mechanism is found.

## 14.4 THORN System Attribute Syntaxes

| Attribute | Syntax |
|---|---|
| thornACL | ThornACL |
| ruleDescription | RDType |
| objectDescription | ODType |
| attributeDescription | ADType |
| knowledgeReference | KnowledgeReference |

The Syntaxes listed above are not recognised by QUIPU, and are thus handled as ASN.1 — see Section 14.6. However, QUIPU compatible syntax handlers for them are available as part of the THORN[FSiro88] project.

### 14.4.1 NRSInformation

| THORN System Attributes |
|---|
| forwardOnlyInformation |
| reverseOnlyInformation |
| forwardAndReverseInformation |

Although essentially a "Thorn" attribute, QUIPU does have a syntax handler for this syntax; however, it is very complex and not defined here. It is defined in [SKill89c].

## 14.5 MHS Attribute Syntaxes

| Attribute | Syntax |
|---|---|
| mhsORaddresses | ORAddress |
| mhsDLMembers | ORName |
| mhsDLSubmitPermissions | DLSubmitPermissions |

The Syntaxes shown above are not currently recognised by QUIPU, and are thus handled as raw ASN.1 (see Section 14.6). However, the PP MHS System has QUIPU compatible syntax handlers that can be easily added to the DISH program, and provides a tool for handling entries of the "distribution list" object class. PP is available under conditions similar to the ISODE,;for details you should contact "PP-Support@cs.ucl.ac.uk."

## 14.6 ASN.1

As the preceding sections in this chapter have mentioned, not all syntaxes have a string representation defined by QUIPU, so are represented by the raw ASN.1.

An example would be:

```
photo= {ASN}0308207b4001488001fd...
```

where 0308...is a hexadecimal representation (encoded using the "Basic Encoding Rules") of the ASN.1 defined attribute.

Attributes stored as ASN.1, will usually be matched correctly, with the following exceptions:

- There is an IMPLICIT Set in the ASN.1. The DSA will not detect the set, and so will not know to match components in arbitrary order.
- If special matching rules apply, for example, special rules to determine equivalence of telephone numbers. Such rules would need to be represented by code in the DSA.

# Chapter 15

# Introduction to Security Features

## 15.1 Passwords

When you bind to a DSA, to get write access you need to tell the DSA who you are — you do this by supplying your distinguished name. So that the DSA can authenticate you, you also need to supply your QUIPU password. Anyone knowing your password can act as you and alter your data. Therefore your password should be well chosen and kept safe.

### 15.1.1 Choosing a Password

- Do not use the same password for QUIPU as you do for login. It is always bad practise (but convenient!) to use the same password on different systems. The manager of your QUIPU DSA can discover your QUIPU password. This doesn't affect the security of QUIPU (as your DSA manager can alter local data anyway), but the QUIPU manager is probably not allowed access to your login account.
- Do not choose an obvious word.

  Your password should **not** be any of the following:

  - Your name, initials, date of birth, place of work or similar personal details.
  - Any girl's name in any language.
  - The name of a film star, television personality, and so forth.
  - The name of a character from a science-fiction or fantasy novel.
  - Computer jargon e.g., "foobar".
  - Any of the above, spelt backwards.
  - Any word from your system's on-line dictionary. Ideally, your password should not be a word at all (it could be the concatenation of two unrelated words, for example).

- Change your password from time to time.

### 15.1.2 Taking Care of Your Password

- Configuration Files. It is possible to put your QUIPU password in a configuration file in your home directory (see the later Chapters on user interfaces). If you do this, you must make sure that the configuration file (.quipurc) is not publicly readable (by using the UNIX *chmod* command, for example).
- Access Control Lists. Your QUIPU password is itself stored in QUIPU, as the *userPassword* attribute of your entry. You should make sure that the access control list for your entry grants public *compare* but not *read* access to this attribute. (The attribute must be publicly comparable so that QUIPU can check that you have presented the right password when you start a session). The next section will explain how to set up access control lists.
- Do not give your password to other people.

  If several people need to be able to modify the same data, the access control lists can be set up so that this is possible without them sharing passwords.
- Do not write your password down!

## 15.2 Discretionary Access Control

"Discretionary access aontrol" is any means by which users can (at their discretion) give other users access to data which they control. In QUIPU, access control lists are used to provide discretionary access control.

### 15.2.1 Model

Each node in the DIT held by a QUIPU DSA has a QUIPU access control list (ACL). The ACL is divided into three parts:

1. Child ACL. This controls who may discover or change which entries are placed immediately below the node in the DIT.
2. Entry ACL. This controls who may access the entry placed at the node.
3. Attribute ACL. For every attribute of the entry, there is an attribute ACL which controls who may access that attribute. To keep the representation compact, each entry has a default attribute ACL. This is used for all the attributes of the entry that have not been explicitly given a different attribute ACL.

Each entry, child, or attribute ACL (henceforth called an object ACL) consists of a list of (access selector, access level) pairs. It associates every distinguished name with an access level, according to the following rule:

> Take every pair where the selector (left hand side) matches the name. The associated access level is the maximum of the corresponding right-hand sides. If no selectors match the name, the associated access level is *none*.

The levels of access are as follows:

**None:** No accesses to the object are allowed.

**Detect:** A DUA can detect that the protected object exists.

**Compare:** A filter (e.g. test for equality to some value) may be applied to the object.

**Read:** The contents of the object may be read.

**Add:** The contents of the object may be added to, but not removed from.

**Write:** The contents of the object may be modified in any way.

The possible Access Selectors are as follows:

**Entry:** Matches the entry itself only.

**Other:** Matches everything.

**Prefix <name>:** Matches <name> and everything below it in the DIT.

**Group <name>:** Matches <name>. (This is not what the 'group' selector was originally designed for, but it is currently what it does!)

The attribute syntax used to represent this is defined in Section 14.2.1, with the ASN.1 definition shown in Figure 15.1.

### 15.2.2 Detect Access

QUIPU treats the access level *none* as though it were *detect.* This means that it is often possible to detect the presence of protected data, even if you have no access to it.

The reason for this is that it is very difficult for the Directory to pretend that data isn't there; carefully chosen queries can catch it out. Access control mechanisms that can be by-passed are very dangerous; they give a false sense of security. Accordingly, we have decided not to implement "undetectable data."

### 15.2.3 Effect of ACLs on Operations

This section explains which ACLs are checked for each of the X.500 operations.

**List:** The child ACL of the target must give at least *read* access. In addition, each child will only be listed if its entry ACL gives at least *read*. Later versions of QUIPU may also require that the attribute ACL of the distinguished (naming) attribute of the child give at least *read* access.

**Search:** To search the immediate descendants of a node, that node's child ACL must give at least *read* access. In addition, each child will only be searched if its entry ACL gives at least *compare* access. The filter "present" may be applied to any attribute. Other basic filters evaluate to *maybe* unless the relevant attribute ACL gives at least compare access. If an attribute within an entry does not have public read access, normally subtree searches on that attribute will fail. This is intentional, as it would be difficult to provide a consistent picture of the DIT, when unauthenticated DSP links are involved in the search. This restriction is lifted if, and only if, the entire subtree to be searched (using master or slave EDB files) is held within one DSA, and the association to that DSA is an authenticated DAP association.

**Read:** The entry ACL of the target must give at least *read* access and the attribute ACL of each attribute read must give at least *read* access.

**Compare:** The entry ACL of the target must give at least *compare* access. The attribute ACL of the tested attribute must give at least *compare* access.

**Modify:** The entry ACL of the target must give at least *add* access if attributes or values are to be added, and at least *write* access if they are to be removed. For each attribute changed, the attribute ACL must give at least *add* access for an attribute or value to be added, and at least *write* access for an attribute or value to be removed.

**Add Entry:** To add an entry below a node, that node's child ACL must give at least *add* access.

**Remove Entry:** To remove an entry, the child ACL of its parent must give at least *write* access. No rights to the entry itself are required.

**Modify RDN:** The child ACL of the target's parent must give at least *write* access. If the operation needs to add an attribute (value), the target's entry ACL must give *add* access and the attribute ACL of the attribute must give *add* access. If the operation needs to remove an attribute (value), the target's entry ACL must give *write* access and the attribute ACL of the attribute must give *write* access.

### 15.2.4 Example Use of ACLs

A node representing a user might be given the following ACL:

- childACL is not applicable, and so omitted.
- EntryACL is {other, read} + {self, write} + {group=<Manager>, write}, so that only the user or a manager can change the entry. Using the ACL syntax, this is expressed as:

```
acl= other # read # entry
acl= self # write # entry
acl= group # <Manager Name> # write # entry
```

- DefaultAttributeACL is {other, read} + {self, write}, which leads to publicly readable attributes modifyable by the user. Using the ACL syntax, this is expressed as:

```
acl= other # read # default
acl= self # write # default
```

- The attribute ACL for ACL is {other, read} + {group = <manager name>, write}, so that only the manager can change the ACL. Using the ACL syntax, this is expressed as:

```
acl= other # read # attributes # acl
acl= group # <Manager Name> # write # attributes # acl
```

- The attribute ACL for Password is {self, write} + {other, compare} so that the user can change the password, DSAs can check the password, and only the user can read it.

```
acl= self # write # attributes # userPassword
acl= other # compare # attributes # userPassword
```

A node representing an organisation or organisational unit might be given the following ACL:

- childACL is {other, read} + {group=<manager name>, write}. Everybody can search the members of the organisation, but only the manager is allowed to add or delete members. This is represented as an attribute with:

```
acl= other # read # child
acl= group # <Manager Name> # write # child
```

- EntryACL is {other, read} + {group=<manager name>, write}. This is represented as an attribute with:

```
acl= other # read # entry
acl= group # <Manager Name> # write # entry
```

- DefaultAttributeACL is {other, read} + {group=<manager name>, write}. This is represented as an attribute with:

```
acl= other # read # default
acl= group # <Manager Name> # write # default
```

Every entry in the QUIPU DIT must have an acl attribute. If you do not supply one, the the default is added. The default ACL is often printed as

```
acl=
```

with no value. The default ACL is everybody read everything, but self can write, in long form this is expressed as:

```
acl= self # write # entry
acl= self # write # child
acl= self # write # default
acl= others # read # entry
acl= others # read # child
acl= others # read # default
```

For many entries this is sufficient.

It can be seen that this scheme gives a great deal of flexibility, without the addition of any protocol elements. The encoding is designed so that the volume overhead is not excessive for sensible access policies.

### 15.2.5 Extended Example

As an extended example, suppose we wanted to set up an ACL for the following situation:

1. Anybody can read most attributes.
2. Nobody can read password except the user.
3. User can modify homeTelephone number, everybody else can read it.
4. Sys Admin can modify workTelephoneNumber and PayrollNumber, everybody else can read them.
5. Only user and Sys Admin can read the PayrollNumber.

The first stage is to consider the requirements of various groups of users, so we could write:

```
acl= group  # c=GB@o=UCL@cn=Admin # write # entry
acl= group  # c=GB@o=UCL@cn=Admin # write # \
            attributes # workTelephone $ PayrollNumber
```

But later on in the ACL definition we will want different ACLs for certain attributes, so we need to split into two different groups at this stage.

```
acl= group  # c=GB@o=UCL@cn=Admin # write # entry
acl= group  # c=GB@o=UCL@cn=Admin # write # \
            attributes # workTelephone
acl= group  # c=GB@o=UCL@cn=Admin # write # \
            attributes # PayrollNumber
```

If you do not do this, the DSA will complain about inconsistent ACL definitions, as it will be unable to determine which ACL line to use for which attribute.

We need to give "self" access to various parts of the entry. We do not need to mention workPhone as the access given to "others" is sufficient. Again we split the attribute definitions into small groups.

```
acl= self   # write # entry
acl= self   # write # default
acl= self   # write # attributes # userpassword
acl= self   # write # attributes # homeTelephone
acl= self   # read  # attributes # PayrollNumber
```

Finally, we need to give others access to required attributes.

```
acl= others # read # entry
acl= others # read # default
acl= others # compare # attributes # userpassword
acl= others # read # attributes # homeTelephone
acl= others # read # attributes # workTelephone
acl= others # none # attributes # PayrollNumber
```

```
ACLInfo ::= SET OF SEQUENCE {
        AccessSelector,
        AccessCategories }

AccessCategories ::= ENUMERATED {
        none (0),
        detect (1),
        compare (2),
        read (3),
        add (4),
        write (5) }

AccessSelector ::= CHOICE {
        entry [0] NULL,
                -- DUA identified by the entry
        other [2] NULL,
                -- This indicates "public" rights
        prefix [3] NameList,
                -- This identifies a prefix name for specified DUAs
                -- e.g., anyone in the UK
        group [4] NameList
                -- For specifying group rights
        }

NameList ::= SET OF DistinguishedName

ACLSyntax ::= SEQUENCE {
    childACL            [0] ACLInfo DEFAULT {{other, read}},
    entryACL            [1] ACLInfo DEFAULT {{other, read}},
    defaultAttributeACL [2] ACLInfo DEFAULT {{other, read}},
    [3] SET OF AttributeACL }
                        -- Defaults to a publicly readable
                        -- read only directory

AttributeACL ::= SEQUENCE {
    SET OF AttributeType,
    ACLInfo }

ACL ATTRIBUTE
    WITH ATTRIBUTE-SYNTAX ACLSyntax
    SINGLE VALUE
```

Figure 15.1: ACL Definition

# Part IV

# QUIPU Manual: Administrator's Guide

# Chapter 16

# Installing QUIPU

This section describes how to install QUIPU, and make it operate in a basic fashion. This is reasonably prescriptive, as it should be possible to install and operate a QUIPU DUA and/or DSA without too much knowledge about how it functions.

QUIPU comes in various separate parts of the ISODE source tree. Only the *libdsap* (3n) library, the DSA *ros.quipu* and the DUA interface DISH are "made" as part of the default installation of ISODE. This section assumes you have installed this part of ISODE. You should consult the *READ-ME* file in the top level of the source tree to find out how to do this. Your attention is drawn to the discussion of the *iaed* and *dased* programs in this *READ-ME* file. This can be used to replace the *isoentities*(5n) and *isoservices*(5n) static files with dynamic directory lookup[1]. Volumes 1–4 of the ISODE manual describe in more detail other features of the installation of ISODE not specific to the directory.

Before you install QUIPU there are various compile time options you could consider setting which control the operation of QUIPU, in particular of the DSA. These options are set in the file *h/quipu/config.h*, and are described in the next section. If you consider yourself a QUIPU "novice", then these are probably best left to their default values initially. However, if you qualify as a "large" site you may want to consider enabling the TURBO_DISK options.

In the *others/quipu/uips/* directory of the ISODE source tree there are various sub-directories, one for each optional user interface (FRED, DSC, sd, POD, *ufn* and Xd). A version of DISH that runs directly from a UNIX shell, *dishinit*; a script to create a default *.quipurc* file for new users, and *sid*: a set of scripts that utilise the shell version of DISH, are all installed from the *dish* sub-directory. The *manage* sub-directory contains an enhanced version of DISH that can be used to manage alias attributes. You should consult *others/quipu/uips/READ-ME*, for precise installation details of all of these interfaces.

Each of these interfaces knows about the "photo" attribute that an entry in the DIT can have. In order to display the photographs, the photo handling code must

[1]In fact, you are encouraged to use these services rather than the static (potentially out of date) files.

be compiled. Instructions on this can be found in Section 18.7.3 of this manual and the file *others/quipu/photo/READ-ME*.

## 16.1 Compile Options

This section describes the options that can be set in the *h/quipu/config.h* before compilation of the QUIPU code.

`#define PDU_DUMP`: If this is defined, and DISH' is invoked with

```
dish -pdu foobar
```

then a directory "foobar" will be created, and will contain logs of all the X.500 PDUs sent to and from the DSA. This is useful for debugging.

`#define NO_STATS`: If defined, the QUIPU will *not* produce statistical and audit logs either the DSA or DUA. These logs are useful to see what has been happening to your system. If logging is allowed it can be turned off at runtime. From the standpoint of security, it is advisable not to select this option. Audit logs are very useful for detecting and tracing attempts to break the security of the system.

`#define CHECK_FILE_ATTRIBUTES`: If an EDB entry contains a FILE attribute, check that the corresponding file exists at load time. This significantly increases the time taken to start a DSA.

`#define QUIPU_MALLOC`: Use a version of malloc() optimised for the memory resident QUIPU DSA database. It is believed to behave about 20% faster than the standard malloc algorithm in QUIPU's case.

`#define TURBO_DISK`: This option is described in the next section of this manual.

`#define TURBO_AVL`: This option is described in the next section of this manual.

`#define TURBO_INDEX`: This option is described in the next section of this manual.

`#define SOUNDEX_PREFIX`: Consider soundex prefixes as matches. For example, make 'fred' match 'frederick'. Defining this option gives approximate matching behavior the same as in QUIPU-6.0.

`#define HAVE_PROTECTED`: If defined, enable use of protectedPassword attribute, and thus enable the use of protected simple authentication.

`#define HAVE_RSA`: This option results in a DSA that can perform strong authentication; see Chapter 19 for details.

**#define COMPAT_6_0:** Operate in a manner compatible with QUIPU-6.0. To be fully compliant with X.500 distributed operations involving subtree searching across multiple DSA, this option should be removed. *However*, it is essential for the pilot service that this option is *set* until QUIPU-support indicates that is it safe to remove it!

**#define USE_BUILTIN_OIDS:** A DSA needs to know the OIDs for various attribute type and object classes. With this option, the OIDs are built into the code (for efficiency, and to remove the table dependency), without it the *oidtables* are used.

For the DISH interface a compile option to allow the use of the GNU "readline" package from the Free Software Foundation can be set in the *quipu/dish/Makefile*. Details are given in the Makefile.

## 16.2 TURBO Options for Large Sites

This section describes three options (TURBO_AVL, TURBO_INDEX, and TURBO_DISK) that can be set in the file *h/quipu/config.h*. All three options are most useful for sites with a large amount of data (e.g., thousands of entries, or hundreds of EDB files). The TURBO_AVL and TURBO_INDEX options are set by default. If your DSA only holds a small amount of data you can skip this section.

The first option, TURBO_AVL, is used to speed the process of loading data from disk during startup (the TURBO_AVL option replaces the TURBO_LOAD option for this purpose), and to reduce DSA paging in many circumstances. With this option defined, code is enabled to keep each in core EDB in an AVL tree, instead of in a linked list. When QUIPU starts, it must check each entry that it loads against those sibling entries already loaded to ensure that each EDB file contains no duplicate RDNs. Normally, this is done by searching a linked list of loaded entries. The TURBO_AVL option causes AVL trees to be built and searched, making the loading process for big EDB files much faster. As an added benefit, fewer entries will be touched when resolving distinguished names, so DSA paging is reduced.

The second option, TURBO_INDEX, can be used to speed certain kinds of searches by building an index based on selected attribute types. There are three DSA tailor file options that are used to specify which attributes and which portions of the tree are to be indexed. They are `optimize_attr`, `index_subtree`, and `index_siblings`. Section 18.3 describes these options in more detail. For the selected attributes and portions of the tree, the index is searched for queries involving equality, approximate equality, initial substring matching, and attribute existence. *and* and *or* combinations of the above queries are also supported. Queries involving negation, inequality, or substring matching with no initial substring supplied are not indexed and will be handled as usual, by a linear search of the database. *Note*: TURBO_AVL must also be defined in order to use TURBO_INDEX.

The third option, TURBO_DISK, can be used to make modify operations much faster, especially on large data sets. It requires the use of the *gdbm* library. *Gdbm* is a library of simple database routines providing functionality similar to *dbm* and *ndbm*, but without the filesystem page size limitations of those systems. *Gdbm* is GNU software and is available from the Free Software Foundation. It is not a part of the ISODE.

Normally, when an entry is modified, QUIPU writes the entire EDB file containing the entry out to disk. If the EDB file is very large, this can take some time, especially on a heavily loaded system. The TURBO_DISK option works by keeping the disk data in *gdbm* files instead of the regular EDB files. This way, when an update is made, only the affected entry need be written. The performance increase is directly proportional to the size of the EDB file. Whereas a normal update operation takes time proportional to the size of the EDB file, with the TURBO_DISK option it takes a small constant amount of time. If you don't have EDB files with at least several hundred entries, it's probably not worth enabling the TURBO_DISK option. *Note*: TURBO_AVL must also be defined in order to use TURBO_DISK.

To use the TURBO_DISK option, add a line like this to the *h/quipu/config.h* file:

```
#define TURBO_DISK /* enable fast EDB update operations */
```

You should also add a line like this to the *config/CONFIG.make* file:

```
LIBGDBM= -lgdbm
```

If you have defined TURBO_DISK, you will have to convert your EDB file hierarchy into a gdbm file hierarchy before running QUIPU. This step is only necessary once. The *quipu/turbo* directory contains some tools to help in this process. The shell script *tree2dbm* will convert an EDB file hierarchy to a *gdbm* file hierarchy. To use it, type "`tree2dbm database-directory`" where database-directory is the directory where the EDB file hierarchy begins. This script does a find starting in the specified directory for files named EDB and runs them through the *edb2dbm* program which creates a file called *EDB.gdbm*. The original EDB file is neither removed nor molested, so you'll need roughly twice the disk space. Alternatively, you can run *edb2dbm* by hand on each EDB file. The reverse operation (converting from a *gdbm* hierarchy to an EDB hierarchy) is done by the *synctree* shell script. It is a good idea to run *synctree* out of *crontab* once in a while to update the EDB file hierarchy.

Finally, it should be noted that parse errors will be reported somewhat differently in the *dsap.log* file with the TURBO_DISK option enabled. Since line numbers do not make much sense in a *gdbm* file, errors will be reported based on the Relative Distinguished Name of the offending entry. If you get a parse error (because of a non-printable character, for example), the best approach is to do something like this:

```
edbcat EDB >bob
```

Edit the file *bob*, locate the entry, fix the problem, then

```
edb2dbm bob
mv bob.gdbm EDB.gdbm
```

where this procedure assumes you are in the directory containing the bad EDB.gdbm file. The *edbcat* program can be found in the *quipu/turbo* directory and is used to convert from *gdbm* back to plain text EDB format.

## 16.3 Files

Regardless of how you install QUIPU and the ISODE, the number of files needed to run QUIPU is quite small.

In ISODE's `BINDIR` directory, typically */usr/local/bin/*, there are a few programs of interest:

**dish:** The DIrectory SHell
This is discussed in Chapter 7.

**bind:** Shell interface to DISH
There are actually several links (listed below) to a program called *bind*. These act to export the DISH interface to the UNIX shell. As such, you can issue commands to DISH from the shell, rather than running DISH directly.

| | |
|---|---|
| add | compare |
| delete | dsacontrol |
| list | modify |
| modifyrdn | moveto |
| search | showentry |
| showname | squid |

**fred:** A white pages user interface
See Chapter 11.

**editentry:** Edit a Directory entry
This is a simple shell script that DISH invokes when you ask DISH to edit an entry in the Directory.

**unbind:** Unbind from DISH
This command is used to terminate DISH.

In ISODE's `SBINDIR` directory, typically */usr/etc/*, the DSA resides:

**ros.quipu:** The QUIPU DSA
This program will be started once, for each DSA you are running, from rc.local. A script is provided to invoke this program, in case you need to restart it.

In ISODE's `ETCDIR` directory, also typically */usr/etc/*, there are a few programs and files of interest:

**oidtable.at, oidtable.gen, oidtable.oc** These define the attribute types, generic object identifiers, and object classes known to the system. (An object identifier is a method used to unambiguously encode, among other things, the names of attributes and object classes.) These files you never deal with unless they are accidentally corrupted.

**dsaptailor** This is the run-time tailor file for the DUAs. You will configure this file initially and then probably leave it alone.

**isoaliases, isobjects, isoentities, isomacros, isoservices** These are various databases used by the ISODE. These files you never deal with unless they are accidentally corrupted.

**isologs** This script runs nightly under *cron*(8) to trim the ISODE log files, kept in ISODE's `LOGDIR` directory, typically */usr/tmp/*. This file you never deal with unless it is accidentally corrupted.

**isotailor** This is the run-time tailor file for the ISODE. You will configure this file initially and then probably leave it alone.

# Chapter 17

# Configuring a DUA

It is suggested that you try to get a DUA operational by connecting to a "well-known" DSA before you attempt to operate a local DSA. Or, if you have a DSA from a previous release of QUIPU — try and connect to that.

## 17.1 Connecting to a DSA

A DUA essentially only needs to know one thing to be able to contact a DSA: that is the OSI network address of the DSA. This parameter is defined in the file *dsaptailor*, together with some other parameters. The full set of parameters is described in Section 17.2.

The `dsa_address` parameter defines a local name and the network address of the DSA to initially contact. For example,

```
dsa_address  vicuna  Internet=bells.cs.ucl.ac.uk+50987
```

declares that the DSA locally referred to by the name `vicuna` is contacted by calling the network address `Internet=bells.cs.ucl.ac.uk`50987. The syntax of network addresses is discussed in briefly in Section 18.2.1 and more fully in Volume 2 of the ISODE manual and [SKill89a].

As shown, the address is preceded by a private key `vicuna`. This can be used in some DUAs (including DISH) to specifying the address of the DSA to contact. If there are more than one `dsa_address` entries, the first entry will be used to supply the default DSA address.

A default *dsaptailor* file (taken from the *dsap/dsaptailor* file of the ISODE source tree) is installed as *dsaptailor* in the ISODE `ETCDIR` directory (usually */usr/etc/*) when the *dsap* library is installed, this supplies the addresses of various DSAs that you may be able to access.

To try to connect to one of the DSAs listed in *dsaptailor*, invoke DISH, with a `-call` flag; e.g., `dish -call giant` will try to contact the DSA "giant" running at

UCL. If the connection is successful, then the prompt `dish ->` will be returned. If the connection fails, the program will exit with an appropriate error message.

If this fails you might want to try connecting to some of the other registered DSAs, for example, try `dish -call alpaca`, `dish -call eel` or `dish -call anaconda`.

Many of these top level DSAs do not allow anonymous connections. If you see the message `inappropriate authentication` as a result of your connection attempt you will probably need to supply a DN using the `-username` flag to dish.

If you fail to contact a DSA at this point, there are likely to be lower level problems. You should turn up the ISODE logging (see Volume 2 of the ISODE manual) to see what is happening to the network calls.

If you invoke DISH without a `-c` flag (using the default *dsaptailor*), it will try to connect to the DSA defined by the first `dsa_address` entry.

DISH is described in full in Chapter 7 of this manual.

## 17.2 Tailoring

The program configuration is tailored to allow you to change logging levels, and other parameters at runtime. It is used by the QUIPU DUA procedures, and by the QUIPU User Interfaces.

The file *dsaptailor* is used for this purpose and consists of single value entries (e.g., oidtable), unless otherwise stated (e.g dsaplog). Each entry has a parameter followed by its value. The various options are:

`oidtable`: The path for the OID definition tables. NOTE: It is best to have this appear as the first entry of the *tailor* file, as other entries may contain attributes that need to be looked up in these tables There are three:

1. *file.gen*, which contains generic names for building OIDs;
2. *file.at*, which contains the OIDs for attributes; and,
3. *file*.oc, which contains the OIDs for object classes.

For example,

```
oidtable    /usr/lib/quipu/OIDTable
```

will direct the DSA to consult:

```
/usr/lib/quipu/OIDTable.gen
/usr/lib/quipu/OIDTable.at
/usr/lib/quipu/OIDTable.oc
```

By default this variable is set to `oidtable` which refers to the tables *oidtable.** in the ISODE `ETCDIR` directory.

`dsa_address`: This parameter is described in Section 17.1.

**dsaplog:** Tailoring for the normal logging file. Each entry consists of one or more key/value pairs expressed as:

```
key=value
```

The keys are:

**file:** The name of the logfile.

**size:** The size in KBytes to which the logfile should be allowed to grow. When the log has reached this size, if the "zero" option below is set, then the log will be truncated; otherwise, no further logging will take place.

**level:** The levels of logging to be written to this log file. This can be any of the following levels:

**fatal:** fatal errors only.

**exceptions:** serious, but hopefully temporary, errors.

**notice:** general logging information.

**trace:** program tracing.

**pdus:** pdu tracing.

**debug:** full tracing of events.

**all:** log all events.

For example to have all errors written to the file you will need

```
dsaplog level=fatal level=exceptions
```

**dlevel:** Do not log the specified log level, this is the opposite of the above entry.

**dflags/sflags:** The flags associated with the log may be set (with `sflag`) or unset (with `dflag`). The allowable options are:

**close:** close the log after each entry.

**create:** create the log file if it does not exist.

**zero:** truncate the file when it gets too big.

**tty:** copy the logging information to the users tty.

An example might be:

```
dsaplog level=notice size=30 file=quipulog dflags=close
```

This says log events at "notice" level into the file *quipulog*, do not let the file grow larger than 30Kbytes; and do not close the file after each logging message.

**stats:** Used to control the level of statistical logging (parameters as for `dsaplog` above).

`local_DIT`: The argument is a distinguished name. When some User Interfaces start, you will be automatically moved to this position in the DIT.

`oidformat`: Defines how object identifiers should be printed. Use

```
oidformat   short
```

to print in short local key form, e.g.,

```
Country
```

or,

```
oidformat   long
```

to print in long object identifier form, e.g.,

```
joint.ds.attributeType.country
```

or,

```
oidformat   numeric
```

to print in numeric form, e.g.,

```
2.5.4.6
```

`photo`: The argument has two parts, a "terminal type" such as "sun" or "xterm"; the second is the name of the process that should handle displaying of photographs; for exampl,

photo xterm Xphoto

tells the DUA to call the process Xphoto to handle photograph attributes if the user is on a terminal of type "xterm." Handling photographs is described more fully in Section 18.7.3.

`quipurc`: If the argument has the value on, then a program called *dishinit* will be run every time a user without a *.quipurc* file tries to access the directory. *dishinit* is discussed in Section 7.7.1.

`sizelimit`: Defines the maximum number of entries a successful list or search should return. For example,

```
sizelimit 20
```

sets the DAP default service control "sizelimit" to be 20 entries.

# Chapter 18

# Configuring a DSA

This chapter discusses how to configure a QUIPU DSA. We recommend that you get a DUA running before you try to get a DSA working.

## 18.1 Basic Formats and Structures

All of the information a DSA requires is stored on disk and is text-structured. This includes various files (described later), and the local DIT database itself. A complete BNF description of the files is given in Appendix B on page 325.

### 18.1.1 Entry Data Block

A key component of the directory database is the entry data block, which is described fully in [SKill89b]. Figure 18.1 shows an example EDB file containing two "person" entries.

An EDB file contains a header, this is optionally but typically followed by a sequence of entries.

The header consists of two lines of text, the first must contain the string "`MASTER`", "`SLAVE`" or "`CACHE`", which indicates whether the data in the EDB file represents the authoritative `master` data, a `slave` copy of all the data, or some cachedd entries.

The next line of the EDB is a string that describes the version of the EDB. Every time the EDB is altered, the version number should be changed, so that `SLAVE` EDBs elsewhere will be automatically updated. When a DSA alters an EDB file, it writes the current (UTC) time in string format as the version string.

Generally following the header are a sequence of blank line separated entries. The concept of a null EDB file that contains just a header is allowed but discouraged. However it is sometimes useful as a temporary measure when creating a database.

An entry consists of a set of attributes, each attribute begins on a new line of the file. Section 6.2 discusses attributes in more detail and Chapter 14 describes the syntaxes used by all the attributes QUIPU recognises.

```
MASTER
19891025113003Z
CN= Colin Robbins
CN= Colin John Robbins
Phone= +44-1-387-7050 ext 3683
Surname= Robbins
Room= G10
Userid= crobbins
userClass= csstaff
rfc822Mailbox= C.Robbins@cs.ucl.ac.uk
Photo= {FILE}crobbins.photo
objectClass =thornPerson & quipuObject
acl=others # none # attribute # photo
acl=self # read # attribute # photo

CN= Steve Kille
CN= Steve E. Kille & Stephen Kille
Phone= +44-1-387-7050 ext 7294
Surname= Kille
objectClass = thornPerson & quipuObject
Room= G24
Userid= steve
userClass= csstaff
rfc822Mailbox= S.Kille@cs.ucl.ac.uk
```

Figure 18.1: Example EDB File

The first line of an entry is the relative distinguished name (RDN) of the entry. The subsequent line contains the non distinguished attributes.

### 18.1.2 Object Class Attribute

Of all the attributes an entry may have, the "objectClass" attribute is one of the most important from the configuration point of view. It defines the set of mandatory and optional attributes that must and may be present in the entry. For example, the object class "person" insists that there is a "surname" attribute, and there may optionally be a "telephone number" attribute. QUIPU knows about all the standard object classes and attributes, some of those defined by the THORN project (see Section 20.2) and those defined by QUIPU itself (see Appendix C). The full set of object classes and attributes a DSA knows about is defined by the "oidtables" which are explained in Section 18.11.

An entry can belong to more that one object class. For example, an entry representing an organisation might have the following object class attribute:

```
objectClass = organization & quipuNonLeafObject
```

And a person within that organisation might use the following object class definition:

```
objectClass = organizationalPerson & quipuObject & thornPerson
```

Every entry in a QUIPU DSA should belong to either the `quipuObject` or `quipuNonLeafObject` object classes[1], as this allows attributes the DSA needs to be added to an entry.

Further, object classes posses the notion of `class inheritance`. This means that an object class can be defined as a subclass of a previously defined object class with additional refinements. As a subclass, the newly defined object inherits all the semantics of its superclass, in addition to having additional semantics.

For example, the Directory defines an object class called `person`. This object class defines the attributes which a person in the real world might have. It may be useful to refine this somewhat to talk about persons who have network access. So, we need a new object class, e.g., `netPerson`. This can be defined in a straightforward fashion:

- The object class `netPerson` is a subclass of the object class `person` which *may* contain an additional attribute, `netMailbox`.

- The syntax of an `netMailbox` is a simple string of printable characters which is not case sensitive when performing comparisons.

[1]An entry may belong to `ExternalNonLeafObject` instead IF it is actually represented in the DIT by a non QUIPU DSA — See Section 18.6.

It is a QUIPU requirement that every entry that is not a leaf of the DIT should belong to the object class `quipuNonLeafObject`.

This class has one mandatory attribute:

**masterDSA:** identifies the Directory entity which is responsible for maintaining the master EDB for the children of this entry. The value is a Distinguished Name.

There is typically a single master for a particular entry in the tree. Hence, this value is usually single-valued. When an entry is to be modified, the Directory must contact the entity responsible for the MASTER EDB for that entry in order to perform the modification.

This class has two optional attributes:

**slaveDSA:** identifies any directory entities which have authoritative copies of the EDB for the children of this entry, and are prepared to resolve operations on that EDB file for a remote DSA. The value is one or more Distinguished Names.

**treeStructure:** identifies the object classes which may exist immediately below this entry. The value is one or more object classes. See Section 18.7.2 for full details of how to set this attribute.

Since a fundamental assumption of the Directory is that reads (queries) occur much more frequently than writes (updates), it is common to have several entities containing authoritative copies of an EDB. By keeping copies locally, queries can be answered with less latency.

### 18.1.3 Database Structure

All the local information held by a QUIPU Directory is held in an in-core database, this is loaded from disk when the DSA starts.

The data on disk is held in a UNIX tree of EDB[2] files that map the DIT. At every level in the DIT for which the DSA holds data, there is a single file called *EDB*. The top level of the DIT is stored in the UNIX directory defined by the `treedir` variable in the *quiputailor* file. For example, the setting

```
treedir      /usr/etc/quipu-db/
```

would define that the top level of the DIT would be found in this UNIX directory. If you hold a copy of the root EDB file, it will be found here.

If an entry defined in an *EDB* file has children stored locally, then the *EDB* file for the children will be found in a subdirectory whose name is the string encoded relative distinguished name of the entry. For example, underneath the root, there

[2] Throughout this section the term EDB is used in the generic sense, and includes *EDB.gdbm* files if the TURBO_DISK compile option is used

are typically countries such as "c=GB". The data for this will be held in the file *c=GB/EDB*, or to give the fullpath name */usr/etc/quipu-db/c=GB/EDB*.

This mapping continues all the way down the DIT hierarchy, so for example, if an *EDB* file has an entry whose RDN is "ou= Computer Science", then if the entry for "ou= Computer Science" has sibling entries and these are stored locally, they can be found in the file *ou=Computer Science/EDB* relative to the directory that contains the EDB file with the "ou=Computer Science" entry.

NOTE that the case sensitivity of the subdirectory naming is one of the few areas within QUIPU where string matching is case sensitive. The case of the attribute type is taken from the definition of the attribute in the oid tables, whereas the case of the attribute value is the same as that found in the EDB file. Spacing is also important. There should be no spaces either side of the "=" sign, and only one space between each word contained in the name.

When an entry is modified, a new *EDB* file is rewritten to disk. The old *EDB* is renamed *EDB.bak* to provide a limited backup.

### 18.1.4 Long Distinguished Names

There is a problem with the above method for naming UNIX subdirectories with some versions of UNIX — particularly System V. In these systems directory names are limited in length. Some versions of UNIX will not allow space characters in filenames (in any case they are hard to manage because of all the quoting required).

To allow for this, any distinguished name can be given a "mapping name", which will be used as the UNIX sub-directory name. For example the entry for "o=University College London", may be mapped onto the name "UCL" and thus stored in the file *UCL/EDB*. The mapping names are specified in a file called *EDB.map*, found in the same directory as the EDB file holding the entry to be mapped. So if the file *c=GB/EDB* contains an entry for "o=X-Tel Services Ltd", then the file *c=GB/EDB.map* may be used to map this onto "X-Tel".

The syntax of the *EDB.map* file is:

```
<Distinguished Name> "#" <Mapped name>
```

so for the example used above, the file will contain:

```
o=X-Tel Services Ltd#X-Tel
```

Only RDNs you want to map need to be in this file. If a name is not found in the mapping file, then the long directory name will be used.

When a DSA needs to create a subdirectory (e.g., after an add operation) it will use the relative distinguished name for each subdirectory, unless the name is longer than the maximum number of allowed characters (usually 15). In this case, the DSA will generate a shorter mapped name and write this to the *EDB.map* file. A generated mapped name is based on the UNIX *mktemp* procedure call and produces names such as "XTelServia01950".

## 18.2 Setting Up an Initial DSA

These instructions are assuming that you are trying to set up a DSA with the following characteristics:

- It is the first DSA in an Organisation.
- It is not the first DSA in the Country.
- It holds a copy of the root EDB.

This is found in the example:

*others/quipu/quipu-db/organisation*

There are two other examples which might also be used as illustrations for national DSAs and organisational DSAs not holding a copy of the root EDB. These are in :

*others/quipu/quipu-db/national*

and

*others/quipu/quipu-db/non-root.*

Note that if you are going to be running a DSA in the United States, then you should skip this section and refer to the document [MRose90b], which is provided in the ISODE documentation set (look in the source tree area for the directory *doc/whitepages/admin/*). This document describes turn-key installation mechanisms for DSAs in the United States.

To start a DSA with one of these example databases go into the relevant database directory and type:

```
$(SBINDIR)ros.quipu -t ./quiputailor
```

The `-t` flag tells QUIPU to use the *tailor* file *./quiputailor* rather than the default file (*quiputailor* in the ISODE `ETCDIR` directory).

This will cause the DSA to print some logging information onto the screen, followed by the message

```
DSA c=GB@cn=toucan has started on localHost=17003
```

The default setup assumes you have TCP/IP access and starts a DSA on the IP address of the local machine (127.0.0.1). If you do not have TCP/IP, you will need to change the address the DSA will attempt to listen on. The next section delves into the world of addresses!

The presentation address of the example DSA is found in the file

*others/quipu/quipu-db/organisation/c=GB/EDB*

```
cn=Toucan
presentationAddress= localHost=17003
edbinfo= #cn=giant tortoise#
description= Demonstration DSA
description= Bird with large colourful bill.
objectClass= quipuDSA & quipuObject
manager= c=GB@o=X-Tel Services Ltd@cn=Camayoc
acl= others # compare # attributes # userPassword
userPassword = toucan
quipuVersion= quipu 6.8 #3 (trellis) of Mon Feb 4 09:26:47 GMT 1991
supportedApplicationContext= QuipuDSP & X500DSP & X500DAP
```

Figure 18.2: Example DSA Entry

The first entry in this file is the entry for a DSA called "c=GB@cn=Toucan", which is the name of the DSA we are trying to start (as defined by the "mydsaname" entry in quiputailor). The entry is shown in Figure 18.2. The attribute `presentationAddress` defines the address that the DSA is going to listen to the network on. If you need to listen on a different address, you should change the value of the attribute to the address you want to listen on.

Having started your DSA you should be able to connect to it by invoking DISH. If you are using the default DSA address, and are using the default *dsaptailor* file, then invoking DISH without arguments is sufficient. If you are not using the default address or *dsaptailor* file, then you will need to edit *dsaptailor* in the ISODE ETCDIR directory. You should add an entry

```
dsa_address  toucan  <presentation address>
```

Note that `<presentation address>` should have *exactly* the same value as the `presentationAddress` attribute in the DSAs entry in the EDB file. Now to contact the DSA use

```
dish -c toucan
```

Once connected to the DSA, try issuing the command:

```
list "@c=GB@o=University College London@ou=Computer Science"
```

You should get a list of four names back:

```
1. commonName=Colin Robbins
2. userid=quipu%commonName=Colin Robbins
3. commonName=Steve Kille
4. commonName=Michael Roe
```

If this happens you have a working DSA. (The entry numbered 2 is an example of an RDN with multiple values !)

### 18.2.1 Presentation Addresses

This section is a brief introduction into presentation addresses, and may be all you need to know. For the brave, more details are given in volume 2 of the ISODE manual and [SKill89a].

The example address used in the previous section for the demonstration DSA was "`localHost=17003`". This is an address using the TCP/IP transport stack, and is the TCP loop back address. You should *not* use this in any DSA involved in the pilot DIT for reasons explained at the end of the section.

If you want to use the TCP/IP transport stack (using RFC1006) there are two possibilites for an address. If you are connected to the Capital-I Intenet network, you can use addresses of the form

```
Internet=128.16.5.31+17003
```

"128.16.5.31" is the IP address of your machine, which can usually be found in the */etc/hosts* file on your system. You can use the DNS name of your host instead, but the ISODE will replace this with the IP address when possible to aid portability of addresses. "17003" is the TCP port number the DSA will listen on.

If you want to use TCP/IP on a local Ethernet[3], that is not connect to the Capital-I Internet, you will need to define a local network community. This process is described in full in Volume 2 of the ISODE manual and should result in addresses of the form

```
LOCAL-ETHER=128.16.5.31+17003
```

Do *not* use Internet= addresses UNLESS you are connected to the Internet.

Now onto the X.25(80) community. If you have IPSS access, you can use addresses of the form

```
Int-X25(80)=23421920030045
```

where 23421920030045 is the DTE of you host. If you plan to have more than just a DSA (e.g., *iaed* or *tsapd*) listening on X.25 on the same machine, we advise the use of a two-digit subaddress (45 in the example). The DTE should have the DNIC included; full details of tailoring DNICs are given in *isotailor* (5n). The X.25 parameters PID and CUDF can be specifed if needed, see [SKill89a] for details.

If you do not have connectivity to the IPSS network, as in the TCP/IP case, you will need to define a local community. The ISODE has knowledge of two such X.25 communites built in. In Europe, the IXI network should be addressed using an address of the form

```
IXI=20433450210398
```

[3] Ethernet is a trademark of the Xerox Corporation.

In Great Britain, the Janet network should be addressed using an address of the form

```
Janet=00002100102998
```

Your DSAs address should contain a component for every network you have access to. Multiple components can be linked using the "|" symbol; for example:

```
Internet=128.16.5.31+17003|IXI=20433450210398
```

Using this addressing mechanism it is possible to use transport, session and presentation selectors; however, in the context of a QUIPU DSA they are unnecessary. Hence we advise against their use; again details can be found in [SKill89a].

Correctly defining your DSA's address is important. A paper [PBark89] describes the problem in detail. Briefly, X.500 was defined assuming a single global network. Unfortunately the world is not yet like that: there are at least two major communities. QUIPU DSAs know about this, and make a careful choice between use of referrals and chaining in an attempt to make sure all operations suceed. If your DSA is incorrectly addressed, other DSAs may make the wrong assumption about your DSA, and so your DSA will not be able to contact certain parts of the DIT, and they will not be able to contact you. For a similar reason you should not use the "localHost" macro for addreses, as other DSAs will think they can connect to the DSA in question.

### 18.2.2 Choosing a Name for Your DSA

Every QUIPU DSA *must* have an entry in the DIT, hence your DSA will need a unique **distinguished** name. This entry is used by other DSAs to identify your DSA, and so is needed if other DSAs are going to be able to see your DSA. The examples are tailored to start a DSA called "toucan", and will be sufficient to get an example DSA started, but it is not unique, so will not be of much use when you want to start adding your own data, and want to connect into the global DIT. *Note* that the DN has to be unique, but not the RDN component, thus both "cn=Wombat" and "c=GB @ cn=Wombat" are allowed!

There are other two aspects to consider in choosing a name for your DSA.

Firstly, it is a QUIPU convention that DSAs should be named after endangered South American wildlife, and that the entry for the DSA should contain a description of the animal or plant in question. Some example animal names are shown in Table 18.1. A more comprehensive list can be found in the IUCN's "Red Book" [IUCN82]. This is not a just a game, there is a serious point. The authors believe it is wrong to name DSA "UCL.DSA" or similar, as this binds the DSA to the organisation too tightly, especially at the higher levels of the DIT.

Secondly, the entry for your DSA must be visible to other DSAs that do not know how to contact your DSA. So, the *master* copy of your DSA's own entry must be held at least one level higher up in the DIT than the part of the DIT it holds as `MASTER` data. For example the DSA which holds "c=GB @ o=University College London @ ou=Computer Science", must be held at the "c=GB @ o=University College London" level (e.g., "c=GB @ o=University College London @ cn=wombat") or above. Such naming also helps prevent loops as described more fully in [SKill89b].

Typically, you will not hold the master EDB file containing your DSA locally. However, you do still have control of the entry as if you held the master copy. This is explained in more detail in Section 18.4.

In practice DSAs should be named fairly high up the tree. Each country should have at least two DSAs named at the root level. Each Organisation should have at least two DSAs named at the national level.

You should use DISH to find out if the name you want is already taken. For example, if you are creating a DSA for an organization in Great Britain, you might use:

```
% dish -c "Giant Tortoise"
Welcome to Dish (DIrectory SHell)
Dish -> search @c=GB -filter objectClass=dsa -nosize
```

This will print out the list of names already in use.

### 18.2.3 Setting up Your DSA

Having chosen a name, you will need to tell your DSA its name, and make sure it can find an EDB file for its own entry.

A DSA finds it own name from the "mydsaname" variable defined in the file *quiputailor* (see Section 18.3 for details). An example `quiputailor` entry would be:

```
mydsaname: "c=GB@cn=a dsa name"
```

Having read this name from `quiputailor`, a DSA will try to find the corresponding entry, in this case by looking in the *c=GB/EDB file*.

If you hold the EDB that the entry should be in, simply make sure the entry is in that EDB and then it will be found. If you do not hold, and do not want to hold the EDB in which your DSA is named (e.g., your DSA is called `c=GB@cn=toucan` but you do not hold the EDB `c=GB`), then you should (normally) supply a cached copy of the EDB which contains only the entry for the DSA, and not all the other entries the full EDB would have. If you do not supply it, your DSA will have to rely on other DSAs before it can start.

Having located its own entry, a DSA will know its network address by looking at the `presentionAddress` attribute, hence it can start listening for operations.

But first it must load the database. This process is described in full in Section 18.8.

| | | | |
|---|---|---|---|
| Agouti | Alpaca | Anaconda | Queen Anglefish |
| Anole | Carpenter Ant | Leaf Cutter Ant | Giant Anteater |
| Two toed Anteater | Antshrike | Aperea | Arapaima |
| Armadillo | Giant Armadillo | Hairy Armadillo | Six-banded Armadillo |
| Brazilian Three-banded Armadillo | Axolotl | Fruit Bat | Vampire Bat |
| Spectacled Bear | Long Haired Beetle | Passionflower Leaf Beetle | Rhinocerous Beetle |
| Emarald Tree Boa | Red-footed Booby | Brocket | Map Butterfly |
| Cacique | Dwarf Caiman | Black-headed Caique | Capuchin |
| Black-capped Capuchin | Capybara | Caracara | Crested Cariama |
| Cascabel | Andean Cat | Pampas Cat | Little Spotted Cat |
| Armoured Catfish | Blue Leopard Catfish | Pimelodid Catfish | Southern Mountain Cavy |
| Weasel Cavy | Cayman | Dragon Finned Characin | Rainbow Characin |
| Chinchilla | Long-tailed Chinchilla | Short-tailed Chinchilla | Cichlid |
| Dwarf Cichlid | Oscar Cichlid | Pike Cichlid | Triangle Cichlid |
| Greater Pichi Ciego | Lesser Pichi Ciego | Coati | Brown Coati |
| Ring-tailed Coati | False Cobra | Condor | Andean Condor |
| Boa Constrictor | Giant Cookroach | Giant Coot | Horned Coot |
| Flightless Cormorant | Land Crab | Rock Crab | Curassow |
| Black Curassow | Brazilian White-headed Curassow | Darter | Marsh Deer |
| Pampas Deer | Argentinian Pampas Deer | Swamp Deer | Bush Dog |
| Small-eared Dog | Amazonian Dolphin | Dourouconli | Inca Dove |
| Scaly Dove | Muscovy Duck | Torrent Duck | Black-chested Buzzard Eagle |
| Harpy Eagle | Ornate Hawk Eagle | Black and White Hawk Eagle | Electric Eel |
| Moray Eel | Plumbeous Forest Falcon | Spotted Silver Dollar Fish | Four-eyed Fish |
| Hatchet Fish | Hillstream Fish | Leaf Fish | Pampadour Fish |
| Pencil Fish | Andean Flamingo | James's Flamingo | Andes Fox |
| Crab-eating Fox | Southern Gray Fox | Greenhouse Frog | Horned Frog |
| Marsupial Frog | Arrow Poison Frog | Surinam Frog | Gallinule |
| Gar | Juan Fernandez Island Goat | Yellow Pocket Gopher | Grison |
| Brazialian Blue Grosbeak | Grunion | Guanaco | Guppy |
| Galápagos Hawk | Humpback Headstander | Little Blue Heron | Yellow-crowned Night Heron |
| Hoatzin | Hornero | North Andean Huemul | South Andean Huemul |
| Small Hummingbird | Hummingbird | Black-chinned Hummingbird | Black Faced Ibis |
| Scarlet Ibis | Iguana | Jaguar | Jaguarundi |
| Pileated Jay | Kinkajou | Everglades Kite | Cayenne Lapwing |
| Teiid Lizard | Llama | Peruvian Longfin | South American Lungfish |
| Mabuya | Macaw | Military Green Macaw | Hyacinth Macaw |
| Scarlet Macaw | Manatee | Amazonian Manatee | Caribbean Manatee |
| Mara | Margay | Buffy-headed Marmoset | Buffy-tufted-ear Marmoset |
| Common Marmoset | Cotton-top Marmoset | Black Eared Marmoset | Goeldi's Marmoset |
| Golden Lion Marmoset | Tassel-eared Marmoset | White Marmoset | Molly |
| Brown Howler Monkey | Red Howler Monkey | Black Spider Monkey | Brown-headed Spider Monkey |
| Geoffroy's Spider Monkey | Long-haired Spider Monkey | Woolly Spider Monkey | Squirrel Monkey |
| Red Titi Monkey | Woolly Monkey | Yellow-tailed Woolly Monkey | Morpho |
| Cypri's Morpho | Anopheles Mosquito | Motmot | Roufous Motmot |
| American Cane Mouse | Red Nosed Mouse | Ocelot | Oilbird |
| Wolly Opossum | American Oriole | Baltimore Oriole | Giant Brazilian Otter |
| Giant Otter | Marine Otter | La Plata Otter | Southern River Otter |
| Roufous Ovenbird | Burrowing Owl | Long Moustached Owl | Spectacled Owl |
| Paca | Pacarana | American Paddlefish | Pangolin |
| Parrakeet | Quaker Parrakeet | Yellow-fronted Amazon Parrot | Blue-headed Parrot |
| Red-fan Parrot | White-fronted Parrot | Chacoan Peccary | Collared Peccary |
| Brown Pelican | Galápagos Penguin | Humbolts Penguin | Rockhopper Penguin |
| Peropatus | Guinea Pig | Fruit Pigeon | Piranah |
| Thin-spined Porcupine | Tree Porcupine | Puculet | Nothern Pudu |
| Southern Pudu | Sooty Capped Puffbill | Puffbird | Puma |
| Forrest Rabbit | Crab-eating Raccoon | Clapper Rail | Giant Wood Rail |
| Chinchilla Rat | Spiny Rat | Rhea | Cock of the Rock |
| Saki | Southern Bearded Saki | Monk Saki | White-nosed Saki |
| Scalare | Screamer | Horned Screamer | South American Sea-lion |
| Elephant Seal | Juan Fernandez Fur Seal | Galápagos Fur Seal | Sloth |
| Maned Sloth | Brazilian three-toed Sloth | Blind Snake | Coral Snake |
| Canana Rat Snake | Urutu Snake | Pygmy Seed Snipe | Solendon |
| Atlantic Spadefish | Couch's Spadefoot | Bird-eating Spider | Silk Spider |
| Roseato Spoonbill | South American Red Squirrel | Variegated Squirrel | Jaribu Stork |
| Sunbittern | Black-necked Swan | Coscorba Swan | Bare-face Tamarin |
| Cotton-top Tamarin | Emperor Tamarin | Golden Lion Tamarin | Golden-headed Lion Tamarin |
| Golden-rumped Lion Tamarin | Red Mantled Tamarin | Pied Tamarin | Black and Red Tamarin |
| White-footed Tamarin | Tanager | Violet headed Tanager | Central American Tapir |
| Young South American Tapir | Mountain Tapir | Tarpon | Buenos Aires Tetra |
| Bentos Tetra | Cardinal Tetra | Bleeding Heart Tetra | Small Scaled Tetra |
| Tinamou | Masked Titi | Burrowing Toad | Columbian Toad |
| Darwin's Toad | Giant Tortoise | Galápagos Giant Tortoise | Yellow-legged Tortoise |
| Toucan | Red Billed Toucan | Saffron Toucan | Trogon |
| Violaceous Trogon | Ocellated Turkey | Black-headed Uakari | Red Uakari |
| Red and White Uakari | Vicuna | Viscacha | Black Widow |
| Maned Wolf | Woodcreeper | Black Cheeked Woodpecker | Bar Winged Wood Wren |
| Yapok | Zebu | | |

Table 18.1: Endangered South American Wildlife

In its own entry it will find a **edbInfo** attribute, this describes which EDBs the DSA is expected to hold. The format of the **edbInfo** attribute is described fully in Section 18.10, but essentially the first parameter supplied says "load this EDB". Thus the attribute

```
edbInfo = ##
edbInfo = c=US@o=The Wollongong Group ##
edbInfo = c=GB ##
```

requests that the EDB files

*quipu-db/EDB*

(signified by no data before the first "#" sign),

*quipu-db/c=US/o=The Wollongong Group/EDB*

and

*quipu-db/c=GB/EDB*

are loaded.

There are a few other important attributes your DSAs entry should have, the "toucan" entry in Figure 18.2 on page 187 gives examples of the other attributes. They are briefly described below.

**description:** A textual message describing the DSA, and the wildlife!

**quipuVersion:** This should contain the version number of the QUIPU software you are using. This can be found by using the dish command `squid -version`. You only have to set this once. From then on the DSA will manage it, updating the entry when required.

**manager:** The DN of the manager of the DSA. This user will not be blocked by access control when modifying the local database over DAP.

**supportedApplicationContext:** This should always have the value

```
QuipuDSP & X500DSP & X500DAP
```

for this version of QUIPU. It is used by remote DSAs to decide which protocols your DSA supports, and thus how best to contact it.

**objectclass:** This must contain "quipuDSA".

**listenAddress:** Sometimes, (particularly in the X.25 world, or when using a transport service bridge), the address a server should listen o, is not the same as the address clients should call. The presentationAddress attribute defines the address clients will always call. If, and only if, this is not the address the server should listen on, the address for the server should be given in the listernAddress attribute.

**acl:** A DSAs entry, like any other, can be protected by access control lists. Care should be taken to make sure all remote DSAs can see all the attributes they need. The following ACL is recommended for use in a DSAs entry. The string "`MANAGER DN`" should be replaced with the distinguished name of the DSA manager as defined by the "manager" attribute.

```
acl= group # MANAGER DN # write # entry
acl= group # MANAGER DN # write # default
acl= others # read # entry
acl= others # read # default
acl= others # read # child
```

A little explaination may help as this might seem somewhat cryptic. The `others # read # child` line is to prevent anybody from adding children to the entry; it is the only line referencing the children, so nobody is given write access. The userpassword attribute in the entry does not need protecting for two reasons. Firstly nothing can make use of it, self has only got read access to the entry (as defined by the others clause). Secondly, the password will probably be in a highly replicated EDB file, so despite the pseudo crypting, is easily breakable.

**relayDSA:** If your DSA is not connected to one of the major networks (Internet, IPSS...), it may from time to time get references to a DSA that it cannot connect to directly. For the operation to succeed, your DSA will need to chain the operation to a DSA that can progress the query.

This attribute is the DN of a DSA or DSAs that are connected to both your network and the major networks you are not connected to. There needs to be an agreement between the managers of the two DSAs because the relay DSA will be asked to perform operations on your behalf. For example, if the DSA "x" has access to IPSS and Internet, but DSA "y" only has IPSS access, DSA "y" might add a relayDSA attribute to it own entry, with the DN of DSA "x" as the value. Then, when DSA "y" gets a reference to an Internet based DSA, it will chain the operation the DSA "x". Clearly, if every DSA chooses the same relay DSA, that DSA will soon become overloaded and reject your association attempts with a "busy" error. So some care is needed in choosing the "right" DSA (The QUIPU team recognise that there needs to be some form of "relay authorisation" and are looking at possible solutions for future versions of QUIPU). Section 18.3 describes how to prevent your DSA (e.g., DSA "x") from chaining operations on behalf of other DSAs.

**photo:** A picture of the wildlife !

Section 18.7 describes how you can add data to your DSA by extending the supplied textual database to include your own data or by sending data to the directory via the DUA modify operations. This may be done independently from connecting to the global directory.

## 18.3 Tailoring

The previous sections have described how to start a basic DSA, and connect a DUA to it. Having done this, there are various configuration options you can set, which are described in this section.

On startup the DSA first consults a runtime tailor file (the default DSA tailor file is called *quiputailor* in the ISODE `ETCDIR` directory, but can be changed with a `-t` parameter to *ros.quipu*; consult *quipu*(8c) for details), which indicates such things as:

- name of the DSA.
- location of the database.
- location and level of the logs that the DSA will produce.
- location of any other DSAs for initial bootstrap

At startup, the *isotailor* (5n) file is also consulted to configure the system-wide ISODE parameters.

The format is identical to the DUA *tailor* file described in Section 17.2, with the addition of the following options:

`mydsaname`: The distinguished name of the DSA. For example,

```
mydsaname   cn=Axolotl
```

declares this DSA to have the common name of `Axolotl`. Quotes will be needed in the name contains a space characer, for example

```
mydsaname   "c=GB@cn=Long Moustached Owl"
```

`parent`: This entry consists of a name/address pair of a parent DSA. The DSA referenced needs to hold a master or slave copy of an EDB higher up in the DIT than the highest locally held EDB. For example,

```
parent C=GB@CN=vicuna Internet=vs1.ucl.cs.ac.uk+50987
```

declares the parent DSA to be C=GB@CN=vicuna at the indicated address. If more than one `parent` tailor entries are found, the DSA will chose which DSA to contact. The first DSA in the list is taken as the master reference, with the subsequent entries as slave references.

If your DSA holds a copy of the ROOT EDB file, this parameter should have just one value which is a reference to the DSA holding the master copy of the root EDB file (currently cn=Giant Tortoise).

**stats:** The value has the same format as the **dsaplog** entry described in Section 17.2, and is used to control the level of DSA statistical logging.

**treedir:** Defines the directory in which the textual database is stored. For example,

```
treedir      /usr/etc/quipu-db/
```

declares the directory */usr/etc/quipu-db/* to contain the local part of the Directory Information Tree. Be sure to remember the trailing slash "/".

**shadow:** When searching, often a large part of the time is involved with chaining off to other DSAs to search aliases. To enhance performance it is sometimes useful to have a cached copy of the alias locally, this tailor variable allows such attributes to be "spot shadowed". The value of this variable is an attribute type. The attribute value associated with this type should have DN syntax. When the database has been loaded, if any instance of this attribute references a DN that is not held locally your DSA will "spot shadow" that entry. That is from time to time it will read the entry from a remote DSA, and cache the result.

**optimize_attr:** If TURBO_AVL and TURBO_INDEX have been defined, this option specifies the attribute types to index. Each attribute type must be on a separate line. For example the lines:

```
optimize_attr commonName
optimize_attr surname
```

would arrange to index both the commonName and surname attributes. Only string attributes are allowed. *Note*: this option must come before any index_subtree or index_siblings options.

**index_subtree:** If TURBO_AVL and TURBO_INDEX have been defined, this option specifies the distinguished name of a subtree to index for subtree searches. Multiple subtrees may be specified by multiple lines. For example, the lines

```
index_subtree "c=US@o=your org"
index_subtree "c=US@o=your org@ou=really big OU"
```

arrange to have two indexes built, one for each subtree specified. Be aware that the indexes take up extra space in core, so care should be taken to index things sparingly.

**index_siblings:** If TURBO_AVL and TURBO_INDEX have been defined, this option specifies the distinguished name of the parent of a group of siblings to index. For example, the line

```
index_siblings "c=US@o=your org@ou=really big OU"
```

arranges to have an index built for one-level searches directly below the specified entry. Multiple indexes may be specified by multiple lines. Be aware that the indexes take up extra space in core, so care should be taken to index things sparingly.

`optimized_only`: If TURBO_AVL and TURBO_INDEX have been defined, the value **on** tells the DSA to refuse any searches that do not consist entirely of optimized attributes and filters. Any such non-indexed queries will be rejected with an "unwilling to perform" service error.

`update`: The value **on** tells the DSA to update slave and cached EDB files when it starts up. See Section 18.10 for further details; by default this parameter is **off**.

`searchlevel`: Defines the level below which users will be able to search the DIT, for example, default 2 (e.g., below organisations). If they try to search from higher up, a n"unwilling to perform" service error will result.

`lastmodified`: If the value is **off**, the attributes `lastmodifiedby` and `lastmodifiedtime` will not be added by the DSA when an entry is altered.

`readonly`: Bring the DSA up in read only mode, that is, prevent user modification. Slave updates are still allowed.

`dspchaining`: The value **on** tells the DSA it is allowed to chain DSP requests to other DSAs if necessary. The default mode of operation is to return a DSA referral, unless a chain is needed due to a disjoint network. The full set of issues deciding whether to use chaining or referrals is discussed in the QUIPU design document ([SKill89b]), and [PBark89].

`adminsize`: The administrative size limit for use on search and list operations.

`admintime`: The maximum time allowed to spend on a user query.

`cachetime`: The length of time to kee /use "cached" information.

`conntime`: The length of time to hold a unused connection open.

`nsaptime`: The length of time to wait before deciding a connection cannot be established for a given NSAP.

`retrytime`: The length of time before deciding it is worth attempting to connect to a DSA that could not be contacted earlier.

`slavetime`: The length of time between attempting to update slave EDB files.

**preferdsa:** When a DSA has creates a reference to other DSAs it tries to discriminate, and choose the "best" DSA to contact. This variable gives you a handle on controlling the choice. For example the lines

```
preferDSA c=GB@cn=Vicuna
preferDSA "cn=Giant Tortoise"
```

tell the DSA to use either c=GB@cn=Vicuna or cn=Giant Tortoise in preference to any other DSA. Furthermore, use the DSA c=GB@cn=Vicuna rather than cn=Giant Tortoise if possible.

**cainfo:** For authentication.

**secretkey:** For authentication.

**bindwindow:** For authentication.

**isode:** The argument is an **isodevariable isodevalue** pair as would be found in *isotailor*. This is used to "override" isotailor settings.

### 18.3.1 Tailoring a Running DSA

The tailoring described above is performed when the DSA is booted. It is sometimes useful to alter the tailor settings after the DSA has started without having to bring the DSA down and reboot. This can be done via the special *dsacontrol* command in the *dish* (1c) program as described in Section 7.5 on page 103.

The DUA invokes a modify operation, with a single special attribute "dSAControl" defined in [SKill89b]. The DSA recognises the special attribute, and provided you are bound as the manager of the DSA, passes the attribute value to the appropriate routine.

[SKill89b] describes this process in full.

## 18.4 Modifying your DSA's Entry

A DSA manages its own entry in the DIT. Generally the master EDB in which your DSAs entry resides is not held by your DSA. For security reasons, this means it is difficult for a DSA to modify its own entry directly, so, for example it cannot keep its version number up to date. However, a DSA holding the master EDB knows that any QUIPU DSA[4] wants to manage its own entry. To allow this to happen, the DSA holding the master EDB "spot shadows" the remote DSA entry. That is, from time to time it connects to the DSA in question, reads its entry, and writes the result back into the master EDB file. So modify operations on the DSA's entry

[4] Any QUIPU DSA for which the version number is 6.8 or greater

can now take place in your local DSA. This has the advantage that attributes such as the version number are kept up to date.

To perform this shadowing, the DSA has to read its own entry across an unauthenticated DSP link; thus it can not read any attributes that are protected by ACLs. So all important attributes in the DSAs entry *must* be publicly readable (this includes the unused userPassword attribute). If they are not readable the shadowing operation will fail.

To keep the database consistent with the master EDB, when a modify takes place, your DSA cannot rewrite the information back to its slave copy EDB. So it writes the entry in a file called *DSA.real* in the top level of your database. If there is an inconsistency found, it is this file that is "trusted."

There is also a file called *DSA.pseudo*, which contains some attributes managed by the DSA, that it does not need to make public (such as which cached EDB files it holds). You should *never* need to edit this file.

There is a problem when modifying the presentation address of a DSA. You must make sure the DSA with the master EDB reads the new address, *before* you move the DSA. If not, it will always attempt to connect to the wrong address to try to shadow the entry, and never find the new address. (Alternatively you could use a ts_bridge to make it look as if the old address still works.) You can check the master EDB has updated by making a DAP bind to the DSA managing the EDB and reading the address it has got. If it is out of date, you should wait for it to be updated; this usually takes place every six hours. To summarise, the sequence of events is

1. Change the address attribute using a DAP modify operation.
2. Wait for the DSA with the master EDB to read the entry.
3. Restart the DSA on the new address.

## 18.5 Connection to Other DSAs

All QUIPU DSAs should be connected. This section describes how you should configure your DSA to connect to other DSAs in order to read the data not held locally. Section 18.5.1 describes how to make sure that other DSAs can access your DSA.

A dynamic approach is used to bootstrap a new DSA. The "global master" DSA is administered at the University of London Computer Center[5] (ULCC), and other DSAs should be configured in relation to this one.

Every DSA needs to know the distinguished name and presentation address of one or more DSAs nearer to, or actually holding, the root EDB. This parameter is supplied in the *tailor* file (see Section 18.3) under the name `parent`. This information is used by the QUIPU DSA when it cannot find a DSA's entry in the local

[5]The DSA has moved from University College London.

database, or can find no pointers in the local database to the whereabouts of the data. If you hold a slave copy of the root EDB, then your parent should be a DSA that is "closer" to the master copy of the root EDB, and probably the master itself.

The example databases are set up with default parents (defined in the file *quipu-db/organisation/quiputailor*). To see if your DSA can contact the "parent", connect to the local test (root holding) DSA using DISH, and type

```
list @
```

This will list the locally held root. Now try

```
list @ -dontusecopy
```

This will try to connect to the parent DSA.

Care should be taken in choosing the parent DSA. If all DSAs have the same parent DSA then that DSA may become overloaded. Typically each site will have several DSAs. One of these should be the default parent for all the other DSAs, with only one DSA having a default parent outside the site.

When "walking down" the DIT, QUIPU needs access to information to tell it on which DSA the next level of the DIT is stored. To do this each nonleaf entry *must* have a "masterDSA" or "slaveDSA" attribute. The value of the attribute is the distinguished name of the DSA holding the next level of the DIT (it may be your own DSA name, if you hold the next level as well). If there is no such attribute, QUIPU assumes the entry is a leaf. If the information required is not held in the local DSA then QUIPU chains the request to the named DSA or returns a referral — depending upon the mode of operation. (The named DSAs entry is read to establish the address. This may mean a connection to another DSA in order to read the entry.)

Once you have started your DSA, you should try to connect to other DSAs using the DISH program (this connects to the local DSA, which will chain requests to other DSAs). Try listing the children of organisations other than yourself, to find which organisations are connected, try listing your countrys' children.

### 18.5.1 Connection to the Global Directory

To enable the global directory to connect to you, you must contact the manager of the DSA immediately above the node you want to added under. Supply them with the entry for your DSA, and the top level entry of the subtree you want to hold. For example, to add the organisation o=foobar below c=US, contact the manager of the DSA holding c=US as a master, giving them the entry for c=US@o=foobar and c=US@cn=foobar_dsa, assuming c=US@cn=foobar_dsa is the name of your DSA (see Section 18.2.2 on naming a DSA).

By convention, to find out who administers the master EDB for a particular node, run the *dish*(1c) program and retrieve the **manager** attribute from the entry for the DSA holding that node.

You can then find a mail address by looking that person up in the directory.

The following example shows you how to get the mail address of the manager of the c=GB subtree.

```
% dish
Welcome to Dish (DIrectory SHell)
Dish -> showentry @c=GB -type masterDSA
masterDSA  - cn = Giant Tortoise
Dish -> showentry "@cn=Giant Tortoise" -type manager -edb
manager= c=GB@o=X-Tel Services Ltd@cn=Camayoc
manager= c=GB@o=University College London@ou=Computer Science@cn=incads
Dish -> moveto "@c=GB@o=X-Tel Services Ltd@cn=Camayoc"
Dish -> showentry -edb
cn= Camayoc
roleOccupant= c=GB@o=X-Tel Services Ltd@cn=Colin Robbins
objectClass= organizationalRole & quipuObject
Dish -> moveto "@c=GB@o=X-Tel Services Ltd@cn=Colin Robbins"
Dish -> showentry -type rfc822mailBox
rfc822Mailbox         - C.Robbins@xtel.co.uk
Dish -> quit
%
```

If you want to add data to the root node of the "global tree." The new entries should be sent to *QUIPU-support* at the address given in Section 5.6.

When you think you are connected to the "global DIT", you should test that you are. To do this use `dish` to connect to a DSA higher than you in the DIT (using the `-call` flag as described in Section 17.2; then see if you can navigate to your own part of the DIT, and look at your data: if you can, then the DSA is connected.

## 18.6 Connecting to a Non QUIPU DSA

QUIPU has the concept of mastering all entries in one EDB file built into its design. Other implementations may not share this model. The entry represented by the non QUIPU DSA can be "spot shadowed." For example, if you wanted to add "o=foobar" to the DIT and this was mastered by a non QUIPU DSA, you would add an entry of the form

```
o=foobar
objectClass= ExternalNonLeafObject & organization
subordinateReference= cn=The DSA # Internet=123.456.1.2+17003
```

where cn=The DSA is the DN of the DSA, and Internet=...is the presentation address of the DSA. Instead of a subordinate reference, a cross-reference or nonspecific subordinate reference can be given using the "crossReference" or "nonSpecificSubordinateReference" attributes respectively.

Although this is entry is in a master EDB file, QUIPU recognises that is may not actually hold the authorative master, and contacts the referenced DSA as required.

## 18.7 Adding More Data

Having got a DSA started, and connected to the global DIT, you should start to add lots of data. There are many sources of such data, and with just a relatively small amount of effort this data can be added to the directory.

There are two ways such data can be added. First of all you can use one of the DUA programs to bind to the DSA as the DSA manager, and send data to the directory via the *add* and *modify* operations (see Sections 7.1.5 and 7.1.8). This is probably the best way to add relatively small amounts of data or make minor changes to the data.

To add a large amount of data (i.e., the initial creation of a large database), it is probably easiest to write a shell script using UNIX tools such as `awk` and `grep` to create the EDB files directly. In the next version of the software there will be tools to facilitate this.

When adding data for users it is advisable to allocate a userPassword, and a suitable ACL to protect this password. Chapter 15 describes how to do this.

### 18.7.1 More on Object Classes

The only object class discussed so far is the quipuDSA object class. When you start to add data, you will probably want to add information about people, sub-divisions of your organisation, and other application entities. This section introduces some of the more important object classes, and the attributes they may contain. In many cases, only the attribute type is specified, for details of typical values and the value syntax you should read Chapter 14.

As already described, every entry in the DIT must belong to the object class `top`, which means every entry must have an `objectClass` attribute. Also, every entry in the QUIPU DIT should belong to either the `quipuNonLeafObject` or `quipuObject`.

The following part of this chapter describes some of the basic object classes and the attributes implied.

#### Person

This is a base object class used to represent a person.

There are two mandatory attributes:

1. **commonName:** which gives a (potentially ambiguous) name for the person. The value of this attribute is a string usually containing the person's first and

last names; e.g.,

```
Marshall Rose
```

This attribute is usually multivalued, containing variations on the first, middle, and last names; e.g.,

```
Colin Robbins
Colin John Robbins
Colin J. Robbins
```

Generally this attribute will supply the distinguished attribute of the entry.

2. **surName:** which gives the person's last name.

The optional attributes are:

```
userPassword                seeAlso
telephoneNumber             description
```

### OrganizationalPerson

This is a subclass of the `person` person object class and introduces the following optional attributes:

```
preferredDeliveryMethod       destinationIndicator
registeredAddress             internationaliSDNNumber
x121Address                   facsimileTelephoneNumber
teletexTerminalIdentifier     telexNumber
physicalDeliveryOfficeName    postOfficeBox
postalCode                    postalAddress
title                         organizationalUnitName
streetAddress                 stateOrProvinceName
locality
```

### ThornPerson

Like `OrganizationalPerson`, this is also a subclass of `person` and introduces the following optional attributes:

```
homePostalAddress             lastModifiedBy
lastModifiedTime              secretary
homePhone                     userClass
photo                         roomNumber
favouriteDrink                info
rfc822Mailbox                 textEncodedORaddress
userid
```

Two example `ThornPerson` entries are given in Figure 18.1 on page 182.

### OrganizationalRole

Entries of this class are used to represent a position or role within an organization.

There is one mandatory attribute:

**commonName:** gives the name of the role. The value of this attribute is a string; e.g.:

```
PostMaster
```

There are many optional attributes including:

**roleOccupant:** the distinguished name of the person who fulfills the role, e.g.:

```
c=US@o=X-Tel Services Ltd@cn=Peter Cowen
```

The other optional attributes are:

```
seeAlso                       preferredDeliveryMethod
destinationIndicator          registeredAddress
internationaliSDNNumber       x121Address
facsimileTelephoneNumber      teletexTerminalIdentifier
telexNumber                   telephoneNumber
locality                      postOfficeBox
postalCode                    postalAddress
description                   organizationalUnitName
streetAddress                 stateOrProvinceName
physicalDeliveryOfficeName
```

### Alias

Objects of this class represent an alias to some other entry in the DIT. It is generally used when an entity belongs in one or more subtrees of the DIT, and is used to "point" one entry at the other.

There are two mandatory attributes:

**commonName:** gives the name of the alias. The value of this attribute is a string; e.g.:

```
Colin Robbins
```

**aliasedObjectName:** a pointer to another object in the Directory; e.g.:

```
c=GB@o=X-Tel Services Ltd@cn=Colin Robbins
```

There are no optional attributes for this object class. An example of an Alias entry is given below:

```
cn= QUIPU-support
aliasedObjectName= c=GB@o=University College London
   @ou=Computer Science@cn=Incads
objectClass= quipuObject & alias & top
```

### OrganizationalUnit

The `OrganisationalUnit` object class is used to represent a unit within your organisation. There is one mandatory attribute

**organizationalUnitName:** which gives the name of the organizational unit. The value of this attribute is a string; e.g.:

```
Research and Development
```

The optional attributes are:

```
userPassword                  seeAlso
preferredDeliveryMethod       destinationIndicator
registeredAddress             internationaliSDNNumber
x121Address                   facsimileTelephoneNumber
teletexTerminalIdentifier     telexNumber
telephoneNumber               physicalDeliveryOfficeName
postOfficeBox                 postalCode
postalAddress                 businessCategory
searchGuide                   description
streetAddress                 stateOrProvinceName
locality
```

### Organisation

Objects of this class represent a top-level organizational entity, such as a corporation, university, government entity, and so on.

There is one mandatory attribute:

**organisationName:** which gives the name of the organisation. The value of this attribute is a string; e.g.:

```
Performance Systems International
```

The optional attributes are:

```
userPassword                  seeAlso
preferredDeliveryMethod       destinationIndicator
registeredAddress             internationaliSDNNumber
x121Address                   facsimileTelephoneNumber
teletexTerminalIdentifier     telexNumber
telephoneNumber               physicalDeliveryOfficeName
postOfficeBox                 postalCode
postalAddress                 businessCategory
searchGuide                   description
streetAddress                 stateOrProvinceName
locality
```

**domainRelatedObject**

If an object has some relationship to the Internet Domain Name System (DNS), then this can be represented in the DIT using this object class.

This class has one mandatory attribute:

**associatedDomain:** identifies the domain which corresponds to this object. The value is a domain string; e.g.:

```
psi.com
xtel.co.uk
```

### 18.7.2 Schemas

Directories should provide a very flexible tool which enable any information to be stored. There is a danger that schemas, as specified in the OSI Directory, will lead to Procrustean directory implementations which impose unreasonable restrictions. The QUIPU Directory does not, per se, place restrictions on what can be placed in a DSA. It does, however, give control so that managers may control what is stored in the directory.

The first aspect of structure is with respect to attributes which may be present in an entry. A QUIPU DSA will allow an entry to belong to one or more object classes which are known to the DSA (stored in a table). An entry will typically have a small number of object classes (e.g., TOP (implicit) + Person + Organisational Person + QUIPU Object). The DSA will maintain a table of mandatory and optional attributes for each object class supported. This will follow the guidelines of the standard or specification identifying the object class in question. From this information, the DSA can determine the permitted and mandatory attributes for a given entry by calculating the union of all the object classes of that entry. Free extension (i.e., the ability to store any attribute) was rejected, as there does not appear to be a reasonable mechanism to manage this. However, it is straightforward for managers to create new object classes as desired.

It is important to allow management control of what is permitted at a given level. Therefore a "treeStructure" attribute may be created. This attribute is defined in Figure 18.3, with the string syntax discussed in Section 14.2.2. This specifies for the level below, what types of object are permitted. Each attribute value identifies a class of object which can exist at the level below, and defines a set of mandatory and optional object classes. This can be considered as defining a (private) object class implied by the combination of these classes.

For each type of object, the attribute types permitted in the RDN are also listed. This is not checked in the current version of QUIPU. The directory knows about the treeStructure attribute and will ensure consistency. When creating an entry, the DSA must check that it conforms to the treeStructure attribute of the parent

```
TreeStructureSyntax ::= SET {
    mandatoryObjectClasses [1] SET OF OBJECT IDENTIFIER,
    optionalObjectClasses [2] SET OF OBJECT IDENTIFIER OPTIONAL,
    permittedRDNs [3] SET OF SET OF AttributeType }

TreeStructure ::= ATTRIBUTE
    WITH ATTRIBUTE-SYNTAX TreeStructureSyntax
    MULTI VALUE
```

Figure 18.3: Schema Definition

entry. When removing information from a treeStructure attribute, the Directory will check that all of the children conform to the modified attribute.

### 18.7.3 Photograph Attributes

The data that a DSA can hold does not have to be limited to data that can be represented by printable strings. Any attribute a QUIPU DSA does not know a string syntax for, will be held as a block of ASN.1. One such attribute is the "photo" attribute. Photographs of people and objects are stored in the directory as a g3fax-encoded block of ASN.1, and are best stored as "file" attributes described in the next section. There is an example of a photograph attribute in the example database. This can be looked at by connecting to the directory with DISH and looking at the entry "Steve Kille, CS, UCL, GB".

Unless you you have compiled and installed the "photo" code as described in Section 16 you will see the message

```
''No display process defined''
```

Having compiled the "photo" code, you will need to add a line such as

```
photo xterm Xphoto
```

to your *dsaptailor* file (see Section 17.2) This says that if the user in logged on to a terminal of the type `xterm` then use the process *g3fax/Xphoto* in the ISODE `ETCDIR` directory to display the photograph.

There are display routines provided for the X Window System, SunView, Tektronix 4014, and "dumb" terminals.

#### Generating Photos

The photograph files used by QUIPU need to be two-dimensionally g3fax-encoded. QUIPU contains some tools to help you get your files into the required format. These are found in the *others/quipu/photo* directory of the ISODE source tree.

Getting pictures onto your machine is a local problem that will need discussing with your system manager. You may have them in a different format from that required by QUIPU.

If they are in SunView *pixrect* format, the tool "pr2pe" can be used to convert them. For other formats, there are two utilities, "pbmtofax" and "faxtopbm", which can convert from the "PBM" format to two-dimension fax, and vice versa. The PBM format is that defined and used by Jef Poskanzer's "pbmplus package." This package can convert a large range of bitmap formats into the PBM format[6]. You will need to obtain this package to compile the "pbmtofax" and "faxtopbm" utilities.

*Note*: with this version of QUIPU, the "pbmtofax" tool should always be used with a "-old" flag to ensure user at remote sites with older code can still decode and display your photograph files.

### 18.7.4 File Attributes

Attributes values are generally stored in the EDB file, and loaded into memory when the DSA starts. For some large attributes such a photos, this is not a sensible approach, so the concept of a "file" attribute is introduced.

If an attribute value is prefixed by `FILE`, then the value is assumed to be stored on disk. For example, if the following were found in an EDB file:

```
photo={FILE}/usr/local/pictures/steve
```

then the value for the photo attribute would be read from the file

```
/usr/local/pictures/steve.
```

The syntax of the data in the file is expected to be the same as the string syntax, except in the case of ASN.1 and photo attributes which are expected to be in raw ASN.1.

If there is not a file name supplied, then a default name is allocated. The default file name is the RDN of the entry the attribute belongs to followed by a dot ".", followed by the attributeType. This file is expected to be in the same directory as the EDB file for the entry. For example the default file for photo attribute, representing the entry for "c= GB @ o= University College London @ ou= Computer Science @ cn= Colin Robbins" would be:

```
cn=Colin Robbins.photo
```

in the directory

```
quipu-db/c=GB/o=University College London/ou=Computer Science
```

[6]You should not confuse "pbmtofax" with the "pbmtog3" tools which are part of the pbmplus package; this uses a one-dimensional encoding scheme

or equivalent mapped file as described in Section 18.1.4.

The process defined so far allows for attributes stored in an EDB in file format to be read by a DSA. Writing the attributes back to files if modified/added by a DUA requires a little more. The DSA needs to know which attributes should be stored on disk. This information is supplied in the attribute "oidtables" which are defined in Section 18.11. For example if the following entry was found in the file *oidtable.at* in the ISODE ETCDIR directory then a "photo" attribute would always be written back to disk.

```
photo:  thornAttribute.7: photo : file
```

### 18.7.5 Attribute Inheritance

Attribute inheritance is a mechanism whereby an entry can get default attribute values from its parent entry. This can make management of common attributes much easier. Inheritance can be used to make the in-core database significantly smaller, which as a side effect should make the DSA run faster. For example, entries of the object class "person" for a particular organisation might all have the same postal address attribute. Using inheritance this attribute can be placed in the organisation entry and inherited down to all "person" entries.

```
InheritedListSyntax ::= SET OF CHOICE {
   AttributeType,          -- Take value from the entry
   Attribute }

InheritedAttributeSyntax ::= SET {
   default [0] InheritedListSyntax OPTIONAL,
      -- default which can be overriden in lower entry.
   always [1] InheritedListSyntax OPTIONAL,
      -- always present in lower entry.
   objectclass OBJECT IDENTIFIER OPTIONAL
      -- object class to inherit to.
      -- The null case means the objectclass attribute
      --    itself is inherited
}

InheritedAttribute ATTRIBUTE
   WITH ATTRIBUTE-SYNTAX InheritedAttributeSyntax
   MULTI VALUE
```

Figure 18.4: Attribute Inheritance

The information is placed in the entry above using the "inheritedAttribute"

attribute type, defined in Figure 18.4. The QUIPU string syntax to represent this is:

```
<InheritedAttributeValue> ::= [ <oid> "$" ]
                          [ "always" <InheritedList> ]
                          [ "default" <InheritedList> ]
<InheritedList> ::= "(" NEWLINE <AttributeSequence>
                          NEWLINE ")"
```

For example, if the following was an attribute of an entry

```
inheritedAttribute = person $ always (
postalAddress= UCL $ Gower Street $ London $ WC1E 6BT
postalCode= WC1E 6BT
) default (
telephoneNumber= +44 71-387-7050
)
```

then all entries of objectclass "person" positioned one level below the entry would always inherit the attributes

```
postalAddress= UCL $ Gower Street $ London $ WC1E 6BT
postalCode= WC1E 6BT
```

and if the entry does not contain a "telephoneNumber" attribute itself, it would inherit

```
telephoneNumber= +44 71-387-7050
```

The attribute value in the inherited attribute can be left blank, for example

```
inheritedAttribute = person $ always (
postalAddress
)
```

in which case the value is taken from the same entry as the inherited attribute itself. This avoids duplicating attributes.

The OID representing the object class can only appear in one attribute value, thus the following, which may seem similar to the above is *not* allowed: the attributes need to be combined.

```
inheritedAttribute = person $ always (
postalAddress= UCL $ Gower Street $ London $ WC1E 6BT
)
inheritedAttribute = person $ always (
postalCode= WC1E 6BT
)
inheritedAttribute = person $ default (
telephoneNumber= +44 71-387-7050
)
```

If the OID representing the object class is omitted, then the values are inherited to entries that themselves do not contain an object class attribute. Thus the inherited attribute must define an object class to inherit down (as schema checking still takes place). For example

```
inheritedAttribute = default (
ObjectClass= person & quipuobject
postalAddress= UCL $ Gower Street $ London $ WC1E 6BT
postalCode= WC1E 6BT
)
```

Inheritance can be used for any attribute with the following exceptions:

- An entry can not inherit its distinguished attributes.
- An inherited "userPassword" attribute in not used to authenticate a user at bind time.
- The following system attributes

| | |
|---|---|
| objectClass | ACL |
| masterDSA | slaveDSA |
| aliasedObjectName | edbInfo |
| presentationAddress | relayDSA |
| treeStructure | supportedApplicationContext |
| inheritedAttribute | |

  can only be used in the "default" clause. They can not appear in the "always" clause as there is the potential for an inconsistency to occur.

- You must hold at least one copy of the EDB file containing the parent entry.

If an entry belongs to more than one object class, and more than one of these classes is listed in the inherited attribute of the parent entry, then only attributes from *one* of these will be inherited into the entry. It is undefined which.

The inheritance described thus far only covers one level of the DIT, whereas it is often useful to inherit attributes down the whole subtree. This can be achieved by inheriting the inheritance attribute! Consider the multivalued attribute

```
iattr= organizationalUnit $ default (
iattr
)
iattr= person $ default (
telephoneNumber
)
```

Every "person" immediately below will inherit the telephone number attribute. Every "organizationalUnit" will inherit the same inheritance attribute, thus any "person" entries below "organizationalUnit" entries will get the telephone number attribute as well. by the same token, this works for multiple levels of "organizationalUnit".

## 18.8 How a DSA Starts

The section gives a brief description of how a QUIPU DSA starts. This is intended to help people who have experienced problems in getting their DSAs started.

First of all the tailor file *quiputailor* in the ISODE ETCDIR directory is read (unless you specify a different tailor file using the -t option to *ros.quipu*). This tells the DSA, amongst other things, its own name, and its parent DSA(s).

The first thing a DSA need to do is find its own entry, thus it tries to load the EDB that should contain it. If it cannot find its own entry, then it will try connecting to the parent DSA to read its own entry. If this fails the DSA will stop.

Having found its own entry, the DSA will check to see if it is a cached entry read fron disk; if so, it will attempt to read a new version from the relevant remote DSA. If successfu,l a new cache EDB file will be written.

Now the rest of the local DIT can be loaded. Each EDB specified in the"edbInfo" attribute is in turn loaded from disk, followed by any cached EDB files.

As each EDB is loaded from disk, it is checked to make sure all the attributes in the entry are allowed, as defined by the "objectClass" attribute, and that the tree shape conforms to that defined by the "treeStruture" attribute. If any EDB fails these checks then the DSA will not start, and an appropriate message will be logged.

Having loaded all its data, the DSA will start listening for DAP and DSP associations.

## 18.9 Adding More DSAs

Many organisations will need to have more than one DSA to meet their requirements. This section suggests how you might arrange your DSAs to get the most out of the system.

You will almost certainly need at least one DSA that holds a copy of the root EDB, and your country EDB. This DSA should also hold the master copy of your organisation's own EDB. Subsequent DSAs that are set up should have this DSA defined as one of their parent DSAs.

For robustness, it is a good idea to have some other DSAs replicating these EDBs, so that if one local machine or DSA becomes unavailable, then there is another copy elsewhere that can be used. EDBs that contain addresses of other DSAs that you may want to contact regularly should also be replicated, to prevent extra associations having to be made just to read DSA addresses. In short, if you know that data from a certain EDB is going to be accessed a lot, replicate it locally. Replication does not have a high cost.

When setting up multiple DSAs be sure to name them as described in Section 18.2.2; ensure the DSA entries are sufficiently high in the DIT, so that other DSAs can read the entry without having to contact the DSA concerned.

## 18.10 Receiving EDB Updates

If your DSA holds a slave copy of one or more EDBs, then it can automatically update these for you. The current approach is very simple minded, but will be extended for future versions.

There are two ways to ask a DSA to update its slave EDBs, either use *dish* program and issue a "dsacontrol -slave" command (see Section 7.5), or set the `quiputailor` parameter "update" to **on** (see Section 18.3), in which case the DSA will try to update its slaves when it starts up.

To update the slaves, the DSA uses the "edbinfo" attribute that the DSAs entry in the DIT *must* have. This attribute specifies which EDBs you hold, and where to get updates of the from. *Note*: you do not necessarily have to get updates from a master EDB, a slave is acceptable. In many cases this will be preferable to prevent the load on the master DSA being too high. For example, a "national" EDB is likely to be highly replicated, it would not be a good idea to have just one DSA handling updates. It would be better to have the load spread over several DSAs.

The syntax of the attribute is

```
edbinfo = EDB concerned # get from # send to
```

It is a multivalued attribute.

A few examples:

```
# cn=Giant Tortoise # cn=Fruit Bat
c=US # # cn=Fruit Bat
c=US # # c=US@cn=Spectacled Bear
c=US@l=NY # cn=Fruit Bat #
```

Note that there is no harm to using multiple `eDBinfo` lines, even if they refer to the same EDB. These lines indicate that:

- The root EDB is read from the `cn=Giant Tortoise` DSA, further the `cn=Fruit Bat` DSA is allowed to read the root EDB from this DSA. This is an important point — A DSA has to explicitly say it will allow you to update from it, before it will send EDB files. Thus if you want to pull EDB files from a remote DSA, you will need to ask the manager to add your DSA to their DSAs "send to" field.

- The `cn=Fruit Bat` DSA and the `c=US@cn=Spectacled Bear` DSA are allowed to read the EDB for `c=US`. Note that the second and third line could be combined as:

  ```
  c=US # # cn=Fruit Bat$c=US@cn=Spectacled Bear
  ```

- The DSA-named `cn=Fruit Bat` supplies the EDB for `c=US@l=NY` to this DSA.

Some EDB files, such as the ROOT, and country level EDB files are highly replicated, and having to list all the DSAs that are allowed to pull such EDBs is too restrictive. Thus the following syntax can be used as an abbreviation:

```
c=US # # c=US
```

This indicates that the c=US EDB file can be sent to DSA named at the c=US level of the DIT, for example;

```
c=US@cn=Wombat
```

is allowed to pull the EDB, but the following are not:

```
cn=Wombat
c=US@o=Foobar Inc.@cn=Wombat
c=GB@cn=Wombat
```

Whether to update is decided upon by looking at the version string; if the two EDB files have a different version string, then the EDB will be updated.

## 18.11 Tables

Throughout QUIPU, all the Object Identifiers that need to be specified are specified using a string representation, for example:

| String representation | Object Identifier |
|---|---|
| attributeType | 2.5.4 |
| surname | 2.5.4.4 |
| streetAddress | 2.5.4.9 |
| organisationName | attributeType.10 |

A set of Object Identifier tables in the ISODE ETCDIR directory are used to provide this mapping (see also Volume 1 of the ISODE manual). In general the default table will be sufficient. This section describes the tables for those who want to extend the default definitions.

This basic format is used to build up the specification of general object identifiers. This file is by default named *oidtable.gen*, and has simple mappings from string to oid. These strings can then be used in the definition of further oids (for example the "organizationName" oid in the table above).

This simple table is extended to give table formats for attributes This file is by default named *oidtable.at*. Each entry in this table is assumed to represent an attribute, so in addition to mapping strings onto oids, it also defines the syntax for that attribute:

| String representation | Object Identifier | Syntax |
|---|---|---|
| objectClass: | attributeType.0: | objectclass |
| aliasedObjectName: | attributeType.1: | dn |
| commonName,cn: | attributeType.3: | caseignorestring |
| searchGuide: | attributeType.14: | asn |
| x121Address: | attributeType.24: | numericstring |
| presentationAddress: | attributeType.29: | presentationaddress |

This says that the attribute named "objectclass" represents the oid "attributeType.0"; using the expansion of "attributeType" ( as defined in the file *oidtable.gen*) thus gives the oid "2.5.4.0". The syntax taken by the attribute value is "objectclass".

Similarly an "aliasedObjectName" has "dn" (DistinguishedName) syntax. The recognised syntaxes are defined in the BNF in Appendix B.

After the "syntax", an extra optional parameter is allowed; if this is the string "`file`" the the relevant attribute is designated a file attribute; see Section 18.7.4 for a description of file attributes.

The file *oidtable.oc* defines the object classes QUIPU knows about. The file again maps strings onto oids. Each string is assumed to represent an object class, and for each it defines the hierarchy (which object classes it is a subclass of), the mandatory attributes of the object class, and the optional attributes of the object class.

For example the entry

```
quipuObject:    quipuObjectClass.2 : top : acl : \
                 masterDSA, slaveDSA, treeStructure
```

defines "quipuObject" to be an objectClass represented by the oid "quipuObjectClass.2". It is a *subclass* of the object class "top". An entry having this object class *must* have the attribute "acl", and *may* have the attributes "masterDSA", "slaveDSA" and "treeStructure" (*Note*: The similarity between this definition and the ASN.1 definition of a "quipuObject" in Appendix C).

To allow for definitions of "attribute sets", there is a simple macro facility provided, for example, using the macro

```
localeAttributeSet = localityName, streetAddress ...
```

every occurrence of "`localeAttributeSet`" will be replaced by the right-hand side expression.

With the definition of the "string" form of the oid it is also possible to specify *one* abbreviation for the name. The standard tables use the following abbreviations:

| | |
|---|---|
| c | countryName |
| o | organizationName |
| ou | organizationalUnitName |
| cn | commonName |
| co | friendlyCountryName |

The abbreviated name may be used anywhere the full name would be allowed.

Every entry stored in the QUIPU DSA is checked against these tables to see if the attributes supplied are allowed in the entry, to make sure the mandatory attributes are present, and the attributes themselves have the correct syntax.

If you wish to add you own definitions to the tables you should add them to the files *isode/dsap/oidtable.at.local*, *isode/dsap/oidtable.oc.local* and *isode/dsap/oidtable.gen.local* in that way, if a new set of tables is issued, your local entries will be preserved.

## 18.12 More Help Installing QUIPU

Contact "QUIPU-support." The mail address is given in Section 5.6.

# Chapter 19

# Security Management

## 19.1 Configuration

There are a number of options that can be set when compiling QUIPU; these are discussed in Section 16.1. Three of the parameters have security implications:

**NO_STATS:** This option results in a DSA that does not record any usage and audit information. From the standpoint of security, it is advisable not to select this option. Audit logs are very useful for detecting and tracing attempts to break the security of the system.

**HAVE_PROTECTED:** This option results in a DSA that can perform protected simple authentication.

**HAVE_RSA:** This option results in a DSA that can perform strong authentication.

To build a DSA that can perform strong or protected simple authentication, you will also need additional files that are not part of the ISODE. These files (the "QUIPU security upgrade") will soon be available and will be distributed by University College London. For further information, contact:

Steve Kille
Department of Computer Science
University College London
Gower Street,
London,
England

Internet: quipu-security@cs.ucl.ac.uk

### 19.1.1 QUIPU Userid

The DSA should not run under the userid of the super-user (root). The reason for this is that no application should be run as root unless it is absolutely necessary, just in case an undetected bug causes it to malfunction. (A process running as an ordinary user will be halted if it starts to misbehave; one running as root might carry on and delete important files, for example).

Ideally, the DSA should be assigned a special userid to run under, called, for example, "quipu". If this is not possible, it should run under the userid of the DSA manager. Whichever option is taken, we shall henceforth refer to the selected userid as "quipu" in the documentation.

### 19.1.2 File Permissions

The EDB files are where QUIPU stores the contents of the Directory. As these files potentially contain sensitive information, they should be readable and writable only by the QUIPU userid.

There are two log files: one for debugging information and one for audit. Both of these files should be readable and writable only by the QUIPU userid. There is a potential problem here, in that ISODE's logging code usually makes log files writable by everybody. To be on the safe side, make a separate directory for QUIPU's logs (*/etc/isode/quipu-logs*, for example). Make this directory only accessible by the QUIPU userid, and change the tailoring parameter *logdir* so that the logs are written there.

## 19.2 Discretionary Access Control

The principles of discretionary access control are explained in the Chapter 15 of this manual. This section gives guidelines on setting the access control lists for entries in the DIT.

### 19.2.1 What Must be Publicly Readable

Some attributes are used by the Directory itself for routing and other purposes. If these attributes are not publicly readable (and hence readable by all DSAs) then the Directory's internal communications may fail. If a DUA gives messages such as "Unavailable" this is one possible cause. Note that there are many other possible causes of such failures; Network congestion or a machine being down is the most likely explanation.

The following attributes ought to be publicly readable:

- masterDSA.
- slaveDSA.

- presentationAddress.
- userCertificate.
- treeStructure.

The *userPassword* attribute ought to be comparable by everybody, but not readable (unless the entry is a spot-shadowed DSA entry, in which case the userPassword must be publically readable, see Section 18.4).

## 19.3 Audit

### 19.3.1 Enabling Auditing

The *stats* parameter in the *quiputailor* file controls how much audit information is kept. It is advisable to enable recording of audit events at the *notice* level. More detailed information is given at the *trace* level. Both are enabled by default.

### 19.3.2 Relating Events to Users

Most events in the usage log contain an *association descriptor* instead of the name of the user who caused the event. An association descriptor is a (small) number which identifies a connection to QUIPU. (It is rather like knowing which terminal line a command came in on.) To discover the user name, it is necessary to scan back through the log to find the record for the start of the association. This will contain the name of the user and how he or she became authenticated.

### 19.3.3 Format of Audit Records

Each record in the log file is formatted as follows:-

```
<AuditRecord> ::= <month> "/" <day> <time> <process>
                  <pid> "(" <userid> ")" <Event>
```

**time:** The time of the event in hh:mm:ss format.

**process:** The name of the program ("quipu").

**pid:** The process id of the DSA.

**userid:** The id of the user who started the DSA running. It is *not* the id of the DUA which caused the event!

**Event:** is the rest of the message. The following sections describe most of the common messages.

### 19.3.4 Start of an Association

```
<BindEvent> ::= "Bind" "(" <Integer> ")"
                "(" <AuthType> ")"
                ":" <DN>
<AuthType> ::= "none" | "simple" | "protected" |
               "strong" | "noauth"
```

For example:

```
Bind (4) (simple): c=GB@o=University College
         London@ou=Computer Science@cn=Steve Kille
```

This means that Steve Kille has started using association descriptor 4, and proved his identity using simple authentication (i.e., a password).

### 19.3.5 End of an Association

```
<UnbindEvent> ::= "Unbind" "(" <Integer> ")" <WhoBy>
      ":" <DN> <WhoBy> ::= "(by this)" | "(by that)"
```

For example:

```
Unbind (4) (by that): c=GB@o=University College
           London@ou=Computer Science@cn=Steve Kille
```

This means that Steve Kille's DUA has disconnected from the DSA, and descriptor 4 is left free for use by someone else. The "(by that)" means that the DUA, rather than this DSA, decided to close the connection.

### 19.3.6 DAP Operation

```
<DAPOperationEvent> ::= <OpType> "(" <Integer> ")"
                        ":" <DN>
<OpType> ::= "Read" | "Search" | "List" | "Compare" |
             "Add" | "Remove" | "Modify" | "ModifyRDN" |
             "Getedb"
```

For example:

```
Read (4): c=gb@o=Nottingham University
```

This means that whoever is using association 4 (Steve Kille in this example) has read the entry for Nottingham University.

### 19.3.7 DAP Result

```
<DAPResultEvent> ::= "Result sent" "(" <Integer> ")"
<DAPErrorEvent>  ::= "Error sent"  "(" <Integer> ")"
```

Each operation will normally be answered by either a result or an error.

### 19.3.8 Chaining

```
<ChainingEvent> ::= "Chain" "(" <Integer> ")"
```

This means that the DSA has decided to contact another DSA in order to perform an operation received previously.

### 19.3.9 Updates

```
<UpdateEvent> ::= "Slave update" <DN> |
                  "Shadow update" <DN>
```

These indicate an EDB file or spot shadow entry have been updated.

### 19.3.10 Other Events

There are a few other less common messages that can be written to the audit log. The text messages should be self-explanatory.

### 19.3.11 Processing the Log Files

A script called *dsastats* may be used to process the log file and produce a report summarising the usage of a DSA. The report shows both the following:

- Who has accessed the DSA.
- Which parts of the DIT have been accessed.

The report summarises the calls received by the DSA according to the degree of authentication. This analysis is given for remote and local access. The report also tries to distinguish between system usage, which includes QUIPU getedb operations, DSA probing and testing by directory system and interface developers, and real usage. The ability to make this distinction rests on user names being supplied in bind requests. A large percentage of binds are currently anonymous; it is hoped that this report encourages directory administrators to install systems such that the provision of user names becomes the norm.

### Configuring dsastats

The usefulness of the report relies on accurate configuration. The key configuration details to be noted are:

**Local Organisation:** Analysis of which parts of the DIT have been accessed is given by organisational unit for the preconfigured local organisation. For all other parts of the DIT, analysis is restricted to being by organisation.

**Local addresses:** A file should be set up (a skeleton is provided) which contains the leading substrings from local DUA and DSA addresses, as they appear in the *quipu.log* file. This file, which is called *quipulocaladds,* might look something like the following:

```
LOCAL-ETHER
Janet=000012345678
Internet=128.9
# file must end with this line
```

**Filtering out system usage:** A file should be set up (again a skeleton is provided) which contains the distinguished names of system users. This will probably include the names of directory software developers, directory administrators and dsa probes. Distinguished names can be specified case independently. The file, which is called *quiputechusers,* might look something like the following:

```
c=GB@o=University College London@ou=Computer Science@cn=incads
c=GB@o=University College London@cn=DSA Probe
# File must end with this line
```

### Running the script

The script can be configured to find the *tailor* files and *log* files. In this case, the script can be run by something like the following:

```
dsastats >usage.report
```

The above will not be possible if you run more than 1 DSA. The recommendation is then that each DSA logs to a file with a name of the form *dsaname.usage*. Usage would now be:

```
dsastats llama.usage >llama.report
```

A report produced by this script should resemble the example given in Figure 19.1.

```
Summary of calls to DSA <giant armadillo>
From  2:48:46 on 04 feb to 13:24:09 on 07 feb

No. of binds                        local  remote

Anonymous                              63      82
Unauth name DAP                        17       3
Unauth name DSP                        22      14
Simple                                  1       9

System usage (calls received)

Binds by Directory technicians              0
Reads of DSA entries                        0
Getedb operations                         953
Spot shadows                                6

Who has used the directory?
*Real* usage by organisation
No. users No. binds
        1       145    anonymous
        1         5    c=gb, o=x-tel services ltd
        ...

Which parts of the Directory have been accessed - real usage?
No. ops  Subtree
Local subtree
     67  c=gb@o=university college london
     14  c=gb@o=university college london@ou=computer science
      1  c=gb@o=university college london@ou=genetics and biometry
      1  c=gb@o=university college london@ou=mathematics
      ...

Other parts of the DIT
      0  root
     66  c=gb
      1  c=gb@o=brunel university
      1  c=gb@o=edinburgh university
      1  c=gb@o=glasgow university
      ...

Which parts of the Directory have been accessed - system usage?
No. ops  Subtree
      ...
```

Figure 19.1: Example Output of dsastats

# Chapter 20

# User Naming Architecture

## 20.1 Overview

The original work in INCA defined a naming architecture. Some of this work has been overtaken by standardisation activity, and other components are not relevant here. A few pieces are retained, as they may be of general use. This is called a *user* naming architecture, as it defines information for the user of the directory. The entire naming architecture is shown in Appendix C on page 331.

## 20.2 THORN

The THORN project is a significant ESPRIT project, which is implementing Directory services[FSiro88]. THORN has defined a naming architecture, which includes a number of nonstandard but useful attributes [SKill89c]. This architecture has been adopted for use in QUIPU at UCL, and for this reason, information in this architecture is not duplicated here. The latest version of the THORN naming architecture (also known as the RARE naming architecture) in available via FTAM from UCL (the address is given in the Preface of this manual) in the files *thorn/thorn-na.txt*, *thorn/thorn-na.ps* or *thorn/thorn-na.ms* depending whether you want a "plain text", "postscript" or "nroff -ms" version. Alternatively you could mail `QUIPU-support` asking for the relevant document (see Section 5.6).

## 20.3 Common Name Forms

ISO 3166 codes should not be used, as they make the DUA perform things which the DSA should do. Therefore a more general country attribute is introduced (see Figure 20.1). The intention is to use this attribute to permit users to search for countries based on familiar strings.

QUIPU supports multiple inheritance, so there is a need to define an QUIPU

```
friendlyCountryName ATTRIBUTE
  WITH ATTRIBUTE-SYNTAX
  caseIgnoreStringSyntax
        ::= {attributeType 8}
                -- example "UK", "United Kingdom" etc.

friendlyCountry OBJECT-CLASS
  SUBCLASS OF country, quipuObject
  MUST CONTAIN { friendlyCountryName }
        ::= {objectClass 3}
```

Figure 20.1: Country

Object class which will permit all of the standard QUIPU attributes to be associated with all objects in the QUIPU directory; the definition can be found in Figure C.1, in Appendix C.

## 20.4 DSA naming architecture

The following Naming Architecture components are needed in order to support the QUIPU mechanism for distributed operations. These are defined here, as a convenient location. Numbers are assigned elsewhere in this manual.

```
QuipuObject ::= OBJECT-CLASS
        SUBCLASS OF top
        MUST CONTAIN {aCL}
        MAY CONTAIN {lastModifiedBy, lastModifiedTime, entrySecurityPolicy}

QuipuNonLeafObject ::= OBJECTCLASS
        SUBCLASS OF quipuObject
        MUST CONTAIN {masterDSA}
        MAY CONTAIN {slaveDSA, treeStructure, inheritedAttribute}

ExternalNonLeafObject ::= OBJECTCLASS
        SUBCLASS OF quipuObject
        MAY CONTAIN {subordinateReference, crossReference,
            nonSpecificSubordinateReference}

QuipuDSA ::= OBJECT-CLASS
  SUBCLASS OF dsa
  MUST CONTAIN { aCL, edbInfo, userPassword, manager, quipuVersion}
  MAY CONTAIN { description, lastModifiedBy, lastModifiedTime,
        dsaDefaultSecurityPolicy, dsaPermittedSecurityPolicy, relayDSA,
        listenAddress, info }

EDBInfoSyntax ::= SEQUENCE {
        edb          DistinguishedName,
        getFromDSA   DistinguishedName OPTIONAL,
                                    -- If omitted DSA is master
                                    -- Determine mode of update from this DSA
        sendToDSAs   NameList,
                                    -- Send these DSAs incremental updates
                                    -- Namelist is defined with the ACLs
        getEDBAllowed NameList
                                    -- List of DSAs allowed to pull EDB
        }

EdbInfo ::= ATTRIBUTE
  WITH ATTRIBUTE-SYNTAX EDBInfo
  MULTI VALUE

MasterDSA ::= ATTRIBUTE
  WITH ATTRIBUTE-SYNTAX distinguishedNameSyntax
                        -- Master QSR
                        -- Usually, but not necessarily single valued

SlaveDSA ::= ATTRIBUTE
  WITH ATTRIBUTE-SYNTAX distinguishedNameSyntax
                        -- Slave QSR

SubordinateReference ::= ATTRIBUTE
  WITH ATTRIBUTE-SYNTAX AccessPoint
```

```
    SINGLE VALUE

CrossReference ::= ATTRIBUTE
    WITH ATTRIBUTE-SYNTAX AccessPoint
    SINGLE VALUE

NonSpecificSubordinateReference ::= ATTRIBUTE
    WITH ATTRIBUTE-SYNTAX AccessPoint

QuipuVersion ::= ATTRIBUTE
   WITH ATTRIBUTE-SYNTAX caseIgnoreStringSyntax

DSAControl ::= ATTRIBUTE
   WITH ATTRIBUTE-SYNTAX caseIgnoreStringSyntax
```

Figure 20.2: Naming Architecture

# Part V

# QUIPU Manual: Programmer's Guide

# Chapter 21

# Programming the Directory

This part of the manual is written for implementors who wish to access the directory using the *libdsap* (3n) library. This might be an OSI application wishing to look up information, or an interactive directory user-interface. The interface to the directory is defined as a series of procedures which closely parallels the service defined in [CCITT88]. This section defines the procedures, and shows how they relate to the standard. To avoid unnecessary wordiness, the user is expected to be familiar with the standard.

## 21.1 Conventions

The library defines various *C* structures, described in the following sections. Associated with the *C* structures, are routines which:

- allocate structures.
- free structures, including sub-structures.
- compare structures.
- copy structures.
- print structures.
- parse structures.

The following conventions are followed in many routines, which are then briefly identified later. For a general structure **x**, there will be the following routines:

- Allocation:

```
struct x *x_alloc ()
```

  Allocate memory for structure x.

- Freeing:

```
x_free (a)
struct x * a;
```

Free structure x, and any nested structures.

If the structure x is a linked-list type of structure, then as well as the routines described above, there will be routines of the form x_comp_function (where function is alloc, free, and so on). These act upon a single element of the list rather than the list as a whole.

- Copying:

```
struct x * x_cpy (a)
struct x *a;
```

Return a copy of structure a.

- Comparing:

```
int     x_cmp (a, b)
struct x *a, *b;
```

Return 0 if the structures a and b same. Return -1 if a<b, or 1 if a>b. For some structures the notion of a>b and a<b is not defined, but will be consistent.

- Printing:

```
int     x_print (ps, a, format)
PS       ps;
struct x *a;
int      format;
```

Print the structure a to the presentation stream ps, using the specified format, either READOUT, for a pretty-printed format (for example the output of a showentry from *dish*); or, EDBOUT, for a format suitable for inclusion in an EDB file. The PS structure is described in Volume 1 of the ISODE manual.

For the structures representing a DN and RDN there is an extra format: DIROUT, which is used to get a representation of the name suitable for inclusion in a UNIX filename (essentially EDBOUT with the @ symbols replaced with / separators).

- String format:

```
struct x * str2x (str)
char * str;
```

Most attribute syntaxes have a string representation. A string of the required syntax can be converted to the relevant *C* structure with the "str2x" function. Each of the string parsers assumes the input string has had multiple spaces and tabs removed, and replaced with single spaces. The function

```
char * Tidy_String (a)
char * a;
```

will do the relevant tidying if required. Strings printed with the EDBOUT format of x_print should be parsable.

*Note:* `str2AttrV()` does not follow the "convention" and has an extra parameter, which is the expected syntax of the string.

The structures following the "convention" are listed below. The "prefix" column shows what value `x` should take to use the routines for the associated structure.

| Structure | Prefix |
|---|---|
| RDN | rdn |
| DN | dn |
| AttributeType | AttrT |
| AttributeValue | AttrV |
| AV_Sequence | avs |
| Attr_Sequence | as |
| EntryInfo | entryinfo |

## 21.2 Attributes

Attributes are fundamental components of the directory. Attributes have two parts, types and values, which are (respectfully) represented by two structures, `AttributeType` and `AttributeValue`.

To represent AttributeTypes, *libdsap*(3n) has a table (described in Section 18.11) which maps a string representation of attribute types onto OIDs.

This table must be loaded by calling

```
load_oid_table(name)
char * name;
```

The `name` parameter should be the name of the oidtable to load. For most purposes this should be "`oidtable`".

Before you load the table, any syntaxes you want special attribute handlers for should be loaded. To do this you will probably want to call

```
quipu_syntaxes()
```

which will load all the syntax handlers defined in Chapter 14. If not all there syntaxes are required, then a subset can be loaded by calling only the handlers required.

The call

```
dsap_init(argc,argv)
int *argc;
char *** argv;
```

can be used to load the oidtable for you, with the additional benifit that it will read the file */etc/dsaptailor* to find the location of the oidtable. The parameters it expects are the pointers to the **argc** and **argv** parameters passed to your "main()" routine. If a "-c" flag is found then this is used as the name of the DSA to contact as per DISH (see Section 7.1.13). A "-t" can be used to specify which *dsaptailor* file to use, and "-T" to define an oidtable. As with loading the tables, the syntaxes you require should have been loaded before you make a call to `dsa_init` (Beware: `dsap_init` removes flags it interprets from the parameter list, if you care, pass a copy of them, or pass nulls!).

The oidtables are represented using the following structures:-

```
typedef struct {
        char    * ot_name;
        char    * ot_stroid;
        OID       ot_oid;
        OID       ot_aliasoid;
} oid_table;
#define NULLTABLE ((oid_table * )0)

typedef struct {
        oid_table oa_ot;
        short     oa_syntax;
} oid_table_attr, * AttributeType;
#define NULLTABLE_ATTR ((oid_table_attr *)0)
#define NULLAttrT ((oid_table_attr *)0)
```

The table consists of two fields, an integer syntax : `oa_syntax`. This is an integer handle onto the abstract syntax of the attribute value. The value "0" indicates an unknown syntax hence "ASN.1" is used.

The second field `oa_ot`, is a reference to an `oid_table` structure, which contains the oid, `ot_oid`; a numeric string representation of the oid, `ot_stroid`; and the local key string, `ot_name`.

The field `ot_aliasoid` is used to store an alternative OID for the same attribute. This is used to allow an attribute to change its OID over a period of time.

To create an `AttributeType` given a string representation of an OID, you should use

```
AttributeType str2AttrT (str)
char   *str;
```

which will look up the string supplied in the relevant OID tables and returns an `AttributeType` pointer into the oidtables.

There are various low level routines to manipulate entries in the OID table; however, the `AttributeType` routines described in Section 21.1 will be sufficient for most uses, so the details of these "invisible" routines are omitted here.

Attribute values are represented by the structure `AttributeValue`:-

```
typedef struct attrVal {
        short       av_syntax;
        caddr_t     av_struct;
} * AttributeValue;

#define NULLAttrV (AttributeValue) NULL
```

The AttributeValue structure can hold attribute values in many formats. Different syntaxes use different specialised *C* structures pointed to by av_struct, the field av_syntax defines the syntax represented by the av_struct field. Unknown syntaxes are represented as a presentation element indicated by the syntax being zero. Section 21.4 describes this more fully.

Attribute values can now be linked together to form a multivalue attribute value. For this the AV_Sequence structure is used.

```
typedef struct avseqcomp {
    attrVal             avseq_av;
    struct avseqcomp    *avseq_next;
} avseqcomp, *AV_Sequence;

#define NULLAV ((AV_Sequence) 0)
```

This is simply a linked list of AttributeValues.

To create an AV_Sequence the two routines

```
AV_Sequence avs_comp_new (av)
AttributeValue av;

AV_Sequence avs_merge (a,b)
AV_Sequence a,b;
```

can be used.

Finally an attribute can now be formed by linking the attribute type, and multiple attribute values using the AttrSequence structure:-

```
typedef struct attrcomp {
    AttributeType       attr_type;
    AV_Sequence         attr_value;
    struct attrcomp     *attr_link;
    struct acl_info     *attr_acl;
} attrcomp, *Attr_Sequence;

#define NULLATTR ((Attr_Sequence) 0)
```

This structure is used singularly to represent an attribute, and as a linked list (linked using attr_link) to represent a set of attributes.

To create an Attr_Sequence the two routines

```
Attr_Sequence as_comp_new (at,as,acl)
AttributeType at;
AV_Sequence as;
struct acl_info * acl;

Attr_Sequence as_merge (a,b)
Attr_Sequence a,b;
```

can be used. The `acl` parameter is only used by the DSA, for use in a DUA it should be set to `NULLACL_INFO`.

The routine

```
Attr_Sequence as_combine (as,str)
AV_Sequence as;
char * str;
```

is also provided, as an optimisation of

```
as_merge(as,str2as(str));
```

The approach to access control is defined in [SKill89b]. The representation of the attribute for access control is given by the structure shown below. This closely follows the ASN.1 definition.

```
struct acl_info {
    int                 acl_categories;
#define ACL_NONE          0
#define ACL_DETECT        1
#define ACL_COMPARE       2
#define ACL_READ          3
#define ACL_ADD           4
#define ACL_WRITE         5
    int                 acl_selector_type;
#define ACL_ENTRY         0
#define ACL_OTHER         1
#define ACL_PREFIX        2
#define ACL_GROUP         3
    DN                  acl_name;
    struct acl_info *acl_next;
};
```

The DN `acl_name` is used for the type `ACL_PREFIX` and `ACL_OTHER` only.

## 21.3 Distinguished Names

The structures which define names are critical. Names are essentially made up of attributes, but because of their importance, a different — more specific structure is used.

```
typedef struct rdncomp {
    AttributeType       rdn_at;
    attrVal             rdn_av;
    struct rdncomp      *rdn_next;
} rdncomp, *RDN;

#define NULLRDN ((RDN) 0)
```

An RDN consists of a set of attribute types (`rdn_at`) and attribute values (`rdn_av`); the set is linked using `rdn_next`.

RDNs can the be joined in a sequence to form a distinguished name (DN):-

```
typedef struct dncomp {
    RDN                 dn_rdn;
    struct dncomp       *dn_parent;
} dncomp, *DN;

#define NULLDN ((DN) 0)
```

The following routines are provided in addition to the routines defined in Section 21.1 to allow the user to create and manipulate names;

- Create a DN given an RDN:

  ```
  dn_comp_new (rdn)
  RDN     rdn;
  ```

- Append a DN to the end of another DN:

  ```
  dn_append (dn1, dn2)
  DN      dn1,
          dn2;
  ```

  `dn2` is added to `dn1`.

- Create an RDN given an AttributeType and AttributeValue:

  ```
  RDN rdn_comp_new (at, av)
  AttributeType  at;
  AttributeValue av;
  ```

- Merge two RDNs:

  ```
  RDN rdn_merge (rdn1, rdn2)
  RDN     rdn1,
          rdn2;
  ```

  RDNs form a set. To make comparisons easier, this implementation assumes them to be ordered sets. This routine takes two ordered RDN sets, and merges them. If RDNs received across the network are not ordered, the decoding process will order them for you.

### 21.3.1 User-Friendly Naming

There are various routines to implement user-friendly naming (UFN)[SKill90]. These are briefly described in this section.

To print a DN to a PStream as a UFN you can use

```
ufn_dn_print (ps,dn,multiline)
PS  ps;
DN  dn;
int multiline;
```

If the `multiline` option is `TRUE` the UFN will be printed on multiple lines, otherwise, a single line of output will be used. The `ufn_dn_print` routine prints each RDN using

```
ufn_rdn_print (ps,rdn)
RDN  rdn;
PS   ps;
```

Parsing a UFN into a DN is a little more complex:

```
ufn_match (argc,argv,interact,result,el)
int argc;
char ** argv;
DNS (* interact) ();
DNS * result;
envlist el;
```

The `argc` and `argv` parameters provide the components of the UFN, which will typically have been generated from a comma separated UFN string. The `el` component is used to pass a UFN environment list to the lookup routine. If this is left as NULL, this is generated from the system wide *ufnrc* file.

A sequence of DNs is returned in the `result` paramenter. `DNS` has the following structure:

```
typedef struct dn_seq {
    DN  dns_dn;
    struct dn_seq *dns_next;
} *DNS;
```

The `interact` parameter if the name of a routine to interact with the user if the UFN process is unclear as to which name to choose.

```
DNS interact (dns,dn,s)
DNS dns;
DN dn;
char * s;
```

The **dns** parameter is the sequence of potential names, **dn** is the DN of the environment below which the names have been, **s** is UFN element being matched. The user should be asked to select which DNs should be used, and the DNs returned. DNs not required in the **dns** passed in should be freed. If user interaction is not required, a simple interact routine to return a NULL DNS should be provided.

## 21.4 Adding New Syntaxes to QUIPU

It will probably be necessary to add knowledge of extra syntaxes to directory user interfaces as the range of applications grow. QUIPU has been designed to make this as easy as possible.

This section describes how you might do this, by adding knowledge of a FOOBAR syntax to *libdsap*(3n) library. FOOBAR is represented by the *C* structure "struct foobar {...};".

The DSA does not need to know about the new structure, as it will handle unknown syntaxes as blocks of ASN.1.

The procedure call

```
add_attribute_syntax (sntx,enc,dec,parse,
                      print,cpy,cmp,sfree,
                      print_pe,approx,multiline)
char *  sntx;
IFP     enc,dec,parse,print,cpy,cmp,sfree,approx;
char *  print_pe;
char    multiline;
```

is used to add knowledge of new attribute syntaxes to QUIPU.

The parameters are used as follows:

**sntx:** The string defining the syntax; in this case it should be Foobar. Any attributes defined as having the syntax "Foobar" in the oidtables will then be handled using the following routines.

**enc:** This is a function pointer to a routine that will convert a *C* structure representation of foobar into a presentation element that can be sent across the network. The routine is given a single parameter, a pointer to the foobar structure, and is expected to return a PE. You are reminded of the *pepy*(1c), *posy*(1c) and *pepsy*(1c) utilities described in Volume 4 of the ISODE manual, they may be of help in creating this encoder.

**dec:** This performs the inverse of the above, it is passed a PE, and should return a *C* structure representation.

**parse:** Each syntax needs to have a representation that can be read from and written to an EDB file. This defined routine should take a single char * argument and return a C structure representation.

**print:** This routine is used to print the syntax to a PStream[1]. The arguments are:

```
foobar_print (ps,fb,format)
PS ps;
struct foobar * fb;
int format;
```

If format is READOUT the structure should be printed to the stream PS in a "human readable" manner; otherwise is should be printed in a form that can be parsed by the "parse" function. *Note*: in many case both formats will be the same.

**cpy:** This function should take a foobar structure as a parameter and returns a copy of it.

**cmp:** A function that takes two foobar structures and compares them; returning 0 if they are the same; 1 if the first is considered "greater" than the second; –1 otherwise. If there is no appropriate ordering for the syntax, returns 2. If an error occurs during the comparison, returns –2.

**sfree:** A routine to free the structure foobar.

**print_pe:** The name of an external process to "exec" when the READOUT option is supplied to the print routine. This is generally set to NULLCP which means the default "print" routine is used.

**approx:** A routine to perform approximate matching (if required). The routine should expect two parameters as shown:

```
foobar_approx (a,b)
    struct filter_item * a;
    AV_Sequence b;
```

The routine should return OK or NOTOK depending on whether any attribute value in the AV_Sequence approximately matches the filter_item.

**multiline:** If TRUE the multivalue attributes will be printed on separate lines:

```
foobar = value1
foobar = value2
```

otherwise the attribute will be printed on one line:

```
foobar = value1 & value2
```

[1]PStreams are discussed in Volume 4 of the ISODE manual.

### 21.4.1 Where to Add the Syntax Definition

Where should you add this procedure call to define the new syntaxes?

This depends on which applications you want to know about the syntax. If you want the DSA and all DUAs to know about the syntax, then this call should be added to *libdsap*, in the directory *dsap/common*. The file *dsap/common/quipu_sntx.c* is where other similar calls are made. A small test program `test` is included in the common directory, and is made with "`make test`". It takes as input a string representation of attributes, and exercises the handlers. If this works for your new attribute, then it should be safe to recompile the DSA/DUA and try them.

If you only wish your DUAs to know about the new syntax, then add the call into your DUA's code, before loading the oidtables or calling `dsap_init`.

# Chapter 22

# The Procedural DUA

The *libdsap*(3n) library defines a set of procedure calls which correspond to each of the X.500 abstract operations. This chapter describes those procedure calls.

## 22.1 Procedure Model

Each operation is accessed via a procedure call of the same name as the X.500 operation, prefixed by "`ds_`". The procedure is supplied an argument structure, and returns either an error or result structure. For example the `read` operation is invoked by calling `ds_read (argument, error, result)`.

The return value of the procedures have the following common values, which indicated whether an error or result is returned:

**`DS_OK`:** Operation completed successfully; the result structure will have the corresponding result (if the operation generates results).

**`DS_ERROR_LOCAL`:** Error within the DUA module.

**`DS_ERROR_CONNECT`:** Failed to connect to a remote DSA.

**`DS_ERROR_PROVIDER`:** Other OSI provider error.

**`DS_ERROR_REMOTE`:** Remote error. Further details will be in the error parameter in the procedure call.

**`DS_X500_ERROR`:** This is the same as `DS_ERROR_REMOTE`.

These values defined in *quipu/ds_error.h*, which must be included in your program (there are other return values defined here, but these should only occur within the DSA, and should not be returned by a DUA call).

## 22.2 Common Parameters

All of the DAP operations described in Sections 22.5 to 22.11.4 have certain common parameters in their arguments and results. These structures are now described.

### 22.2.1 Arguments

The common arguments are represented by the following structure:

```
typedef struct common_args {
    ServiceControl        ca_servicecontrol;
    DN                    ca_requestor;
    struct op_progress    ca_progress;
    int                   ca_aliased_rdns;
#define CA_NO_ALIASDEREFERENCED -1
    struct security_parms * ca_security;
    struct signature      * ca_sig;
    struct extension      * ca_ext;
} CommonArgs;
```

The fields ca_ext, ca_progress, ca_requestor and ca_aliased_rdns are provided as they are defined within X.500. Neither the QUIPU DSA or DUA use these fields.

The field ca_servicecontrol is used to select the type of service the DSA should provide, the structure is given below

```
typedef struct svccontrol {
    int           svc_options;
#define SVC_OPT_PREFERCHAIN                 0X001
#define SVC_OPT_CHAININGPROHIBIT            0X002
#define SVC_OPT_LOCALSCOPE                  0X004
#define SVC_OPT_DONTUSECOPY                 0X008
#define SVC_OPT_DONTDERFERERENCEALIAS       0X010
    char          svc_prio;
#define SVC_PRIO_LOW     0
#define SVC_PRIO_MED     1
#define SVC_PRIO_HIGH    2
    int           svc_timelimit;
#define SVC_NOTIMELIMIT -1
    int           svc_sizelimit;
#define SVC_NOSIZELIMIT -1
    int           svc_scopeofreferral;
#define SVC_REFSCOPE_NONE        -1
#define SVC_REFSCOPE_DMD         0
#define SVC_REFSCOPE_COUNTRY     1
} svccontrol, ServiceControl;
```

The values takes by each field within the ServiceControl structure are described in full in [CCITT88].

### 22.2.2 Results

```
typedef struct common_results {
    DN      cr_requestor;
    char    cr_aliasdereferenced;
    struct security_parms  * cr_security;
    struct alg_id          * cr_alg;
    char                   * cr_tmp;
    int                      cr_len;
} common_results, CommonResults;
```

The filed cr_aliasdereferenced is set to TRUE if the base object of the operation was an alias, and was dereferenced.

The other fields are not used by the current version of QUIPU.

## 22.3 Continuation References

"Continuation References" are returned by the directory when the operation asked for could not be fully completed, in which case the structure ContinuationRef is returned as part of the error or results structures. The structure is explained below:

```
typedef struct continuation_ref {
    DN            cr_name;
    struct op_progress cr_progress;
    int           cr_rdn_resolved;
#define CR_RDNRESOLVED_NOTDEFINED  -1
    int           cr_aliasedRDNs;
#define CR_NOALIASEDRDNS -1
    int           cr_reftype;
#define RT_UNDEFINED    -1
#define RT_SUPERIOR      1
#define RT_SUBORDINATE   2
#define RT_CROSS         3
#define RT_NONSPECIFICSUBORDINATE 4
    struct access_point * cr_accesspoints;
    struct continuation_ref *cr_next;
}continuation_ref, *ContinuationRef;
```

**cr_name:** The DN that has only been partially explored.

**cr_rdn_resolved:** The number of RDNs in the name that have been examined; hence, how far down the DIT the query has been taken.

**cr_aliasedRDNs:** If TRUE then some of the RDNs were aliases.

**cr_reftype:** The type of reference that was used to get this information.

**cr_accesspoints:** The access point of the DSA to contact. The structure for an access point is as follows:

```
struct access_point {
    DN                   ap_name;
    struct PSAPaddr      *ap_address;
    struct access_point  *ap_next;
};
```

**ap_name:** The DN of the DSA to contact.

**ap_address:** The address of the DSA (derivable from the name).

**ap_next:** There may be more than one access point, hence they form a linked list structure.

**cr_next:** There may be more than one access point; if so they form a linked list structure.

## 22.4 Errors

All DAP operations return a common error structure, which maps closely onto the service definitions. An error is only returned if the operation failed; if successful (indicated by the return value DS_OK) the error structure returned is undefined.

```
struct DSError {
    int dse_type;
#define DSE_INTR_ABANDON_FAILED -5
#define DSE_INTR_ABANDONED      -4
#define DSE_INTRERROR           -3
#define DSE_LOCALERROR          -2
#define DSE_REMOTEERROR         -1
#define DSE_NOERROR             0
#define DSE_ATTRIBUTEERROR      1
#define DSE_NAMEERROR           2
#define DSE_SERVICEERROR        3
#define DSE_REFERRAL            4
#define DSE_ABANDONED           5
#define DSE_SECURITYERROR       6
#define DSE_ABANDON_FAILED      7
#define DSE_UPDATEERROR         8
#define DSE_DSAREFERRAL         9
```

```
        union {
            struct DSE_attribute     dse_un_attribute;
            struct DSE_name          dse_un_name;
            struct DSE_service       dse_un_service;
            struct DSE_referral      dse_un_referral;
            struct DSE_abandon_fail dse_un_abandon_fail;
            struct DSE_security      dse_un_security;
            struct DSE_update        dse_un_update;
        }  dse_un;
    };
```

The field dse_type is used to indicate what sort of error has occurred, and hence which structure from the union is used.

The value DSE_LOCALERROR is used to indicate that the error came from within the DUA; there is no associated structure in the union for this error.

The value DSE_REMOTEERROR is used to indicate that an error occurred at the DSA end, and the request was rejected; again there is no associated structure in the union for this error.

The structures in the union for the other error conditions are as described in the following sections.

### 22.4.1 Attribute Error

```
    struct DSE_attribute {
        DN DSE_at_name;
        struct DSE_at_problem DSE_at_plist;
    };
```

**DSE_at_name:** The name of the entry causing the error.

**DSE_at_plist:** A list of the errors:

```
        struct DSE_at_problem {
            int                        DSE_at_what;
        #define DSE_AT_NOSUCHATTRIBUTE          1
        #define DSE_AT_INVALIDATTRIBUTESYNTAX   2
        #define DSE_AT_UNDEFINEDATTRIBUTETYPE   3
        #define DSE_AT_INAPPROPRIATEMATCHING    4
        #define DSE_AT_CONSTRAINTVIOLATION      5
        #define DSE_AT_TYPEORVALUEEXISTS        6
            AttributeType              DSE_at_type;
            AttributeValue             DSE_at_value;
            struct DSE_at_problem * dse_at_next;
        };
        #define DSE_AT_NOPROBLEM ((struct DSE_at_problem*)0)
```

The fields are used as follows:

**DSE_at_what:** Indicates which error has occurred.

**DSE_at_type:** The attribute type causing the error.

**DSE_at_value:** The associated value (if any).

**dse_at_next:** There may be more than one such error; if so, they form a linked list.

### 22.4.2 Name Error

```
struct DSE_name {
    int DSE_na_problem;
#define DSE_NA_NOSUCHOBJECT             1
#define DSE_NA_ALIASPROBLEM             2
#define DSE_NA_INVALIDATTRIBIBUTESYNTAX 3
#define DSE_NA_ALIASDEREFERENCE         4
    DN  DSE_na_matched;
};
```

DSE_na_matched is the part of the DN successfully matched.

### 22.4.3 Referral Errors

```
struct DSE_referral {
    ContininuationRef DSE_ref_candidates;
    DN                DSE_ref_prefix;
};
```

The continuation reference supplies information on how to continue the query. The structure is described in Section 22.3

The field DSE_ref_prefix is for DSP only. You should generally chase such referrals.

### 22.4.4 Security Error

```
struct DSE_security {
    int DSE_sc_problem;
#define DSE_SC_AUTHENTICATION           1
#define DSE_SC_INVALIDCREDENTIALS       2
#define DSE_SC_ACCESSRIGHTS             3
#define DSE_SC_INVALIDSIGNATURE         4
#define DSE_SC_PROTECTIONREQUIRED       5
#define DSE_SC_NOINFORMATION            6
};
```

### 22.4.5 Service Error

```
struct DSE_service {
    int DSE_sv_problem;
#define DSE_SV_BUSY                         1
#define DSE_SV_UNAVAILABLE                  2
#define DSE_SV_UNWILLINGTOPERFORM           3
#define DSE_SV_CHAININGREQUIRED             4
#define DSE_SV_UNABLETOPROCEED              5
#define DSE_SV_INVALIDREFERENCE             6
#define DSE_SV_TIMELIMITEXCEEDED            7
#define DSE_SV_ADMINLIMITEXCEEDED           8
#define DSE_SV_LOOPDETECT                   9
#define DSE_SV_UNAVAILABLECRITICALEXTENSION 10
#define DSE_SV_OUTOFSCOPE                   11
#define DSE_SV_DITERROR                     12
};
```

### 22.4.6 Update Error

```
struct DSE_update {
    int DSE_up_problem;
#define DSE_UP_NAMINGVIOLATION          1
#define DSE_UP_OBJECTCLASSVIOLATION     2
#define DSE_UP_NOTONNONLEAF             3
#define DSE_UP_NOTONRDN                 4
#define DSE_UP_ALREADYEXISTS            5
#define DSE_UP_AFFECTSMULTIPLEDSAS      6
#define DSE_UP_NOOBJECTCLASSMODS        7
};
```

### 22.4.7 Abandon Failure

If an abandon operation fails then the following is used:

```
struct DSE_abandon_fail {
    int DSE_ab_problem;
#define DSE_AB_NOSUCHOPERATION  1
#define DSE_AB_TOOLATE          2
#define DSE_AB_CANNOTABANDON    3
    int DSE_ab_invokeid;
};
```

### 22.4.8 Error Handling Procedures

The *libdsap*(3n) library has three routines for handling errors:

```
ds_error (ps,error)
PS ps;
struct DSError * error;
```

This routine will take the error, and pretty-print the contents to the PStream ps.

```
log_ds_error (error)
struct DSError * error;
```

This routine will take the error, print a simple message in *dsap.log* at LLOG_EXCEPTIONS logging level, and a more detailed report at LLOG_TRACE logging level.

```
ds_error_free (err)
struct DSError * err;
```

This frees the embedded structures within the error structure, *but not* DSError itself.

## 22.5 Binding and Unbinding

Before operations may be invoked, the DUA must BIND to the DSA.

The bind procedure

```
secure_ds_bind (arg, error, result)
    struct ds_bind_arg          * arg;
    struct ds_bind_arg          * result;
    struct ds_bind_error        * error;
```

is used for this purpose.

You will need to include *quipu/bind.h* to use this procedure.

The ds_bind_arg structure is defined as follows.

```
struct ds_bind_arg {
    int  dba_version;
#define DBA_VERSION_V1988 0
    int dba_auth_type;
#define DBA_AUTH_NONE      0
#define DBA_AUTH_SIMPLE    1
#define DBA_AUTH_STRONG    2
#define DBA_AUTH_EXTERNAL  3
#define DBA_AUTH_PROTECTED 4
    char  *dba_time1;
    char  *dba_time2;
```

```
        struct random_number dba_r1;
        struct random_number dba_r2;
        DN      dba_dn;
        int     dba_passwd_len;
    #define DBA_MAX_PASSWD_LEN 512
        char    dba_passwd[DBA_MAX_PASSWD_LEN];
        struct signature        *dba_sig;
        struct certificate_list *dba_cpath;
        char * dba_vtmp;
        int     dba_vlen;
    };
```

**dba_version:** should always be set to DBA_VERSION_V1988.

**dsa_auth_type:** is used to select the type of authentication required.

**dba_dn:** is the name of the entity you wish to bind as, this can be NULLDN if you only require access to "publically readable" information.

**dba_passwd:** The password required to bind as the entity. This will be checked against the "userPassword" attribute in the entity.

**dba_passwd_len:** The length of the string in dsa_passwd.

**dba_sig:** The strong authentication signature (which must be provided if strong authentication is used in the bind call).

**dba_cpath:** The strong authentication certification path (optional).

**dba_time1:** Used for protected and strong authentication.

**dba_time2:** Optionally used for protected simple authentication.

**dba_r1:** Random number used for protected and strong authentication.

**dba_r2:** Optionally used for protected simple authentication.

**dba_vtmp:** Unused.

**dba_vlen:** Unused.

The bind operation will try to connect to the DSA, whose address is defined in the external "char *". "dsa_address", the syntax of the string is that of an ISODE PSAP address.

If secure_ds_bind() returns DS_OK, then you have a successful connection, otherwise a ds_bind_error structure will inform you of the error condition.

```
struct ds_bind_error {
    int  dbe_version;
    char dbe_type;
#define DBE_TYPE_SERVICE  1
#define DBE_TYPE_SECURITY 2
    int  dbe_value;
};
```

The filed dbe_value takes a value as defined for a DSE_security or DSE_service error shown in Sections 22.4.4 and 22.4.5.

### 22.5.1 No Authentication

To bind without using any authentication, dsa_auth_type should be set to DBA_AUTH_NONE. The fields dba_version and dba_dn must be filled in.

### 22.5.2 Simple Authentication

To bind using simple authentication, the dsa_auth_type field should be set to the value DBA_AUTH_SIMPLE. The dba_version, dba_dn, dba_passwd and dba_passwd_len fields must be filled in.

For backwards compatibility the routine

```
ds_bind (arg, error, result)
    struct ds_bind_arg        * arg;
    struct ds_bind_arg        * result;
    struct ds_bind_error      * error;
```

is still supplied, and gives you an unprotected simple bind request.

### 22.5.3 Protected Simple Authentication

To bind using protected simple authentication, the dsa_auth_type field should be set to to the value DBA_AUTH_PROTECTED. The fields dba_version, dba_dn, dba_time1, dba_r1, dba_passwd and dba_passwd_len must be filled in. The fields dba_time2 and dba_r2 must be either filled in or set to NULL.

### 22.5.4 Strong Authentication

To bind using strong authentication, the dsa_auth_type field should be set to the value DBA_AUTH_STRONG. The fields dba_version, dba_dn, dba_time1, dba_r1, and dba_sig must be filled in. The field dba_cpath must be either filled in or set to NULL.

## 22.6 Unbind

The unbind operation has no parameters.

```
ds_unbind ()
```

and is used to disconnect from the directory.

## 22.7 Read

The read operation is used to access information from a particular entity in the DSA.

```
ds_read (arg, error, result)
    struct ds_read_arg          * arg;
    struct ds_read_result       * result;
    struct DSError              * error;
```

You will need to include *quipu/read.h* to use this procedure.
The argument **ds_read_arg** is used to formulate the DAP request:

```
struct ds_read_arg {
    CommonArgs           rda_common;
    DN                   rda_object;
    EntryInfoSelection rda_eis;
};
```

The parameters are used as follows:

**rda_common:** The common arguments as described in Section 22.2.1.

**rda_object:** The DN of the object you want to read.

**rda_eis:** The "Entry Information Selection", which defines which attributes you want to be returned, this is defined in Section 22.7.1.

The results returned on a **DS_OK** return form the structure shown below:

```
struct ds_read_result {
    CommonResults rdr_common;
    EntryInfo     rdr_entry;
};
```

**rdr_common:** The common results as described in Section 22.2.2.

**rdr_entry:** This is a pointer to the "Entry Information" which contains the attributes you requested. This structure is defined in Section 22.7.2.

### 22.7.1 Entry Information Selection

Operations that return an Entry Information structure, will have an "Entry Information Selection" in their arguments to specify exactly what the DSA should return. The structure is represented thus:

```
typedef struct {
    char               eis_allattributes;
    Attr_Sequence      eis_select;
    char               eis_infotypes;
#define EIS_ATTRIBUTETYPESONLY  0
#define EIS_ATTRIBUTESANDVALUES 1
} EntryInfoSelection;
```

The parameters are used as follows:

**eis_allattributes:** If TRUE the all attributes are required.

**eis_select:** If eis_allattributes is FALSE then this field is used to specify the attributes you want. *Only* the attribute types of this structure need to be set; any attribute values will be ignored.

**eis_infotypes:** If EIS_ATTRIBUTETYPESONLY is set, then only attribute types will be returned; otherwise the values will also be returned.

### 22.7.2 Entry Information

The structure "Entry Information" is used by some of the operations to return data to the DUA.

```
typedef struct entrystruct {
    DN                 ent_dn;
    Attr_Sequence      ent_attr;
    int                ent_iscopy;
#define INFO_MASTER 0x001
#define INFO_COPY   0x002
#define INFO_CACHE  0x003
    char               ent_pepsycopy;
    time_t             ent_age;
    struct entrystruct *ent_next;
} entrystruct, EntryInfo;
```

The parameters are used as follows:

**ent_dn:** The DN of the entry.

**ent_attr:** The requested attributes of the requested entry.

**ent_iscopy:** This is either INFO_MASTER or INFO_COPY indicating whether master data or copied data was used to generate the results. INFO_CACHE is not applicable to a DUA.

**ent_pepsycopy:** Unused.

**ent_age:** This field is the age of the entry, used to expire cached information.

**ent_next:** There may be many results, this is used to link them.

## 22.8 Compare

The compare operation is used to compare an asserted attribute with an attribute in the directory.

```
ds_compare (arg, error, result)
    struct ds_compare_arg       * arg;
    struct ds_compare_result    * result;
    struct DSError              * error;
```

You will need to include *quipu/compare.h* to use this procedure.
The argument is as follows:

```
struct ds_compare_arg {
    CommonArgs cma_common;
    DN         cma_object;
    AVA        cma_purported;
};
```

**cma_common:** The common arguments as described in Section 22.2.1.

**cma_object:** The DN of the object you want to compare an attribute against.

**cma_purported:** The attribute you want to compare. This structure is defined in Section 22.8.1.

If successful, the result structure is as follows:

```
struct ds_compare_result {
    CommonResults cmr_common;
    DN            cmr_object;
    char          cmr_matched;
    char          cmr_iscopy;
    char          cmr_pepsycopy;
    time_t        cmr_age;
};
```

**cmr_common:** The common results as described in Section 22.2.2.

**cmr_object:** The DN of the entry the attribute was compared against. This may not be the same as the DN supplied in the argument (e.g., if an alias was dereferenced).

**cmr_matched:** If TRUE then the attributes were the same, otherwise they were different.

**cmr_iscopy:** If TRUE then the compare took place against a copy of theattribute.

**cmr_pepsycopy:** Unused.

**cmr_age:** Unused.

### 22.8.1 Attribute Value Assertion

An "Attribute Value Assertion" is used by some of the operations to specify an attribute type/value pair, the structure used in this case is shown below.

```
typedef struct {
    AttributeType  ava_type;
    AttributeValue ava_value;
}AVA;
```

## 22.9 List

The list operation is shown below. This returns a list of subordinates of the specified entry.

```
ds_list (arg, error, result)
    struct ds_list_arg           * arg;
    struct ds_list_result        * result;
    struct DSError               * error;
```

You will need to include *quipu/list.h* to use this procedure.

```
struct ds_list_arg {
    CommonArgs lsa_common;
    DN         lsa_object;
};
```

**lsa_common:** The common arguments as described in Section 22.2.1.

**lsa_object:** The DN of the object you want to list the children of.

The results of a successful list form the following structure:

```
struct ds_list_result {
    CommonResults           lsr_common;
    DN                      lsr_object;
    time_t                  lsr_age;
    struct subordinate * lsr_subordinates;
    POQ                     lsr_poq;
    struct ds_list_result * lsr_next;
};
```

**lsr_common:** The common results as described in Section 22.2.2.

**lsr_object:** The DN of the entry whose children were listed. This may not be the same as the DN supplied in the argument (e.g., if an alias was dereferenced).

**lsr_age:** Not currently used.

**lsr_subordinates:** This structure contains the RDNs that were found below the base object. The structure is as follows:

```
struct subordinate {
    RDN                     sub_rdn;
    char                    sub_aliasentry;
    char                    sub_copy;
    struct subordinate * sub_next;
};
```

**sub_rdn:** The RDN of this child.

**sub_aliasentry:** If TRUE then it is an alias entry.

**sub_copy:** If TRUE then the list took place against a copy of the object.

**sub_next:** A pointer to the next element in the list.

**lsr_poq:** A partial outcome qualifier. The structure is as follows:

```
#define LSR_NOLIMITPROBLEM      -1
#define LSR_TIMELIMITEXCEEDED   0
#define LSR_SIZELIMITEXCEEDED   1
#define LSR_ADMINSIZEEXCEEDED   2
typedef struct {
    int             poq_limitproblem;
    ContinuationRef poq_cref;
    char            poq_no_ext;
} POQ;
```

**poq_limitproblem:** Used to indicates which type of limit has been reached.

**poq_cref:** A list of continuation references. Continuation References are described in Section 22.3.

**poq_no_ext:** Not used

**lsr_next:** A pointer to the next element if the list is uncorrelated. QUIPU will always return correlated results..

## 22.10 Search

The search operation performs a key directory functionality. This is done on the basis of filters as described in Section 22.10.1 below. The operation is defined as:

```
ds_search (arg, error, result)
    struct ds_search_arg        * arg;
    struct ds_search_result     * result;
    struct DSError              * error;
```

You will need to include *quipu/ds_search.h* to use this procedure.

```
struct ds_search_arg {
    CommonArgs          sra_common;
    DN                  sra_baseobject;
    int                 sra_subset;
#define SRA_BASEOBJECT          0
#define SRA_ONELEVEL            1
#define SRA_WHOLESUBTREE        2
    Filter              sra_filter;
    char                sra_searchaliases;
    EntryInfoSelection sra_eis;
};
```

**sra_common:** The common arguments as described in Section 22.2.1.

**sra_baseobject:** The DN of the object you want to start the search from.

**sra_subset:** This specifies which part of the DIT to search.

**sra_filter:** The filter to apply to the searched entries to see if the entry is required. Filters are discussed in Section 22.10.1

**sra_searchaliases:** If TRUE, aliases encountered below the search baseobject are dereferenced, and the dereferenced object searched. Note how this is different from the service control
"**dontderferencealiases**" which is used to control dereferencing of entities above the base object.

**sra_eis**: The "Entry Information Selection", which defines which attributes you want to be returned (if the filter is matched), this is defined in Section 22.7.1.

The results form the following structure:

```
struct ds_search_result {
    char  srr_correlated;
    union {
        struct ds_search_unit    * srr_unit;
        struct ds_search_result * srr_parts;
    }     srr_un;
    struct ds_search_result * srr_next;
};
```

**srr_correlated**: If TRUE the the results are said to be correlated; that is, there will only be one element in the list of search results. A DSA may return uncorrelated result, in which case the routine

```
correlate_search_results(sr_res)
struct ds_search_result * sr_res;
```

can be called, which will correlate the results.

*Note*: QUIPU DSAs will always return correlated results.

**srr_un**: If the results are uncorrelated then the union will contain a nested ds_search_result structure, which contains a list of the uncorrelated results.

If the results are correlated, then this union will contain a pointer to the correlated results. These form the structure

```
struct ds_search_unit {
    CommonResults   srr_common;
    DN              srr_object;
    EntryInfo     * srr_entries;
    POQ             srr_poq;
};
#define CSR_common        srr_un.srr_unit->srr_common
#define CSR_object        srr_un.srr_unit->srr_object
#define CSR_entries       srr_un.srr_unit->srr_entries
#define CSR_limitproblem srr_un.srr_unit->\
                              srr_poq.poq_limitproblem
#define CSR_cr            srr_un.srr_unit->\
                              srr_poq.poq_cref
```

*Note*: the #defines to access the elements of this structure. The fields are used as follows:

**srr_common:** The common results as described in Section 22.2.2.

**srr_object:** The DN of the entry used as the base object of the search. This may not be the same as the DN supplied in the argument (e.g., if an alias was dereferenced).

**srr_entries:** A pointer to the "Entry Information", which will contain the attributes you requested (if present in the entry). The EntryInfo structure is defined in Section 22.7.2.

**srr_poq:** A partial outcome qualifier. This is the same as for the list operation described in the previous section.

**srr_next:** This is a pointer to the next result in a list of uncorrelated results.

### 22.10.1 Filters

A filter in its simplest sense is a single `filter_item`. This is used to perform one of six basic tests on one attribute of an entry. If the "match" is good, then the entry is returned as part of the search result structure. The six basic types of `filter_item` are represented by the structure below:

```
struct filter_item {
    int         fi_type;
#define FILTERITEM_EQUALITY       1
#define FILTERITEM_SUBSTRINGS     2
#define FILTERITEM_GREATEROREQUAL 3
#define FILTERITEM_LESSOREQUAL    4
#define FILTERITEM_PRESENT        5
#define FILTERITEM_APPROX         6
    union {
        AttributeType     fi_un_type;
        AVA               fi_un_ava;
        Filter_Substrings fi_un_substrings;
    }           fi_un;
    IFP         fi_ifp;
};
```

**fi_type:** Defines the type of `filter_item` being represented.

**fi_un.fi_un_type:** FILTERITEM_PRESENT matches. Just supply an AttributeType, an entry matches if this attribute exists within the entry.

**fi_un.fi_un_ava:** FILTERITEM_EQUALITY,
FILTERITEM_GREATEROREQUAL,
FILTERITEM_LESSOREQUAL,
and FILTERITEM_APPROX searches all take an Attribute Value Assertion (AVA)

structure, and return the entries for which the attribute in the entry matches the asserted value. The AVA structure is defined in Section 22.8.1.

**fi_un.un_substrings**: **FILTERITEM_SUBSTRING** matches. Use the substring structure defined below, to specify which substrings to look for in the appropriate attribute.

```
typedef struct {
            AttributeType fi_sub_type;
            AV_Sequence   fi_sub_initial;
            AV_Sequence   fi_sub_any;
            AV_Sequence   fi_sub_final;
            char         *fi_sub_match;
        } Filter_Substrings;
```

The AV_Sequence structure is used to represent a string, and should be treated as essentially a linked list of char * parameters.

**fi_sub_type**: The attribute that you want to perform a substring search on.

**fi_sub_initial**: This contains a single attribute value, that must appear at the start of the string.

**fi_sub_any**: A set of values, which must appear in order in the middle of the string.

**fi_sun_final**: This contains a single attribute value, that must appear at the end of the string.

**fi_sub_match**: For DSA use only.

**fi_ifp**: For DSA use only.

The single filter items can now be linked into a filter structure to build more complex search definitions:

```
typedef struct filter {
    char          flt_type;
#define FILTER_ITEM 1
#define FILTER_AND  2
#define FILTER_OR   3
#define FILTER_NOT  4
   struct filter * flt_next;
   union {
        struct filter_item   flt_un_item;
        struct filter      * flt_un_filter;
   }                  flt_un;
}filter, *Filter;
```

**flt_type:** This defines whether the filter is a single item, or a more complex filter made up of one or more components.

**flt_un.flt_un_item:** If the filter represents a filter_item, then the item is placed here.

**flt_un.flt_un_filter:** AND, OR and NOT filters apply to a linked list of "children" filters. This element is a pointer to the head of that list.

**flt_next:** If the parent filter is an AND, OR. or NOT filter, then the component filters are linked using this field. *Note*: that NOT filters should contain a list of one child only.

As an example, lets us consider a filter to represent a person whose name is either "Robbins" *or* ( "Steve" *and* "Kille" ). The structure would look something like:

```
flt_type = FILTER_OR
        - The filter is an OR filter
flt_un_filter.flt_type = FILTER_ITEM
        - First component or the OR is an item
flt_un_filter.flt_un_item = filter_item (Robbins)
        - The item should match "robbins"
flt_un_filter.flt_next->flt_type = FILTER_AND
        - Second component or the OR is an AND filter
flt_un_filter.flt_next->flt_un_filter.flt_type = FILTER_ITEM
        - First component or the AND is an item
flt_un_filter.flt_next->flt_un_filter.flt_un_item =
                                            filter_item (Steve)
        - The item should match "Steve"
flt_un_filter.flt_next->flt_un_filter.flt_next->flt_type =
                                            FILTER_ITEM
        - Second component or the AND is an item
flt_un_filter.flt_next->flt_un_filter.flt_next->flt_un_item =
                                            filter_item (Kille)
        - The item should match "Kille"
```

## 22.11 Modification Operations

There are four operations available to modify the directory.

*Note*: with this version of QUIPU, modify operations are only allowed over DAP, attempts to modify over DSP will return referral errors.

### 22.11.1 Add

To add an entry to the DIT use

```
ds_addentry (arg, error)
    struct ds_addentry_arg      * arg;
    struct DSError              * error;
```

You will need to include *quipu/add.h* to use this procedure. The argument you must supply is made up as follows:

```
struct ds_addentry_arg {
    CommonArgs    ada_common;
    DN            ada_object;
    Attr_Sequence ada_entry;
};
```

**ada_common:** The common arguments as described in Section 22.2.1.

**ada_object:** The DN of the object you want to add.

**ada_entry:** The attributes you want to add for this entry. This must contain the RDN of the entry, and an "objectclass" attribute. Then, the other attribute *must* conform to the set of "optional" and "mandatory" attribute for that object class.

### 22.11.2 Remove

This is used to remove an entry from the DIT. Only leaf entries can be removed.

```
ds_removeentry (arg, error)
    struct ds_removeentry_arg   * arg;
    struct DSError              * error;
```

You will need to include *quipu/remove.h* to use this procedure. The argument you must supply is made up as follows:

```
struct ds_removeentry_arg {
    CommonArgs rma_common;
    DN         rma_object;
};
```

**rma_common:** The common arguments as described in 22.2.1.

**rma_object:** The DN of the object you want to remove.

### 22.11.3 Modify

`ModifyEntry` is used to modify the attributes of the specified entry. There are strong restrictions on this operation as required by X.500. Invalid operations result in errors, and as such none of the requested modifications are made. To modify an attribute you must first **remove** it then **add** a new attribute. You cannot modify the RDN; you must use the `ModifyRDN` operation described in Section 22.11.4 to do this.

```
ds_modifyentry (arg, error)
    struct ds_modifyentry_arg   * arg;
    struct DSError              * error;
```

You will need to include *quipu/modify.h* to use this procedure. The argument you must supply is made up as follows:

```
struct ds_modifyentry_arg {
    CommonArgs          mea_common;
    DN                  mea_object;
    struct entrymod * mea_changes;
};
```

**mea_common:** The common arguments as described in Section 22.2.1.

**mea_object:** The DN of the object you want to modify.

**mea_changes:** A tree structure defining the changes you want to make to the entry.

```
struct entrymod {
    int                 em_type;
#define EM_ADDATTRIBUTE          1
#define EM_REMOVEATTRIBUTE       2
#define EM_ADDVALUES             3
#define EM_REMOVEVALUES          4
    Attr_Sequence       em_what;
    struct entrymod * em_next;
};
```

**em_type:** The type of modification this is.

**em_what:** The attribute you want to add or remove. If the operation type is remove, then this structure should only contain an attribute type, and not a value.

**em_next:** A modify operation is built up with a series of small modifications. Hence this structure is a linked list. The operation is seen as one atomic operation.

### 22.11.4 ModifyRDN

To modify the distinguished attribute values of an entry, you must use this operation; `modifyEntry` cannot be used.

```
ds_modifyrdn (arg, error)
    struct ds_modifyrdn_arg      * arg;
    struct DSError               * error;
```

You will need to include *quipu/modifyrdn.h* to use this procedure.

The arguments are:

```
struct ds_modifyrdn_arg {
    CommonArgs mra_common;
    DN         mra_object;
    RDN        mra_newrdn;
    char       mra_deleterdn;
};
```

**mra_common:** The common arguments as described in Section 22.2.1.

**mra_object:** The DN of the object you want to modify the name of.

**mra_newrdn:** The new RDN.

**mra_deleterdn:** if TRUE then the old RDN will be deleted as an attribute; otherwise it will remain as a nondistinguished attribute.

## 22.12 Abandon

The abandon operation shown below is slightly different from the other DUA operations. It does not make much sense for a synchronous interface to handle abandon directly. In the next release, transparent use of abandon will be provided.

```
ds_abandon (arg, error)
    struct ds_abandon_arg        * arg;
    struct DSError               * error;
```

The argument structure contains a single parameter supplies the operation invocation id.

```
struct ds_abandon_arg {
    int aba_invokeid;
};
```

In the synchronous interface, an operation may be abandoned by the user entering a "control–c" (unless trapped by user code). In this case, the abandon will be handled by the lower layers of QUIPU, and the outstanding operation will return. It may have results if the abandon operation failed, or may indicate "abandon successful" via the DAP error structure!

## 22.13 Multiple Associations

The procedural interface described so far has been based on the assumption of a connection to a single DSA. However, it is possible to make connection to multiple DSAs.

### 22.13.1 Multiple Binds

The bind and unbind routines needed to make multiple association are as follows:

```
dap_bind (ad, arg, error, result, addr)
    int                          * ad;
    struct ds_bind_arg           *arg;
    struct ds_bind_arg           *result;
    struct ds_bind_error         *error;
    struct PSAPaddr              *addr;

dap_unbind (ad)
    int                          ad;
```

The **arg**, **error** and **result** arguments are as defined in Section 22.5 for the routine **secure_ds_bind**.

The argument **ad** is the association descriptor of the association. It will be different for each association.

The **addr** argument is the address of the DSA you wish to contact.

### 22.13.2 Other DAP Operations

The other DAP operations (read, list, modify...), use the same format as already described, but with two extra integer parameters; thus

```
ds_read (arg, error, result)
```

becomes

```
dap_read (ad, id, arg, error, result)
```

where **ad** is the association descriptor returned by the bind, and **id** uniquely identifies the operation with respect to other operation on the same association.

# Chapter 23

# The Async DAP Procedural Interface

Originally, the procedural interface providing a representation of the X.500 DAP operations was only required to provide synchronous behaviour. It is likely that many useful applications will be written which only require synchronous representation of operations; so that having bound to a DSA, operations are constructed in some way and then the routine representing the relevant operation is called and will block until an appropriate response has been received from the DSA.

However, in more sophisticated DUAs it will be desirable to have asynchronous or non-blocking routines representing the various DAP operations, so that the DUA can construct and send operations, perform useful work whilst waiting for the operations to complete, and collect and use the responses to operations as they become available.

For the above reasons, a new set of procedure calls has been written as part of the *libdsap* (3n) library. These calls provide a representation of the X.500 operations (including the bind operation) which can be used to program asynchronous performance of operations within a DUA. This chapter describes those routines and their intended use.

To use the async DAP interface described here it is necessary to include the file *quipu/dap2.h*.

## 23.1 Procedure Model

### 23.1.1 Styles of Behaviour

The routines which it is desirable to have to represent X.500 DAP operations depends on the behaviour required within a DUA. A simple DUA may be more easily developed by expecting a synchronous behaviour from routines representing operations; DAP operations are invoked as routines which block until a response to the operation arrives and the DUA can then continue according to that response.

If, for whatever reasons, it is undesirable to block every time a DAP operation is requested, then a different behaviour is required from the routines representing operations; the operation request should be issued and the routine returned. Subsequently a routine should be available to accept a response to the request issued and process that response.

An additional twist is that there are actually three styles of behaviour which it is desirable to make available to DUA programs: a simple synchronous interface, an interruptible synchronous interface, and an asynchronous interface.

The interruptible synchronous interface is the style of behaviour described in the previous section. If an operation is called synchronously and then interrupted (a Control-C to the user interface for instance) during performance of the operation, then an abandon DAP operation should automatically be invoked on the outstanding operation and appropriate responses gathered from the DSA before returning to the user. The interruptible synchronous style of behaviour is only available for the remote operations of the directory access context (read, add entry, ...) and not for the bind and unbind operations.

Mixing of styles of behaviour is deprecated, although there are no known problems. An asynchronous operation request followed by a synchronous operation request may well get the response to either operation, which means checking the responses to all synchronous requests in the same ways as the responses to asynchronous requests must be checked, thus losing most of the advantages that make the synchronous style worthwhile in the first place.

In order to enable the incorporation of all three styles, a generalised interface has been written over which the interruptible synchronous interface described in Section 22.1 has been reimplemented. Thus, the routines in that previous section can be thought of as a specialised restriction of the interface described here.

The generalised interface also differs, in that it does not provide automatic decoding of results and errors into particular parameters, instead returning an indication parameter which may include decoded structures within it. This means that the implementation of the old style interface using the generalised routines is not as straightforward as the above comments might suggest.

Future revisions should take on board the separation of the provision of routines which perform DAP operations from the provision of routines which provide DUA services in the construction of DAP operations (e.g., getting passwords for a bind request is a high-level DUA task; parameterisation which allows the use of pre-allocated result and error return parameters is a lower-level DUA task). All that the DAP operations should provide is the encoding of arguments, sending of operations and appropriate subsequent behaviour. Hopefully, future documentation will be produced which is structured so as to enable a clearer relationship between the different interfaces and behaviour styles provided for DAP operations.

Where each routine of the synchronous interface described in the previous chapter had a prefix of "`ds_`" (when using an implicit association identifier) or of "`dap_`" (when using an explicit association identifier), all the routines in the asynchronous interface have a prefix of "Dap". All operations in the asynchronous interface take an explicit association identifier.

For each of the DAP bind operations, the DAP unbind operations and the DAP remote operations (read, list, search, addentry, removeentry, modifyentry, modifyrdn and abandon) a request routine is provided. The request routine takes a parameter indicating the style of behaviour to be used (synchronous, or asynchronous for the bind and unbind operations requests; synchronous, interruptible or asynchronous for the DAP remote operations).

If the style indicated is synchronous, then the request routine will attempt to construct and send the appropriate operation and wait for a response. If the operation completes successfully (a result or an error is returned) then the routine returns `OK`. Otherwise, on failure, the routine returns `NOTOK`.

If the style indicated is interruptible, then the operation is sent and an interruptible wait initiated for a response from the DSA. If an interruption occurs (see a description of the routine `RoIntrRequest` in the rosap module for details of what constitutes an interruption and how it is indicated), then an abandon operation is sent for the outstanding operation and responses from the DSA are awaited for both the abandon operation and for the outstanding operation. Except in the case of an interruption the style of behaviour is exactly the same as the synchronous style.

If the style indicated is asynchronous, then the operation is sent and the routine returns. For the DAP bind and DAP unbind operations a retry routine is provided for each operation which when called will either complete the outstanding operation or indicate that it is not yet complete. For the DAP remote operations a single wait routine is available which will complete an outstanding operation, if there is one which can be completed, or indicate that there is no completable operation.

The value used to indicate the style of behaviour is borrowed from the "`rosap`" module:

**`ROS_SYNC`:** Simple synchronous behaviour: block until DSA responds.

**`ROS_INTR`:** Interruptible synchronous behaviour: block until DSA responds or an interruption occurs. (Untidily, the definition of the value `ROS_INTR` is currently contained in *quipu/dap2.h*.)

**`ROS_ASYNC`** : Asynchronous behaviour: send operation, do not block.

### 23.1.2 Arguments

Arguments taken by async DAP request operations are, in general, a binding (or association) identifier which identifies the association on which to invoke the operation; an operation identifier which it is the responsibility of the DUA to generate, maintain and use as a reference (e.g., for abandoning a previously requested operation); a representation of the argument for the operation; an indication return parameter through which information on the outcome of the operation can be returned to the invoker of the routine; and of course the behaviour style indicator.

### 23.1.3 Indications

All of the routines representing X.500 operations in this procedural interface take an indication parameter, the type of which is a pointer to a pre-allocated DAPindication structure.

```
struct DAPindication {
    int      di_type;
#define DI_RESULT       2
#define DI_ERROR        3
#define DI_PREJECT      4
#define DI_ABORT        6
    union {
        struct DAPresult        di_un_result;
        struct DAPerror         di_un_error;
        struct DAPpreject       di_un_preject;
        struct DAPabort         di_un_abort;
    } di_un;
#define di_result di_un.di_un_result
#define di_error di_un.di_un_error
#define di_preject di_un.di_un_preject
#define di_abort di_un.di_un_abort
};
```

This structure is a discriminated union (tag element followed by a union). Depending on the routine called, style of behaviour requested, and the value returned by the routine the contents of the indication should be readily retrievable.

For the bind and unbind routines the DAPindication structure is only updated on failure and will contain an abort indication.

For the DAP remote operations the DAPindication structure is used to indicate failure of the association, failure of the request, an error response to a request, or a result response to a request.

When the DAPindication structure is used to indicate a failure of the association it will contain a DAPabort structure.

```
struct DAPabort {
    int      da_source;

    int      da_reason;

#define DA_SIZE 512
    int      da_cc;
```

```
        char    da_data[DA_SIZE];
    }
```

**da_source:** the source of the abort, one of:

| Value | Source |
|---|---|
| DA_USER | service-user (peer) |
| DA_PROVIDER | service-provider |
| DA_LOCAL | local DAPM |

**da_reason:** The reason for aborting the association (if known).

**da_data/da_cc:** a diagnostic string from the provider.

When the DAPindication structure is used to indicate a rejection it will contain a DAPpreject structure.

```
    struct DAPpreject {
        int             dp_id;

        int             dp_source;

        int             dp_reason;

    #define DP_SIZE 512
        int     dp_cc;
        char    dp_data[DP_SIZE];
    }
```

**dp_id:** the operation identifier of the operation rejected.

**dp_source:** the source of the abort, taking the same values as da_source in the DAPabort structure described above.

**dp_reason:** The reason for rejecting the operation (if known).

**dp_data/dp_cc:** a diagnostic string from the provider.

When the DAPindication structure is used to indicate a result in response to a previously issued remote operation request it will contain a DAPresult structure.

```
    struct DAPresult {
        int                     dr_id;
        struct DSResult         dr_res;
    }
```

**dr_id:** the operation identifier of the operation for which this is the result.

**dr_res:** the decoded result structure.

The operation identifier should be used on the receipt of an operation result to determine the operation the result applies to, and the result structure handled appropriately.

When the DAPindication structure is used to indicate a error in response to a previously issued remote operation request it will contain a DAPerror structure.

```
struct DAPerror {
    int                 de_id;
    struct DSError      de_err;
}
```

**de_id:** the operation identifier of the operation for which this is the error response.

**de_err:** the decoded error structure.

The operation identifier should be used on the receipt of an operation error to determine the operation the error applies to, and the error structure handled appropriately.

### 23.1.4 Return Values

The values returned by the various routines in this interface and their meanings are more complicated than may be entirely reasonable. However, a quick overview goes as follows:

- for bind and unbind operations synchronous style and DAP remote operations in synchronous or interruptible style, the request routines may return NOTOK on failure and OK on success.
- for bind and unbind operations asynchronous style, the request routines may return NOTOK on failure, DONE on completion, and CONNECTING_1 or CONNECTING_2 when incomplete.
- for DAP remote operations asynchronous style, the request routines may return NOTOK on failure, OK on successful invocation.

## 23.2 Binding and Unbinding

### 23.2.1 Binding

To be able to send DAP remote operations to a DSA it is necessary to establish an association with the DSA using a DAP bind operation. This can be accomplished either synchronously or asynchronously using the routine DapAsynBindReqAux.

```
int        DapAsynBindReqAux (callingtitle, calledtitle,
                callingaddr, calledaddr, prequirements,
                srequirements, isn, settings, sf,
                bindarg, qos, dc, di, async)
AEI                       callingtitle;
AEI                       calledtitle;
struct PSAPaddr         * callingaddr;
struct PSAPaddr         * calledaddr;
int                       prequirements;
int                       srequirements;
long                      isn;
int                       settings;
struct SSAPref          * sf;
struct ds_bind_arg      * bindarg;
struct QOStype          * qos;
struct DAPconnect       * dc;
struct DAPindication    * di;
int                       async;
```

This routine will attempt to call a DSA at the called address and/or with the called title, to establish a directory access association using the directory bind argument provided.

Often, all that is required for many of these parameters is that they are initialised to appropriate values. The routine DapAsynBindRequest is provided which sets up sensible defaults for most of the parameters before calling the routine DapAsynBindReqAux.

```
int DapAsynBindRequest (calledaddr, bindarg, dc, di, async)
struct PSAPaddr         * calledaddr;
struct ds_bind_arg      * bindarg;
struct DAPconnect       * dc;
struct DAPindication    * di;
int                       async;
```

**calledaddr:** the address of the DSA to send the bind request to. The PSAPaddr structure is described in Volume 2 of the ISODE manual), and more general discussion of addresses is given in Volume 1 of the ISODE manual).

**bindarg:** is a representation of the argument of the DAP bind operation. The ds_bind_arg structure is described in Section 22.1.

**dc:** is used to return bind response information when a response is received. The DAPconnect structure comprises connection information from the underlying association and a structure containing a representation of the bind response (bind result or bind error) if any.

**di:** is the indication parameter described above in Section 23.1.3.

**async:** can take one of two values: ROS_ASYNC or ROS_SYNC. If the value is ROS_SYNC, then the routine will await a response to the association request and attempt to decode the value returned in that response. If the value is ROS_ASYNC, then the routine may return without receiving an association response, which may be checked for later using the DapAsynBindRetry routine.

The DAPconnect structure is used to return the response to a DAP bind operation:

```
struct DAPconnect {
    int     dc_sd;
    int     dc_pctx_id;
    struct AcSAPconnect dc_connect;

    int     dc_result;
#define DC_RESULT       1
#define DC_ERROR        2
#define DC_REJECT       3

    union {
        struct ds_bind_arg          dc_bind_res;
        struct ds_bind_error        dc_bind_err;
    } dc_un;
};
```

**dc_sd:** the association identifier assigned to the bound association.

**dc_pctx_id:** the identifier of the directory access context in the negotiated list of presentation contexts.

**dc_connect:** the connect information for the underlying association.

**dc_result:** the type of response received.

**dc_bind_res:** the decoded bind result if the response is a result.

**dc_bind_err:** the decoded bind error if the response is an error.

For explanations of the other parameters to DapAsynBindReqAux see the description of the AcAssocRequest routine in the ISODE Manual).

When the asynchronous style of behaviour is selected for a bind request, the DapAsynBindRetry can be used to attempt to complete the bind and process any response. In order to determine when to call DapAsynBindRetry, the methods for asynchronously establishing connections described in the ISODE Manual should be applied. Essentially, the values CONNECTING_1 and CONNECTING_2, are used to determine whether the association establishment is currently blocked on reading or writing, and is used in constructing a call to xselect to determine if further progress can be made. If the call to xselect indicates that further work can be done then DapAsynBindRetry should be called.

```
int         DapAsynBindRetry (sd, do_next_nsap, dc, di)
int                            sd;
int                            do_next_nsap;
struct DAPconnect            * dc;
struct DAPindication         * di;
```

sd: the association descriptor returned in the DAPconnect structure after an asynchronous call to DapAsynBindReqAux.

do_next_nsap: is used to specify whether the association should be retried on the same NSAP of the called address originally passed to DapAsynBindReqAux or whether to give up on the current NSAP and go on to the next (if any). A value of zero will specify retrying on the same NSAP, a non-zero value specifies retrying on the next NSAP. This is somewhat messy as it forces the calling code to keep track of how long a particular NSAP has been tried for and when to try another. If there are no more NSAPs when the next NSAP is requested, then the association attempt is deemed to have failed and an appropriate indication is generated.

dc: if the routine returns DONE then this structure will contain the connect information as described for DapAsynBindReqAux above.

di: if the routine returns NOTOK then this structure will contain the indication information.

### 23.2.2 Unbinding

When a DUA no longer needs to be bound to a DSA it can issue a DAP unbind operation to unbind from the DSA and end the association. This is achieved by using the DapUnBindRequest routine.

```
int         DapUnBindRequest (sd, secs, dr, di)
int                            sd;
int                            secs;
struct DAPrelease            * dr;
struct DAPindication         * di;
```

sd: the association identifier for the association from which the DUA wishes to unbind.

"secs: the number of seconds to spend trying to unbind.

dr: the result of unbinding when complete.

di: an indication.

If the unbind operation fails then the routine will return NOTOK and an appropriate indication.

If the unbind operation completes successfully within secs seconds then the routine will return OK and the DAPrelease structure will be filled out.

If no unbind response is received within secs seconds the routine will return a value of DONE and the unbind should be completed using the routine DapUnBindRetry.

```
int       DapUnBindRetry (sd, secs, dr, di)
int                     sd;
int                     secs;
struct DAPrelease      * dr;
struct DAPindication   * di;
```

Which takes exactly the same parameters and has similar behaviour to the routine DapUnBindRequest above.

## 23.3 DAP Remote Operations

For each DAP remote operation (read, abandon, add entry, ...) there is a routine in the asynchronous interface to request that operation. The DapRead routine will be described in detail, which taken in conjunction with the descriptions of arguments given in Section 22 should also provide adequate description of the routines DapCompare, DapAbandon, DapList, DapSearch, DapAddEntry, DapRemoveEntry, DapModifyEntry, and DapModifyRDN.

All these routines can be invoked with synchronous, interruptible or asynchronous styles of behaviour. In the synchronous and interruptible cases the call will not return until a response is received (in the interruptible style an interruption will cause an automatic sending of an abandon request for the operation requested by the routine and will await and return the response to that operation). In the asynchronous case the routine will return after the request has been sent and specific procedures for receiving responses must be undertaken using the DapInitWaitRequest routine.

### 23.3.1 Invoking Requests

```
int       DapRead (ad, id, arg, di, asyn)
int                     ad;
int                     id;
struct ds_read_arg     * arg;
```

```
    struct DAPindication    * di;
    int                       asyn;
```

ad: the association identifier for the bound association over which to send the read operation.

id: the operation identifier to assign the the read operation.

arg: the read argument.

di: an indication parameter, only used if the request fails.

asyn: the behaviour style selector.

If DapRead is invoked with synchronous behaviour, then it will block until a response arrives, and hope that the response is for the operation just requested, although no guarantees are made that this is so.

If the interruptible style is selected then the call may be interrupted by some signals and an abandon operation for the operation requested is generated when this occurs, with the routine then awaiting both the response to the abandon operation and to the original operation before returning.

If the asynchronous style is selected, then the call issues the request and returns, the response should be expected in a subsequent call to the routine DapInitWaitRequest.

### 23.3.2 Receiving Responses

```
int       DapInitWaitRequest (sd, secs, di)
int                      sd;
int                      secs;
struct DAPindication   * di;
```

sd: the association identifier.

secs: the number of seconds to spend waiting for a response; OK will produce a polling effect and NOTOK will produce a blocking effect.

di: the indication structure.

If the DapInitWaitRequest routine returns OK then there is a response contained in the indication parameter. If it returns DONE then there was no response available within the specified time.

## 23.4 Programming Comments

This interface has been written with expectations of the following sort of program structure in mind.

Through interaction with a user or from arguments or tailoring, a DUA will undertake to attempt one or more DAP bind operations to one or more DSAs.

An asynchronous call to DapAsynBindReqAux should be made using an appropriate bind argument for each DSA that the DUA wishes to bind to. If the association completes then operations can be constructed and invoked on the bound association identified by the value returned in the dc_sd fields of the DAPconnect structure dc_sd.

If the value returned by the DapAsynBindRequest procedure call is either CONNECTING_1 or CONNECTING_2 then this value should be recorded along with the value returned in the dc_sd field of the dc parameter, which identifies the association even though it is not yet complete. Operations *must not* be invoked using this identifier until the bound association is completely established.

At a later stage, for each outstanding association request, depending on whether the last value returned for the association attempt on that association identifier is CONNECTING_1 or CONNECTING_2, the routine xselect should be used to check for writing or reading on the value returned by PSelectMask for the given association identifier.

If the call to xselect indicates that writing (or reading) is available then the routine DapAsynBindRetry should be called for that association identifier.

This should be repeated until the association attempt fails or is completed, at which point operations can be constructed and invoked over the bound association. This is done using the appropriate routine for the required operation.

If operations are invoked asynchronously, then a call to the procedure DapInitWaitRequest will need to check for responses to outstanding operations and to return such a response as an indication if there is one available. The DUA can then process responses to the operations it invoked.

When the DUA no longer needs to be bound to a DSA, the procedure DapUnBindRequest can be used to initiate the termination of a bound association, and if necessary, the DapUnBindRetry routine used to complete the binding.

# Chapter 24

# Caching in a DUA

This part of the manual is written for implementors who wish to perform caching in their DUA. This used to require the use of the the *libquipu* (3n) library. However the functionality has now been rolled into the *libdsap* (3n) library and the *libquipu* (3n) library removed.

The library provides some routines to manage the data returned by the DUA procedure calls described in Chapter 22.

## 24.1 The Entry Structure

The Entry structure is used by the QUIPU DSA to store the data in the local DIT. This structure can also be used by a DUA to cache information from a successful read operation, and so the structure is described. In fact, this is how DISH maintains its cache.

The structure is shown below. Many of the fields are not appropriate to a DUA, but are briefly described for completeness.

```
typedef struct entry {
    RDN             e_name;
    Attr_Sequence   e_attributes;
    InheritAttr     e_iattr;
    char            e_leaf;
    char            e_complete;
    int             e_data;
#define E_DATA_MASTER           1
#define E_TYPE_SLAVE            2
#define E_TYPE_CACHE_FROM_MASTER 3
#define E_TYPE_CONSTRUCTOR      4
    char             e_allchildrenpresent;
    struct acl      * e_acl;
    DN               e_alias;
    struct dsa_info * e_dsainfo;
```

```
        char            * e_edbversion;
        AV_Sequence       e_oc;
        AV_Sequence       e_inherit;
        struct entry    * e_parent;
#ifdef TURBO_AVL
        Avlnode         * e_children;
#else
        struct entry    * e_sibling;
        struct entry    * e_child;
#endif
        time_t            e_age;
        char              e_lock;
        char              e_external;
                          /* 0 -> Quipu, 1 -> External */
        union  {
           struct {
           AV_Sequence un_master;
           AV_Sequence un_slave;
           } un_in;
           struct {
           int          un_reftype;
           AV_Sequence  un_reference;
           } un_out;
        } e_un;
#define e_master         e_un.un_in.un_master
#define e_slave          e_un.un_in.un_slave
#define e_reference      e_un.un_out.un_reference
#define e_reftype        e_un.un_out.un_reftype

        int          e_refcount;
} entry, *Entry;
```

**e_name:** The RDN of the entry, to find the DN, use the routine

```
DN get_copy_dn (entryptr)
Entry entryptr;
```

**e_attributes:** The attributes returned by the DSA.

**e_iattr:** pointer to attributes inherited into the entry. This will always be NULL in a DUA — all attributes whether or not inherited will be in the `e_attributes` field.

**e_leaf:** Set to `TRUE` if the entry is known to be a leaf.

**e_complete:** Set to `TRUE` if it is know that we have *all* the attributes.

**e_data:** This takes one of four values. in the DUA only two apply. E_TYPE_CACHE_FROM_MASTER implies the entry has data that has been read from the DSA. E_TYPE_CONSTRUCTOR is used when the entry has been "made" by the caching mechanism to fill in a missing part of the DIT on the way down to another entry. An entry of this type will contain no data except from the RDN of the entry.

**e_allchildrenpresent:** Set to TRUE when it is known that all the children are held. This is a DSA-specific field.

**e_acl:** A pointer to the "Access Control List" attribute.

**e_alias:** Set to TRUE if the entry represents an alias. This is a DSA specific field.

**e_dsainfo:** pointers to the "EDBInfo" and "PresentationAddress" attribute of entries representing DSAs.

**e_edbversion:** This is a DSA specific field representing the EDB version number of the children.

**e_parent:** Pointer to the parent entry.

**e_sibling:** Pointer to other nodes at this level in the tree.

**e_child:** Pointer to the children.

**e_children:** Pointer to the children (if using AVL trees).

**e_age:** If the data type is E_TYPE_CACHE_FROM_MASTER, then the entry is time stamped. This enables the cache to be "timed out". *Note*: in a DUA all entries are cached!

**e_lock:** This field has a dual purpose! In the DSA it is used to prevent an entry from being modified. In the DUA, if FALSE, then is suggests that in the field e_attributes there are only the attribute types for some attributes, this is a result of caching an results from an operation in which the entry info selection requested that attribute type only were returned (see Section 22.7.1).

**e_external:** Indicates type of reference — QUIPU or nonQuIPU.

**e_master:** Pointer to the "MasterDSA" attribute.

**e_slave:** Pointer to the "SlaveDSA" attribute.

**e_reftype:** Type of a reference to a nonQuIPU DSA.

**e_reference:** Reference to a nonQuIPU DSA.

**e_refcount:** Reference count used to make sure entry is not freed too early.

Using this structure a tree, mapping the DIT can be built up. The tree is rooted by the external `Entry` "`database_root`". This entry will *never* have any attributes or siblings, *only* children.

## 24.2 Caching Results

There are four routines to create a cache from results of DAP operations:-

To cache results returned from a `read` or `search` operation call

```
cache_entry (ptr, complete, vals)
EntryInfo      *ptr;
char            complete;
char            vals;
```

The `complete` parameter should be `TRUE` if all attributes were requested and returned.

The `vals` parameter should be `TRUE` if the attribute values were asked for.

The external `Entry` "`current_entry`" will be a pointer to the newly created entry.

To remove an entry from the cache use:

```
delete_cache (adn)
DN              adn;
```

## 24.3 Finding Data in the Cache

The procedure

```
Entry local_find_entry (object,deref)
DN                        object;
char                      deref;
```

is used to find an entry in the cache. If the entry exists, it will be returned, otherwise `NULLENTRY` will be returned. `object` is the DN of the entry you want to find. If `deref` is `TRUE` then any aliases encountered in trying to find the entry will be de-referenced.

The cache is only maintained for the period specified in a `cache_timeout` external variable (this is initially set to six hours). If the cache expires then `local_find_entry` will return `NULLENTRY`. To prevent timeouts, the routine `local_find_entry_aux` will return the cached entry even if the timeout has expired.

## 24.4 Caching List Results

List results are cached slightly differently, as only the RDN is known.

```
cache_list (ptr, prob,dn,sizelimit)
struct subordinate *ptr;
int             prob;
DN              dn;
int             sizelimit;
```

The parameters are as follows:-

**ptr:** A pointer to the subordinates returned by the search.

**prob:** The `srr_limitproblem` field of the search results, see Section 22.10.

**dn:** The DN of the entry that has been listed.

**ptr:** The `svc_sizelimit` field of the common argument of the list argument (see Section 22.2.1).

To inspect the cache use

```
struct list_cache *find_list_cache (dn,sizelimit)
DN dn;
int sizelimit;
```

The `sizelimit` parameter is the sizelimit you would send in the list request.

This returns a `list_cache` structure; if the result is NULL, then the entry is not cached, or has less than "sizelimit" results.

```
struct list_cache {
        DN              list_dn;
        struct subordinate *list_subs;
        struct subordinate *list_sub_top;
        int             list_count;
        int             list_problem;
        struct list_cache *list_next;
};
```

The subordinates can be found in `list_sub_top`. The other field should be ignored, as they are for internal management only.

## 24.5 Changes

To conclude this part of the manual, a brief summary of the changes between this version and the QUIPU-6.0 version of the *libdsap* (3n) library is given.

Calls to the `x_decode()` routines are no longer required and should be removed. All the decoding is performed as the attributes come across the network.

The AttributeType structure is now just a pointer into the OID tables, thus "at_table" structure reference is no longer needed. Code of the form

```
at->at_table.oa_syntax
```

should be replaced with

```
at->oa_syntax
```

and

```
at->at_oid
```

replaced with

```
at->oa_at.ot_oid
```

# Part VI

# QUIPU Manual: Design

# Chapter 25

# Overview

## 25.1 Introduction

This part of the manual describes aspects of the design of QUIPU which are not needed to be known by the administrator or user of QUIPU. However, it documents important design decisions and protocol, which are of interest to understand how QUIPU works, and in some specific circumstances (e.g., solving interoperability problems). A summary of the main features of QUIPU is also given.

QUIPU fully implements both of the OSI directory protocols, and a number of extensions. The highlights of the QUIPU directory service implementation are:

- Use of memory structures to provide fast access, without use of complex keying techniques.
- Activity scheduling within the DSA to allow for multiple accesses.
- General and flexible searching capabilities.
- A mechanism to provide nonlocal access control.
- A mechanism to provide external schema management.
- A sophisticated approach for management of distributed operations and replication.

The current implementation provides a DSA, and a procedural interface to the directory abstract service and the associated directory access protocol (DAP), which will enable other applications to use the directory.

## 25.2 General Aims

To understand the rationale behind some of the decisions, it is useful to consider the original aims of the QUIPU project. These can then be mapped onto a number of more technical considerations:

- To produce an implementation which followed the emerging standards. This is an aim in itself.
- Flexibility, to enable the system to be used for experimentation and research into problems relating to directory services.
- To provide a vehicle for experimentation in the area of distribution and replication.
- To provide some level of real usage. This sort of work is useless if entirely confined to the laboratory. It is important that it is capable of use for some level of experimental service. However, it is not consciously designed to evolve into a full-fledged product.

As the work has evolved, the following goals have emerged as additional to the original ones listed above:

- To provide a public domain OSI directory implementation as a part of the ISODE package.
- To provide integrated support for the ISODE Applications.
- To be used as a part of the initial pilot directory service in the UK academic community and in other pilots.

## 25.3 Technical Goals

The major goals of the QUIPU directory service are:

- Full support of the directory access protocol and directory system protocols [CCITT88].
- Support of the majority of the service elements specified in the OSI directory.
- Full interworking with other OSI directory implementations.
- Very full searching and matching capabilities, beyond the minimum required by the OSI directory.
- Provision of a system which has potential for very high distribution.
- Support of distributed operations in a manner which is in full conformance with respect to nonQUIPU systems, and provides additional functionality for QUIPU systems.

The following areas were not intended as goals in the initial system. Some discussion is given as to how these areas might be tackled in future versions.

- The QUIPU directory is not intended for very large scale systems (i.e., millions and tens of millions of entries per DSA or hundreds of megabytes of data per DSA).
- Substantial data robustness is not required: there is no need to employ complex data backup techniques, such as replicated hardware.

- The security aspects of the OSI directory were initially omitted, as not required by the general aims. At this point, there is no reason why this aspect should not be integrated.

## 25.4 Further QUIPU Documents

The following documents are available, in addition to this manual:

- A paper on the original design, which is mainly of historical interest [SKill87].
- A paper presented at the 1988 IFIP 6.5 conference, which gives a general overview [SKill88a].
- A paper presented at ESPRIT Conference Week 1988, which describes the distributed operations [SKill88b].
- A paper presented to the Dutch UNIX User Group in November 1989, which describes how QUIPU DSAs navigate the DIT [PBark89].

These papers, except the first, are distributed online with QUIPU.

# Chapter 26

# General Design

## 26.1 Overview

This chapter describes general decisions. In particular, issues relating to use of the OSI directory are covered, rather than system implementation decisions. However, the two are somewhat bound up. Attention is drawn to the protocol extensions defined in section 29.1. Note that this does *not* affect interactions with non-QUIPU DSAs (or DUAs). The following aspects of the OSI directory are not handled in the current version of QUIPU:

- The protocol elements for support of directory use of authentication are handled in a conformant manner, but the associated services are not available to the end user.
- Search is always supported by multicasting. This does *not* affect the basic service offered to the user, but means that prohibition of chaining is not possible in all cases.
- Partial outcome qualifier is not supported for List.
- There are some aspects of distributed operation, where interaction withanother conforming system would not be fully general. In particular, QUIPU might not be able to be configured with references to point at a complex configuration where not all sibling entries are held.

Otherwise, QUIPU is believed to conform to the standard.

## 26.2 Service Controls

QUIPU use of service controls conforms to the OSI directory. Comments are made on those controls where QUIPU makes a choice with respect to some option given by the OSI directory.

**preferChaining:** Chaining will be done.

**chainingProhibited:** Chaining will not be done. For some cases of the search operation, this means that the QUIPU directory Service will not be able to provide the service, and will return a "chaining required" error.

**localScope:** The scope will be restricted to the DSA concerned (i.e., no chaining will be done).

**dontUseCopy:** If this is set, the master data will be used. This may have a significant impact on performance for operations on entries which are high up the tree and for the DSAs which master this information. These issues need study.

**dontDereferenceAliases:** Followed as per the OSI directory.

**priority:** This is used to help control scheduling within the DSA. High priority tasks are dealt with before low priority tasks (Note: there are no checks here, so this is open to mis-use !)

**timeLimit:** Followed as per the OSI directory.

**sizeLimit:** Followed as per the OSI directory.

**scopeOfReferral:** The OSI directory is followed, although QUIPU does not make use of this control.

# Chapter 27

# Distributed Operation

## 27.1 Overview

Distributed Operation is a major aspect of the QUIPU directory service. Sadly, the OSI directory specifications in this area are, in the author's opinion, rather unsatisfactory. Therefore, the QUIPU distributed operations are described in a slightly different manner. The concept of "naming context" is not used, and the significance of "knowledge" is deemphasised. The external view of this functionality is fully in line with the standard.

Some of the concepts defined in this chapter do *not* correspond to the ISO/CCITT terms, and so new terminology is introduced. Standard terminology is used in the standard way.

## 27.2 DSA/DUA Interaction Model

There are some interesting choices to be made between DSA Referral and Chaining. A DUA will start by contacting a local DSA, specifying that chaining is preferred (i.e., DSA referrals should not be passed back to the DUA). After that, the first DSA will proceed by use of DSA Referral, except for operations where this is not possible in the QUIPU framework (some cases of search). The advantages of this approach are:

- The DUA code can be kept to a minimum, as there is no need to handle referrals. This does mean that the DUA must always interact with the directory Service through a DSA which supports chaining (which might exclude some implementations).
- Always going through a local DSA allows a "per system" cache to be maintained in a coherent manner.
- The overhead of maintaining chained connections is not passed on too far.

Note that whilst the DUA procedural does not handle referrals transparently, they are defined in the service interface, so that an application can choose to handle the referrals directly if it wishes to do so.

## 27.3 Model of Data Distribution

This is a critical section of the design. It is essential to understand it before studying distributed operation.

### 27.3.1 Entry Data Blocks

For the root and every nonleaf vertex, there will be an *entry data block* (EDB) which contains *all* information pertaining to the next level down in the DIT. Figure 27.1 gives an ASN.1 description of the entry data block format.

```
<entrydatablock> ::= <type> <CRLF> <version> <CRLF> <data>
<type>           ::= "MASTER" | "SLAVE" | "CACHE"
<version>        ::= <printablestring>
<data>           ::= <entry> | <entry> <CRLF> <data>
<entry>          ::= <rdn> <CRLF> <attributelist> <CRLF>
<attributelist>  ::= <attribute> | <attributelist> <CRLF> <attribute>
```

Figure 27.1: entry data block Format

It should be noted and remembered that the entry data block associated with an entry and described as "the entry data block of the entry" contains the entry's children (i.e., their attributes and RDNs) and not the attributes of the entry itself. This is *not* necessarily intuitive.

### 27.3.2 Masters and Slaves

Every entry data block has "Master" and "Slave" copies. There will typically be only one master (although there may be multiple master copies, where data is maintained "out of band"). Slave copies are automatically replicated from a master EDB. This may be direct or indirect. The full propagation path must be acyclic (loop free).

A DSA has either all or none of an entry data block as a master or slave (viz: entry data blocks are atomic). Any other DIT information it contains is treated as cached data. A DSA does not need to have any master or slave data.

DSAs are named, and represented in the DIT. One of the reasons for this is to enable use of the directory to identify the OSI location of DSAs. This OSI location can then be adjusted transparent to the logical mapping of the DIT onto DSAs.

This can be seen as treating a DSA in the same manner as any other Application Entity. This simplifies the implementation, as there does not need to be specific storage of additional configuration information (knowledge).

An important piece of information stored in the entry of each DSA is the list of EDBs and how they are replicated. This information is the basis for automatic replication.

### 27.3.3 QUIPU Subordinate References

An entry has associated with it attributes which indicate the DSAs which have master or slave entry data blocks for the entry in question. These pointers are known as "QUIPU Subordinate References" (QSR). For every QSR, the DSA must have a master or slave copy of the EDB, as implied by the QSR. The converse it not true: DSAs may have copies of EDBs without there being QSRs. The DSAs with QSRs have the information *and* are prepared to answer public queries about the entry data block in question. DSAs with EDBs (typically slave copies) and no QSRs usually have copies for performance or robustness reasons.

The QUIPU subordinate reference is similar to the standardised nonspecific subordinate references (NSSR). There are the following differences:

- QSRs admit to replication, and therefore there are master QSRs and slave QSRs.
- A QSR always points to all of the relevant information, whereas an NSSR may only point to a part of it and must be used in "and" conjunction with other NSSRs.

### 27.3.4 Access to the Root EDB

There is no requirement for a given DSA to hold a copy of the root entry data block. However, to be able to systematically process all queries, there must be direct or indirect access to the root entry data block. Therefore, every DSA which does not have a copy of the root entry data block must know the name and address of one or more DSA which either has a copy of the root entry data block, or is closer (in terms of these references) to a DSA which has a copy. This approach is similar to, but not the same as, use of superior references defined in the standard.

## 27.4 Standard Knowledge References

In addition to the QUIPU specific QSRs, an entry might also contain standard Knowledge References, as defined in the OSI directory. This is used to point to data not contained in a QUIPU DSA. There are three types of reference defined in the standard:

**Subordinate Reference:** Pointer to an entry.

**Cross Reference:** From the QUIPU standpoint, the same as a subordinate reference.

**Non Specific Subordinate Reference:** Pointer to multiple subordinates which must be queried for the next level down. QSRs are similar to this (see previous section).

In the first two cases, the entry in the entry data block is considered to be "knowledge only" (although other entry information may be cached). In the third case the entry will also have full information on itself. If any of these are present, there will be no QUIPU master or slave pointers. These three types of pointer are mutually exclusive.

## 27.5 Navigation

Given this data model, a straightforward navigation algorithm can now be specified. The requirement is to locate the entry associated with a specified distinguished name. When the entry is arrived at, the operations will behave as proscribed.

The basis of the navigation strategy is that the first DSA (i.e., the one accessed by the DAP) does all of the hard work. Other DSAs, accessed by DSA referral, either answer the question or return an error. This is important, as it is the basic strategy by which the system ensures completion of queries. There are times when the DSA may depart from this model. These are discussed in Section 27.8 and [PBark89].

First consider the behaviour of a DSA accessed by the directory system protocol (DSP):

1. Look up the distinguished name.
2. If the distinguished name is found, go to step 6.
3. If there is a local copy of the entry data block of the parent, return a nameError. The "matched" parameter should be set to the distinguished name of the entry data block (i.e., the level above the offered name). This is an authoritative *no*
4. Strip the lowest component off the distinguished name, and go to step 1. If there are no more components, go to step 5. This process checks for authoritative *no*.
5. At this point, the name has not been found, and no relevant entry data block has been found. This implies that the DSA does not hold the root entry data block. Therefore the DSA should return a DSA Referral. The DSA Referral should be the list of DSAs (names and addresses) which are known to be closer to the root.

6. We now have an entry which matches some or all of the original distinguished name. Consider this entry.
7. If the entry contains an *alias* attribute, dereference, and go to step 1. Note that if a referral is returned, that the appropriate parameters should be set to indicate all dereferences.
8. If the entry is the one specified in the query, return the answer to the query, or the appropriate (authoritative) error.
9. If the entry is of object class "QuipuNonLeafObject," return a referral. This is simply a redirect to a DSA which can take the query at least one step further. The names for the DSA referral should be taken from the master and slave QUIPU subordinate references. Where the calling DSA is a non-QUIPU DSA, the presentation address of the master DSA must be looked up, and only this one returned.
10. If the entry contains a reference, the appropriate referral should be returned.
11. The query refers to an entry below the bottom of the DIT. An authoritative nameError can be returned.

Now consider the slightly more complex case of the initial DSA (doing the DSA referral). Steps 1-4 are followed as above, to determine authoritative NO.

5. At this point, the name has not been found, and no relevant entry data block has been found. This implies that the DSA does not hold the root entry data block. The list of DSAs which are known to be closer to the root is the starting point for the iterative query. Go to step 12.
6. We now have an entry which matches some or all of the original distinguished name. Consider this entry.
7. If the entry contains an *alias* attribute, apply the relevant dereference to the original query, and go back to the start.
8. If the entry is the one specified in the query, return the answer to the query, or the appropriate (authoritative) error.
9. If the entry is of object class "QuipuNonLeafObject," this gives a list of QSRs to start the iterative query. Go to step 12.
10. If the entry contains a standard knowledge reference, then go to step 12. Note that for nonspecific subordinate references, *all* of the references must be followed before giving up.
11. The query refers to an entry below the bottom of the DIT. An authoritative nameError can be returned,
12. Select one of the DSAs from the referral list. The order to try the DSAs is arbitrary. However, it is attempted to select ones with the topologically closest name first (e.g., a UK DSA will prefer to query another UK DSA before asking a French one). Try DSAs in turn until one gives an answer or you get bored. Consider the answer. Authoritative answers (yes or no) should be passed back to the DUA. If a referral is received, recurse to step 1, watching carefully for loops.

It can be seen that this navigation is relying on data being distributed correctly, and DSAs other than the one doing the work behaving in a correct manner. Information provided in the referral should be used to ensure that the iteration is progressing, and thus detect livelock situations.

## 27.6 List

The entry data block concept allows the list operation to fall out in a straightforward manner. Navigation to the entry data block belonging to the name provided, will give access to the full result for the list operation.

Note that where cross/subordinate references are involved, it will be assumed that these are not alias entries (reasonable in practice). This will allow list to be performed in a single DSA in all cases.

## 27.7 Search

This section describes how the OSI directory search is supported. This is one of the hardest parts of the implementation, and care must be taken. Note that the DAP argument in DSP is always that provided by the DUA[1]. This means that the work done by a given DSA must be in relation to the target object. With other operations, this is (fairly) straightforward, as the target object always references the base object of the operation. For searching, care must be taken to verify correctly whether the base object has been reached. This is done by use of the operation progress information, setting the name resolution phase to completed.

The search operation functions by searching the part of the tree implied by the "subset" specification. Rather than returning all of the information, the queried DSA will apply the associated filter to the entries in question, and return the filtered result, along with appropriate continuation pointers. This should minimise network traffic.

The case of "subset = baseObject" is handled by navigating to the entry data block of the object's parent, and applying the given filter. If the entry is a cross-reference or subordinate reference, the reference should be followed (using the same query).

The case of "subset = oneLevel" is handled by navigating to the object's own entry data block. There the filter is applied to each of its children. If any of the children are alias entries, the alias should be dereferenced, and a baseObject search applied to the new entry. For each child which is a cross-reference or subordinate reference, the references should be followed, setting the target object to be the child.

[1]Whilst this is in principle one of the key aspects of the way the DSP works, the recommendations for distributed operations violate this principle when dealing with aliases during search.

The case of "subset = wholeSubtree" is handled by navigating to the object's own entry data block. There, the filter is applied to the object and to each of its children. If any of the children are *alias* entries, the alias should be dereferenced, and a wholeSubtree search applied to the new entry. For each child which has QUIPU children (determined by the presence of a masterDSA attribute), the search should be applied to the master or one of the slave DSAs, with target object set to the child. For each child which is a cross-reference or subordinate reference, the references should be followed, setting the target object to the child. For each child which has nonspecific subordinate references, the search should be applied to *all* of the referenced DSAs, with the target object set to the child.

There are three procedures for operating:

1. Everything handled by the first DSA, with other DSAs returning a mixture of results and partial outcome qualifiers.
2. Proceed by referral until a DSA is reached which has a copy of the base object. Then this DSA proceeds by referral, and returns the full result to the first DSA. This is how the current version of QUIPU works. It has the advantage of often accumulating search results in a local environment, and so is selectable (possibly in a complex manner).
3. Proceed by referral until a DSA is reached which has a copy of the base object. Then proceed entirely by chaining.

There is potential for looping in this procedure. This will be detected and broken by noting loops in the DSA trace information. This takes account of the fact that some distribution will allow for a query to reenter the same DSA a number of times.

The search and list operations make use of the "partial results" functionality to return information if a time or size limit is reached. Thus, setting a low size limit will allow a user easily to examine sample information (either by list or search).

## 27.8 Selecting a DSA

In QUIPU-5.0 the chain/refer choice was very ad hoc. For a DSA, the best choice is usually to give a referral, except where this will not work. To make this calculation, it is necessary to determine if two DSAs can communicate directly. This is done by deriving from the presentation address of a DSA a list of connected networks. This can then be used to determine if a pair of DSAs can communicate directly, and is the basis for the chaining/referral choice. This will need the extension of the network address, to allow encoding of private networks other than the three well-known ones.

There is an analogous problem when a DSA needs to access a DSA which cannot be accessed directly. Each DSA which does not have full connectivity, will have an attribute which indicates network/DSA pairs. This indicates a DSA which may be used (bilateral agreement) to access a given network by application relay.

The following sections discuss briefly how these choices are made; [PBark89] describes the process more fully.

### 27.8.1 DSA Quality

Replication gives a choice of DSAs to direct a given query to. The following criteria are relevant:

- Use an existing association if possible.
- Prefer a QUIPU DSA.
- Prefer a reliable DSA.
- Prefer a "local" DSA.

The first two are straightforward. A local DSA can be selected using the following:

1. Prefer to use networks in the order specified by ts_communities. This will encourage access over a local Ethernet or preferred network.
2. Pick a DSA with a close name (e.g., prefer one in the same country)
3. Pick a DSA in the same DMD. This would need to add a DMD attribute to the DSA entry (encoded as DN) [Not yet implemented].

Picking a reliable DSA is achieved using the following information:

```
DSAInfo ::= SEQUENCE {
      dsa DistinguishedName,
      lastAttempt UTCTime,
      lastSuccess UTCTime OPTIONAL,
      failures-since-last-success INTEGER }
```

Thus a DSA will be able to check if it knows about the DSAs in question, and can make a choice based on past results. This should operate dynamically, without operator interference. Information on DSAs not contacted for a given period should be expunged. It is hoped to store this as an attribute of a DSA in future versions of QUIPU.

### 27.8.2 Unavailable DSAs

In the case where a DSA is unavailable, and chaining is preferred, a reference will be returned by a QUIPU DSA. A QUIPU DUA, which knows it is talking to a QUIPU DSA can rely on this behaviour, and simply use the referral as a diagnostic to the user. It is hoped that the next version of the standard will add an obvious extra parameter.

### 27.8.3 Operating When DSAs are Not Fully Interconnected

Whilst global interconnection of all application entities is an OSI ideal, it will not be achievable in the short or medium term. Application relaying by DSAs will be needed to achieve full directory connectivity.

In general, it is not desirable for DSAs to proceed by chaining — it wastes unnecessary application level resources. Later, there may be policy reasons to prefer chaining, but these are ignored for now. The internal structure of network addresses allows a DSA to determine if two DSAs can communicate directly.

## 27.9 The External View of QUIPU

To a nonQUIPU system, QUIPU will appear to work exactly according to the standard.

When a QUIPU DSA interacts with another DSA, it will look up its object classes (and probably other information). This will allow it to determine if the other DSA is a QUIPU DSA. When interacting with another QUIPU DSA, the following deviations from the standard are possible. These are primarily concerned with the introduction of replication:

- Presentation address might be omitted from access point (always present in the current QUIPU version).
- Cross references and subordinate references have multiple values (although QUIPU will probably never send these to itself).
- Multiple values of nonspecific subordinate references are assumed to have *or* conjunction (i.e., they are really QSRs).
- Use of QUIPU Access control as described in Section 28.3.5.

When a QUIPU DSA returns references which are derived from reference attributes, it will return them as specified. If it returns information derived from QUIPU internal pointers, it will return a nonspecific subordinate reference. If the DSA being communicated with is not a QUIPU DSA, it will return only a reference to the selected DSA (as replication is not admitted within the protocol).

## 27.10 Cached Data

Cached data is not mentioned in the basic algorithm. However, the algorithm can utilise cached data in some circumstances. This is because of the manner in which identification of copy data has been introduced in the final stage of the OSI directory specification. Cached data may be used whenever this is not prohibited by the service controls. The standard does not clearly define what "copy" data is. In general, QUIPU treats master and slave data as authoritative. Both slave and cached data are returned to the user as "copy" data. For this reason, the distinction between slave and copy data can only be internal to QUIPU.

There is no time to live or age information in the OSI directory Protocols. When caching, care must be taken that spurious information is not passed around indefinitely between DSAs.

When QUIPU holds cached data, it will notes how long it has had it, and will "time out" the data after a tailorable period.

This section is open ended. The exact approaches to caching and determining suitable timeout values will be the subject of experiment.

The important thing about managing cached data is to handle timeouts sensibly. Data cached from a cache may have an indeterminate age. It is important that this data be given a relatively short timeout, to prevent it being circulated indefinitely amongst a set of DSAs. However, *if* the data can be verified by usage (e.g., correctly connecting to a DSA verifies a presentation address), it should then be treated as if cached from a master/slave. Non-verified data should be treated in the same manner as user data, which is described in the next section. Data cached from master/slave information should be given a longer timeout. Data is discarded, rather than refreshed automatically. A timeout of some number of days seems appropriate for most data.

## 27.11 Configuration and Slave Update

A given DSA will have copies of zero or more entry data blocks. A DSA may either be a master for a given entry data block, or a slave. If there are multiple master copies, it is assumed that these are kept coherent by some out-of-band mechanism. For example, one of them is the "real" master, and the others are updated by file transfer when modifications occur. This discussion will proceed for the single master case.

There are three distinct types of DSA:

1. A DSA with a master copy of the root entry data block.
2. A DSA with a slave copy of the root entry data block.
3. A DSA with no copy of the root entry data block.

As noted in Section 27.3, DSAs of types 2 and 3 will have pointer(s) to a DSA which is "closer" to the master copy of the root entry data block. Specifying this hierarchical distribution, as opposed to requiring direct access to the master (as in earlier versions of the OSI directory) means that there can be many copies of information which needs to be highly replicated, without excessive redundant copying across the wide area network. This will be particularly important for the root entry data block.

DSAs of type 2 will only need the pointer information for initial startup or recovery after catastrophic corruption. When the slave copy of the root entry data block has been obtained for the first time, this will supersede the pointers. DSAs of type 3 will usually use cached information in preference to these pointers, and will only need the pointers if cached information is (or appears to be) invalid.

The only information which a DSA has to obtain locally at initial boot time, other than the DSA pointers, is its own name. All other information may be obtained from the directory. Beyond this, the directory service manages its own configuration. There is little point in having a directory service providing general high speed access to global information, and then requiring an additional system (knowledge) to deal with its own configuration.

Associated with the DSAs entry in the DIT is a specification of the entries for which the DSA is a master, and for which it is a slave. A DSA will be able to derive the location of an entry data block for which it is master from this information. Thus at initial boot, a DSA will utilise its initial DSA pointers to read its own entry. The location of master entry data blocks will be derivable from their name, and so their existence can then be verified by the DSA in question. A DSA which is a master for the root entry data block will have no pointers. However, it can go straight to the master root entry data block, read the information about itself, and proceed as for other DSAs.

It is believed that for early pilots, a high level of copying configuration data will be desirable to achieve robustness. The root and national EDBs will be very highly replicated, even though QUIPU can operate with a rather low level of replication.

## 27.12 DSA Naming

### 27.12.1 Choice of Names to Prevent Loops

Care must be taken to prevent the situation where the location of a DSA is only known through itself (and other more complex variants). A simple rule for naming DSAs will ensure that this cannot happen. The master DSA for a given entry (i.e., the DSA controlling the entry data block of containing the entry's children) should have its name in the entry data block of the entry's parent or at a level higher in the DIT. For example, the master DSA of

```
Country=UK, Org=University College London, OU=Computer Science
```

which contains information on entries below Computer Science, may be labelled

```
Country=UK, Org=University College London, DSA=Three Toed Sloth
```

or

```
Country=France, DSA=Capybara
```

It may not be labelled

```
Country=UK, Org=University College London, OU=Computer Science,
        DSA=Alpaca
```

or

```
Country=France, Org=Inria, DSA=Llama
```

A little more flexibility could be allowed; however, this rule is simple, it prevents deadlock, and allows for reasonable labelling practices. The restriction may be relaxed somewhat, when the concept of directory management domains is introduced more formally.

# Chapter 28

# Access Control and Authentication

## 28.1 Models

### 28.1.1 Access Control

QUIPU uses access control lists to represent access rights; the subjects are DUAs (represented by DNs) and the objects are entries in the DIT, attributes of entries, and the child-of relation for each entry (all represented by DNs, and, in the case of attributes, the attribute type as well).

Furthermore, objects can be *containers* that hold other objects. To access an object within an container, it is necessary to have access rights both to the object and the container that holds it. In particular, entries in the DIT are containers. The attributes of the entry and the list of its children are contained within the entry. The children themselves are *not* contained within the parent.

The possible levels of access are as follows: *none*, *detect*, *compare*, *read*, *add* and *write*.

### 28.1.2 Security Domains

The DIT is a global database, maintained by many separate organisations. It is possible for the manager of DSA to change its interpretation of the access control rules, in order to obtain access fraudulently to information held by other DSAs.

As a result, data in a DSA may need to be protected from the managers of other DSAs, as well as from users. This means that special checks must be performed on DSP operations that come from untrusted DSAs.

In order to decide to trust a DSA, it is necessary to be able to authenticate it and to know that it should be trusted. The current version of QUIPU can do neither of these, and so assumes that *all* DSAs are untrusted.

```
ProtectedPassword ::=
    SEQUENCE {
    algorithm [0] AlgorithmIdentifier OPTIONAL,
    salt [1] SET {
        time1 [0] UTCTime OPTIONAL,
        time2 [1] UTCTime OPTIONAL,
        random1 [2] BIT STRING OPTIONAL,
        random2 [3] BIT STRING OPTIONAL}
        OPTIONAL,
    password [2] OCTET STRING}
```

Figure 28.1: ProtectedPassword

# 28.2 Representation in the DIT

## 28.2.1 Simple Authentication

DUAs which use simple authentication have their password stored in the *userPassword* attribute of their entry.

## 28.2.2 Protected Simple Authentication

QUIPU represents both passwords (the $K_A$s) and authenticators by the ASN.1 type *ProtectedPassword* shown if Figure 28.1.

When this structure represents a password, *algorithm* indicates which one-way function is being used and *password* is the (unencrypted) password. The other fields are not supplied.

When this structure represents an authenticator, *password* is the hash value $f_1(K_A, t_1, q_1)$, where $t_1$ is *time1*, $q_1$ is *random1* and $K_A$ is the password. *algorithm* is not supplied.

A relation $\geq$ can be defined on the set of passwords and authenticators as follows: If $a$ is a password, $b$ is an authenticator, and $a$ matches $b$, then $a \geq b$. (Also, $a \geq a$). It can be shown that this relation is a partial ordering of the set, justifying our use of the symbol "$\geq$". We could have defined an attribute syntax for which the above relation corresponded to "greater than or equal to" without violating any of the implied semantics of X.500. However, the DAP *compare* operation cannot be used to test "greater than or equal to", only "equal to", and we wanted an easy way to ask the Directory to check this relation. To achieve this, we made the relation correspond to "equals" for the *ProtectedPassword* attribute syntax.

## 28.2.3 Access Control Lists

The access control list for an entry is held in that entry's *accessControlList* attribute.

### 28.2.4 Security Policies

The *entrySecurityPolicy* attribute of an entry is used to indicate the amount of care that should be taken to preserve the integrity and confidentiality of that entry. While the *accessControlList* indicates who should have access to the entry, the *entrySecurityPolicy* indicates which steps should be taken to prevent unauthorized access.

The *dsaDefaultSecurityPolicy* attribute of a DSA indicates which precautions the DSA will take when dealing with entries that do not have an *entrySecurityPolicy* attribute.

The *dsaPermittedSecurityPolicy* attribute of a DSA indicates which security policies the DSA is prepared to enforce. A DSA may not support a security policy either because it lacks the necessary software or because its manager wishes to forbid use of that policy.

The security policy attribute syntax is not yet implemented.

### 28.2.5 Labels

Security labels are one means of enforcing rule-based access control (sometimes referred to as mandatory access control). QUIPU does not provide mandatory access control in any form.

## 28.3 Distributed Operations

### 28.3.1 (Protected) Simple Authentication

If the responding DSA holds the initiator's entry, then it may check the password directly. Otherwise, the responder will formulate a DSP compare operation to check it. If the result is *true*, the bind will be accepted.

This approach can only be used to check a DAP bind; if it were used in DSP, there would be a danger of livelock. Hence, QUIPU will not attempt to verify the password in a DSP bind.

### 28.3.2 Strong Authentication

In strong authentication, it is necessary to build a certification path for the originator that will be believed by the recipient. From the standpoint of the protocol, the originator builds the certification path and sends it to the recipient. However, the originator does not know for certain which CA's the recipient trusts, and so cannot be sure of constructing a valid path.

QUIPU solves this problem by treating the presented certification path as a hint. The recipient tries to build an acceptable certification path out of the components of the presented path and the certificates it has cached.

### 28.3.3 Restricting Read Access

To maintain the confidentiality of data, results from read, search etc. must not be passed to another DSA unless that DSA has rights to them. The current version of QUIPU solves this problem in the manner described below.

When a DUA requests private data via an untrusted DSA, QUIPU checks whether any of the requested information can be seen by the DUA but not by the DSA. If it can, the security error "inappropriate authentication" is sent to the untrusted DSA. (Otherwise, the data can be safely sent over DSP).

QUIPU DSAs will interpret this error if it is sent by another QUIPU DSA to mean that they are not trusted, and will pass a referral back to the DUA. (Other DSAs may behave differently; X.500 ought to be clarified in this area).

The DUA will chase the referral, and repeat its query directly to the DSA holding the data. The DSA will then give the DUA the results.

### 28.3.4 Restricting Write Access

To maintain the integrity of the data, requests to modify data over DSP must not be accepted unless they are signed or can be performed by anyone.

QUIPU solves this problem as in the read access case, by returning a security error. When strong authentication is added to QUIPU, modify requests will be accepted over DSP provided that they are signed by the DUA.

As an optimisation, QUIPU DSAs never chain modify requests unless they are signed. (The operation will probably be rejected, so it is quicker to give a referral to the DUA immediately, rather than trying to chain.)

### 28.3.5 Caching

DSAs try to improve performance by caching the results of DSP operations. Caching interferes with access control in two ways:

1. The cached data may be incomplete. The DUA that requested it may not have had rights to all the data, or the DSA that held the data may not have been prepared to send all of it over DSP.
2. Caching can prevent access control. The original data may have been subject to access controls which the holder of the cache is unaware of.

QUIPU has a special solution that only works between QUIPU DSAs (using the QUIPU DSP application context): the ACL is sent along with the data across DSP.

QUIPU DSAs will only cache data if they have the ACL to go with it. This ensures that the same access controls will be applied to a cache as to the master copy. It also enables a DSA to tell if the cache is complete. The required information is checked against the ACL in the cache; if any of it is not publicly readable, then it will not have been returned over DSP and the cache cannot be used.

### 28.3.6 Replicated Data

The mechanism originally envisaged for replicating data was "reliable ROS": remote operations carried by X.400(88). DSAs could use the security mechanisms in X.400(88) to provide both integrity and confidentiality for the EDB updates. This would make the slave updates the only place in QUIPU where cryptographic techniques are used to provide confidentiality, as opposed to integrity. The provision of confidentiality here is justified in view of the sensitivity of entire entry data blocks; many of them will contain user's passwords, for example.

However, X.400(88) is not yet widespread, and hence cannot be used as the primary means of replicating data. In the interim, the *getEDB* mechanism is used. This provides neither confidentiality nor integrity, and is not even subject to access control (as DSP is unauthenticated).

# Chapter 29

# Replicating Updates

## 29.1 Basic Update Approach

QUIPU supports a simple automatic update mechanism. This allows for copying of entry data blocks, but with a simple check to ensure that only new information is copied. slave copies are obtained by use of a new remote operation. The argument to the operation is the name of the entry, and the version number of the copy of the entry data block held locally. A *full* copy of the entry data block is returned if this version is out of date. In the DSAs entry, there is a list of entry data blocks for which the DSA has master or slave copies, and the DSA which it gets updates from. For each entry data block, there is the list of DSAs which pull the entry data block, and for slave copies, which DSA the update should come from. It is assumed that this operation will be invoked sufficiently often for it to be acceptable to consider the slave data as "official". For the type of usage being considered, this probably means several times per day. Within QUIPU, this operation is in a new protocol (QUIPU DSP), which will also contains the DSP ASEs. The operation is specified in Figure 29.1.

```
GetEntryDataBlock ABSTRACT-OPERATION
        ARGUMENT GetEntryDataBlockArgument
        RESULT GetEntryDataBlockResult
        ERRORS {NameError,ServiceError,SecurityError}

getEntryDataBlock GetEntryDataBlock ::= 10

                                    -- will make this an OBJECT IDENTIFER
                                    -- when ISODE can support this form
                                    -- of operation code

GetEntryDataBlockArgument ::= SET {
        entry [0] DistinguishedName,
        sendIfMoreRecentThan [1] EDBVersion OPTIONAL
                              -- if omitted, just return version held
                              -- To force send, specify old version
}

GetEntryDataBlockResult ::= SEQUENCE {
                versionHeld [0] EDBVersion
                [1] EntryDataBlock OPTIONAL
        }
}

EDBVersion ::= UTCTime
```

Figure 29.1: EDB Access Operation

Note that a DSA receiving a GetEDB operation should check the associated EDBInfo to ensure that the DSA in question is allowed to pull a copy of this EDB.

The operation may be used to determine which version of the EDB is currently master. This might be used when a query with dontUseCopy arrives, in order to determine whether slave information is accurate. This would be a big performance win for search and list operations, due to potential reduction in information transferred.

# Chapter 30

# Implementation Choices

## 30.1 DSA Structure

Whilst the operation of a QUIPU DSA is fast, its startup procedure is not, due to reading all of its data from a text file on disk. This long startup means that applications must be able to use multiple DSAs, to prevent lockout whilst the local DSA starts up. Also, the process structure of DSAs must be static. To provide a system with reasonable availability, particularly in view of the system's ability to perform extravagant searching, the basic DSA must be able to handle multiple calls. For this reason, apart from conformance issues, the DSA will be inherently asynchronous, and will need to have its own internal scheduling. Initially, this can be simple minded. However, we are providing a framework for a system which is very sophisticated in this area.

The basic approach of the DSA is to have two (conceptually) coroutined modules, which are interfaced by in-core *C* structures. The first module is the DSA engine, which resolves inbound queries either by looking them up in its in-core data structures or by generating further queries. The second module is the protocol engine. This is responsible for opening and closing calls, and for mapping between OPDUs on the network and *C* structures to be handled by the DSA engine. The interface provided to the DSA is largely independent of DAP vs. DSP.

### 30.1.1 Memory Structures

There are a number of structures which are of particular importance. They are summarised here:

- The entry is as the basic component of the in-core tree, which is linked upwards and downwards between parents and children. The tree always starts at the root, even if there is no information beyond the RDN present. Where an entry corresponds to the base of an entry data block, the parameters of the entry data block are present. Siblings are linked in a chain. Each entry is represented by a *C* structure, which contains:

  - Information on the linkage (hierarchical, and between siblings).
  - How entry data blocks are managed.
  - How the "special" attributes (ACL, Schema, Alias, Password, DSA location info) are held.

- There is a structure associated with each connection. This is used to represent actual and desired connections. These structures are linked into a list, and are the key point for the protocol module. They indicate a list of operations and tasks associated with each connection. When the DSA engine needs a connection, it will see if one is already open to the DSA in question. If it is not, a connection structure will be created, which the protocol engine will act on in due course. Similarly, the protocol engine will close down unneeded connections, possibly after some (intentional) delay.
- There is a Task structure associated with each query which arrives. This holds the *full* state of the task, so the the DSA can switch between tasks at intervals (typically when a network connection blocks). This points to the list of operations which have been generated by the task. This is the key structure for the DSA Engine.
- There is an Operation structure, associated with each pending operation. These structures are in mesh structure, arranged both by Task and Connection.

Multi level priorities are associated with tasks and operations, which are used by both engines to control scheduling. This is done in QUIPU on two bases:

- The user-specified priority.
- The progress of the operation (long searches are downgraded in priority).

### 30.1.2 Malloc

The above is optimised by careful use of *malloc* (3), which is a the UNIX memory allocation procedure. A purpose-built malloc is used; this knows about the memory-intensive DSA, and tries to ensure that data accessed at similar times during the DSA operation will be stored in the same page of core memory. This has the effect that the number of page faults generated is significantly reduced (early results indicate a twenty percent improvement over the standard malloc supplied with SunOS4).

### 30.1.3 Disk Structures

All of the data for a given QUIPU DSA will be contained under a single (UNIX) directory. There will be a directory for each RDN, where the DSA in question has an entry data block (which may be master, slave, or cached). The name of directory being that of the QUIPU text-encoded RDN. Thus there will be a UNIX directory structure which corresponds to the portion of the DIT held in the DSA. There will be file in each RDN directory called "EDB", which has the authoritative version of the data, and one called "EDB.bak", which has the previous version. This might be extended to provide more comprehensive backup.

When the system is booted, the following steps will be carried out:

1. Read tailoring information.
2. Look for sequence of entry data blocks implied by the DSAs name. These will usually be cached for later reuse. If not, the default addresses must be used.
3. With the DSA's own information available, read in the other master and slave entry data blocks.
4. Read in other entry data blocks, checking for consistency.

## 30.2 OSI Choices

ROS (1988) and the implied protocols (ACSE and presentation) will be used. Other combinations (e.g., TP0 over TCP or TP4 over CLNS may be used by bilateral agreement between DUA and DSA or DSA and DSA).

To ensure full connectivity of the QUIPU directory service, one of the following conditions must be met:

1. Support of transport class 0 over international X.25(80) (This condition will be changed to support of CONS with access to the international X.25 subnetwork, when such a statement is realistic).
2. Access to a DSA which will perform application relaying in line with the procedures of Section 27.8.3. This will need a bilateral agreement. It is hoped to establish "well-known" DSAs which can serve this function for the following well known networks:
   - Janet.
   - The DARPA/NSF Internet.

# Part VII

# QUIPU Manual: Appendices

# Appendix A

# The QUIPU Pilot DIT

Table A.1 show the number of registered QUIPU DSAs at the top two levels in the DIT as of $5^th$ February 1991. The number of entries is an estimation of the number of entries held by the DSAs in those countires. As not all DSAs were contactable when the figures were calculated, this is almost certainly an underestimate. As the table shows, the QUIPU pilot is now active in 13 countries, with 177 DSAs, holding data for about 370 organisations. Bearing in mind these figures only take account of DSAs at the top two levels of the DIT, and several DSAs are known to be represented lower down in the tree, we can estimate that there are about 200 DSAs in all holding close to 400, 000 entries.

Table A.1: Countries Involved in QUIPU Pilot

| Country | DSAs | Organisations | Entries |
|---|---|---|---|
| Australia | 14 | 15 | 16536 |
| Canada | 10 | 10 | 21300 |
| Denmark | 1 | 1 | 16 |
| Finland | 10 | 13 | 10316 |
| Germany | 9 | 85 | 9026 |
| Iceland | 1 | 1 | 185 |
| Netherland | 2 | 69 | 2132 |
| Norway | 3 | 40 | 3714 |
| Spain | 2 | 3 | 141 |
| Switzerland | 5 | 9 | 4554 |
| Sweden | 6 | 17 | 3035 |
| United Kingdom | 38 | 33 | 67345 |
| United States | 66 | 74 | 167577 |
| Total | 177 | 370 | 296440 |

As an example of the typical spread of data, Table A.2 shows the organisations participating in the United Kingdom pilot. The size figure is only an estimate, and based on the information held by the relative DSAs.

Table A.2: The c=GB Node of the QUIPU Pilot

| Organisation | DSAs | Size |
|---|---|---|
| l=Nottingham<br>X-Tel Services Ltd | 3 | 3714 |
| Aston University | 1 | 935 |
| Bell-Northern Research<br>Northern Telecom | 2 | 453 |
| Bradford University | 1 | 169 |
| Brunel University | 1 | 6900 |
| Cambridge University | 3 | 10647 |
| Concurrent Computer Corporation | 1 | 2660 |
| Data General | 1 | 24 |
| Edinburgh University | 2 | 3063 |
| GID Ltd<br>STC | 1 | 19330 |
| Glasgow University | 1 | 2 |
| Heriot-Watt University | 1 | 20 |
| Hewlett-Packard | 1 | 7 |
| Imperial College | 1 | 2218 |
| Joint Network Team | 1 | 131 |
| Manchester Computing Centre | 1 | 73 |
| Nottingham University | 2 | 3647 |
| Oxford University | 1 | 89 |
| Rutherford Appleton Laboratory | 1 | 1710 |
| Salford University Business Services Ltd | 1 | 4 |
| Salford University | 1 | 4 |
| Sussex University | 1 | 1054 |
| The University of Birmingham | 1 | 1573 |
| University College London | 2 | 5101 |
| University of Bath | 1 | 1565 |
| University of Exeter | 1 | 26 |
| University of London Computer Centre | 1 | 148 |
| University of Stirling | 1 | 275 |
| University of Strathclyde | 1 | 1718 |
| University of Warwick | 1 | 85 |

# Appendix B

# BNF used by QUIPU

This appendix gives the BNF definitions used by QUIPU.

Figure B.1 shows the BNF used for the oidtables described in Section 18.11.

Figure B.2 shows the BNF used to define Attributes and hence Distinguished Names; this is discussed in Section 6.2.3. The syntaxes used to represent attribute values are discussed fully in Chapter 14, and so are not repeated here.

Figure B.3 shows the BNF definition of the EDB files discussed in Section 18.1.1.

```
-- This specification is in BNF
-- Comments start with two dashes

<a> ::= any of the 52 upper and lower case IA5 letters
<d> ::= any IA5 digit 0-9
<k> ::= any of th 52 upper and lower case IA5 letters, IA5 digits,
          and "-" (hyphen)
<p> ::= any IA5 character in ASN.1 PrintableSting
<CRLF> ::= IA5 Newline
<letterstring> ::= <a> | <a> <letterstring>
<numericstring> ::= <d> | <d> <numericstring>
<keystring> ::= <k> | <k> <keystring>
<printablestring> ::= <p> | <p> <printablestring>
-- The first notation is to specify Object Identifiers.
-- These have the basic (BNF):

<numericoid> ::= <numericstring> | <numericstring> "." <numericoid>


-- We define a table which gives a mapping of generic OIDs to strings:
-- and a possible abbreviated form of the name

<oidkeytable> ::= <oidkeyentry> | <oidkeyentry> <CRLF> <oidkeytable>
<oidkeyentry> ::= <abbrstring> ":" <oidnumber>
<abbrstring>  ::= <keystring> | <keystring> "," <keystring>
<oidnumber>   ::= <numericoid> | <numericoid> "," <aliasoid>
<aliasoid>    ::= <numericoid>

-- For example:
-- UCL :0.3.2342.19200149
-- country,c :2.5.4.6

-- Tables of this form will be read in by every QUIPU DSA, to give it a set
-- of OID strings forms, and abbreviations

-- A general BNF of oid is now given:

<oid> ::= <keystring> "." <numericoid> | <keystring> | <numericoid>

-- For example, "UCL.5" gives OID 5 as allocated by UCL, "C" gives the
-- standard country oid.

- We define a table for attribute values:

<attrTable> ::= <attrEntry> | <attrEntry> <CRLF> <attrTable>
<attrEntry> ::= <oidkeyentry> ":" <attrEncoding>
<attrEncoding> ::= "ObjectClass" | "DN" | "CaseIgnoreString" |
            "CaseExactString" | "PrintableString" | "CountryString" |
            "Guide" | "PostalAddress" | "TelephoneNumber" |
            "telexNumber" | "TelexTerminalIdentifier" |
```

```
            "FacsimileTelephoneNumber" | "NumbericString" |
            "DestinationString" | "PresentationAddress" |
            "OID" | "OctetString" | "IA5String" | "Photo" |
            "Mailbox" | "UTCTime" | "DeliveryMethod"
            "Integer" | "Boolean" | "Password"
            "ACL" | "Schema" | "Update" |
            "Audio" | "CaseIgnoreList" | "VisibleString" |
            "Certificate" | "CerfiticatePair" | "CertificateList" |
            "ProtectedPassword" | "AccessPoint" | "Edbinfo" |
            "InheritedAttribute" | "NRSInformation" |
            <attrASN>

<attrASN> ::= <keystring>
    -- defined, but unknown syntax - treated as "ASN"

-- For example:
-- description: attributetype.13: CASEIGNORESTRING

-- Finally we define an object class table:

<ocTable> ::= <ocEntry> | <ocEntry> <CRLF> <ocTable>
<ocEntry> ::= <ocData> | <ocMacro>
<ocData>  ::= <oidkeyentry> ":" <strList> ":" <strList> ":" <strList>
--                          :(hierarchy):(must contain):(may contain)
<ocMacro>   :: = <keystring> "=" <strList>

<strList> ::= <keystring> | <keystring> "," <strList> |
-- Note the final "|" to permit the null string

-- For example;
-- localeAttributeSet = facsimileNumber,isdnAddress,telephoneNumber, ...
-- country: objectclass.2 : top: countryname: description,searchguide
-- organisationalPerson: person: : localeAttributeSet,OU,title,...
```

Figure B.1: BNF Used for oidtables

```
<attribute-value> ::= <NumericValue>
                | <ASNValue>
                        -- For unknown syntaxes & photos
                | <DNValue>
                | <OIDValue>
                        -- OID & ObjectClass
                | <PSAPvalue>
                | <StringValue>
                        -- Used for:
                        --      CaseIgnoreString, CaseExactString,
                        --      PrintableString, CountryString,
                        --      OctetString, IA5String, Password
                        --      TelephoneNumber
                | <GuideValue>
                | <TelexNumberValue>
                | <TeletexTerminalIdentifierValue>
                | <FacsimileTelephoneNumberValue>
                | <PostalAddressValue>
                | <MailboxValue>
                | <UTCTimeValue>
                | <DeliveryValue>
                | <IntegerValue>
                | <BooleanValue>
                | <ACLValue>
                | <SchemaValue>
                | <EdbInfoValue>
                | <otherValues>

<otherValues>  ::= ANY -- can be user defined.

<namevalue>    ::= <namelist> ["#"]
<namelist>     ::= <name> | <namelist> "$" <name>

<attribute>    ::= <oid> "=" <avlist>
<avlist>       ::= <attribute-value> | <avlist> "&" <attribute-value>
<rdn>          ::= <attribute> | <attribute> "%" <rdn>
<name>         ::= <rdn> | <rdn> "@" <name>
                        -- most significant first

-- An example name might be:
--        "c=GB @ o=UCL % locality=London @ ou=CS"
-- Finally, this can be assembled together to give a format for a textual
-- representation of an Entry Data Block.
```

Figure B.2: BNF Used in Names

```
<entrydatablock> ::= <type> <CRLF> <version> <CRLF> <data>
<type>           ::= "MASTER" | "SLAVE" | "CACHE"
<version>        ::= <printablestring>
<data>           ::= <entry> | <entry> <CRLF> <data>
<entry>          ::= <rdn> <CRLF> <attributelist> <CRLF>
<attributelist>  ::= <attribute> | <attributelist> <CRLF> <attribute>
```

Figure B.3: BNF Used in EDB Files

# Appendix C

# The QUIPU Naming Architecture

---

```
QuipuNameDefinitions DEFINITIONS ::=

BEGIN

IMPORTS
ABSTRACT-OPERATION, ABSTRACT-ERROR
   FROM AbstractServiceNotation
         {joint-iso-ccitt mhs-motis(6) asdc(2) modules(0) notation(1)}

NameError, ServiceError, SecurityError
   FROM DirctoryAbstractService
         {joint-iso-ccitt ds(5) modules(1) directoryAbstractService(2)}

DistinguishedName, RelativeDistinguishedName, Attribute,
ATTRIBUTE, ATTRIBUTE-SYNTAX, OBJECT-CLASS
   FROM InformationFramework
         {joint-iso-ccitt ds(5) modules(1) informationFramework(1)}

caseIgnoreStringSyntax
   FROM SelectedAttributeTypes
         {joint-iso-ccitt ds(5) modules(1) selectedAttributeTypes(5)}

TreeStructure, ACL, EDBInfo, MasterDSA, SlaveDSA, DSA, QuipuVersion,
InheritedAttribute, SubordinateReference, Crossreference,
NonSpecificSubordinateReference,
QuipuDSA, QuipuObject, QuipuNonLeafObject, ExternalNonLeafObject,
   FROM QuipuDirectoryDefinitions;

quipu OBJECT IDENTIFIER ::= {ccitt data(9) pss(2342) ucl(19200300) quipu(99)}
                                   -- interim QUIPU OID

attributeType OBJECT IDENTIFIER ::= {quipu attributeType(1)}
```

```
attributeSyntax OBJECT IDENTIFIER ::= {quipu attributeSyntax(2)}

objectClass OBJECT IDENTIFIER ::= {quipu objectClass(3)}

treeStructure TreeStructure ::= {attributeType 1}

acl ACL ::= {attributeType 2}

eDBInfo EDBInfo ::= {attributeType 3}

masterDSA MasterDSA ::= {attributeType 4}

slaveDSA SlaveDSA ::= {attributeType 5}

control DSAControl ::= {attributeType 15}

quipuVersion QuipuVersion ::= {attributeType 16}

ProtectedPassword ::=
      SEQUENCE
      {
            algorithm [0] AlgorithmIdentifier OPTIONAL,
            salt [1] SET {
                  time1 [0] UTCTime OPTIONAL,
                  time2 [1] UTCTime OPTIONAL,
                  random1 [2] BIT STRING OPTIONAL,
                  random2 [3] BIT STRING OPTIONAL
                  }
                  OPTIONAL,
            password [2] OCTET STRING
      }

protectedPassword ATTRIBUTE
   WITH ATTRIBUTE-SYNTAX   ProtectedPassword
      ::= {attributeType 17}

SecurityPolicy ::= ANY
                  -- to be defined

entrySecurityPolicy ATTRIBUTE
   WITH ATTRIBUTE-SYNTAX
   SecurityPolicy ::= {attributeType 18}

dsaDefaultSecurityPolicy ATTRIBUTE
   WITH ATTRIBUTE-SYNTAX
   SecurityPolicy ::= {attributeType 19}

dsaPermittedSecurityPolicy ATTRIBUTE
   WITH ATTRIBUTE-SYNTAX
   SecurityPolicy ::= {attributeType 20}
```

```
inheritedAttribute InheritedAttribute ::= {attributeType 21}

execVector ATTRIBUTE
   WITH ATTRIBUTE-SYNTAX
   PrintableString ::= {attributeType 22}

relayDSA ATTRIBUTE
   WITH ATTRIBUTE-SYNTAX
   distinguishedNameSyntax ::= {attributeType 23}

audio ATTRIBUTE
   WITH ATTRIBUTE-SYNTAX
   OCTECT STRING ::= {attributeType 24}

subordinateReference SubordinateReference ::= {attributeType 25}

crossReference Crossreference ::= {attributeType 26}

nonSpecificSubordinateReference NonSpecificSubordinateReference
                        ::= {attributeType 27}

listenAddress ATTRIBUTE
   WITH ATTRIBUTE-SYNTAX
   PresentationAddress ::= {attributeType 28}

cachedEDB ATTRIBUTE
   WITH ATTRIBUTE-SYNTAX
   distinguishedNameSyntax ::= {attributeType 29}


quipuDSA QuipuDSA ::= {objectClass 1}

quipuObject QuipuObject        ::= {objectClass 2}

quipuNonLeafObject QuipuNonLeafObject ::= {objectClass 6}

externalNonLeafObject ExternalNonLeafObject ::= {objectClass 9}

quipuSecurityUser OBJECT-CLASS
   SUBCLASS OF quipuObject
   MUST CONTAIN {protectedPassword}
       ::= {objectClass 7}

iSODEApplicationEntity OBJECT-CLASS
   SUBCLASS OF applicationEntity
   MUST CONTAIN {execVector}
       ::= {objectclass 8}

friendlyCountryName ATTRIBUTE
  WITH ATTRIBUTE-SYNTAX
  caseIgnoreStringSyntax
```

```
        ::= {attributeType 8}
                -- example "UK", "United Kingdom" etc.

friendlyCountry OBJECT-CLASS
  SUBCLASS OF country, quipuObject
  MUST CONTAIN { friendlyCountryName }
        ::= {objectClass 3}


END
```

Figure C.1: The QUIPU Naming Architecture

# Appendix D

# ASN.1 Summary

This appendix summarises the ASN.1 used (or planned for use) in QUIPU, and incorporates the system naming aspects.

---

```
QuipuDirectoryDefinitions
DEFINITIONS ::=

BEGIN

                          -- give the module an identifier in QUIPU 6.0

IMPORTS
EVERYTHING
   FROM QuipuNameDefinitions

mhs-or-addresses
   FROM MHSDirectoryObjectsAndAttributes
         {joint-iso-ccitt mhs-motis(6) arch(5) modules(0) directory(1)}

ABSTRACT-OPERATION, ABSTRACT-ERROR
   FROM AbstractServiceNotation {joint-iso-ccitt mhs-motis(6) asdc(2) modules(0) notation(1)}

NameError, ServiceError, SecurityError
   FROM DirctoryAbstractService {joint-iso-ccitt ds(5) modules(1) directoryAbstractService(2)}

DistinguishedName, RelativeDistinguishedName, Attribute, AttributeType,
ATTRIBUTE, ATTRIBUTE-SYNTAX, OBJECT-CLASS
   FROM InformationFramework {joint-iso-ccitt ds(5) modules(1) informationFramework(1)}

distinguishedNameSyntax, commonName, description, presentationAddress
   FROM SelectedAttributeTypes {joint-iso-ccitt ds(5) modules(1) selectedAttributeTypes(5)}

top, dsa
   FROM SelectedObjectClasses {joint-iso-ccitt ds(5) modules(1) selectedObjectClasses(6)}

AccessPoint
   FROM DistributedOperations {joint-iso-ccitt ds(5) modules(1) distributedOperations(3)} ;
```

```
QuipuObject ::= OBJECT-CLASS
        SUBCLASS OF top
        MUST CONTAIN {aCL}
        MAY CONTAIN {lastModifiedBy, lastModifiedTime, entrySecurityPolicy}

QuipuNonLeafObject ::= OBJECTCLASS
        SUBCLASS OF quipuObject
        MUST CONTAIN {masterDSA}
        MAY CONTAIN {slaveDSA, treeStructure, inheritedAttribute}

ExternalNonLeafObject ::= OBJECTCLASS
        SUBCLASS OF quipuObject
        MAY CONTAIN {subordinateReference, crossReference,
            nonSpecificSubordinateReference}

QuipuDSA ::= OBJECT-CLASS
   SUBCLASS OF dsa
   MUST CONTAIN { aCL, edbInfo, userPassword, manager, quipuVersion}
   MAY CONTAIN { description, lastModifiedBy, lastModifiedTime,
        dsaDefaultSecurityPolicy, dsaPermittedSecurityPolicy, relayDSA,
        listenAddress, info }

EDBInfoSyntax ::= SEQUENCE {
        edb          DistinguishedName,
        getFromDSA   DistinguishedName OPTIONAL,
                                     -- If omitted DSA is master
                                     -- Determine mode of update from this DSA
        sendToDSAs   NameList,
                                     -- Send these DSAs incremental updates
                                     -- Namelist is defined with the ACLs
        getEDBAllowed NameList
                                     -- List of DSAs allowed to pull EDB
        }

EdbInfo ::= ATTRIBUTE
   WITH ATTRIBUTE-SYNTAX EDBInfo
   MULTI VALUE

MasterDSA ::= ATTRIBUTE
   WITH ATTRIBUTE-SYNTAX distinguishedNameSyntax
                          -- Master QSR
                          -- Usually, but not necessarily single valued

SlaveDSA ::= ATTRIBUTE
   WITH ATTRIBUTE-SYNTAX distinguishedNameSyntax
                          -- Slave QSR

SubordinateReference ::= ATTRIBUTE
```

```
   WITH ATTRIBUTE-SYNTAX AccessPoint
   SINGLE VALUE

CrossReference ::= ATTRIBUTE
   WITH ATTRIBUTE-SYNTAX AccessPoint
   SINGLE VALUE

NonSpecificSubordinateReference ::= ATTRIBUTE
   WITH ATTRIBUTE-SYNTAX AccessPoint

QuipuVersion ::= ATTRIBUTE
  WITH ATTRIBUTE-SYNTAX caseIgnoreStringSyntax

DSAControl ::= ATTRIBUTE
  WITH ATTRIBUTE-SYNTAX caseIgnoreStringSyntax

TreeStructureSyntax ::= SET {
   mandatoryObjectClasses [1] SET OF OBJECT IDENTIFIER,
   optionalObjectClasses [2] SET OF OBJECT IDENTIFIER OPTIONAL,
   permittedRDNs [3] SET OF SET OF AttributeType }

TreeStructure ::= ATTRIBUTE
   WITH ATTRIBUTE-SYNTAX TreeStructureSyntax
   MULTI VALUE

InheritedListSyntax ::= SET OF CHOICE {
   AttributeType,              -- Take value from the entry
   Attribute }

InheritedAttributeSyntax ::= SET {
   default [0] InheritedListSyntax OPTIONAL,
       -- default which can be overriden in lower entry.
   always  [1] InheritedListSyntax OPTIONAL,
       -- always present in lower entry.
   objectclass OBJECT IDENTIFIER OPTIONAL
       -- object class to inherit to.
       -- The null case means the objectclass attribute
       --    itself is inherited
}

InheritedAttribute ATTRIBUTE
   WITH ATTRIBUTE-SYNTAX InheritedAttributeSyntax
   MULTI VALUE

ReliableROSData ::= SEQUENCE {
   rosOperation INTEGER,
                               -- the operation being applied
   data ANY,
                               -- the Operation Argument
   oldVersion ANY
                               -- data version to which operation should be applied
```

```
                                -- version syntax will be defined by the
                                -- Reliable ROS user
  newVersion ANY
                                -- version number which results from operation
  }

GetEntryDataBlock ABSTRACT-OPERATION
        ARGUMENT GetEntryDataBlockArgument
        RESULT GetEntryDataBlockResult
        ERRORS {NameError,ServiceError,SecurityError}

getEntryDataBlock GetEntryDataBlock ::= 10

                                        -- will make this an OBJECT IDENTIFER
                                        -- when ISODE can support this form
                                        -- of operation code

GetEntryDataBlockArgument ::= SET {
        entry [0] DistinguishedName,
        sendIfMoreRecentThan [1] EDBVersion OPTIONAL
                                -- if omitted, just return version held
                                -- To force send, specify old version
}

GetEntryDataBlockResult ::= SEQUENCE {
                versionHeld [0] EDBVersion
                [1] EntryDataBlock OPTIONAL
        }
}

EDBVersion ::= UTCTime

ACLInfo ::= SET OF SEQUENCE {
    AccessSelector,
    AccessCategories }

AccessCategories ::= ENUMERATED {
    none (0),
    detect (1),
    compare (2),
    read (3),
    add (4),
    write (5) }

AccessSelector ::= CHOICE {
    entry [0] NULL,
        -- DUA identified by the entry
    other [2] NULL,
        -- This indicates "public" rights
    prefix [3] NameList,
```

```
        -- This identifies a prefix name for specified DUAs
        -- e.g., anyone in the UK
    group [4] NameList
        -- For specifying group rights
    }

NameList ::= SET OF DistinguishedName

ACLSyntax ::= SEQUENCE {
  childACL             [0] ACLInfo DEFAULT {{other, read}},
  entryACL             [1] ACLInfo DEFAULT {{other, read}},
  defaultAttributeACL [2] ACLInfo DEFAULT {{other, read}},
  [3] SET OF AttributeACL }
                     -- Defaults to a publicly readable
                     -- read only directory

AttributeACL ::= SEQUENCE {
  SET OF AttributeType,
  ACLInfo }

ACL ATTRIBUTE
  WITH ATTRIBUTE-SYNTAX ACLSyntax
  SINGLE VALUE

END
```

Figure D.1: Summary of ASN.1

# Appendix E

# Attribute Matching

An important part of QUIPU is the ability to search for specified attributes. This appendix describes the attribute you can search for and the type of search that is valid, using the standard tables.

## E.1 Approximate Matches

The attributes shown in Figure E.1 take a "string" value, and perform approximate matching if asked. Substring matches are allowed. Exact matches are case independent.

Table E.2 shows the attributes for which matches are case sensitive.

## E.2 Exact Matches Only

Table E.3 shows attributes for which matches are for equality only. The syntax of the value is a formatted string; the syntax of which is shown.

| Attribute | Abbreviation |
|---|---|
| knowledgeInformation | |
| commonName | cn |
| surname | |
| serialNumber | |
| countryName | c |
| localityName | l |
| stateOrProvinceName | st |
| streetAddress | |
| organizationName | o |
| organizationalUnitName | ou |
| title | |
| description | |
| businessCategory | |
| postalAddress | |
| postalCode | |
| postOfficeBox | |
| physicalDeliveryOfficeName | |
| userid | uid |
| textEncodedORaddress | |
| rfc822Mailbox | mail |
| info | |
| favouriteDrink | drink |
| roomNumber | |
| userClass | |
| host | |
| documentIdentifier | |
| documentTitle | |
| documentVersion | |
| documentLocation | |
| friendlyCountryName | co |
| orAddressComponent | |

Table E.1: Case Independent Attributes

| Attribute |
|---|
| telephoneNumber |
| telexNumber |
| teletexTerminalIdentifier |
| facsimileTelephoneNumber |
| iSDNAddress |
| registeredAddress |
| destinationIndicator |
| preferredDeliveryMethod |

Table E.2: Case Sensitive Attributes

| Attribute | Syntax |
|---|---|
| objectClass | objectclass |
| x121Address | numericstring |
| supportedApplicationContext | oid |
| aliasedObjectName | dn |
| member | dn |
| owner | dn |
| roleOccupant | dn |
| seeAlso | dn |
| manager | dn |
| documentAuthor | dn |
| masterDSA | dn |
| slaveDSA | dn |
| filestore | dn |

Table E.3: Exact Match Only Attributes

# Bibliography


[BKern78] Brian W. Kernighan and Dennis M. Ritchie. *The C Programming Language. Software Series*, Prentice-Hall, Inc., Englewood Cliffs, New Jersey, 1978.

[CCITT88] The Directory — Overview of Concepts, Models, and Service. International Telegraph and Telephone Consultative Committee, December, 1988. Recommendation X.500.

[FSiro88] F. Sirovich and M. Antonellini. The THORN X.500 Distributed Directory Environment. In *Esprit '88: Putting the Technology to Use*, pages 1711–1720, North Holland, November, 1988.

[ISO88] Information Processing Systems — Open Systems Interconnection — The Directory — Overview of Concepts, Models, and Service. International Organization for Standardization and International Electrotechnical Committee, December, 1988. International Standard 9594-1.

[IUCN82] The IUCN Mammal Red Data Book. International Union for Conservation of Nature and Natural Resources, 1982. Unwin Brothers Limited, The Gresham Press, Woking, Surrey, UK. ISBN 2–88032–600–1.

[JPost81] Jon B. Postel. *Transmission Control Protocol.* Request for Comments 793, DDN Network Information Center, SRI International, September, 1981. See also MIL-STD 1778.

[MRose86] Marshall T. Rose and Dwight E. Cass. OSI Transport Services on top of the TCP. *Computer Networks and ISDN Systems*, 12(3), 1986. Also available as NRTC Technical Paper #700.

[MRose90a] Marshall T. Rose. *PSI White Pages Pilot Project: User's Handbook.* 1990. ISODE documentation set.

[MRose90b] Marshall T. Rose. *PSI White Pages Project: Administrator's Guide.* 1990. ISODE documentation set.

[MRose90c] Marshall T. Rose. *The Open Book: A Practical Perspective on Open Systems Interconnection.* Prentice-hall, 1990. ISBN 0–13–643016–3.

[PBark89] P. Barker and C.J. Robbins. Directory navigation in the quipu x.500 system. In *UNIX & Connectivity*, pages 235–244, National UNIX Systems User Group The Netherlands, November, 1989.

[SKill87] Stephen E. Kille. INCA Directory Services. In *Esprit '87: Achievements and Impact*, pages 1472–1476, North Holland, September, 1987.

[SKill88a] S.E. Kille. The QUIPU directory service. In *IFIP WG 6.5 Conference on Message Handling Systems and Distributed Applications*, pages 173–186, North Holland Publishing, October, 1988.

[SKill88b] S.E. Kille and C.J. Robbins. Distributed operations in QUIPU. In *Esprit Conference Week*, North Holland Publishing, November, 1988.

[SKill89a] Stephen E. Kille. *A string encoding of Presentation Address.* Research Note RN/89/14, Department of Computer Science, University College London, February, 1989.

[SKill89b] Stephen E. Kille. *The Design of QUIPU.* Research Note RN/89/19, Department of Computer Science, University College London, March, 1989.

[SKill89c] Stephen E. Kille. *The THORN X.500 Naming Architecture.* THORN Project Internal Report UCL-45, revision 6.1, University College London, January, 1989.

[SKill90] S.E. Kille. *Using the OSI Directory to achieve User Friendly Naming.* Research Note RN/90/29, Department of Computer Science, University College London, February, 1990.

# Part VIII

# PP Manual: Introduction

# The PP Manual

Steve Kille
Department of Computer Science
University College London

Julian Onions
X-Tel Services Ltd

# Chapter 31

# Overview

## 31.1 What is PP?

PP is a message transfer agent (MTA), which supports a number of message transfer protocols, including:

- X.400 (1984) P1 [CCI84].
- X.400 (1988) / ISO 10021 P1 [CCI88].
- A number of RFC 822-based protocols [Cro82].

It is based on experience with previous MTAs, and has the following aims:

- Use for switching large volumes of messages in a service environment.
- Management features, suitable for complex sites.
- Protocol conversion facilities, particularly for mapping between RFC 822 and X.400 according to RFC 987 [Kil86] and RFC 1148[Kil89].
- Body part format conversion.
- Support for development of advanced user agents, particularly those wishing to use X.400 and/or multimedia capability.

For a technical overview of PP, the paper by Kille is recommended [Kil88]. PP is implemented in *C*, and runs on a range of UNIX and UNIX-like operating systems. The current release includes the following modules:

- X.400 (1984) P1 protocol.
- JNT mail (grey book) Protocol.
- Simple mail transfer protocol (SMTP / RFC 821).
- UUCP mail transfer.
- Distribution list expansion and maintenance.
- RFC 822-based local delivery.
- Delivery time processing of messages.

- Conversion between X.400 and RFC 822 according to RFC 1148 and RFC 987
- Conversion support for reformatting body parts and headers.
- X-Window-based management console.
- Message Authorisation checking.
- X.400 (1988) P1 protocol (beta test).
- X.500-based distribution list facility using the QUIPU directory (beta test).

## 31.2 The PP Documentation

This manual refers to a pre-release PP version 6.0. There are no substantial differences expected between this and the final version. Any differences will be clearly documented in the 6.0 release.

The PP manual is divided into three volumes and the information in this part of the book which introduces PP and contains general information relevant to all of the other volumes. Each volume is represented as a part of this book.

**Part IX (Volume 1):** Installation and Operations. This describes all that is needed to install PP and how to administer PP as part of an operational service.

**Part X (Volume 2):** Programmer's Guide. This describes programming interfaces for submission of messages into PP, and for channels which deliver messages locally or remotely.

**Part XI (Volume 3):** User's Guide. In general, PP should not be visible to the end user. There are some associated tools, which are needed, and are described in this part.

## 31.3 A Brief History of PP

PP began in 1985, when several of us wished to produce a system to support X.400. It was clear that MMDF (our favourite MTA at that time) was not going to be extensible to do all that we wanted. Steve Kille had looked at the EAN MTA at the end of 1984. Whilst this was an impressive development at the time, it did not really meet our needs, although our initial plan was to use the OSI layers from EAN.

Two meetings were held in September 1985 to consider the possibilities of future MTA development:

- At CWI, discussion took place between: Doug Kingston (CWI/BRL), Piet Beertma (CWI), Miriam Amos (DEC/UCB), Kevin Dunlap (DEC/UCB), Daniel Karrenberg (Uni Dortmund), and Steve Kille.

- At UCL, discussion took place between: Phil Cockcroft (UCL), Doug Kingston, Steve Kille, and Julian Onions.

These meetings, and following messages, resulted in some of the initial PP design. As a result of the second meeting, Phil Cockcroft and Julian Onions started to write large chunks of code, and Steve Kille wrote some small chunks of code.

By April 1986, a system was starting to come together, which was being called PP. Marshall Rose was starting work on his *ASN.1* tools, which were clearly going to be a part of PP! In July, the mechanisms for representing multimedia messages in the queue were designed and evolved.

By October 1986, it was time to design the QMGR fully. Steve Kille had been at the infamous CCITT Directory meeting in Munich in February, and so specified a QMGR design in the new ASDC (abstract service definition conventions). Phil Cockcroft left UCL at the end of 1986, which was a big loss to the effort.

In February 1987, there was a basic system working, which talked SMTP and X.400. Filling in the holes took much longer than we expected! The first priority was to replace the shell script QMGR. Julian Onions was then working on the ISODE ROS tools (ROSY and POSY), and so it was decided to use ROS to implement the QMGR. The QMGR and the tools proceeded in parallel. In 1988 Alina daCruz (UCL) rewrote the access libraries, Pete Cowen (Nottingham) worked on a range of formatting tools, and Bruce Wilford (UCL) redid all of the channel binding and domain handling. Mike Roe (UCL) started work on LISP code to produce a first cut at the 1988 X.400 protocol. Discussions with Piete Brookes (Cambridge) led to the initial design of the JNT mail channel. In October 1988, Steve Kille presented a paper on PP at the IFIP WG 6.5 conference, but there was still no PP ready for release. By the end of 1988, there was a PP which had been radically changed and looked much more like the final system.

PP received its first public airing at CEBIT (Hannover Fair) in March 1989, where it carried ODIF over X.400, and converted into Diamond format by use of private conversion tools. It interworked with a number of X.400(84) systems at this point. This was as a part of the ESPIRIT PODA project.

In 1989, the X MTA Console (Pete Cowen) and authorisation (John Taylor) were added in, and the internal structures fully upgraded to X.400(88). PP 3.0 was cut in July 1989, and was used as the basis for UK to full X.400 relaying. This system was released outside UCL and Nottingham on a very selective basis.

PP 4.0 was released at the very end of 1989 to 15 beta sites. Three more beta releases were made during 1990 to an increasing number of beta sites. During this time, the upgrade to RFC 1148 was made, and initial implementations of P1(1988) and directory-based distribution lists (Colin Robbins) added.

PP 5.0, the first openly available release, was cut in September 1990.

## 31.4 Etymology

PP is not an acronym. There is no truth in the rumour that PP stands for "Postman Pat," a famous British postman.

## 31.5 Acknowledgements

PP funding has come from a number of sources. In particular the UK Joint Network Team (JNT) has funded a significant part of the PP development. Jim Craigie of the JNT has been helpful and encouraging in this. The Alvey-sponsored COSMOS project funded a major part of the initial development of PP. The Alvey-sponsored Locator project funded work on PP to provide hooks for security features. Use of PP as infrastructure in the ESPRIT PODA project has led to many improvements in the current release.

Prof. Peter Kirstein of University College London (UCL) and Dr. Hugh Smith of Nottingham University have been particularly tolerant of the excessive resources consumed by this development.

The major work of coding PP (apart from the authors) has been done by Phil Cockcroft, Alina da Cruz, and John Taylor of UCL and Pete Cowen of Nottingham University. Code has also been written by Adrian Joseph, Mike Roe, Colin Robins, and Bruce Wilford of UCL. Irene Hassel of UCL helped to write documentation. John Andrews of UCL has helped to bring PP into service at UCL.

Piete Brooks of Cambridge Computer lab has been a faithful alpha test site, and has contributed code to integrate UNIX-NIFTP and C-NRS. He has made many useful comments and contributed a number of bugfixes. Andrew Macpherson of STL has contributed a number of bugfixes and tools to help Sendmail sites convert to PP.

The ISODE from Marshall T. Rose of NYSERNet is an essential component of PP.

Useful comment and fixes have been provided by our beta test sites. Particularly useful help has come from: Andrew Findlay of Brunel; Juha Heinanen of FUNET; Simon Poole of SWITCH; Ole Bjørn Hessen of University of Oslo; George Michaelson of University of Queensland; and Peter Yee of NASA.

# Chapter 32

# Using PP

## 32.1 Conditions of Use

PP is an openly available suite of software. There are no restrictions on its usage. The authors accept no liability resulting from use of PP.

## 32.2 Comments and Discussion

Comments and problems on PP should be sent electronically to the PP support mailbox. The RFC 822 form of this is:

`<pp-support@cs.ucl.ac.uk>`

Bug reports (and fixes) to this address are welcome. These reports will be dealt with on a best-effort basis.

The X.400 form is:

| | |
|---|---|
| Surname | PP-Support |
| Org Unit | CS |
| Organisation | UCL |
| PRMD | UK.AC |
| ADMD | Gold␣400 |
| Country | GB |

If this is not possible, comments may be sent to:

Postal Address: Steve Kille
Department of Computer Science
University College London
Gower Street
WC1E 6BT
UK

Telephone: +44-1-380-7294

There is an electronic discussion list:

`<pp-people@cs.ucl.ac.uk>`

All interested parties are encouraged to join this list by sending to:

`<pp-people-request@cs.ucl.ac.uk>`

# Chapter 33

# Obtaining PP

The PP version 6.0 software is planned to be available in the following ways from these places:

## DISTRIBUTION SITES

### NIFTP

If you run NIFTP over the public X.25 or over Janet, and are registered in the NRS at Salford, you can use NIFTP with username "guest" and your own name as password, to access UK.AC.UCL.CS to retrieve the file pp/`pp-6.tar`. The file `<PP>pp-6.tar.Z` is the *tar* image after being run through the compress program (approx 2Mb).

### FTP

If you can FTP to the Internet from outside Europe, then use anonymous FTP to uu.psi.com [136.161.128.3] to retrieve the file `pp-6.tar.Z` in binary mode from the isode/ directory. This file is the *tar* image after being run through the compress program and is approximately 2Mb in size.

If you can FTP to the Internet from Europe, then use anonymous FTP to nic.eu.net [192.16.202.1] to retrieve the file `pp-6.tar.Z` in binary mode from the network/isode/ directory. This file is the *tar* image after being run through the compress program and is approximately 2Mb in size.

### EUROPE (tape and documentation)

For mailings in EUROPE, send a cheque or bankers draft and a purchase order for 200 Pounds Sterling to:

Postal address: Department of Computer Science
Attn: Natalie May/Dawn Bailey
University College London
Gower Street
London, WC1E 6BT
UK

For information only:

| | |
|---|---|
| Telephone: | +44 71–380–7214 |
| Fax: | +44 71–387–1397 |
| Telex: | 28722 |
| Internet: | `natalie@cs.ucl.ac.uk` |
| | `dawn@cs.ucl.ac.uk` |

Specify one:

1. 1600bpi 1/2–inch tape, or
2. Sun 1/4–inch cartridge tape.

The tape will be written in *tar* format and returned with a documentation set. Do not send tapes or envelopes. Documentation only is the same price.

### EUROPE (tape only)

Tapes without hardcopy documentation can be obtained via the software distribution service of the European UNIX User group (EUUG). The PP-5 distribution is called "EUUGD22 - PP (5.0)".

Postal address: EUUG Software Distributions
c/o Frank Kuiper
Centrum voor Wiskunde en Informatica
Kruislaan 413
1098 SJ Amsterdam
The Netherlands

| | |
|---|---|
| For information only: | |
| Telephone: | +31 20–5924121 |
| | (or +31 20–5929333) |
| Telex: | 12571 mactr nl |
| Telefax: | +31–20–5924199 |
| Internet: | `euug-tapes@cwi.nl` |

Specify one:

1. 1600bpi 1/2–inch tape: 130 Dutch guilders.
2. 800bpi 1/2–inch tape: 150 Dutch guilders.
3. Sun 1/4–inch cartridge tape (QIC-24 format): 190 Dutch guilders.
4. Sun 1/4–inch cartridge tape (QIC-11 format): 215 Dutch guilders.

If you require DHL, this is possible and will be billed through. Note that if you are not a member of EUUG, then there is an additional handling fee of 300 Dutch guilders (please enclose a copy of your membership or contribution payment form when ordering). Do not send money, cheques, tapes or envelopes; you will be invoiced.

## NORTH AMERICA

For mailings in NORTH AMERICA, send a check for 375 US dollars to:

| | |
|---|---|
| Postal address: | University of Pennsylvania<br>Department of Computer and Information Science<br>Moore School<br>Attn: David J. Farber (PP Distribution)<br>200 South 33rd Street<br>Philadelphia, PA 19104-6314<br>U.S.A. |
| Telephone: | +1 215–898–8560 |

Specify one:

1. 1600bpi 1/2–inch tape, or
2. Sun 1/4–inch cartridge tape.

The tape will be written in *tar* format and returned with a documentation set. Do not send tapes or envelopes. Documentation only is the same price.

## AUSTRALIA and NEW ZEALAND

For mailings in AUSTRALIA and NEW ZEALAND,

1. If you already have ISODE-6.0, send a cheque for 100 dollars Australian to the following address. You will recieve only the PP manuals and a PP tape. **Clearly specify on the cheque and order that you only want PP.**
2. If you do not have ISODE-6.0, send a cheque for 300 dollars Australian to the following address. You will recieve a tape containing both ISODE-6.0 and PP, together with manuals for both ISODE-6.0 and PP.

| | |
|---|---|
| Postal address: | CSIRO DIT<br>Attn: Andrew Waugh (ISODE Distribution)<br>55 Barry Street<br>Carlton, 3053<br>Australia |

For information only:

| | |
|---|---|
| Telephone: | +61 3–347–8644 |
| Fax: | +61 3–347–8987 |
| Internet: | `ajw@ditmela.oz.au` |

Specify one:

1. 1600/3200/6250bpi 1/2–inch tape, or
2. Sun 1/4-inch cartridge tape in either QIC-11 or QIC-24 format.

The tape will be written in *tar* format and returned with a documentation set. Do not send tapes or envelopes. Documentation only is the same price.

### FTAM on Janet or PSS

The source code is available by FTAM at the University College London over X.25 using Janet (DTE 00000511160013), PSS (DTE 23421920030013) or IXI (DTE 20433450420113) with TSEL 259 (ASCII encoding). Use the "anon" user-identity and retrieve the file `pp-6.tar`. The file `pp-6.tar.Z` is the *tar* image after being run through the compress program (2Mb).

### FTAM on the Internet

The source code is available by FTAM over the Internet at host `osi.nyser.net` `[192.33.4.10]` (TCP port 102 selects the OSI transport service) with TSEL 259 (numeric encoding). Use the "anon" user-identity, supply any password, and retrieve `pp-6.tar.Z` from the isode/ directory. This file is the *tar* image after being run through the compress program and is approximately 2Mb in size.

### Online Postscript

For distributions via FTAM, the file service is provided by the FTAM implementation in ISODE 5.0 or later (IS FTAM).

For distributions via either FTAM or FTP, there are additional files available for retrieval, called `pp-6-ps-a4.tar.Z` and `pp-6-ps-us.tar.Z` which are compressed *tar* images (1.5MB) containing the entire documentation set in PostScript format, for A4 and US paper respectively.

## SUPPORT

A UK company has been set up to provide support for the ISODE, PP, and associated packages: X-Tel Services Ltd. This company provides an update service, general assistance and site specific support. This company is closely associated with the development of PP.

| | |
|---|---|
| Postal Address: | X-Tel Services Ltd.<br>Nottingham University<br>Nottingham, NG7 2RD<br>UK |
| Telephone: | +44 602-412648 |
| Fax: | +44 602-790278 |
| Internet: | support@xtel.co.uk<br>xtel@cs.nott.ac.uk |

# Bibliography


[CCI84] Message Handling Systems: System Model-Service Elements, October 1984. International Telegraph and Telephone Consultative Committee.

[CCI88] Message Handling: System and Service Overview. International Telegraph and Telephone Consultative Committee, 1988. Recommendation X.400.

[Cro82] David H. Crocker. Standard for the Format of ARPA Internet Text Messages. Request for Comments 822, DDN Network Information Center, SRI International, August 1982.

[Kil86] Stephen E. Kille. Mapping between X.400 and RFC822. Request for Comments 987, DDN Network Information Center, SRI International, June 1986. Also available as UCL Technical Report number 120 and Mailgroup Note number 19.

[Kil88] S.E. Kille. PP - a message transfer agent. In *IFIP WG 6.5 Conference on Message Handling Systems and Distributed Applications*, pages 115–118. North Holland Publishing, October 1988.

[Kil89] Stephen E. Kille. Mapping between X.400(1988)/ISO10021 and RFC822. Request for Comments 1148, DDN Network Information Center, SRI International, July 1989.

# Part IX

# PP Manual: Installation and Operation

# PP

## *Volume 1: Installation and Operation*

Julian Onions
X-Tel Services Ltd

Peter Cowen
X-Tel Services Ltd

Alina da Cruz
Department of Computer Science
University College London

Steve Kille
Department of Computer Science
University College London

# Preface

This part describes the installation and general operation of the PP software. More details about its history, development and objectives can be found in Part VII (PP Manual: Introduction.)

A general overview of PP is given in Part I.

A guide to writing programs that interact with PP is given in Part X (PP Manual: Programmer's Guide.)

A guide to the user-visible parts of PP can be found in Part XI (PP Manual: User's Guide.)

# Chapter 34

# General Considerations

## 34.1 Overview

Before rolling the tape onto a disk, there are some general issues which it is useful to consider. If you are planning to install PP on more than one machine, you should read the latter parts of this chapter carefully.

## 34.2 General Requirements

### 34.2.1 Systems

PP is designed to be portable to a wide range of UNIX[1] systems. Configurations are given for the following systems:

- Sun 3 using SunOS 3.X.
- Sun 3 using SunOS 4.X.
- Sun 4 using SunOS 4.X.

It is also known to run on the following systems:

- Vax Ultrix.
- Mips.

### 34.2.2 Disk space

A fair amount of space must be made available for the system. The figures given below are only a guide.

The basic distribution tape contains sources amounting to around 7Mb.

You will need approximately 40Mb of headroom extra to compile everything, although you can do it in stages if you do not have that much space.

The installed binaries will take up somewhere around 20-30Mb.

[1]UNIX is a trademark of AT&T Bell Laboratories.

The routing table files plus local tables may take up about 1Mb if you have a lot of connectivity.

The *dbm* database built from these tables, perhaps another 1-2Mb.

Of course you must also allow plenty of space for the mail passing through!

This suggests that you should allow about 50Mb of space for building everything, and when built, about 25Mb to run the system with whatever room you feel reasonable for spooling of messages (phew!).

This figure is less in later versions of ISODE that make use of shared libraries under SunOS.

### 34.2.3 Communications Requirements

PP uses OSI/ROS for its internal communication, using the ISODE implementation of ROS and the lower layers[Ros89]. It is assumed that ISODE is installed and available on the system in question. ISODE *ASN.1* tools are also required to build parts of PP. This version of PP assumes ISODE version 6.0.

### 34.2.4 X Window System

The system has a very useful monitoring tool which is written using the X Window System[2] which is used for managing the MTA as a whole. It is possible to run an MTA without the console, but not so easily. The console depends on X11 release 4 and the Athena Widget set. It will not work under earlier releases of X11.

There are also present some small programs to do X-based alert of new mail. These programs have the same X requirements.

All binaries should work against X11 release 3 servers.

### 34.2.5 QUIPU

This release has no requirements on the QUIPU X.500 directory service agent. There is a prototype list channel that utilises the directory but this is optional. Future releases of PP will require a QUIPU DSA.

## 34.3 Specific Channel Requirements

Some of the channels in PP have external dependencies.

**SMTP:** The Simple Mail Transfer Protocol channel requires the use of TCP/IP. If the domain name server is to be used, then the BIND[Dun] resolver library must be provided (see Table 35.1 on page 376).

[2]The X Window System is a trademark of the Massachusettes Institute of Technology

**JNT Mail:** This is integrated with the UNIX-NIFTP package, available from Cambridge (UK) at the following address:

```
Piete Brooks (pb@cl.cam.ac.uk)
Cambridge University Computer Laboratory,
Cambridge
ENGLAND
```

X.25 access is usually required for this channel.

**X.400:** This uses the ISODE lower layers (both 1984 and 1988 variants). For most services X.25, CONS, or CLNP is required to run this channel, although it can be run over TCP/IP using RFC-1006[RC87].

**UUCP:** This channel requires a working UUCP installed on the given machine.

**DECNET:** This requires the Sunlink DNI (version 7.0 or later) package.

## 34.4 User Agents

This version of PP does not support any sophisticated user agents. It provides a mail-sending interface of the same approximate functionality of */bin/mail*. It is strongly recommended that the MH[Ros86] user agent is considered for use with PP. MH should be configured with the SMTP transfer option which will connect to PP though the SMTP protocol (configuration option `mts send/smtp`). This also allows PP to be accessed from hosts not running PP directly but with SMTP connectivity.

**Warning:** MH should be compiled without the `BERK` option.

## 34.5 Compatibility with Older MTAs

PP is designed as a replacement for *sendmail*(8) and MMDF. As such it is capable of the majority of functions of both (and a great deal more). However, there are some differences.

### 34.5.1 MMDF

PP does not support the MMDF syntax that allows users to give an address as `user=string@host.domain`.

### 34.5.2 Sendmail

PP does not support sendmail style mailboxes by default. These can created by a variety of mechanisms listed later.

Some programs that send mail have compiled into them the *sendmail* program. To deal with these, a fake sendmail is provided that emulates some of the sendmail options.

As PP does not have sendmail's general rewriting rules, it can not in general be programmed to "fix up" strange addresses. This applies particularly to address formats such as DECnet and Xerox-style addresses. To handle this sort of address an inbound channel should be written that can parse these addresses and convert them to RFC-822 addresses.

## 34.6 MTA Layout

Usually PP will support sites with many hosts. It is possible, but not desirable, to run a copy of PP on each host. An MTA is defined by the existence of a queue (spool area). Each queue should be managed (in human terms) in order to guarantee good service.

For this reason, the number of MTAs should be kept small, and other mechanisms used for delivery to local hosts. Possibilities include:

- NFS. This simply consists of NFS-mounting (possible through use of an automounter) the necessary files systems for delivery.
- Remote access protocols. Use of services such as POP[Ros88] may be an alternative.
- Delivery to a central place which is NFS-mounted by clients.

For these reasons, some of the PP utility programs may be accessed remotely using *rsh*(1).

A site with 1000 users and 100 hosts might consider installing between one and four MTAs. Reasons for choosing MTAs might include:

- External communication links.
- Large host with many users.
- Fileservers used substantially for mail.
- Separate administration domains.

## 34.7 Performance

Currently, not many statistics have been collected on the performance of PP, and little effort has been made on tuning as yet. However, some observed results may be useful.

PP has been running on a Sun 4/330 at UCL handling a large percentage of the electronic mail. This consists of around 50,000 messages a week consisting of around 175Mb of data. This system is also providing a directory service and does not show signs of saturation as yet.

# Chapter 35

# Installing PP

This is a description of things to do when installing PP. The basic information is described in *pp-gen*(8), but this section gives the full details. It is recommended that you read this section before compiling or installing the software.

## 35.1 Compile Time Configuration

Most of the definitions that have to be set before compiling PP are given in *Make.defs* in the top level of the source tree, and *config.h* in the `h/` directory.

### 35.1.1 Make.defs

A number of *make* variables can be set. These variables come in two classes. The first are variables that are truly site specific. These are listed in Table 35.1. The second class are variables that you can probably leave as the defaults. These are listed in Table 35.2. For each entry a reasonable default is given.

A number of these variables are important, so care must be taken when configuring these variables. A description of each of these variables is now given, however Tables 35.1 and 35.2 give a good overview of the variables.

**`CMDDIR`:** This is the directory into which most of the PP core commands are placed. This is usually the directory that contains subdirectories for channel and formatting programs.

**`CHANDIR`:** This directory is normally a subdirectory of `CMDDIR`. It contains all the channel programs that PP knows about.

**`FORMDIR`:** This directory contains the formatting programs that are run by *filtercontrol*. These are either binary executables or shell scripts.

| Variable | Example | Description |
|---|---|---|
| TAILOR | /usr/lib/pp/tailor | Location of the pp tailor file |
| CMDDIR | /usr/lib/pp | Directory for PP basic commands |
| CHANDIR | /usr/lib/pp/chans | Directory for channel programs |
| FORMDIR | /usr/lib/pp/format | Directory for the simple formatting channels |
| TOOLDIR | /usr/lib/pp/tools | Directory for miscellaneous shell scripts and debugging tools |
| LOGDIR | /usr/lib/pp/logs | Directory for PP logs |
| QUEDIR | /usr/spool/pp | Location of the PP queue directory |
| TBLDIR | /usr/lib/pp/tables | The directory containing the table files |
| LIBSYS | -lisode | External libraries required - must include ISODE |
| LIBRESOLV | -lresolv | Resolver library for bind (empty if nameserver not required) |
| USRBINDIR | /usr/local/bin | Directory for user binaries |
| OPTIONALCHANS | list 822-local smtp | List of optional channels you require |
| OPTIONALFILTERS | | List of optional filters |
| MANDIR | /usr/local/man | Directory to place manual pages under |
| MANOPTS | -bsd42 | Manual page installation options |
| NIFTPSRC | /usr/src/niftp | Directory containing the source to unix-niftp package. (Only required if you wish to run grey book mail). |
| NIFTPINTERFACE | sun | Niftp interface being used (restrictions as above) |

Table 35.1: Make Variables That Should Be Set

| Variable | Default | Description |
|---|---|---|
| CC | cc | The *C* compiler to use |
| CCOPTIONS | -O | *C* compiler options |
| LIBCCOPTIONS | -O | *C* compiler options specific to library files |
| OLDCC | cc | Other cc if gcc is used |
| LDOPTIONS | -s | Loaded options |
| PEPY | pepy | The *pepy* ASN.1 parser/compiler |
| POSY | posy | The *posy* stub generator |
| ROSY | rosy | The *rosy* remote operations stub generator |
| PEPSY | pepsy | The *pepsy* program |
| X11 | true | Does the system have X11? |
| LIBX | -lXaw -lXmu -lXt -lX11 | The X11 libraries - may need -lXext for X11R4 |
| LINT | lint | The *lint* (1) command |
| LINTFLAGS | -hbuz | Lint flags |
| PGMPROT | 755 | Program protection mode |
| PPUSER | pp | The user id PP will run as |
| ROOTUSER | root | The user id for privileged channels |
| CHOWN | chown | The *chown*(8) command |
| CHMOD | chmod | The *chmod*(1) command |
| BACKUP | cp | A command to back up the old binary |
| INSTALL | cp | A command to install a new binary |

Table 35.2: Make Variables That Can Be Defaulted

**TOOLDIR:** This directory is where a number of miscellaneous tools are placed. These are useful programs that aid in the day-to-day running of PP but are not usually used directly by the PP system.

**LOGDIR:** This directory is where the logging files are written to by default. These logs are used for a variety of purposes, including debugging and statistics gathering. You should allow for a reasonable amount of space.

**TAILOR:** This specifies the location of the PP tailor file. It is important you get this right. Almost every PP variable can be changed in the PP tailor file, but obviously the location of the PP tailor cannot. If you get this wrong, you will need to relink all the PP binaries against an updated *libpp.a*.

**QUEDIR:** This is the directory under which the PP queue is maintained. As all messages sent are queued here, you should allow enough room to handle all the mail you are likely to receive. A busy site with just a day or two's network outage can gather several megabytes of mail.

**TBLDIR:** This is the directory in which all the PP routing tables and similar configuration files are kept.

**LIBSYS:** This variable contains all the external libraries that you may require when building most of the PP binaries. It should contain at least the ISODE library and possibly other libraries such as the *dbm* (3) library and any machine specific libraries you may need.

**LIBRESOLV:** This variable contains the library for the bind domain name server (or equivalent). It is only required if you are making use of the DNS (see Section 35.1.2). Leave it empty otherwise.

**USRBINDIR:** This is a directory where binaries that are used by users are placed. This includes a simple mail interface, and some delivery time processors.

**OPTIONALCHANS:** PP requires a certain core set of channels to operate at all, plus a number which are used in all normal configurations. However, there are a number of protocol and experimental channels which can be included if required. This variable specifies which of the optional channels and protocols you wish to support. Currently this consists of a list made from the following:

**822-local:** Basic RFC 822 delivery.

**list:** Support for distribution lists.

**grey:** Support for JNT mail protocol (Grey book).

**shell:** Support for delivery to programs.

**slocal:** Support for structured local delivery (experimental).

**smtp:** Support for the SMTP protocol.

**uucp:** Support for the UUCP protocols (primitive).

**x40084:** Support for the X.400 P1(1984) protocol.

**x40088:** Support for the X.400 P1(1988) protocol.

**dirlist:** Experimental X.500 distribution list channel.

**fax:** Experimental fax delivery.

**decnet:** Contributed DECnet[1] MAIL11 channel.

**OPTIONALFILTERS:** PP has a number of filters that can be used. Some are built by default; others are only useful if you plan to support the given style of content. Leave this empty initially if you are unsure; the defaults are usually sufficient.

**MANDIR:** This is the directory under which manual pages are placed. The installation process understands about most layouts of manual pages, so this is usually a base directory.

**MANOPTS:** This variable configures the style of manual pages to be installed. It can take the following values:

| Option | Format |
|---|---|
| -bsd42 | man<N>/file |
| -bsd44 | cat<N>/file.O |
| -ros | man<N>/file – using /etc/install |
| -sys5 | <a\|p\|u>_man/man<N>/file |
| -local | manl/file.l |
| -l | man<N>/file.<N>l |
| -hpux | HP manual style |

**NIFTPSRC/NIFTPINTERFACE:** These two variables control the PP interfacing with the unix-NIFTP code. These variables are ignored unless grey book mail is being installed. The variables should be set to the source directory of the unix-NIFTP package, and the particular interface the grey book channel will use. Suitable interface settings include:

- sun (this is the only version currently in use.)
- inet.
- ubc.
- dexpand.
- x25b.
- yorkbox.

[1]DECnet is a trademark of Digital Equipment Corporation.

CC: The *C* compiler to use. The PP system has been compiled with a number of *C* compilers.

> **Warning:** If you wish to use the *gcc* compiler on sparc-based system, you must compile files making use of *dbm*-style routines with *cc*. (The compiler will normally warn about these files.) See OLDCC below.

OLDCC: The *C* compiler to use on dbm-related files. This is to work around a problem with *gcc*; it should usually be set to *cc*.

CCOPTIONS: This contains global *C* compiler options. If your include files for ISODE are in a non standard place, a "-I" flag or two may be necessary here.

LIBCCOPTIONS: This contains global *C* compiler options to use when compiling files to place in libraries. In normal use this will be the same as CCOPTIONS.

LDOPTIONS: This variable contains global loader flags. It is normally empty or just contains the "-s" flag.

PEPY/POSY/ROSY/PEPSY: These variables are the *pepy*, *posy*, *rosy* and *pepsy* programs. Normally they just contain those names, but may be full pathnames if they are not in the standard search path.

X11: If you have X11 then set this variable to *TRUE*. Leave it empty and no X-based programs will be compiled.

LIBX: The X11 libraries. This contains a list of the X libraries necessary to compile the few X-based programs in the distribution. This distribution is aligned to the X11R4 release; it will *not* run under earlier versions of X.

LINT: The *lint* (1) command. This is not normally used unless you are doing development work.

LINTFLAGS: A list of global lint flags. This variable is also not normally used unless development work is being done.

PGMPROT: This is the default mode to install programs as. Some programs need special modes, but these are handled separately.

PPUSER: This is the username that most PP programs are installed under. It is usually pp, but need not be.

ROOTUSER: The super user.

CHOWN: The *chown* (8) program. This may need to be a full pathname.

CHMOD: The *chmod* (1) program. This is normally ok as just chmod.

**BACKUP:** When PP installs a program, it normally takes a copy of the existing program for safety. If you wish this behaviour then you should set this variable to *cp* (1). If not, setting it to something harmless like ":" or *echo* (1) which will disable this action.

**INSTALL:** The command used to install a new binary. This is normally either *cp* (1) or *install* (1).

### 35.1.2 h/config.h

The only other tailoring that should be done before compiling is setting of `#defines` in the file *h/config.h*. These affect the more global options and there are very few of these.

**DBM/NDBM:** One of these values must be defined. It is *strongly* advised that you use *ndbm* (3) if you have it at all; the *dbm* (3) routines can create havoc if you are using another package that uses dbm too. If you are certain you don't have *ndbm* (3) then use *dbm* (3) and add `-ldbm` to your `LIBSYS` make variable.

**PP_DEBUG:** This variable should be set to one of the following:

| Level | Meaning |
|---|---|
| PP_DEBUG_ALL | Include all debugging code |
| PP_DEBUG_SOME | Include basic debugging code |
| PP_DEBUG_NONE | Don't include any debugging code |

**NAMESERVER:** If you wish to make use of the BIND nameserver for the SMTP channels, you should define this.

**HAS_FSYNC:** This variable should be defined if your system has the *fsync* (2) system call. This is defined for you if the system is BSD based.

## 35.2 Overview of Channels

This is a brief overview of the channels distributed with PP. The binaries of these channels are installed in the *CHANDIR* directory.

### 35.2.1 Mandatory Channels

The channels under this section must be installed with all configurations of PP. They are mostly "housekeeping" channels used by the *qmgr*.

**qmgrload:** The *qmgr* maintains its own model of the queue, separate to the master model stored under the *quedir* directory. The *qmgrload* channel is used to initialise the *qmgr*'s model when the *qmgr* starts up. When running, the *qmgr* periodically uses *qmgrload* to check the consistency between its model and reality.

**msg-clean:** After all work has been done on a message and that message is no longer of interest to PP, the *qmgr* removes the message from the *quedir* directory via the *msg-clean* channel.

**trash:** From time to time, the *qmgr* invokes the *trash* channel. This channel hunts around the *quedir* directory for files and directories that are no longer of interest to PP and removes them.

**timeout:** When a message has been in the queue for too long, the *qmgr* uses the *timeout* channel to send a message back to its originator, telling him or her that PP timed out the original message.

**dr2rfc:** The *dr2rfc* channel is used to construct delivery receipt notifications or error messages for channels that cannot handle these types of messages directly. It converts delivery reports into standard RFC 822 messages which can then be sent back to the sender.

### 35.2.2 Optional Channels

The channels under this section are optional. To see how they are combined to produce various configurations see Section 35.3.

**822-local:** The *822-local* channel is used to deliver messages to local users in RFC 822 format. It can deliver by a number of methods. For more details see Section 37.10 on page 429 and also Part XI (PP Manual: Users Guide.)

**slocal:** The *slocal* channel (structured local channel) should be used if local users are to receive structured messages, that is, if the MTA is to deliver messages made up of different parts, such as multi-media messages, which cannot be appended to a single file but which must be delivered as a directory of files. The *users* table will indicate, for each user, whether *slocal* is an optional channel.

> **NOTE:** This channel is still experimental and not designed for an operational configuration.

**X400-84:** Inbound and outbound channels for handing X.400 P1(84) messages are available. The channels will run over any media that ISODE can support transport connections on.

**X400-88:** Inbound and outbound channels for handing X.400 P1(88) messages are available. The channels will run over any media that ISODE can support transport connections on. This software should be considered as "*beta test*" software in the current release.

**SMTP:** An *smtp* channel is available for use over TCP/IP. It may be used over networks such as a local Ethernet or WAN such as the DARPA Internet.

**JNT Mail:** The JNT mail channel is used over X.25 networks, particularly in the U.K. The unix-niftp package is used to provide the blue book file transfer part of this.

**UUCP:** A channel that will interface with the UUCP protocols.

**Note:** This channel has not been tested extensively by the developers. Others have reported that it is satisfactory, however.

**DECnet MAIL11:** A channel that implements the DECnet protocol. This is contributed software.

**p2explode:** The *p2explode* channel is a restructuring channel that is used to explode a general p2 message into its separate component bodyparts. Note the same binary can explode p2(84) and p22(88). It is used on an incoming X.400 message when the MTA needs to manipulate the separate components of that message.

**p2flatten:** The *p2flatten* channel is a restructuring channel that is used to combine all the separate components of a message into one p2 file. It is the exact inverse of *p2explode.*

**P2toRFC:** The *P2toRFC* channel is a reformating channel that is used to convert an X.400 style header encoded in p2(84) or p2(88) to an RFC 822-style header. This conversion is performed according to RFC 1148[Kil89] .

**RFCtoP2:** The *RFCtoP2* channel is a reformating channel that is used to convert an RFC 822 style header to an X.400 style header encoded in p2 (84) or p2 (88). This conversion is done as described in RFC 1148.

**rfc934:** The *rfc934* channel flattens an RFC 822-style message which may contain forwarded messages, into a flat RFC 822 message. The flattening is done as described in RFC 934[Mar85].

**list:** The *list* channel expands a distribution list into its component members. The original message is then sent to each of these members. The channel uses the associated *list* table as described in Section 37.13 on page 433.

**dirlist:** The *dirlist* channel expands a distribution list into its component members. However, this list channel makes use of the X.500 directory to retrieve the members of the list. This channel is experimental in this version of PP.

**shell:** The *shell* channel runs a specific process for the originator of the message. This allows delivery of a message to a special process rather than to a user. The mapping from the address the message is sent to and the process to run is described by the *shell* table, see Section 37.14 on page 434.

**fcontrol:** The *fcontrol* channel is used to run various filters on the bodyparts of the message. These filters can only affect the contents of the bodyparts and cannot affect the overall structure of the message. The filters are usually installed in the *FORMDIR* directory.

Here is a brief description of the filters distributed with PP:

`rfc822norm`**:** The filter is used for conversion between various styles of RFC 822 headers.

`removebp`**:** The filter is used to replace bodyparts that the MTA cannot support with a simple text message reflecting this fact.

## 35.3 Example Configurations

This section gives some details about the example configurations included in the distribution. These configurations should be looked on as a sample first step to allow a working system to be installed easily. This should then be evolved to meet local requirements. To use one of these configurations, do the following.

1. Change to the *examples* directory.
2. Select one of the configurations shown below, and change into that directory.
3. Read the *README* file, and carry out the instructions given in there.

This should give you a *very basic* working system.

### Local SMTP

This configuration assumes a simple host doing local deliveries and passing all other messages to another host. It requires the *smtp* channel, the *822-local* channel and optionally the *list* channel.

### SMTP mail

This configuration assumes a simple host doing SMTP relaying and local delivery only. It is similar to the above, but can handle Internet connectivity by use of the domain nameserver.

### Janet mail

This host is assumed to be on the Janet network and has local SMTP capability. It is a skeleton only as for proper operation NRS data is necessary to identify the necessary domain and routes.

## 35.4 Configuration of User Agents

PP is a message transfer agent, and does not contain a sophisticated X.400 user agent. It is hoped that the interface documented in Part X will be useful in the development of new user agents or the interfacing of existing UAs. The latter should be straightforward for most RFC 822-based interfaces.

MH[Ros86] can be used directly with PP if compiled with the SMTP transfer interface.

PP provides a */bin/mail* emulation. This should be installed in the normal installation. Also provided is a *sendmail*(8) emulation program that can be used to intercept those programs that insist on calling sendmail directly (e.g., *cron*(8)).

## 35.5 Checking the Configuration of Your System

Following installation, it is *strongly* recommended to use *ckconfig* (8) to ensure that the PP directory structure is correct and all the channel programs are correctly in place. *ckconfig* is described in Section 39.4.2.

# Chapter 36

# Configuring PP

This chapter is principally concerned with the *tailor* file and how it is configured. The *tailor* file contains the runtime MTA configuration information. This chapter describes how to construct this information.

The information in the *tailor* file may duplicate that in the *Make.defs* in some cases. In these cases, the *tailor* file settings will override the *Make.defs* settings.

There are four basic types of entries in the *tailor* file:

- Variable entries.
- Logging entries.
- Table entries.
- Channel entries.

The following sections describe how to construct these entries. Appendix A contains a complete example *tailor* file.

Since the construction of the information is complex, it is *strongly* recommended to use *ckconfig* (8). *ckconfig* applies several sanity checks to the information contained in the *tailor* file and generally ensures that the information represents a logically correct configuration. *ckconfig* is described in Section 39.4.2.

## 36.1 The General Syntax of Tailor File Entries

A comment starts with an unescaped hash (#) and finishes at the end of the line. Other lines are split into components separated by white space or commas (or both). A line may be extended onto the next line by starting that next line with some white space. A field may be enclosed by quotation marks ("<field>"); this disables special characters such as field delimiters.

## 36.2 Variable Tailor File Entries

Variable entries take the form of a keyword and its value, separated by white space. Each key/value pair should be on a separate line and start in the first column. For example:

```
cmddir   /usr/pp/cmds
tbldir   /usr/pp/tables
```

There are a finite number of tailoring variables that can be referenced in the *tailor* file. These tailoring variables are divided into two types, mandatory tailoring variables and optional tailoring variables. They are listed and described in the sections below.

### 36.2.1 Mandatory Tailoring Variables

The following tailoring variables *must* be included in the *tailor* file:

**loc_dom_mta:** This is the full domain name of the local mta. It is used for trapping routing loops and so should be globally unique. For example: `sheriff.cs.nott.ac.uk`.

**loc_dom_site:** This is the full domain name of the local site. This is used to reference the site, and may refer to a group of MTAs collectively. For example: `cs.nott.ac.uk`.

**loc_or:** This is the local O/R address defaults given in X.400 RFC 1148 encoding form. For example:

```
"/OU=CS/O=NOTT/PRMD=UK.AC/ADMD=GOLD 400/C=GB/"
```

*Note*: If the name contains spaces or other special characters, it must be quoted as above.

**qmgrhost:** This is the name of the machine on which the QMGR is running. For example, you could give the output of *hostname* (1) here.

**postmaster:** This is the address of the local mail system administrator. Typically of the form: `Postmaster <postmaster@cs.nott.ac.uk>`.

**bodypart:** This is a list of bodyparts that are recognised by the system. This line may occur several times in the tailor file, each time appending its arguments to the list of body parts.

**headertype:** This is a list of headers that are recognised by the system. This line like the above line may occur several times each time appending to the list.

**pptsapd_addr:** This is the address that the *pptsapd* listens on for incoming connections. For example the QMGR uses it to connect to channel processes. The default value is: `Internet=localhost+20001`. This is suitable if you are an internet site, but not if you have just your own ethernet which is not connected to the internet. In this case a more suitable value might be `LOCAL-ETHER=localhost+20001` or `localHost=20001`.

This indicates that processes can communicate with the *pptsapd* daemon via a TCP/IP connection to the local machine on Port 20001. The address could just as easily be a remote machine name specifying an X25 address or a real NSAP.

### 36.2.2 Optional Tailoring Variables

The tailoring variables in this section are less critical, having defaults that are normally suitable.

**cmddir:** This is a directory and is the default place to find all the main PP commands. It should be a fully qualified pathname, i.e., starting with a forward slash.

**tbldir:** This is the directory where all the table files are located and should be a fully qualified pathname; it is used by `dbmbuild` to generate the hashed database and for address lookups when tables are defined in `linear` mode.

**quedir:** This is the base directory for the PP queue. It should be a fully qualified pathname.

**logdir:** This is the directory where log files will be written in by default.

**chandir:** This is the directory where the executable channel programs are found. It defaults to a directory called *chans* within the *cmddir*. When defined, if it is a relative name, i.e., not starting with a forward slash, then it will be assumed to be a subdirectory of the *cmddir*.

**formdir:** This is the directory where the simple programs run by the *fcontrol* are found. Not usually tailored, it defaults to being the same as *chandir*. When it is defined, it is taken as relative to the *cmddir* unless a full pathname is given.

**dbm:** This is the name of PP database. It is assumed to be relative to the *tbldir* directory unless a full pathname is given. The default is *ppdbm*.

**pplogin:** This is the user id that most of the PP programs will run under. It defaults to pp and should be a username found in the */etc/passwd* file.

**isode:** This variable allows the tailoring of any ISODE parameter specified in the *isotailor* (5) file. However, the ISODE logging levels are better handled by the **isodelogs** tailor line.

**authchannel:** This gives the default policy for channel authorisation; it is in the form of a *channel-auth* record (see Section 37.16). The default is **block**. This determines the policy for any inbound/outbound channel pairing not explicitly entered in the channel authorisation table *channel-auth*.

**authloglevel:** This sets the level of authorisation logging. Three levels are defined:

> **low:** One line of statistical information is generated for each recipient, giving the outbound channel if authorisation succeeds, or the first (of possibly several) channels to be tested which failed. (It is anticipated that the tables will be configured so that channels will be tested in order of ascending 'cost'.)
>
> **medium:** One line is generated for each potential output channel which fails authorisation tests in the cases where no successful channel is found, but only a single line where authorisation is successful for that recipient.
>
> **high:** As for **medium**, but a line is produced for every channel which fails authorisation tests, whether or not the recipient is ultimately successful.

The default is **low**.

**wrndfldir:** This is a directory to hold warning message files which can be sent automatically to sender or recipients when authorisation fails. It may be a fully qualified pathname starting with "/", or else is taken relative to the table directory **tbldfldir**.

The default is **warnings**.

*Note*: Warnings are not used in this release.

**warninterval:** This is the time in hours after which to send a warning to the sender of the message telling him or her that the message is stuck in the MTA.

The default is one day.

*Note*: Warnings are not used in this release.

**nwarnings:** This is the maximum number of warnings to send.

The default is two warnings.

*Note*: Warnings are not used in this release.

**returntime:** This is the time in hours after which to expire an undelivered message. By default, this time is doubled for low priority messages and halved for high priority messages. However, these other values can be overridden by specifying two other times in hours after the normal return time, the first of these being the return time for high priority messages and the second for low priority messages.

The default normal time out is three days, giving about a day for high priority messages and just less than a week for low priority messages. Messages that pass through the list channel are set to low priority.

**lockstyle:** This is the style of locking to be used when it is necessary to lock a file. It may be one of the following:

| Value | Meaning |
|---|---|
| `flock` | Use the *flock* (2) system call. |
| `fcntl` | Use the *fcntl* (2) system call. |
| `file` | Use lock files that are created and removed. |
| `lockf` | Use the *lockf* (3) library call. |

The default style is `flock` but may be changed if you have doubts about the interaction of *flock* (2) and nfs. This is a run time configuration variable, and it will depend on what platform you are running as to whether all the above will be supported. The file locking mechanism will always be available, though.

**lockdir:** If the +file+" style of locking is to be used, this is the directory to create the files in. It defaults to */tmp* and should be cleaned out at reboot time. It is ignored otherwise.

**maxloops:** This is a number indicating the number of times a message may pass thorough this mta before being rejected. The default is 5.

**maxhops:** This is a number indicating the number of trace fields a message may contain. If it has more than this number, the message will be rejected as looping. The default is 25.

**x400_mta:** This is the name of this MTA in the X.400 world. It defaults to the same as `loc_dom_mta`.

**submit_addr:** This is a list of comma-separated submit addresses. By default a user interface program or channel will directly invoke submit, but with this option it will call a submit daemon. The specification is

```
<hostname> [ ":"<port> ]
```

The hostname is a TCP hostname, the port reference is either a number or a port reference found in the services database. In this mode, *submit* is usually run under *inetd* (8). For example the following *tailor* file entry

```
submit_addr lancaster.xtel.co.uk:pp-submit
```

might be combined with the following *inetd.conf* entry

```
pp-submit stream tcp nowait pp
    /usr/lib/pp/cmds/submit submit
```

**dap_user:** This is an X.500 directory distinguished name used when PP binds to the directory. It is useful to use this in versions of ISODE greater than 6.8 to distinguish PP use of X.500 from other users.

**dap_passwd:** A password to be used in conjunction with the dap_user variable in binding to the directory.

**queuestruct:** This is a variable used to control the structure of the queue. This is only useful to change if you are expecting very large queues (> 2000 messages in the queue at one time.) It takes two numbers. The first number specifies the fan out of the queue. With a value of 100 messages will be put in 100 sub-directories of the main queue file. This cuts down the searching of the main directory but is only useful for very large queues. The second optional number is the level of sub-directories to create. By default this is one indicating an indirection of one directory. Again this parameter should not be changed unless extremely large queues are expected (say > 50,000.)

**fsync:** This is a boolean variable which controls the use of the *fsync* (2) call. Fsync is normally used, but can be switched off by a value of no if you consider that it is too expensive.

## 36.3 Logging Tailor File Entries.

This section describes how to tailor the logging produced by PP.

There are four main groups of logging; covering normal events, unusual operational events, authorisation, and ISODE. By default, each group will describe in a single file, the appropriate activities of all the programs that provide logs. However, the *tailor* file may be used to separate out logging on a per-program or per-channel basis. Thus, for example, all normal activities may be logged in one file except *submit* which may be logged in a different file, and at a different level.

All logging entries are comprised of a standard set of key/value pairs, described below.

**file=xxx:** Set the log file to xxx. This is either a fully qualified filename, or more usually just a relative pathname which is taken relative to the *logdir*.

**level=value:** This adds to the logging levels the given value. Legal values are `all`: Enable all logging (this fills disks very quickly!).

`fatal`: Enable reporting of fatal errors.

`exceptions`: Report exceptional happenings.

`notice`: Report interesting happenings.

`trace`: Trace the programs flow (very detailed).

`debug`: A full debugging trace.

`pdus`: Show protocol data units.

The last three levels are only available if PP was compiled with `PP_DEBUG` defined to a suitable level. The value `all` is special, in that it sets all values. The other levels only set the individual values (e.g., `debug` does not imply settings of any other values).

The default level is to enable `notice`, `exceptions` and `fatal`.

`dlevel=value`: This unsets a logging level. Legal values of this are the same as the above.

`sflags=value`: This sets the logging flags to a given value; the value being one of:

`close`: Close the log file after each entry is made.

`create`: Create the log file if it doesn't already exist.

`zero`: Zero the log file when it gets too big.

`tty`: Log to the standard error as well as to the file. This should be used only when debugging.

The default is to `create` new files.

`dflags`: This unsets one of the above levels for the log.

`size`: Set the maximum size in Kilobytes to which the log should be allowed to grow. The default is not to limit the log size. What happens when the logfile reaches the specified maximum is governed by the flags. If `zero` is not in force, logging will just stop. If `zero` is in force, then the log will be truncated and restarted.

There are currently four logging variables that can be specified although there are several logging structures.

The logging variables are:

`normlog`: This is the log where the bulk of the logging is done.

`operlog`: This is where urgent messages are logged. In the normal course of events no entries should be made in this log unless something serious has happened.

**authlog:** This indicates where authorisation tracing will be logged.

**isodelog:** This line allows the tailoring of specific ISODE tracing levels. The first argument is an ISODE logging level. The rest of the line is interpreted as a normal log tailoring line. Valid ISODE logging levels are:

> **compatlevel:** Compatibility level.
>
> **addrlevel:** Addressing level.
>
> **tsaplevel:** Transport level.
>
> **ssaplevel:** Session level.
>
> **psaplevel:** Presentation structures.
>
> **psap2level:** Presentation level.
>
> **acsaplevel:** Association level.
>
> **rtsaplevel:** Reliable transfer level.
>
> **rosaplevel:** Remote operations level.

By default, all the ISODE logging is directed at the normal log. An example of logging tailoring is shown in Figure 36.1.

Notice that for a given program or channel, the logging information can be diverted. If a logging entry starts with the name of the binary then that line is specific to that program; e.g.:

```
submit normlog file=submit
```

makes a *submit*-specific normlog tailoring entry. Hence all logging from *submit* directed at the normlog will go to the file *submit* instead of the file associated with normlog. The net result is that all the normal logging messages from *submit* end up in the file *submit* in the log directory.

## 36.4 Table Tailor File Entries

This section describes how the tables of aliasing and addressing information, referenced by *submit* and the channel programs, are defined in the *tailor* file.

Generally each table's entry is comprised of a line with several key/value pairs. The line starts with the keyword tbl which is followed by a string setting the default name for the table and the plain text file in *tbldir*. Then come the key/value pairs, described below.

**name=value:** Name this table with the given value (to override the default – see above). This is included only for completeness; it is not normally used.

**file=value:** The tables contents are found in the given file (to override the default).

```
authlog             level=notice,      size=400
operlog             level=all,         size=400
normlog             level=notice,      size=400

submit              normlog file=submit        level=notice, size=400
qmgr                normlog file=qmgr          level=notice, size=400
x400in84            normlog file=x400in84      level=notice, size=400
x400out84           normlog file=x400out84     level=pdus,   size=400

isodelog compatlevel      level=pdus
isodelog tsaplevel        level=pdus
isodelog ssaplevel        level=pdus
isodelog rtsaplevel       level=pdus
```

Figure 36.1: Example of Log Tailoring

`show="value"`: A descriptive string used when printing messages about this table, mainly for logging purposes.

`flags=value`: A set of flags that specifies how this table operates. It should be one of the following:

- `dbm`: This table is stored in the database for fast access (the default).
- `linear`: This table is searched with a linear pass through the file in *tbldir* (this is slow, but does not require rebuilding the database, and changes take immediate effect). Linearly searched files are still built into the database.

An example of table tailoring is shown in Figure 36.2.

```
tbl    aliases   show="Aliases:  mapping -> local id",
                 flags=dbm,file=local-aliases
tbl    domain    show="Mapping domain key ->full domain/MTA",
                 flags=dbm
tbl    or        show="Mapping O/R Address -> MTA",flags=dbm
tbl    or2rfc    show="RFC 987:  X.400 -> RFC 822",flags=dbm
tbl    rfc2or    show="RFC 987:  RFC 822 -> X.400",flags=dbm
tbl    channel   show="Binding MTA -> Channels",flags=dbm
tbl    auth.qmgr show="Qmgr authorisation",flags=linear
```

Figure 36.2: Example of Table Tailoring

## 36.5 Channel Tailor File Entries

Channels are perhaps the most complex aspect of tailoring. There are several types of channels. Input channels carry messages into the system. Output channels carry messages out of the system. Reformatting channels change the message structure in the queue. Finally there are a few miscellaneous channels that do other jobs such as message deletion.

The *channel tailor* file entries each consist of the keyword chan followed by a value which, by default, names the channel and the program associated with it; then comes a list of key/value pairs which provides more information on the channel.

A number of the values can be applied to a pair of channels differently depending on whether the channel is being used in outbound or inbound mode. Where the distinction is significant, there are separate tailor variables prefixed by `in` and `out`.

The key/value pairs consist of the following:

**name=value:** The name of the channel (overrides the default).

**prog=value:** The program associated with this channel, i.e., the actual binary to run (overrides the default).

**key:** A key by which this channel is known. This can be used to map several logical channels onto one. See Section 36.7 on channel pairing on page 402.

**show="value":** A descriptive string used in pretty printing. If this string starts with the keywords `with` or `via` then this value is included in `Received` lines generated for RFC 822 messages.

**type=value:** This parameter is *mandatory* and indicates the type of channel this is. This *must* be set to one of the values shown below:

| Value | Type of Channel |
|---|---|
| `in` | An incoming channel. |
| `out` | An outgoing channel. |
| `both` | Both incoming and outgoing. |
| `shaper` | A reformatter that changes the shape of the message. |
| `warn` | A warning channel. |
| `delete` | A message deletion channel. |
| `qmgrload` | A queue manager loading channel. |
| `debris` | A debris collection channel. |
| `timeout` | A timeout channel. |

**drchan=value:** This value must be set for outbound channels that cannot handle real delivery reports. At present, it is only the X.400 channels and the X.400-based delivery channels that can handle delivery reports. Other channels should set this to a suitable channel that can transform DRs into suitable messages. Currently this is always *dr2rfc*.

**content-in=value:** The content of this channel if it allows incoming messages. It is normally either p2, p22 or 822. It should be empty if the message is submitted in structured form.

**content-out=value:** The content of this channel if it allows outgoing messages. Values are as for `content-in`.

**cost=value:** The cost of running this channel. This is used in the reformatting calculations to decide the best conversion path. The lowest cost route will be chosen, all other things being equal. Costs are relative; a cost of 0, the default, means that this channel essentially makes no changes to the message. Higher costs make the channel less favourable.

As a rule of thumb, any channel that makes a real change to a message should have a positive cost. Thus *rfc822norm* channels should have a small cost as they make small changes to the message. A channel such as *P2toRFC* should have a larger cost as this conversion should not be done unless needed. A channel that removes a content type by *removebp* should be given a large cost as this should only be run if there is no alternative. However, a channel such as *p2flatten* should have a zero cost as it makes no change to the message content, just combining it into one file.

**sort=value:** This value is a series of keys that are used for sorting purposes by the queue manager. The first key is the primary sort key and must be either `mta` or `user` (or none). The remaining keys are secondary sort keys and are taken in order. The values for this field are any of those shown below:

| Value | Meaning |
|---|---|
| `mta` | Sort by destination MTA. This is the most common primary sort key. |
| `user` | Sort by username. This is useful for local deliveries. |
| `priority` | Sort by the priority of the message. |
| `time` | Sort by queued time. |
| `size` | Sort by the size of the message. |
| `none` | Don't attempt to sort |

By default, all outbound channels are sorted by `mta`. Local channels should be sorted by `user`. Reformatters and other channels are normally sorted by none.

However if you require a number ofthe same reforatter to run concurrently, you can try sorting them by `mta` or `user`.

**`out-info=value/in-info=value:`** This contains channel-specific information that can be used for a variety of purposes. For example, the `out-info` field is used by the simple formatters to give the real program to run. Typically a simple formatter is a shell script or similar, with *fcontrol* indicated as the program. In such cases the *fcontrol* program is then responsible for queue manager interaction and it runs the program in the info field as a subprocess.

**`inadr=value/outadr=value:`** The type of addressing that is used by this channel. The value is one of those below:

| Value | Meaning |
|---|---|
| x400 | X.400 addressing |
| 822 | rfc822 addressing |

**`insubadr=value/outsubadr=value:`** The type of subaddressing used by a channel, if appropriate. Currently this is only relevant in conjunction with a definition of `inadr=822` or `outadr=822`. The value is one of those below:

| Value | Meaning |
|---|---|
| real.rfc822 | normal rfc822 style addressing |
| real.rfc733 | rfc733 style addressing |
| jnt | JNT style addressing |

This list will change in the next release.

For inbound channels, if `insubadr` is set to either `real.rfc733` or `jnt` then *submit* will recognise percentages as characters with routing properties. If `insubadr` is not set to either of these, *submit* views percentages as characters with no special properties.

**`adr-order=value:`** The ordering of addresses on this inbound channel. This is one of the following:

| Value | Meaning |
|---|---|
| usa | Internet style addressing is insisted upon. |
| uk | JNT style addressing is insisted upon. |
| usapref | Internet style addressing is preferred but both types will be tried. |
| ukpref | JNT style is preferred but both types will be tried. |

The default value is `usa`. Normally only UK sites will need to modify this variable.

**bptin=value:** A list of body parts that the channel accepts as input. This must be one of the types defined in the **bodypart** tailoring item defined in Section 36.2.1 on page 388.

**bptout=value:** A list of body parts that the channel will output. The possible values are the same as for those for bptin.

**hdrin/hdrout:** These variables are much the same as the **bptin/bpout** variables but apply to the headers instead.

**outtable=value:** A table associated with this channel.

**mtatable:** A table that is used in binding locating an appropriate channel. See Section 36.7 on page 402 on channel pairing for use of this feature.

**mta=value:** A destination MTA for this channel. If this is set, all messages will be delivered to this MTA regardless of the destination MTA given in the message. This is useful for relaying all messages for a given channel via another MTA.

**access=value:** The type of access this channel requires; only applicable to inbound channels. The value is either **mta**, in which case the channel must be run by a trusted user-id, or else **mts** in which case authentication of messages is enabled. The default is **mta**.

**domain-norm=value:** The amount of domain normalisation of MTS addresses on inbound channels. The value is one of those below (the default is **partial**):

| Value | Meaning |
|---|---|
| full | all domains in an MTS address are normalised |
| partial | only the next hop of an MTS address is normalised |

**maxproc=value:** This is the maximum number of instances of the channel the QMGR is allowed to run at any time. A value of 0 indicates that there is no maximum to the number of instances the QMGR can run. The default is 0.

**auth-table=value:** This is a table which contains the authentication data for the channel if it is an **mts** submission channel. The format is described in Section 37.15 on page 435.

**conv:** This variable specifies what effect the channel has on a message. This is used to check on conversion restrictions; in particular the X.400 and RFC 1148 conversion semantics. It may take one of the following values:

| Value | Meaning |
|---|---|
| none | channel does no conversion |
| 1148 | channel does RFC 1148/987 header mappings |
| conv | channel does conversion |
| loss | channel does conversion with loss |

The default value is none. Channels that do mapping of P2 to RFC 822 *headers* and the reverse should use the value `1148` to indicate that conversion can be carried out even in the presence of the conversion-prohibited flag of X.400. This will allow messages with header mappings and no body part conversions to go through an RFC 1148/987 gateway.

Channels that change formats without loosing information (except RFC 1148/987 channels) should be marked as `conv`. Channels which lose data (such as, say, G3Fax to Ia5) should be marked as loss (they should also be given a high cost).

`probe`: This variable states whether this channel can support X.400 style probe messages. It has values `y` and `n`. The default is `n`. This should be set for X.400 channels. If submit determines the channel cannot support probes it will return a delivery report.

`trace`: This variable tells *submit* what sort of trace element to generate. This is only applicable to RFC 822-based protocols, and can be set to either `received` to generate Received lines or `via` for Via lines.

An example of a channel tailoring is shown in Figure 36.3 and will help to make things a little clearer. The descriptions above can be used to determine exactly what each channel does.

```
chan    822-local prog=local,
        show="Local 822 Delivery channel",type=both,
        sort="user time",adr=822,adr-order=ukpref,
        hdrout=822, bptout=ia5, content-out=822,
        table=local,access=mts

chan    x40084 prog=x400out84,show="X400 1984 channel",
        type=both, adr=x400, adr-order=ukpref,
        intable=x400in84, outtable=x400out84

chan    qmgr-load prog=qmgr-load,show="Loading the QMGR",
        type=qmgrload

chan    p2flatten prog=p2flatten,show="Structured body -> P2",
        type=shaper,content-out=p2

chan    g3faxtotxt        prog=fcontrol,type=shaper,bptin=g3fax,
        bptout=ia5,table=none,info=f-fax2txt,
        show="Fax -> Text mapper"
```

Figure 36.3: Example of Channel Tailor Entry

## 36.6 ISODE Runtime Tailoring

### 36.6.1 Queue Manager Tailoring

Information relating to the MTA, its QMGR, and their addresses are normally obtained from the file *isoentities* and take the general form:

```
vs2 "pp qmgr" 1.17.6.2.1 #1001/Internet=vs2+18000
```

The first field is the designator of the machine that the QMGR is running on. It is usually the name of the machine. The second is the QMGR service; this should not be changed. The same goes for the other fields, except for the last one. This specifies the transport selector that the QMGR listens on (1001 in this case) and the NSAP address. In this case it is in internet form, with hostname `vs2` and TCP port number `18000`.

In later releases of ISODE, this information will be obtained from the directory.

### 36.6.2 X.400 Tailoring

If the X.400 is going to be used, then a definition of this must be placed in the file */etc/isoservices*. A suitable definition might look like this:

```
"tsap/p1"  "591"   /usr/lib/pp/chans/x400in84
```

This shows the service name `tsap/p1`, the transport selector `"591"` and indicates the location of the program. You should use a numeric IA5 form of TSEL for X.400(84) compliance.

For more details of the formats of these files, see *The ISO Development Environment: Users Manual.*

## 36.7 Channel Pairing

Many of the channels within PP naturally fall into pairs. For instance, it is usual to have an inbound X.400 channel and a corresponding outbound X.400 channel.

As this is a common occurence, one channel definition in the *tailor* file can be used to define both channels. Such a channel should be marked as type `both`. Where both sides of the channel require a parameter, such as a table, there is an explicit in and out value.

Channel pairing can bring several benefits. If the QMGR knows about paired channels, it can make some optimisations. When a message is received for an MTA on the inbound side of a paired channel, it can, if there are messages waiting to go out on that channel, assume that this MTA has just come up and schedule a retry immediately.

A side effect of channel pairing can help with authorisation. An incoming channel usually has a fixed name. However, if a number of channels are defined in the tailor file with a `key` of that value, then all of these channels are potentially usable. In this case, the MTA that the message was received in is looked up in the `mtatable` table. The first channel to match is the one that is chosen. Authorisation is then done on this basis. One of the channels may not have an `mtatable` associated with it, in which case this is the default channel to use.

As an example, consider a host on the internet which wishes to authorise usage on the basis of whether the user is "local" or "remote". This might be achieved by the following:

```
chan smtp-local key="smtp",mtatable=localhosts,...
chan smtp-internet key="smtp",...
```

The incoming channel then claims to be "smtp". If the MTA the message is received from is in the localhosts table, then `smtp-local` is used as the channel, and authorisation done on that basis. Otherwise it is assumed to be `smtp-internet` and potentially different authorisation is applied.

On a smaller site, this same feature can be used to map many channels onto one. For instance, the *greyin* channel selects one of `gb-janet` `gb-pss` or `ipss` depending on which network the call originated. If this distinction is not important, all three can be mapped to one channel by tailoring:

```
chan gb-janet key="gb-pss,ipss",...
```

## 36.8 Tailoring of Common Channels

Channels perform operations on messages. Intermediate channels for reformatting and other manipulation are considered later. The following terms apply to endpoint channels:

**outbound:** A channel which delivers messages out of PP.

**inbound:** A channel which passes messages into PP (through *submit*).

**active:** A channel which is initiated by the QMGR.

**passive:** A channel which is not initiated by the QMGR (typically by a user or server).

The most common types of channel are passive inbound and active outbound.

### 36.8.1 Protocol Channels

Protocol channels are channels that talk to the outside world. There are a number of these supplied with PP. Those that have special requirements or are optional are described here.

### SMTP channel

The *smtp* channel comes in two parts, the outbound part and the inbound daemon. The inbound daemon can have a number of arguments to it, and can be run either under the control of *inetd* (8) or under the standalone server *smtpd*. To configure it to run under *inetd* the following entry in the file */etc/inetd.conf* might be appropriate (but see *inetd.conf* (5) for more details).

```
smtp stream tcp nowait pp \
    /usr/lib/pp/cmds/chans/smtpsrvr smtpsrvr smtp
```

If, however, you prefer to run a standalone smtp server, the command is something like this (usually included in *pp.start*):

```
/usr/lib/pp/cmds/smtpd /usr/lib/pp/cmds/smtpsrvr smtp
```

The following arguments are supported by the *smtpd* program.

**`-p port`:** Specify a different TCP port to listen on when running standalone.

**`-i maxcon`:** Set the maximum number of simultaneous smtp connections that are supported. Only obeyed when running standalone.

**`-t timeout`:** Set a default timeout for use with the nameserver. This is only used if the server is compiled with nameserver support included.

The two mandatory arguments for *smtpd* are the name of a server program to interpret the smtp protocol, and the name of a channel that incoming messages will arrive on.

Finally, the smtp server makes use of one additional tailoring variable in the channel specification. If the `in-info` element of the channel tailoring entry contains the string `sloppy` then any connection will be allowed. If this is not the case, connections are only supported from hosts that can be reversed translated (e.g., the IP number can be converted back to a host name).

The smtp outbound channel has only one special option. It can be given a flag `-p port` to tell it to connect to a different tcp port other than the default. This can be set up by setting the tailor entry to something like the following:

```
chan smtp-odd pgm="smtp -p 2001",show="Odd smtp"...
```

### X.400 inbound channel

The X.400(84) inbound channel (*x400in84*) takes note of the `in-info` part of the tailoring information. If this is set to the string `sloppy` then no checking of MTA name and password is done for any connection incoming on that channel. Also, if the NSAP cannot be looked up in the channel table the connection is still allowed.

X.400 inbound also has an optional flag; this is as follows:

**-c channelname:** Claim to be the given channel name on input. You may have a number of X.400 inbound channels, selected initially by T-Selector or network address. If you wish to split up traffic in this way, possibly for authorisation reasons, you should set the channel name in this way in the *isoservices* file. By default the channel is assumed to be the name of the program itself.

### UUCP Channel

The uucp channel interfaces to the UUCP system. It uses the `out-info` string of the channel to tailor the interface. This string is a key value pair that can set various parameters. The key/value pairs are separated by a comma. The possible keys are:

**uux:** Set the uux pathname and arguments. This parameter must be present.

**host:** When constructing the uucp from line, use this value as the host name.

An example configuration might be:

```
chan uucp-out prog=uucp-out,show="UUCP outbound channel",
    type=out, adr=822,adr-order=ukpref,table=uucp
    out-info="uux=/usr/bin/uux - -r,host=nott-cs"
```

### DECnet MAILL11 channel

The *decnet* channel implements the DECnet mail protocol. It is currently only available for the Sun implementation of DECnet (Sunlink DNI, V7.0 onward). The channel comes in two parts, the outbound part and the inbound server. The inbound server is run under the control of the DECnet spawner (the DECnet equivalent of *inetd*) and will require an entry of the form

```
27     MAIL    /usr/lib/pp/cmds/chans/decnetsrvr
```

in the *dniserver.reg* configuration file. It is not possible to pass any arguments into the server due to limitations of the *dniserver*, so the server takes its tailoring from a channel with the hardwired name of `decnet-in`.

The *decnet* channel makes use of a number of tailoring options. The `info` element of the channel tailoring entry may be set to any combination of the following options. If more than one option is selected then the options are separated by commas and the whole string must be enclosed in quotes.

**strip:** If this option is selected, all headers except for To:, From: and Subject: will be stripped off and thrown away, otherwise they will be moved into the message body. This is for the benefit of VMS users who tend to be panicked by what they see as UNIX style headers.

**mrgate:** Select this option if the MTAs contacted by this channel are running DECs mail router software. This makes a small but significant change to the addresses presented to such sites.

**map_space:** This option enables the mapping of space to underbar in the incoming channel and vice versa in the outgoing channel. This caters for sites running All-in-One and/or mail router which have chosen to have mail addresses with spaces in them.

Domain and channel table entries for the *decnet* channel are similar to those for the *smtp* channel.

Note that incoming connections are only allowed from hosts for which a reverse mapping exists in the DECnet database. There is no equivalent of the *smtp* `sloppy` option.

### 36.8.2 Filter Control and Common Filters

Filters can be called via a special channel called *fcontrol*. This channel can be used in a variety of guises to run various filters on messages and, in particular, on the body parts within the messages. It should only be used for filters where there is a one-to-one mapping between incoming body parts and outgoing body parts; i.e., the contents of the body parts, and possibly their names, may be altered by a filter, but the structure of the message will remain the same.

A filter reads an incoming body part from the standard input, does the required filtering, and writes the outgoing body part to the standard output. Any error or logging messages produced by the filter should be written onto the standard error. *fcontrol* logs these messages at the `LLOG_NOTICE` level. The filter should exit with a value of 0 to indicate success. Any other exit value is taken as failure.

To create a channel which runs a given filter, an entry has to be made in the *tailor* file. The entry should be constructed in the normal way with the following provisos:

**prog:** This should contain the filename of the filter controller, *fcontrol*.

**out-info:** The pathname of the filter's executable program should be placed in the `out-info` field, followed by any arguments that are to be passed to the filter. If the given name is not a fully qualified pathname, the filter controller assumes the executable to be under the *formdir* directory. Arguments of the form `$(key)` will be expanded to the entities described in Table 36.1. The key is case independent.

**bptin/bptout** Filters should not change the structure of the message. `bptin` should only contain one type of bodypart. This type is the bodypart type that the filter converts. `bptout` should also only contain one type of bodypart. This

| Key | Expansion |
|---|---|
| sender | the address of the sender of the message (format unspecified) |
| 822sender | the address of the sender (rfc822 format) |
| 400sender | the address of the sender (x400 format) |
| recip | the address of the recipient of the message (format unspecified) |
| 822recip | the address of the recipient (rfc822 format) |
| 400recip | the address of the recipient (x400 format) |
| qid | the queue id of the message (e.g., msg.a000000) |
| ua-id | the user agent id of the message |
| p1-id | the P1 id of the message |
| recipient | the recipient in local format |
| userid | either the username if available else the uid |
| groupid | the group id of the user being delivered to |
| size | the message size |
| channelname | the name of the channel doing the delivery |

Table 36.1: Filter Control Expansion Macros

bodypart type is the result of the filter's conversion. i.e., the filter converts bodypart `bptin` into bodypart `bptout`.

`hdrin/hdrout` This fulfills the same type of function as `bptin/bptout` but for the headers of the messages. The header must be one of those defined in `headertype`.

`type` The type should be set to `shaper`.

Example *tailor* file entries of filters running in conjunction with *fcontrol* are shown in Figure 36.4.

Trivial filters such as voice to ia5 mappings can be done by a simple shell script of the type shown in Figure 36.5.

Here are descriptions of some common filters run in conjunction with *fcontrol*:

```
chan 822touk prog=fcontrol,type=shaper,
           hdrin=822,hdrout=822-jntmail,
           out-info="rfc822norm -jnt -jntsender $(sender) -fold 50"

chan g3faxtotxt prog=fcontrol, type=shaper, bptin=g3fax,
             bptout=ia5, info='removebp "Group 3 Fax"',
             show="Fax -> Text Mapper"

chan dmd2odif prog=fcontrol, type=shaper, bptin=dmd,
            bptout=odif, info=f-dmd2odif,
            show="Diamond -> Odif"
```

Figure 36.4: Example of Filter Control Tailoring

```
#! /bin/sh

#
# Voice -> IA5 conversion filter
#

echo "********************"
echo "There was a voice body part here, which was"
echo "removed in the conversion process"
echo "********************"
exit 0
```

Figure 36.5: Simple Shell Script Filter

### RFC 822 Filter

The RFC 822 filter *rfc822norm* is used in conjunction with the general filter controller *fcontrol*, for dealing with RFC 822 and related headers. It takes a generic RFC 822 header as input, and outputs a "normalised" form. A normalised header is one in which all addresses are fully qualified and are in the correct order. For this reason, the `hdrin` and `hdrout` fields in any associated *tailor* file entry should be some extended version of 822, e.g `822-us`, `822-uk`, etc.

The filter affects the following fields of the RFC 822 header:

- All of the addressing fields in RFC 822.
- The Acknowledge-To field (JNT Mail).

The filter's behaviour may be altered by specifying various options. These options are passed through *fcontrol* to the filter by use of the `out-info` element of the channel structure. One possible `out-info` string is as follows:

```
rfc822norm -822 -striptrace -jntsender $(822sender)
```

The RFC 822 filter can be used in a variety of guises. For example, in appendix A the combination of *fcontrol* and *rfc822norm* appears twice, so providing two different channels, *822touk* and *822tous*.

The filter takes the following options:

**-822:** Format source routes according to RFC 822.

**-733:** Format source routes with a "%" notation (default).

**-bigend:** Format domains big–endian.

**-littleend:** Format domains little–endian (default).

**-jnt:** A combination of the `-bigend` option and the `-733` option.

**-striproutes:** Removes any source routes (733 or 822) from the header. This removal starts after the first valid domain in each address.

**-stripdomain <domain>:** Like -striproutes, except that only the specified domain is stripped.

**-striptrace:** Remove all trace fields from the header.

**-jntsender <sender>:** This applies the rules of mailgroup note 15, to ensure that the JNT Mail return path correctly identifies the P1 originator. Typically, this will involve adding a Sender Field to the message, and possibly modifying existing trace fields.

**-msgid:** This flag ensures the presence of a message id in the message. If there is no message id, the RFC 822 filter will create one and append it to the header.

**-percent:** This flag indicates that the % character should be treated as a @ character when parsing addresses. This flag also indicates that all domains in addresses should be normalised. By default, only the next hop of an address is normalised.

**-hidelocal <pattern>:** Apply a host-hiding heuristic to "clean-up" mail sent from other hosts on site which is going off site. Pattern can be a simple domain or a domain with wildcard subdomains, for example:

```
*.icl.stc.co.uk
and
stl.stc.co.uk
```

but not domains of the form

```
frodo.*.co.uk
```

*Warning*: this flag should be used with care and should not normally be required.

**-changedomain <from> <to>:** Change occurances of domain from to domain to. This flag is useful when running PP as a gateway between two or more networks and a specific domain is known by different names on different networks. Note that this replacement may only work on normalised domains. So to normalise all domains and guarantee the replacement, the -percent should also be used.

**-fold <number>:** This indicates the length for displaying RFC 822 header fields. The default value is 79; alternately with a value of -1 there will be no folding. Whatever the value, folding will only occur at higher level breaks, and not within an address.

### Body Part Deleting Filters

In the *formdir* directory there is a general shell script that can be run as a filter to remove body parts. It ignores its input and writes out a short message indicating that the body part has been removed. This can be used as a trivial filter in say, fax to ia5, to indicate that a fax body part has been deleted. The out-info string for such a channel might be:

```
out-info='removebp "Group 3 Fax"'
```

An example *tailor* file entry for such a filter is shown in Figure 36.4.

### ODIF filters

There exist some filters that will convert between BBN Slate format and ODIF. These filters are not publicly available as they were developed under an ESPRIT PODA project. However, anyone interested in these filters should contact Prof. Peter Kirstein (P.Kirstein@cs.ucl.ac.uk).

### 36.8.3 The List Channel

This channel should be tailored in a content independent fashion. This means that the following fields should `NOT` be set:

`content-in`

`content-out`

`bptin`

`bptout`

`hdrin`

`hdrout`

Note that it is not possible to mix different forms of addresses on lists. This is because of the different meanings of symbols between the different forms of addressing. For example, with an X.400 address `(a)` is a printable string encoding of the `@` symbol but with an RFC 822 address it is just a comment. This means that lists with X.400 forms of addresses **must** only contain X.400 addresses and must be expanded by a list channel that is tailored with `adrout=x400`. Similarly lists with RFC 822 forms of addresses **must** only contain RFC 822 addresses and must be expanded by a list channel that is tailored with `adrout=822` (this is the default value for the `adrout` field).

It may be necessary to set the field `adr-order` in the tailoring for a list channel. The default for this field is `usonly`. If you have some UK ordering of domains in your lists you should set `adr-order=ukpref` or `adr-order=uspref`.

A valid content independent entry for the list channel is as follows:

```
chan list prog=list,show="List channel",type=both,
          table=list,drchan=dr2rfc
```

The value of the `out-info` field can alter the behaviour of the list channel. The values that can be set in the `out-info` field are:

**`dosublists:`** This enables the expansion of sublists contained within a list. This will improve performance if there are a number of nested lists *BUT* this behaviour may cause problems with the sender field. If a sublist is expanded, it will be submitted with the sender relating to the main list and not relating to the sublist. By default, the expansion of sublists is disabled.

**`linked:`**

**`notlinked:`** These two values indicate the mechanism used for resubmitting the body of a message. If the `linked` value is set, the body of the message is resubmitted using the UNIX link facility. This is more efficient in terms of speed and space. If the `notlinked` value is set, the body of the message is resubmitted by copying. The default behaviour is `linked`.

### 36.8.4 The RFC 1148 Channels

The *P2toRFC* and *RFCtoP2* channels perform RFC 1148 conversions on the headers of messages. The tailoring of these channels is as with other channels with the proviso that the conv entry is set to `1148`.

The output of the 1148 channels maybe be altered by use of the `out-info` tailor entry.

With the *P2toRFC*, if the `out-info` entry contains the string `uk`, all rfc822 addresses in the produced header will be output in the uk order of domains.

With the *RFCtoP2*, if the `out-info` entry contains the string `rfc987`, the conversion from rfc822 to P2 will adhere to the RFC 987 mapping rather than the RFC 1148. Note that these mappings are very similar anyway.

### 36.8.5 Shaping Channels

Shaping channels alter the structure of the message. This section describes tailoring requirements of the common shaping channels.

#### RFC 934 Channel

The *rfc934* channel flattens an RFC 822 style message as specified by RFC 934. The tailor file entry for such a channel should be constructed with the following provisos:

**`type`:** This field should be set to `shaper` as the channel alters the shape of the message.

**`content-out`:** This field should contain the value 822 to indicate that it converts contents to RFC 822 format.

Note that the *rfc934* channel only recognises three types of bodyparts: RFC 822 headers, which it recognises as starting with the string `hdr.822`; text bodyparts, which it recognises as being of the form `n.ia5` where `n` is a number; and forwarded messages, which it recognises as being subdirectories. If there is a bodypart in the message that it does not recognise, the *rfc934* channel will fail. The key strings `hdr.822` and `ia5` are hardwired into PP. They can only be changed by editing the relevant entries in the file *Lib/pp/static.c* within the source tree.

#### P2flatten Channel

The *p2flatten* channel combines all the separate components of a message into one file of p2 or p22, depending on how the channel is tailored. The tailor file entry for such a channel should be constructed with the following provisos:

**`type`:** This field should be set to `shaper`, as the channel alters the shape of the message.

`content-out`: This field should contain the content that the channel outputs. It should be either p2 or p22. If it is set to p2, *p2flatten* will output a file of p2 (i.e., a message suitable for transfer via X.400(84)). If it is set to p22, *p2flatten* will output a file of p22 (i.e., a message suitable for transfer via X.400(88)).

#### P2explode Channel

The *p2explode* channel explodes a p2 or p22 message into its separate component bodyparts. The tailor file entry for such a channel should be constructed with the following provisos:

`type`: This field should be set to `shaper` as the channel alters the shape of the message.

`content-in`: This field should contain the inbound content, either p2 or p22.

### 36.8.6 Miscellaneous Channels

Miscellaneous channels groups together the "special" channels required by PP. This section describes tailoring requirements of these "special" channels.

#### Qmgrload Channel

The *qmgrload* channel is used to refresh the QMGR model of the queue by reading the model stored on disc. The only proviso for the tailor file entry of this channel is that the `type` is set to `qmgrload`. This channel takes note of the `out-info` field in the *tailor* file. This, if present, should be a number indicating how many messages to load into the QMGR at one time. It defaults to 50 which is a sensible value for most sites.

#### Msg-Clean Channel

The *msg-clean* channel is used by the QMGR to free the storage associated with a message once all activity to do with that message has finished. For the tailor file entry of this channel, `type` is set to `delete`.

#### Debris Channel

The *debris* channel is used by the QMGR to free any storage which no longer is of interest to the mail system. The *tailor* file entry of this channel should have `type` set to `debris`.

#### Timeout Channel

The *timeout* channel is used to time messages out once they have been around for a given time. The tailor file entry of this channel should have `type` set to `timeout`.

### Dr2rfc Channel

The *dr2rfc* channel constructs receipt notifications or error messages in the form of RFC 822 messages. Once constructed these messages are then submitted to the QMGR for return to the sender. The channel's behaviour can be altered by various key/value pairs which may appear in the `out-info` entry of the channel's tailor entry. These pairs are as follows:

**`order=value`:** If the `value` equals **uk**, *dr2rfc* produces UK-ordered domains in its output. By default, *dr2rfc* produces US-ordered domains.

**`submit=value`:** This alters the method used to submit any return of contents. `value` can have one of two values - `linked` or `copy`. If the value is `linked`, *dr2rfc* will submit the return of contents via the use of links wherever possible. If the value is copy, *dr2rfc* will copy the return of contents on *submit*. The default value is `linked`.

**`return=value`:** This key/value pair tailors the amount of the original message that will be submitted as return of contents. If the value is `all`, the whole of the original message is returned. By default, the return of contents is subject to the constraints described below. Otherwise the value must have the syntax of a number followed by a letter (e.g., 10k or 2000l). This provides an upperbound on certain aspects of the return of contents. The letter must either be an `l` or a **k** indicating which aspect is constrained. `l` constrains the number of lines the return of contents can contain. **k** constrains the size of the return of contents (note that the number before the letter is multiplied by 1000 to get the actual constraint). The default values for these constraints are 5k for the size and 10 lines. Note that return of contents is subject to availability and if available the header of the original message is always returned irrespective of any return of contents constraints.

## 36.9 How Channels Work

A channel is called by the QMGR, and initialised. Then it is told to process a given message and a set of recipients. All of the identified recipients will be on the same MTA, or require the same conversion. The channel will then attempt to do the work. After this it will update the queue in the following way for each recipient:

- If a conversion succeeded, it will increment the reformat counter.
- If a delivery succeeded, it will set the status to DONE or DR, dependent on whether a positive Delivery Report is needed.
- If the operation failed, it will set the status to DR.

If the status is set to DR, the DR should be generated before updating the queue status. When the queue is updated, the QMGR should be informed of the final status of each recipient. The QMGR will then give the channel more work, or close it down. Connections to MTAs should be kept open, the QMGR will attempt to sort the queue by MTA.

# Chapter 37

# PP Tables

This chapter describes the purpose and syntax of the various tables used by PP. There are five basic tables used by PP, the *aliases* table, the *users* table, the *domain* table, the *channel* table and the *or* table. How these are combined and used to deliver and route messages is described below.

There are also a set of tables containing authorisation information and a family of tables that provide mappings between X.400 O/R names and RFC 822 domain names. Specific channels may also have their own tables containing the information they require.

## 37.1 Basic Operation of the Tables

When a message arrives, *submit* identifies if it is to be delivered by the local MTA or if it is to be routed to a remote host/MTA. It does this by first attempting to parse the address, and, if this succeeds, it attempts to validate the address.

If the message is to be delivered by the local MTA, *submit* references the *aliases* table to translate any aliases to the real addresses they point to; and then looks at the *users* table to determine which local channel is appropriate for that address (for example, ordinary *822-local* or *list* channel).

If the message is for a remote host/MTA, *submit* references either the *domain* table to discover the fully-qualified for RFC 822-style addresses, or the *or* table for X.400 style addresses. If necessary the address is mapped from one form to another (e.g., RFC 822 to X.400) by use of the mapping tables *or2rfc* and *rfc2or*. This produces the canonical name for the host. The *channel* table is then used to determine a list of channels that can be used to reach the host in question.

At this stage the channels are sorted in the preferred order of use and then checked in this order for authorisation until a channel or mta or user succeeds. Once this is achieved the necessary reformatting channels are calculated and the message is then accepted.

## 37.2 The General Syntax of Table Entries.

In general, entries in the tables are in the form:

```
<key> ":" <value>
```

The only special character is : which if it appears on the LHS must be preceded by a backslash "\" to escape it. All other characters are copied verbatim. However, some tables undergo further processing and may need other escape sequences.

The purposes and details of the various tables now follow.

## 37.3 The Aliases Table

The *aliases* table governs the handling of aliases for user names. It is used for several reasons. These include:

- Mapping non-users to usernames. (e.g., "postmaster" to some "user").
- Redirecting users who have moved (e.g., "fred" to "fred@foo.edu").
- Rewriting users addresses (e.g., "jpo" to "j.onions").
- Mapping aliases. (e.g., "j.p.onions" to "j.onions").

Entries in this table are constructed as follows:

```
<key> ":" <type>  <value> <qualifier>
```

The `type` describes the user name or address. This may be one of:

**`alias:`** a new address is given, but this name does *not* replace the original value. Aliases are not expanded for originators whereas synonyms are.

**`synonym:`** a new address, this name replaces the original value.

The `<value>` is an address. It can be local or remote.

The `<qualifier>` gives the interpretation of the value. By default this is assumed to be a local user. However, full address can be specified with the appropriate qualifier. These are:

**`822:`** a remote RFC 822 user address is specified.

**`x400:`** a remote X400 user address is specified.

**`external:`** If this qualifier is present the name will not be lookup up again in the *aliases* file. This can be used for complex mappings.

A value resulting from searching the alias table is then used as the key for repeated search if the key is an **alias** or **synonym** without any qualifier. This continues until it fails, either by not finding another alias or by detecting a loop. If the final value is for a local address then that value will be used as a key to look up the *users* table; if the final value is an RFC 822 address an RFC 822 delivery channel will be used; or if the final value is an X400 address an X400 delivery channel will be used.

The format is best illustrated by a sample extract of the table as shown in Figure 37.1.

```
################### extract of 'aliases' table ################
#
mailgroup-request:alias Irene.Hassell
postmaster:alias Irene.Hassell
pp:alias postmaster
#
a.dacruz:synonym Alina.DaCruz
alina:synonym Alina.DaCruz
#
jpo:alias jpo@uk.ac.nott.cs 822
#
pc:alias "/I=P/S=Cowen/O=xtel/PRMD=xtel services/ADMD= /c=gb/" x400
#
```

Figure 37.1: Example of Alias Table

The table includes an entry for a local alias `mailgroup-request` The value `Irene.Hassell` is used as a key for a further search, but will not replace the alias in the message header; if no match is found, and since the entry is of type `alias`, the address is assumed to be a local one and used for accessing the *user* table. Also, if a local submission arrives from `mailgroup-request` then checking and authorisation will be done on the basis of `mailgroup-request` rather than `Irene.Hassell`.

The next entry indicates that `a.dacruz` and `alina` are both synonyms for `Alina.DaCruz`. Here, the user's address will be converted to Alina.DaCruz, and this value will be used in future table searches.

An entry is given for a remote RFC 822 user, `jpo`. The value of `jpo@uk.ac.nott.cs` is parsed and routed on as a remote RFC 822 address.

Then follows an entry for a remote X400 user, pc: The value

```
"/I=P/S=Cowen/O=xtel/PRMD=xtel services/ADMD= /c=gb/"
```

would be parsed and routed on an X.400 delivery channel. The quotes (") are needed as the entry contains a space which is normally a separator.

## 37.4 The Users Table

The *users* table determines the local delivery channel for a particular local user. It is formatted in the form:

```
<username> ":" <channel> [ <mta> ]
                  ["," <channel> [ <mta> ] ...]
```

`Channel`: specifies the name of a local delivery channel on `mta`.

`Mta`: is the local machine on which the mailbox resides. If no MTA is indicated, the channel may be used for delivery by any local machine. If an MTA is present and is not the local machine (`loc_dom_mta`) then the message will be sent to that MTA by an appropriate channel. This should only be used for internal shuffling between several MTAs that are responsible for one domain.

A user can have several channels for local delivery. For example, in Figure 37.2 `John.Taylor` can have his mail delivered either by the *822-local* channel or by the *slocal* channel. Which of these two channels is actually used for delivery depends on the format of the message being delivered. This allows a user to have, for instance, X.400 format mail delivered by one channel, and RFC 822 mail by another channel.

```
##################### extract of 'users' table ####################
#
Alina.DaCruz:822-local vs2.cs.ucl.ac.uk
Steve.Kille:822-local pyr1.cs.ucl.ac.uk
John.Taylor:822-local vs2.cs.ucl.ac.uk, slocal vs2.cs.ucl.ac.uk
Postie.Pat:822-local vs2.cs.ucl.ac.uk
x400-users:list
warning:shell
#
```

Figure 37.2: Example of Users Table

Figure 37.2 illustrates how the various local users will receive mail and on which machines their mailboxes reside. An entry for a distribution list is also shown, and the entry for `warning` shows the *shell* channel rather than a local delivery channel.

## 37.5 The Domain Table

The *domain* table is used by *submit* to derive a fully-qualified domain from any aliases or short-form names. See Section 39.6 on page 478 for a description of how to go about constructing this table. Entries in this table are encoded in the form:

```
<dmn> ":" <key> ["=" <value>] [<key>["="<value>]] ...
```

dmn has two possible constructions:

***.dmn** This construction is used to specify partial domain matches. Unless altered by the min and max keys described below, constructions of this form will match domains with at least one subdomain (i.e., min=1 and max=infinity).

**dmn** This construction is used for exact matches.

There are several possible types for key:

**synonym=<dmn-name>:** This identifies a synonym. The dmn should be replaced by <dmn-name> and parsing continues by looking for the new dmn in the domain table.

**mta=<dmn-name>:** This identifies the domain name to replace dmn with. If no key is present in the rest of the entry, then <dmn-name> is used for lookup in the channel table.

**key=<chan-ref>:** This identifies the key for lookup in the channel table.

**local=<subtbl-name>:** This indicates that <dmn> is local. With no <subtbl-name> then this indicates that <dmn> is a local reference with no special tables. With a <subtbl-name> specified, this indicates separate local alias and user tables. This feature is used when one MTA is supporting multiple local organisations, each with its own user and alias tables. This is described in Section 37.8.

**max=<number>:** This specifies the maximum number of subdomains this entry can have. This key is only applicable to <dmn> entries of the partial form (i.e., with the suffix *.)

**min=<number>:** This specifies the minimum number of sub domains this entry can have. Again this is only valid with partial domain constructions.

**valid:** This means that the dmn is a valid partial domain but cannot be directly mapped to a fully qualified domain.

The following examples will illustrate some uses of the syntax:

```
*.edu:key=edu
*.fr:key=fr
fr:key=fr
cs.nott.ac.uk:mta=cs.nott.ac.uk
*.cs.nott.ac.uk:mta=cs.nott.ac.uk max=1
```

This implies the following actions:

- The edu domain will match all domain names with the most significant component of edu and at least one subdomain. Thus, the hosts ucbarpa.berkeley.edu, prep.ai.mit.edu and foo.edu would all be matched by this entry. However an address of user@edu would not be matched. The key edu will be used in the lookup of the channel table to find delivery channels to edu.
- The two exmaples fr and *.fr together match all domain names with the most significant component of fr. Note that this includes fr itself.
- The cs.nott.ac.uk domain will match the explicit name of cs.nott.ac.uk. The second entry, *.cs.nott.ac.uk will allow at most one domain component below cs.nott.ac.uk, such as john.cs.nott.ac.uk.

An example segment of a domain table is shown in Figure 37.3.

```
# top level entries
edu:mta = 1:*
mil:mta = 1:*
pt:mta = 1:*
# local entries
cs.ucl.ac.uk:mta =
cs.ucl.ac:synonym cs.ucl.ac.uk
cs.ucl:synonym cs.ucl.ac.uk
cs.nott.ac.uk:mta cs.nott.ac.uk
# note the above is equivalent to
# cs.nott.ac.uk:mta =
cs.nott.ac:synonym cs.nott.ac.uk
cs.nott:synonym cs.nott.ac.uk
cs:synonym cs.nott.ac.uk
#
# NRS derived entries
alass.nott.ac.uk:mta alass.nottingham.ac.uk
alass.nott.ac:synonym alass.nottingham.ac.uk
alass.nott:synonym alass.nottingham.ac.uk
alass.nottingham.ac.uk:mta =
alass.nottingham.ac:synonym alass.nottingham.ac.uk
alass.nottingham:synonym alass.nottingham.ac.uk
clan.nott.ac.uk:mta clan.nottingham.ac.uk
clan.nott.ac:synonym clan.nottingham.ac.uk
clan.nott:synonym clan.nottingham.ac.uk
clan.nottingham.ac.uk:mta =
clan.nottingham.ac:synonym clan.nottingham.ac.uk
clan.nottingham:synonym clan.nottingham.ac.uk
```

Figure 37.3: Example of Domain Table

## 37.6 The O/R Address Table

The *or* family of tables provides mappings between X.400 O/R names and RFC 822 domain names, to be used by channels concerned with conversion in accordance with the RFC 1148. Lines are encoded in the form:

```
<key> ":" <type> <value> ...
```

In the `<key>` field, the character ":" and "." must be preceded by a "\" character.

Values are separated by white space, and so any space characters must similarly be preceded by either "\" or else the value should be encapsulated in double quotes.

The characters "\" and "." in a `<value>` field must always be preceded by a "\".

The *or* table is used to evaluate O/R addresses. The `<key>` is encoded as dmn-orname (see RFC 1148). The default algorithm for O/R Name analysis should be considered as "tree-walking." The O/R address components are sorted, and components are looked up: first level 1; then level 1 + level 2 and so on. So repeated lookups are carried out, using this table.

There are four possible types on the RHS, much like the domain table:

`valid`: This means that this part of the tree is OK.

`mta <mtaname>`: This identifies the MTA `<mtaname>` as being associated with this vertex of the tree. This `<mtaname>` is a key to the PP channel tables. The search should *not* stop at this point, as further tree searching may determine a more optimal site.

`synonym <dmn-orname>`: This identifies a synonym, and indicates that all O/R components matched so far should be replaced with those identified on the RHS, and the search should now resume from the root. For historical reasons, this encoding has a second equivalent form; `alias <dmn-orname>`.

`local <subdom-name>`: This identifies a local O/R Address. The remainder of the O/R address should be used to determine a local mailbox. As with the similar feature in the domain table, this feature is used when one MTA is supporting multiple local organisations, each with their own user and alias tables. This is described in Section 37.8.

Figure 37.4 gives an example which shows the validity of some Country, ADMD, and PRMD values, and indicates which MTAs will deal with which PRMDs. The MTA value given here is internal to the PP lookup system, providing a key with which to reference the channel table.

```
#
# extract of 'or' table
#
#       -*** gb ***-
#
C$GB:valid
C$UK:synonym C$GB
ADMD$GOLD 400.C$GB:valid
PRMD$UK\.AC.ADMD$GOLD 400.C$GB:valid
#
#
#       -*** sites connecting via gold 400 ADMD ***-
#
PRMD$DIGITAL.ADMD$GOLD 400.C$GB:mta bt-gold
PRMD$TELECOM GOLD.ADMD$GOLD\ 400.C$GB:mta bt-gold
OU$CS.O$UCL.PRMD$UK\.AC.ADMD$GOLD\ 400.C$GB:local
#
#
#       -*** france ***-
#
C$FR:valid
ADMD$PTT.C$FR:mta emu-france
ADMD$ATLAS.C$FR:mta emu-france
PRMD$BULLMTS.ADMD$ATLAS.C$FR:mta MYBULL
PRMD$DERIEUX.ADMD$ATLAS.C$FR:mta persona
#
```

Figure 37.4: Example of Or Table

## 37.7 The Channel Table

Every remote host/MTA has an entry in this table. *Submit* uses it to discover the channel, and in some cases relaying host, that must be used to send to the host in question. See Section 39.6 on page 479 for a method of building this table. The format of an entry has the form:

```
<key> ":" [ <mtaname> ] "("<channel>")"
          ["," [ <mtaname> ] "("<channel>")" ...]
```

**key:** is the fully qualified name derived from the *domain* table.

**mtaname/channel:** the mtaname derived from this lookup will be used as a key in the appropriate channel table. If there is no mtaname present, then the MTA key is reached directly through that channel. This sort of action is appropriate if the channel uses external information (such as the DNS) to look up the domain.

There may be a number of possible channels for each host. Figure 37.5 illustrates an extract of this table.

An entry with an empty RHS is allowed and indicates that this is a valid domain name, but not a valid delivery route. This is usually used to allow checking to proceed when the address should be mapped to a different form of address.

## 37.8 Supporting Multiple Organizations on One MTA

In some situations one may want PP to behave like two or more distinct mail hubs, e.g., cs.nott.ac.uk and physics.nott.ac.uk. This behaviour is possible using the 822-synonym and x400-synonym keywords in the *aliases* table and the local keyword in the *domain* table.

To get this behaviour, the following actions should be followed.

First create, in separate files, the *aliases* and the *users* tables for each hub. These files should have the names of the form hubname-aliases and hubname-users. So for physics.nott.ac.uk, create the *aliases* table physics-aliases and the *users* table physics-users.

Then place one entry for each local hub in the *domain* table. This entry should have the form:

```
<fullname> ":" "local=" <hubname>
```

Now for physics.nott.ac.uk create the following entry in the table:

```
#
#
a.cs.uiuc.edu:a.cs.uiuc.edu(smtp)
#
bsec.abcy.uwist.ac.uk:bsec.abcy.uwist.ac.uk(gb-janet)
bt-gold:bt-gold(x400out84)
bte:bte(x400out84)
abcl.co.uk:ukc.ac.uk(gb-janet),ukc.ac.uk(gb-pss)
btvax.ulster.ac.uk:btvax.ulster.ac.uk(gb-janet)
bull:bull(x400out84)
bunny.ulcc.ac.uk:bunny.ulcc.ac.uk(gb-janet)
#
emu-france:emu-france(x400out84)
#
torch.co.uk:ukc.ac.uk(gb-janet),stl.stc.co.uk(gb-pss)
#
# These are resolved directly by the DNS - no relay
edu:(smtp)
gov:(smtp)
com:(smtp)
us:(smtp)
mil:(smtp)
org:(smtp)
```

Figure 37.5: Example of Channel Table

```
physics.nott.ac.uk:local=physics
```

Finally an entry for each user in each hub should be placed in the main *aliases* file. This entry should have the type `822-synonym` and/or the `x400-synonym`.

With these actions taken, PP will then act like two or more hubs.

For example for inbound message, if a message is addressed to the mailbox `jpo@physics.nott.ac.uk` then the lookup in the *domain* table would identify this as a local address for the hub with the name `physics`. PP would then look up the tables `physics-aliases` and `physics-users` to find out how to deliver the message.

On the outbound side, if `jpo` sent out a message, his user agent would probably fill in his address in terms of the default local hub (`cs.nott.ac.uk` in this case). PP could then correct this address to refer to the right hub by looking up the information placed in the main *aliases* file (`822-synonym` and `x400-synonym` entries).

## 37.9 RFC 1148 Mapping Tables

These mappings are used in gateways to convert between X.400 addressing and RFC 822 addressing. The mappings involved are not algorithmic making necessary the use of such tables.

### 37.9.1 The O/R to RFC 822 Table

The table *or2rfc*, exemplified in Figure 37.6, is for mapping OR names into RFC 822 addresses. The `<key>` is encoded as domain-syntax (see RFC 987 and RFC 1026) and `value` as dmn-orname. The longest possible match is sought.

### 37.9.2 The RFC 822 to O/R table

Performing exactly the reverse operation is *rfc2or*, which has the `<key>` encoded as dmn-orname and the `<value>` as domain-syntax. An example of the format is given in Figure 37.7.

### 37.9.3 The Known RFC 1148 Gateway Table

The *rfc1148gate* table has the same syntax as the *rfc2or* table. Its entries represent gateways between X.400 and RFC 822 (via RFC 1148). This table is used in the cases where RFC 822 messages are relayed across an X.400 link. In such cases mapping to X.400 addresses may not always make sense as there will effectively be routing information encapsulated in the address. Normally this would cause the message to fail. However, if it is known that the destination is an RFC 1148 gateway, then the mapping can proceed in the expectation that the other end can unwrap the message.

```
#
#       -*** general GB ***-
#
PRMD$UK\.AC.ADMD$GOLD 400.C$GB:ac.uk
ADMD$GOLD 400.C$GB:gold-400.gb
#
#       -*** via gold 400 ADMD ***-
#
PRMD$TELECOM GOLD.ADMD$GOLD 400.C$GB:telecom-gold.gold-400.gb
PRMD$DIGITAL.ADMD$GOLD 400.C$GB:digital.gold-400.gb
#
#       -*** france ***-
#
ADMD$ptt.C$fr:ptt.fr
PRMD$aristote.ADMD$ptt.C$fr:aristote.fr
PRMD$BULLMTS.ADMD$ATLAS.C$FR:bullmts.fr
#
```

Figure 37.6: Example of or2rfc Table

```
#
# extract of 'rfc2or' table
#
gold-400.gb:ADMD$GOLD 400.C$GB
#
#       -*** via gold 400 ADMD ***-
#
telecom-gold.gold-400.gb:PRMD$TELECOM GOLD.ADMD$GOLD 400.C$GB
digital.gold-400.gb:PRMD$DIGITAL.ADMD$GOLD 400.C$GB
#
#
#       -*** france ***-
#
fr:PRMD$fnet.ADMD$ptt.C$fr
ptt.fr:ADMD$PTT.C$Fr
aristote.fr:PRMD$aristote.ADMD$PTT.C$Fr
bullmts.fr:PRMD$BULLMTS.ADMD$ATLAS.C$FR
derieux.fr:PRMD$DERIEUX.ADMD$ATLAS.C$FR
#
```

Figure 37.7: Example of rfc2or Table

An example RFC 1148 gateway file is shown in Figure 37.8.

```
ca:O$ubc.PRMD$cdn.ADMD$telecom\.canada.C$ca
uk:OU$CS.O$UCL.PRMD$UK\.AC.ADMD$GOLD
```

Figure 37.8: Example of RFC 1148 Gateway Table

## 37.10 The 822 Local Table

The *ch.local* table is an example of a table accessed by different channels; both *822-local* and *slocal* channels use it in order to find out where to deposit mail to a specific mailbox address, to be dealt with by the user agent. The format is of the form "key=value" on the RHS. The following table of key/value pairs are allowed:

**uid** The numeric user id to deliver the message as.

**gid** The numeric group id to deliver the message as.

**username** A username found in the password file. If this entry is set, it sets default for uid,gid,shell,home and directory.

**directory** the directory to deliver the message in.

**mailbox** The name of the mailbox if default delivery is being done.

**shell** The user's shell.

**home** The user's home directory.

**mailformat** The default format to deliver mail in; this can be either pp or unix for sendmail compatible style (the default is pp).

**restricted** this is set to true if the user is restricted. In restricted mode the user cannot run arbitrary programs on delivery.

**mailfilter** The mailfilter file to use. This defaults to the name of the mailfilter global tailor variable in the users home directory. A value of none disables this feature.

**sysmailfilter** The system default mailfilter file. This defaults to the global tailor entry. A keyword of none disables this facility.

**searchpath** The directory to look for binaries that the user can run in restricted mode.

**opts** other options; not currently used.

If the `resticted` mode is in force, then the *.mailfilter* file processing is reduced in functionality as follows:

- The user is not allowed to set the variable PATH to search other directories for programs. (Actually this variable can be set, it is just ignored.)
- The processes executed by the `pipe` command must be in the directory named in `searchpath` (defaults to `USRBINDIR` defined in the *Make.defs* file).
- The processes executed by the `pipe` command must be executable by the system call *exec*(2). (E.g. redirection and shell syntax will not be obeyed).

*Note*: for compatability with earlier releases the following format is allowed:

```
name ":" <unix ID> [<home directory> [<file>]]
```

For an entry in this table to be valid, it must either contain at least a UNIX login id, or have a userid/groupid/directory to deliver to.

For example:

```
Alina.DaCruz:username=alina home=/cs/users/vs1/alina
John.Taylor:username=jtaylor
Postie.Pat:username=pp
bug-filer:uid=32767 gid=1001 directory=/usr/spool/mail bugs
```

## 37.11 The X.400 (1984/1988) Outbound Table

This table is used by the outbound X.400 channels, allowing them to map the host name to the information needed for addressing and connecting to the remote MTA. The key in this table is the value representing the MTA derived from the "mtaname" field of the *channel* table. The value is a set of `key=value` fields separated by white space and/or commas.

```
mta key:rmta=xx,rpass=xx,rpsap='"591"/Janet=000005110000',
```

The `mta key` is the key from the address lookup. This is the remote host to which the outgoing connection it to be made. The following keys are recognised in the value field:

`lmta`: The name of the local mtaname to pass in the RTS connect parameters. This defaults to local site name if not set.

`lpass`: The passwd of the local site to pass in the RTS connect parameters. This defaults to the default password specified in the *tailor* file.

`rmta`: The name of the remote MTA to pass in the RTS connect parameters. If this is not set, then no authentication will be specified in the RTS connect.

**rpass:** The name of the remote password to pass in the RTS connect parameters. There is no default for this and it should be set if the `rmta` is set.

**rpsap:** The remote presentation address. This is specified in the string encoded format. Note that session selectors and presentation selectors should always be absent in the 1984 RTS.

**lpsap:** The local presentation address. This is only necessary if you need to claim to originate from a specific selector or network address. Normally this parameter is not specified.

**mode:** The mode of RTS connection. This is either `mon` for monologue (the default) or `twa` for two way alternate. This only governs the mode passed initially, it does not imply that the channel will work in TWA mode.

**type:** The type of RTS connection. This is one of the following:

| Value | Meaning |
|---|---|
| 1984 | Use the 1984 protocol mode (default). |
| 1988-X410 | Use the 1988 X.410 mode protocol, |
| 1988-normal | Use the 1988 normal mode protocol. |
| 1988 | Use the 1988 normal mode protocol. |

Obviously, this information is dependent on the capabilities of the channel (a 1984-based channel will not be able to use the 1988 protocol).

**trynext:** A key to another entry in the table. If a connection using the current information fails, look up this key and try making a connection using that data.

**tracing:** The style of tracing information to use. It may take one of the following values:

| Value | Meaning |
|---|---|
| admd | Remove all but the first tracing component. |
| nointernal | Remove all internal tracing components. |
| local-internal | Keep only internal trace related to the current PRMD. |
| all | keep all tracing information |

The `admd` mode should only be used when talking to a particularly restrictive ADMD. Again, it depends on the capabilities of the channel how closely this information can be followed.

**rname:** The "real" name of the MTA. This is an entry that is suitable for lookup in the domain table. It is not used for the outbound channel.

**fix-orig:** This applies an on-the-fly change to the originator address. The syntax is

```
"fix-orig=" <old-or> "->" <new-or>
```

and might be applied as

```
fix-orig="/ADMD= /C=GB/->/ADMD=Gold 400/C=GB/
```

to change the ADMD from space, to `Gold 400` in the originator for outgoing messages to specific hosts.

**other:** Other information. This is a string and is interpreted by the channel to allow other types of operation to be specified. It is not currently used in the X.400 outbound channels.

If an entry with a key `default` exists in the table, then this may be used to set default setting for all entries. The value `default` is looked up first and values filled in from that setting, then the real entry is looked up and those values override the default entry.

An example is shown in Figure 37.9 (lines are folded for clarity).

```
default:lmta="us",lpass=" ",
germany-nixdorf:rmta="nme",rpsap='Int-X25(80)=26245300042203'
france-derieux:rmta="persona",rpsap='Int-X25(80)=208075200131'
france-reunir:rmta="sunir.reunir.fr",
               rpsap='Int-X25(80)=20803500034996'
pp-nottingham:rmta="pp.cs.nott.ac.uk",
               rpsap='"591"/Janet=000021000018+PID+03010100'
vs2.cs.ucl.ac.uk:rmta="vs2.cs.ucl.ac.uk",
               rpsap='"591"/Internet=vs2.cs.ucl.ac.uk'
```

Figure 37.9: Example of X.400 Outbound Channel Table

## 37.12 The X.400 (1984/1988) Inbound Table

This table is used by the inbound X.400 channels, and allows the channels to obtain the MTA name and other information from the OSI calling address. The syntax is the same as the X.400 outbound table, only the key is different.

The key here is the information given in the session connection of the remote calling host; the values are as indicated for the outbound table. It is encoded in the string encoding for presentation addresses using no macro substitution. Therefore, the keys look pretty horrible. It is usual to maintain these tables with keys in macro form and run them through the utility *nsapexpand* to expand the macros.

The matching of incoming information with an entry in this table provides the major security checking. Again an entry `default` in the table may be used to default many of the fields.

An example is shown in Figure 37.10 (again lines are folded for clarity).

```
default:lmta="us",lpass="bar"
"3459"/Int-X25(80)=208006030203:rname="france-kwai",
                   rmta="kwai.inria.fr"
"425"/Int-X25(80)=26245622190113:rname="germany-ibm",
                   rmta="foo",rpass="foo"
Janet=000021000018:rname="pp-nottingham",rmta="cs.nott.ac.uk"
Janet=000005111680:rname="pp-vs2",rmta="cs.ucl.ac.uk"
```

Figure 37.10: Example of X.400 inbound Channel table

## 37.13 The List Table

The *ch.list* table is used by the *list* channel to expand local distribution lists. Entries in this table have the format:

```
<listname> ":" [<moderator> "|" ...] ","
      file=<filename> | <mail address> "|" ... ","
      description
```

`listname`: The name of the distribution list, e.g., `listname` or in X.400 perhaps `/S=listname/`. Note that in order for the list to form a valid local address, the local part of the name, `listname` in the above examples, must have an entry in the local *users* table, specifying that messages addressed to the list should be delivered via the list channel.

`moderator`: The UNIX ids/login names of the moderators of the list. This element of the table entry is purely for the use of the distribution list management tool, *mlist* (see Part XI (The PP Manual: User's Guide)). Anyone with one of the specified uids may use *mlist* to modify the contents of the list.

`file`: The file containing the members of the list. If `<filename>` is not a fully qualified pathname, the required file will be assumed to be under the *tbldfldir* directory structure. The format of such files is one member's address per line. Note that the file must exist for *mlist* to be able to be used on the corresponding list.

`mail address`: An address of a member of the list. Note that because they are specified in the list table itself, *mlist* cannot be used to modify such members.

`description`: A short description of the purpose of the list. This description is output by *mlist* when requested.

Note that in order to form a valid entry in the list table, each entry must be on one line and must contain three and only three commas.

Comment line in tables start with a `#`. The list table extends this mechanism further. Comment lines that are printed by *mlist* start with `#Comment:`. This allows the list table to have two levels of comments, one for the editor of the list table and one for the user of *mlist*.

```
#
# extract of 'list' table
#
#Comment: -*- Example lists -*-
filelist:pac,file=/crg/pp/mainlist,a list with members in a file
strlist:pp|pac,p.cowen|j.onions|g.lunt,a list with members in line
mixedlist:jpo,j.onions|file=mixedlist,another list
#
```

Figure 37.11: Example of List Table

If you have a large sendmail alias file to convert, you may find the utility *make-lists*(8) in the *Tools* directory. This utility attempts to convert lists of names into a format suitable for use in the list channel of PP. Note: it does *not* convert all alias table entries, only lists.

## 37.14 The Shell Table

The *ch.shell* table is referenced by the *shell* channel when converting from the recipient address to the commands to execute in its place. Entries in this table have the format:

```
<address> ":" <user id> "," [<timeout period>['|'<qualifier>]]
            "," <command line to execute>
```

`address`: specifies the recipient address, e.g., `shellprog` or the X.400 form `/S=shellprog/`. Note that in order for this to form a valid local address, the local part, `shellprog` in the examples, must have an entry in the local *users* table, specifying that messages sent to the address should be delivered via the *shell* channel.

**user id:** specifies the user to run as when executing the commands. This id is resolved using */etc/passwd*. Alternatively it may be specified as <uid>/<gid> to run as an arbitrary user and group.

**timeout period:** specifies how long, in seconds, the commands should be allowed to run before the *shell* channel kills them off. If the timeout period is not specified, the commands are allowed to run for the default period of time, five minutes. If the period is zero then the *shell* channel will not kill the commands off.

**qualifier:** qualifies the behaviour of the shell channel. This qualifier is optional appended to the timeout period with a | seperating the two values. If the qualifier is set to the string solo then the shell channel will restart(fork) the command line for each bodypart i.e. solo processing.

**command line:** specifies the command line to execute. If the program name is not a fully qualified pathname, the program is assumed to be under the directory specified by *chandir*. Arguments of the form **$(key)** will be expanded as described in Table 36.1 on page 407.

When running, the *shell* channel pipes all the message body parts, in order, to the program's standard input. The *shell* channel understands an exit code of 0 as success and otherwise as failure.

An example of a *shell* table is shown in Figure 37.12.

```
##################### extract of 'shell' table ####################
#
nullshell:pac,60,sh -c "/bin/cat > /dev/null"
usefulshell:jpo,,usefulshellprog $(ua_id)
lynx:pp,0|solo,/usr/ucb/lpr -Plynx
#
```

Figure 37.12: Example of Shell Table

## 37.15 Authentication

Components of PP must do appropriate checking that they are being invoked correctly. Note that authentication is complementary to authorisation. It is also a prerequisite.

### 37.15.1 Submit Authentication

*Submit* needs to verify the source of an inbound message. For messages from an inbound channel (protocol server) accessing the MTA Abstract Service, this means verification of the UID of the channel (typically to be "root" or "pp"). For the MTS Abstract Service, the identity of the P1 originator must be verified. These two verifications use the same mechanism. There are two cases:

1. Submission from a local process using pipes. In this case, the UID of the invoking process is available, and can be the basis for authentication.
2. For remote submission, the UID is not available, and so a password based mechanism is used. This may also be used locally.

A password and the corresponding name are carried in the initial protocol handshake. This may be overridden for later messages.

Each (inbound) channel has an "auth-table" variable, which identifies a table which is used in the manner described below. The authentication table has three columns. These have meaning:

1. String-encoded address, in the preferred format of the channel:
   - X.400 O/R Address.
   - RFC 822 address.
2. List of valid UIDs.
3. Password (as in /etc/passwd).

Example files:

```
#
# Start of dummy 822 file
#
S.Kille@cs.ucl.ac.uk:steve|aiohpefcn

#
# Dummy X.400 file
#
/i=s/s=kille/ou=cs/o=ucl/prmd=uk.ac/admd= /c=gb/:steve,pp
/i=j/s=onions/o=nott/prmd=uk.ac/admd=gold 400/c=gb/:jonions
```

## 37.16 PP Authorisation

Authorisation is applied after address parsing and validation, to establish whether the message is permitted to be transferred on a per recipient basis. Address lookup may establish several possible outbound channels for each recipient; authorisation selects one of these after applying tests based on entries in the three authorisation tables ***auth.channel***, ***auth.mta***, and ***auth.user***.

Access policy for channel pairs ( inbound + outbound ) determines how the rights for the four entities: sender, recipient, sending MTA, and destination MTA, are to be interpreted. ( "Rights" means one of the four values in/out/both/none and a fifth value "unset" to indicate that no table entry is present.)

The intention is that one of these four may be shown to be authorising the message (i.e., willing to pay for it).

It should be noted that authorisation is not applied to delivery report messages.

### 37.16.1 Access Policy

The access policy is one of the following:

**none:** Message may not be transferred.

**free:** No constraints on the four entities.

**block ( i.e., "blockable" ):** - at least one of the four must enable the message by specifying "in" or "both" for the inbound channel and "out" or "both" for the outbound channel. The message may not be transferred if none of the four methods enable it. Therefore the default is to not let messages through.

**negative:** Any one of the four may stop transfer by disabling the message. This implies the default state is to let everything through, and special cases are stopped by explicit configuration.

When determining rights for a proposed transfer the following algorithm is followed:

- Determine the inbound and outbound channels and look up this pair in the *auth.channel* file.

  If there is no entry in this file, take the default from the tailoring variable as the access policy for the channel.

- If the access policy is free or none, then the message is allowed through or rejected respectively.

- If the access policy is negative, check the MTA and user tables, *auth.mta,* and *auth.user* to see if this route is explicitly disabled.

- If the access policy is block, check the user and MTA tables to see if the route is explicitly enabled.

### 37.16.2 Table Formats

There are three tables associated with authorisation, plus the tailor variables. The first of these tables is the *auth.channel* table. This contains the overall policies for channel to channel relaying. As the key, the table has the syntax:

```
<inchannel> "->" <outchannel>
```

If no value is found for the above, then as a fallback the values

```
<inchannel> "->" "*"
"*" "->" <outchannel>
"*" "->" "*"
```

are checked in that order.

The values that the table can have are as follows:

`<policy>`: Any of the above mentioned policies (`free`, `block` etc.).

`warnsender=<file>`: Send a warning message to the sender, with text taken from the given file.

`warnrecipient=<file>`: Send a warning message to the recipient with text taken from the given file.

`sizelimit=<digits>`: Enforce the given size limit on messages. No messages larger than this size will be relayed. This is obeyed regardless of the overall policy of the channel. (I.e., A channel may be marked as free with a sizelimit, and the sizelimit will still be enforced.)

`test`: This setting modifies the checking procedure always to allow the message through. However, all the checking is carried out and the result is logged. This is useful to test out the results of a setting for a while before fully applying them.

An example of this format might look like the following:

```
822-local->pss:free
822-local->local:block
822-local->slocal:free
822-local->smtp:free, sizelimit=5000, warnsender=smtpwarnsender
822-local->janet:block, sizelimit=4000
x400in84->x400out84:none
x400in84->local:free
822-local->x400out84:block,sizelimit=10000,warnsender=restricted
smtp->smtp:block, test
```

The next table is the MTA policy table in file *auth.mta*. This governs the policy for a given MTA if the channel is not `free` or none. The key used in this table is the source MTA and the destination MTA. Each of these are looked up separately to determine policies.

The allowed values for this field are any of the following in a comma-separated list:

`<channel>=<direction>`: This specifies for given channels what directions are allowed for this MTA. The possible directions are:

**in:** Allow inbound traffic for this channel.

**out:** Allow outbound traffic for this channel.

**both:** Allow both inbound and outbound traffic for this channel.

**none:** Allow no access for this channel.

**default=<direction>:** This specifies the default directions that traffic can flow in the absence of a particular channel being specified.

**requires=<pattern>:** This MTA requires that the user being authorised to send to this matches the given pattern. This is a standard regular expression as specified in *regex* (3).

**excludes=<pattern>:** The MTA requires that the user being authorised does not match the given pattern.

**bodypart-excludes=<bodyparts>:** This specifies a list of bodyparts that the MTA will not accept. These bodyparts are taken from the list of standard bodyparts as described in Section 36.2.1 on page 388.

**sizelimit=<digits>:** The MTA will not relay messages larger than the given sizelimit.

An example of this table might look like the following:

```
vs2.cs.ucl.ac.uk:default=both, smtp=out, x400out84=out,
        822-local=in, excludes="A.DaCruz.*"
localhost:default=in, x400in84=out, smtp=both,
        822-local=none, sizelimit=654321
```

(Lines are folded for readability.)

Finally, the user table is where both the recipient and originator are looked up to determine access rights if none of the other tests proves conclusive. The key is either the full normalized name of the user, or if local, just the local part of the name. The values may contain any of the following:

**<channel>=<direction>:** This specifies, much as for the MTA, what directions are allowed for this user.

**default=<direction>:** This gives the default directions allowed for this user.

**bodypart-excludes=<bodyparts>:** A list of bodyparts that are not allowed to be sent to the user.

**sizelimit=<digits>:** Disallow messages larger than this sizelimit.

An example of the user authorisation table is:

```
j.taylor@cs.ucl.ac.uk:default=both
/I=J/S=Taylor/OU=cs/O=ucl/PRMD=uk.ac/ADMD=gold 400/C=gb/:\
  bodypart-excludes=g3fax|dmd, sizelimit=100000, 822-local=both
a.dacruz@cs.ucl.ac.uk:default=both
s.kille@cs.ucl.ac.uk:default=both
p.cowen@computer-science.nottingham.ac.uk:default=both, \
       822-local=in, x400out84=none
j.onions@computer-science.nottingham.ac.uk:default=both
```

### 37.16.3 Statistical Logging

Each line in the statistics log ("stat") either logs the status of inbound messages, or delivery reports that are generated, or notes a message that is delivered. Amongst the parameters logged are:

- A success indicator ( e.g., "ok" or "DR" ).
- Unique message id.
- A P1 message ID.
- Inbound channel→outbound channel.
- Sender.
- Sending MTA.
- Recipient.
- Destination MTA.
- Message size.
- A diagnostic message.

Fields are space-delimited and double quoted where necessary.

Duplicate recipients are eliminated (second and subsequent) if there is an exact match on the 822 or X.400 address (as appropriate), *not* the original entry.

Channel binding is performed after all other tests have been passed, and takes into account any body parts actually received but not specified in the message header.

Unsuccessful recipients are flagged to generate nondelivery reports.

## 37.17 QMGR Authentication

The *MTAconsole* can connect to the *qmgr* in two distinct modes. These are

`no authentication`**:** In this mode, no authentication is done for the user.

`weak authentication`**:** In this mode a name and password are passed across in the bind, so there is some limited authentication of the initiator.

When an incoming call is received by the qmgr, authentication information is checked in the *auth.qmgr* table. The format of this table is:

```
<name> ":" "passwd=" <password> "," "rights=" <rights>
```

These parameters are interpreted in the following way:

**name:** This is the name given in the bind parameters. If the connection was bound with no authentication, the name **anon** is used for the lookup. If the name is not found in the table, then if the user bound with authentication, the request is refused. If the user bound without authentication, and the name **anon** is not present in the table, then limited access is allowed.

**passwd:** This value takes an encrypted passwd, which can be generated with the utility *mkpasswd*. The password passed in the bind information is encrypted and compared against this value if present. If no **passwd** field is present, then a passwd is not required.

**rights:** This value is used to indicate the rights that the initiator will be allowed. It may be one of the following values:

| Value | Meaning |
|---|---|
| none | The association is refused. |
| limited | The initiator is allowed to examine the queue but not to change any parameters. |
| full | The initiator is allowed to examine the queue and modify queue paramters |

If it is missing, then limited access is assumed.

For example:

```
anon:rights=none
admin:passwd=YNKJHgaawczz,rights=limited
pp:passwd=YNKcye0sT6Fqc,rights=full
```

In this case the following is true:

**anon:** Unauthenticated users are not allowed any access to the QMGR.

**admin:** The user admin with the correct password is allowed to view the queue.

**pp:** The user pp, with the correct password, is allowed full access to control the queue manager.

By arranging permissions differently loose to highly restricted access is possible. If no table is specified, limited access is allowed for any connection.

# Chapter 38

# Setting Up X.400 Links

This chapter shows how to go about setting up X.400 interconnection with other sites.

Information on X.400 routing and connection establishment is entirely table driven. There is no standardised support by the message directory service. This section describes how to set up the *or* routing tables, and the tables needed for bilaterally agreed linkage.

To set up an X.400 connection, information about the remote site needs to be obtained and an entry needs to be inserted in the PP tables.

## 38.1 Remote Site Information

Obtain the information below prior to setting up an X.400 link.

| | | |
|---|---|---|
| | Technical Contact: | The person you contact if things go wrong. |
| | Telephone: | Telephone number of the technical contact. |
| * | O/R Address: | Address of a contact person. |
| * | MTA Name: | Name by which the remote site identifies itself. |
| * | MTA Password: | Password by which the remote site identifies itself. |
| * | Transport Selector: | A port identifier at the transport level. |
| | Network Address: | The X.25 DTE and/or IP address of the remote site. |
| * | X.25 Protocol ID: | A port identifier at the X.25 level. |
| * | ManagementDomains: | Any management domain/s (MD) that the remote site provides a connection to. |

Any information prefixed with an "*" may be optional.

Examples of the format are shown in Tables 38.1 and 38.2.

| | |
|---|---|
| `Technical Contact:` | Peter Yee |
| `Telephone:` | not known |
| `O/R Address:` | C=US; ADMD=TELEMAIL; PRMD=ARC; O=NASA; S=yee; |
| `MTA Name:` | titan.arc.nasa.gov |
| `MTA Password:` | " " (i.e a one character space) |
| `Transport Selector:` | 591 (ascii) |
| `TCP IP Address:` | "128.102.128.5" |
| `X.25 DTE Address:` | not known |
| `X.25 Protocol ID:` | not known |
| `ManagementDomains:` | C=US;ADMD=TELEMAIL; PRMD=ARC; |

Table 38.1: Example of X.400 Information for NASA

| | |
|---|---|
| `Technical Contact:` | John Andrews |
| `Telephone:` | 01-387-7050 ext 3691 |
| `O/R Address:` | C=GB; ADMD=GOLD 400; PRMD=UK.AC;<br>O=UCL; OU=UCL; S=Postmaster; |
| `MTA Name:` | UK.AC.UCL.CS |
| `MTA Password:` | " " (i.e a one character space) |
| `Transport Selector:` | 591 (ascii) |
| `TCP IP Address:` | 128.16.5.31 |
| `X.25 DTE Address:` | 23421920030080 |
| `X.25 Protocol ID:` | not needed |
| `ManagementDomains:` | C=GB; ADMD=GOLD 400; PRMD=UK.AC<br>C=GB; ADMD=BTMHS; PRMD=UK.AC<br>C=GB; ADMD= ; PRMD=UK.AC |

Table 38.2: Example of X.400 Information for UCL

### 38.1.1 Conventions

These are some of the conventions that PP uses for X.400 links. These need not be followed strictly but make a good starting point.

- ISODE uses a transport selector. This should be ASCII-encoded and should be all numeric (to conform to X.400(84)). The value "591" is often used.
- The MTA name is usually an appropriate domain. In the UK this is in NRS (i.e., big endian domain) order.
- The MTA password is usually a single space.

## 38.2 Setting Up the Routing Tables

The following steps need to be taken to set up the X.400 routing tables.

### 38.2.1 Routing and Mapping tables

First, a number of mapping tables need to be installed. If you do not have a copy of them, you will need to get one. Copies should be obtained from University College London (see Appendix D for details).

`or`: The O/R Table (See Figure 38.1 below and Section 37.6).

`rfc2or`: The RFC 822 to O/R Table (See Figure 37.7) .

`or2rfc`: The O/R to RFC 822 Table (See Figure 37.6).

`rfc1148gate`: The RFC 1148 known gateways file.

The *rfc2or* and *or2rfc* are the RFC 1148/987 tables. Incorporate these RFC 1148 tables in the Table directory.

### 38.2.2 Editing the O/R Table

Replace the `_DEFAULT_MTA_` occurrences with appropriate remote site names. These are the names by which the sites are internally identifiable within PP. The choice of name is up to the PP administrator, and is used for identification purposes only.

Local information should be prepended to this table, and will override later entries.

When observing the example O/R tables on pages 446 and 447 please note that:

- The O/R skeleton table in Figure 38.1 on page 446 is a truncated example of the *retrieved* UCL O/R master table.
- The O/R skeleton table in Figure 38.2 on page 447, is a truncated example of an *edited* UCL O/R master table.

```
# A Truncated example of the UCL O/R Master Table
#
#       -*** United Kingdom ***-
#
C$GB:valid
C$UK:alias C$GB
C$US:valid
ADMD$BTMHS.C$GB:valid
ADMD$ .C$GB:valid
ADMD$GOLD 400.C$GB:mta _DEFAULT_MTA_
ADMD$GOLD-400.C$GB:alias ADMD$GOLD\ 400.C$GB
ADMD$ATTMAIL.C$US:mta _DEFAULT_MTA_
PRMD$UK\.AC.ADMD$GOLD 400.C$GB:valid
PRMD$AC\.UK.ADMD$GOLD 400.C$GB:alias PRMD$UK\.AC.ADMD$GOLD\ 400.C$GB
PRMD$UK\.AC.ADMD$BTMHS.C$GB:alias PRMD$UK\.AC.ADMD$GOLD\ 400.C$GB
PRMD$UK\.CO.ADMD$GOLD 400.C$GB:valid
PRMD$BDAC.ADMD$ .C$GB:mta _DEFAULT_MTA_
PRMD$DTIIED.ADMD$GOLD 400.C$GB:mta _DEFAULT_MTA_
O$UCL.PRMD$UK\.AC.ADMD$GOLD 400.C$GB:mta _DEFAULT_MTA_
#
#       -*** australian sites ***-
C$AU:valid
ADMD$OTCDIA.C$AU:valid
ADMD$OTC.C$AU:valid
PRMD$EDU.ADMD$OTCDIA.C$AU:mta _DEFAULT_MTA_
PRMD$DITMELPP.ADMD$OTC.C$AU:mta _DEFAULT_MTA_
#
#       -*** french sites ***-
C$FR:valid
ADMD$PTT.C$FR:mta _DEFAULT_MTA_
ADMD$ATLAS.C$FR:mta _DEFAULT_MTA_
PRMD$REUNIR.ADMD$ATLAS.C$FR:mta _DEFAULT_MTA_
#
# -*** usa sites ***-
ADMD$UM.C$US:valid
ADMD$ATT.C$US:valid
PRMD$NREN.ADMD$UM.C$US:mta _DEFAULT_MTA_
PRMD$ARC.ADMD$TELEMAIL.C$US:mta _DEFAULT_MTA_
PRMD$WOLLONGONG.ADMD$ATT.C$US:mta _DEFAULT_MTA_
```

Figure 38.1: Example of an O/R Table to Edit

```
#   A Truncated example of a
#   UCL O/R Master Table after being edited by
#   a PP Administrator
#
#       -*** United Kingdom ***-
#
C$GB:valid
C$UK:alias C$GB
C$US:valid
ADMD$BTMHS.C$GB:valid
ADMD$ .C$GB:valid
ADMD$GOLD 400.C$GB:mta gb-ucl
ADMD$GOLD-400.C$GB:alias ADMD$GOLD\ 400.C$GB
ADMD$ATTMAIL.C$US:mta gb-ucl
PRMD$UK\.AC.ADMD$GOLD 400.C$GB:valid
PRMD$AC\.UK.ADMD$GOLD 400.C$GB:alias PRMD$UK\.AC.ADMD$GOLD\ 400.C$GB
PRMD$UK\.AC.ADMD$BTMHS.C$GB:alias PRMD$UK\.AC.ADMD$GOLD\ 400.C$GB
PRMD$UK\.CO.ADMD$GOLD 400.C$GB:valid
PRMD$BDAC.ADMD$ .C$GB:mta gb-ucl
PRMD$DTIIED.ADMD$GOLD 400.C$GB:mta gb-ucl
O$UCL.PRMD$UK\.AC.ADMD$GOLD 400.C$GB:mta gb-ucl
#
#       -*** australian sites ***-
C$AU:valid
ADMD$OTCDIA.C$AU:valid
ADMD$OTC.C$AU:valid
PRMD$EDU.ADMD$OTCDIA.C$AU:mta au-goanna
PRMD$DITMELPP.ADMD$OTC.C$AU:mta au-manta
#
#       -*** french sites ***-
C$FR:valid
ADMD$PTT.C$FR:mta fr-kwai
ADMD$ATLAS.C$FR:mta fr-kwai
PRMD$REUNIR.ADMD$ATLAS.C$FR:mta fr-reunir
#
# -*** usa sites ***-
ADMD$UM.C$US:valid
ADMD$ATT.C$US:valid
PRMD$NREN.ADMD$UM.C$US:mta us-destroyer
PRMD$ARC.ADMD$TELEMAIL.C$US:mta us-nasa
PRMD$WOLLONGONG.ADMD$ATT.C$US:mta us-wollongong
```

Figure 38.2: O/R Table after Editing

### X.400 Outbound Procedures

A brief description of how the X.400 outbound table is used within PP follows:

- PP connects to a remote site using its specified network address (in the `rpsap` field). If it cannot connect, because the remote site's X.25 or IP listener is not running for some reason, and if more than one address is specified, then all addresses are tried in the order specified by the `ts_communities` tailor variable in *isotailor*, until either failure occurs or a connection is made. If a specific order is required then use may be made of the `trynext` field.
- When the connection is requested, PP gives its local MTA name and password as identification.
- The remote site *either* accepts connection and returns its own MTA name and password *or* it rejects the connection and gives as its reason "validation failure".
- If the remote site rejects the connection, PP terminates the X.400 connection.
- If the remote site has accepted the connection, PP matches the returned MTA name and password against the values held for the remote site, in the X.400 outbound table (i.e the `rmta` and `rpass` fields).
- If the remote site's MTA name and password match up, PP starts to transmit a message; otherwise PP terminates the X.400 connection.

## 38.2.3 Editing the X.400 Outbound Table

Insert a default entry in the X.400 outbound table if it does not exist, where the key has the value "default" with the following fields set. These are the default values by which the the local PP identifies itself to a remote site when an outgoing X.400 connection is made. Refer to the X.400 outbound table on page 450 when doing this.

`lmta`: Local MTA name.

`lpass`: Local password.

`lpsap`: Local network address (same format as `rpsap`).

When the O/R table was previously edited, the remote site names that were chosen by the PP administrator should have been carefully recorded. These are the names that are now used to "key" into the X.400 outbound table. In addition to this, the information below is also required (refer to page 443).

- MTA name and password (both optional).
- Network address (mandatory)
- Transport selector (optional)

- Protocol ID or PID (optional).

If a remote site has more than one network address, the PP administrator will need to decide:

- Which network address should be always tried first.
- Whether all the network addresses should be entered (maximum 4).

If all network addresses are entered, then the one that is always used, is specified first in the `rpsap` field whose formats are described on page 450.

Insert an entry in the X.400 outbound table, where the remote site information maps into the following fields. Refer to the X.400 outbound table on page 450 when doing this.

- remote site name - `key`.
- MTA name - `rmta`.
- Password - `rpass`.
- Network address, TSAP and PID - `rpsap`.

## NOTE

- All keys in the X.400 outbound table must be unique.
- One or more of the "default" fields (`lmta`, `lpass`, `lpsap`) are only set within a remote site entry when they are to possess values different from those of the `default`. If these values are set within a remote site entry then, when a connection is requested to that particular remote site, the local PP will identify itself differently from normal. This is only set in very rare cases, for example, if a remote site cannot cope with a special character in the `lpass` field.
- If the `rmta` and `rpass` are not specified, this means that the remote site is using *either* some other method of validation *or* no validation at all.
- The `rpsap` field has a number of different types of formats, some of which may be seen on page 450. The formats depend on whether the network address is an X.25 DTE or an IP one, and if an X.25 DTE, on whether the PID field is specified.
- The `trynext` field is optional, and may be used when there is an alternative remote site willing to accept mail on behalf of another. If this field is used, 2 or more remote sites will be tried in succession. See Section 37.11 for more details. See also page 450 for an example of how this field may be used.
- The `tracing` field is optional and is only used if trace compression is required. See Section 37.11 again for more details.

The X.400 outbound table below gives the NASA and UCL entries using the remote site information specified in Figures 38.1 and 38.2. Some possible `rpsap` formats are also shown.

```
#-*************************************
#
#
# -*** UCL's default local entry ***-
# -*** this is different for every PP site ***-
# (lines folded for readability)
default:lpsap='"591"/Internet=bells',lmta="UK.AC.UCL.CS",lpass=" "
#
#
-*** NASA ***-
#
us-nasa:rmta="titan.arc.nasa.gov",
  rpsap='"591"/Internet=128.102.128.5'
#
# -*** UCL ***-
gb-ucl:rmta="UK.AC.UCL.CS",rpass=" ",
  rpsap='"591"/X121+23421920030080'
#
# -*** when pid is specified, the rpsap format below is used ***-
#
eg_site1:rmta="SiteName1",
  rpsap='"999"/Int-X25(80)=23421234005004+PID+03010100'
#
# -*** when more than one network address is specified ***-
# -*** note the network addresses are seperated by '|' ***-
#
eg_site2:rmta="SiteName2",
  rpsap='"400"/X121+23427351714799|X121+23428490013799'
#
# -*** when trynext is specified, the format below is used ***-
#
eg_site3:rmta="SiteName3",rpsap='"999"/X121+234212340050',
  trynext="eg_site2"
#
#
au-manta:rmta="manta.cng.dit.csiro.au",rpass=" ",
  rpsap='"591"/Int-X25(80)=50523343000180+PID+03010100|Internet=128.250.1.100'
#
#
#
#-*************************************
```

Figure 38.3: Example of X.400 Outbound Table

### 38.2.4 Channel Table Usage

The section describes briefly the actions that are taken to validate an X.400 address.

1. Parse an address in X.400 style using the *rfc2or* and *or2rfc* tables if necessary to convert from RFC 822 format.
2. Use the *or* table to try and locate a remote site name, through which the address may be relayed
3. If a remote site name is associated with the address, then look at the channel table to locate the cheapest route by which that remote site may be reached.

### 38.2.5 Edit the Channel Table

The channel table below gives the NASA and UCL entries using the remote site information specified in the tables on page 444.

- Note that the key to this table has the same value as that in the X.400 outbound table on page 450.
- Also, note that the name specified in the rounded brackets is the name of the X.400 outbound channel, and possesses the same value as that specified in the *tailor* file.

```
#-***************************
#
#       -*** nasa ***-
us-nasa:us-nasa(x400out)
#
#       -*** ucl ***-
gb-ucl:gb-ucl(x400out)
#
#-***************************
```

Figure 38.4: Example of Channel Table

### 38.2.6 X.400 Inbound Procedures

A brief description of how the X.400 inbound table is used within PP.

- A remote site requests a connection with the local PP system, and within the request its remote network address, MTA name and password are specified.
- The local PP uses the remote network address as a key into the X.400 inbound table.
- If the key is invalid, then the local PP sends a rejection back to the remote site, giving "validation failure" as the reason.

- If the key is valid, then the remote site's MTA name and password are checked against its *rmta* and *rpass* values specified within the X.400 inbound table.
- If the values match, then the local PP accepts the request by returning its MTA name and password, and begins to get ready for remote message transmission.
- If the values do not match, then the local PP sends a rejection back to the remote site, giving "validation failure" as the reason.

**NOTE:** 2 additional fields may be set to facilitate X.400 inbound connection testing.

- *info=sloppy* set in the *tailor* file, allows the acceptance of all incoming connections. All validation checks are bypassed.
- *other=sloppy* set in the *X.400 inbound table* against a particular remote site entry bypasses the validation checks for that site's remote MTA name and password.

### 38.2.7 Editing the X.400 Inbound Table

Before editing this table the PP administrator needs to:

- Decide whether or not to be selective over the acceptance of remote site connections. If *all* remote site connections are to be accepted, then in the *tailor* file the X.400 inbound channel is tailored with *info=sloppy*, and *no* entries need to be registered in this table. If entries are registered, they will be bypassed.
- Decide whether or not remote site MTA name and password validation checks are to be done. This decision should only be taken if *info=sloppy* is not set in the *tailor* file for the X.400 inbound channel. If no MTA name and password validation checks are to be carried out, then for that remote entry in the X.400 inbound table, set *other=sloppy*.

Please note when taking these decisions:

- If *info=sloppy* is set within the *tailor* file for the X.400 inbound channel, the network address of a remote site is still used as a key into the X.400 inbound table to obtain its remote site name (*rname*). If the key is invalid, then the remote site name is set to its network address. This will cause problems, if delivery notifications are requested by such a site, as the local PP would be unable to use the remote site name to key into the X.400 outbound table. Therefore *info=sloppy* should be set for testing purposes only.
- That for each remote site an X.400 inbound and outbound entry should exist. Otherwise if *info=sloppy* is set, and a remote site's network address keys successfully into the X.400 inbound table, unless there is a corresponding entry in the X.400 outbound table, no mail will be able to be sent to that site.

When the X.400 outbound table was previously edited, the following remote site information should have been obtained:

- remote site name (chosen by the PP administrator).
- MTA name and password (both optional).
- Network address (mandatory).
- Transport selector (optional) .

As the X.400 inbound table is very similar to the X.400 outbound table the same information is again required, only this time, instead of making a connection to a remote site, the concern is centered on a remote site requesting a local connection.

The fields in the X.400 inbound table (see page 454) are very similar to the ones in the X.400 outbound table (see page 450), and should be set accordingly, except for two main differences:

- *rpsap* acts as the table entry key.
- *rname* is an extra parameter which specifies the remote site name. This should have the same value as the remote site *key* in the X.400 outbound table.

The X.400 inbound table below gives the NASA and UCL entries using the remote site information specified on page 444.

In Figure 38.5 above, it can be seen that:

- The PID field is *never* used in the rpsap key.
- If a remote site has a number of network addresses, all may be specified in the rpsap of the remote site's X.400 outbound entry (see page 450) *but* there will need to be a number of inbound rpsap entries for each network address belonging to that remote site. Though all other details (rname, rmta, rpass) would be the same.

### 38.2.8 Testing Outbound Connections

- Go to the PP log directory.
- Look at the X.400 incoming log. The log should look like those in Figure 38.6.

From this log, the following remote site information may be obtained, which can then be inserted as two entries in the X.400 inbound and outbound tables.

- The TSAP: None for the first entry and "PHL" for the second.
- The Network Address: 5052334300018 for the first entry and 302049600717 for the second.
- The MTA Name: "manta.cng.dit.csiro.au" for the first entry and "foo" for the second.
- The password - " " for the first and "foobar" for the second.

```
#-***********************
#
#
#       -*** UCL's default local entry ***-
#       -*** this is different for every PP site    ***-
#
# (Folded for readabilty)
#
default:lpsap='"591"/Internet=bells',
     lmta="UK.AC.UCL.CS",lpass=" "
#
#       -*** NASA ***-
#
"591"/Internet=titan.arc.nasa.gov:rname="us-nasa",
    rmta="titan.arc.nasa.gov",rpass=" "
"591"/Internet=128.102.128.5:rname="us-nasa",
    rmta="titan.arc.nasa.gov",rpass=" "
#
# -*** UCL ***-
#
"591"/X121+23421920030080:rname="ucl",
   rmta="UK.AC.UCL.CS",rpass=" "
#
#
#-***********************
```

Figure 38.5: Example of X.400 Inbound Table

```
2/ 7 15:41:38 x400in   22798 (#52     ) Starting x400in (via X400(84) inbound)
2/ 7 15:41:41 x400in   22798 (#52     ) Connection from
key='X121+5052334300018'   mta='manta.cng.dit.csiro.au'  password=' '
2/ 7 15:41:41 x400in   22798 (#52     ) No information found in the
X.400 incoming tables
2/ 7 16:41:41 x400in   22799 (#52     ) x400in/main error: rts_decode_request
2/ 7 16:41:38 x400in   22799 (#52     ) Starting x400in (via X400(84) inbound)
2/ 7 16:41:41 x400in   22799 (#52     ) Connection from
key='"PHL"/X121+302049600717'  mta='foo'  password='foobar'
2/ 7 16:41:41 x400in   22799 (#52     ) No information found in the
X.400 incoming tables
2/ 7 16:41:41 x400in   22799 (#52     ) x400in/main error: rts_decode_request
```

Figure 38.6: Example of X.400 Incoming Logs

However, note that:

- A remote site does not have to be specified in the X.400 inbound table for a connection to be successful. If in the *tailor* file the X.400 Inbound Channel is tailored with *info=sloppy*, then *all* remote connections are accepted.
- If on the other hand MTA name and password validation is to be ignored, then for that remote entry in the X.400 inbound table, *other=sloppy* is added.

### 38.2.9 How to make a test X.400 connection to a remote site

- Go to the table directory.
- Put the remote site information in the appropriate tables.
- Use the program rtsping84, located in the PP *TOOLDIR*, to make an RTS connection to the remote site. For information on how to use rtsping84 see its manual page. In the meantime, try running:

  rtsping84 -c*x400out-channel-name RemoteSiteName*

  For example

  ```
  rtsping84 -cx400out gb-ucl
  ```

- Check the PP logs. The failure/success will be recorded there.
- The following failure reasons may be given:
  - "Validation failure": The remote site has either got an erroneous PP entry in their tables, or they haven't recorded your entry at all.
  - "Unacceptable dialogue mode": Either the remote site does not support monologue or the RTS ASN.1 encoding is bust.
  - "Connect request refused on this network connection": remote site is either down or its network listener is not running.
  - "Busy": remote site is busy, try again later.
  - "Protocol Error": protocol problems.
  - "Remote system problem": remote site's process has terminated abruptly.
  - "Timer expired": remote system's process is looping.
- If rtsping84 was successful, then try transmitting a proper message, using the 'mail' program. If during transmission a protocol error is received then this needs to be resolved. To analyse this problem, it may be necessary to obtain the required X.400 information by turning up the rts, session, and transport logging in the PP *tailor* file. This can be done by adding the following 3 entries:

isodelog rtsaplevel file=rts level=pdus

isodelog ssaplevel file=session level=pdus

isodelog tsaplevel file=transport level=pdus

### 38.2.10 A Common X.400 Incoming Connection Problem

Sometimes a remote site attempts to do an RTS recovery, due to some transmission failure. PP at the moment, does not support recovery, and so a "cannotRecover" reason is given. This sometimes does not terminate the connection due to a bug in the remote site's software, and so it keeps on trying, which leads to much network activity.

The X.400 Incoming logs will look something like:

```
2/ 8  8:30:31 x400in    01392 (#52      )
      Starting x400in (via X400(84) inbound)
2/ 8  8:30:33 x400in    01392 (#52      )
      RtBInit, [Congestion at RtSAP]
      rejecting attempted recovery
```

To get the network address of the remote site attempting the recovery, look at the ISODE tsapd.log, and then match the network address against the X.400 inbound table keys.

# Chapter 39

# Managing PP

This chapter covers the tools which allow the system administrator to keep up to date with the status of the system and to take action to fix or avoid problems. It also gives some guidance on what is entailed in daily maintenance of the system, and how new users and MTAs may be added.

## 39.1 QMGR

The QMGR operates without ever reading the queue. The key ASN.1 structure is MsgStruct. This is the ASN.1 representation of the message as helped by the queue manager. This is held in a sparse matrix, initially sorted by channel, host/user, and priority. The queue manager is not, inherently, a trusted process, as it does not access the queue directly. The protocol is listed in Appendix F in Figure F.1.

### 39.1.1 Message Submission

When *submit* is started, it asynchronously establishes an association with the QMGR. When a message is submitted to the queue, a ROS message is sent to the queue manager which will hold all of the information needed by the QMGR. This allows the message to be processed without the QMGR actually reading the queue.

### 39.1.2 Queue Reading

A ROS operation allows the queue to be read. This is used at startup and for occasional refresh.

### 39.1.3 Active Channel

An active channel is invoked by the QMGR, which starts a ROS association. The channel is synchronous. The first operation is ChannelInitialise, which identifies the channel to the process (which may act as several channels). Subsequent ChannelInitialise operations serve to change the role of the channel. The ProcessMessage operation allows the QMGR to control the channel, which will access the queue directly.

### 39.1.4 Passive Channel

Passive channels have not yet been implemented.

### 39.1.5 Cleanups, Timeouts, and Debris

Message are deleted by the *msg-clean* channel. This is invoked after all recipients have been processed.

Messages are returned after a certain time by the QMGR invoking the *timout* channel. This process creates a delivery report and changes the status of the message to non-delivery.

Partially submitted messages are cleaned up quietly by debris channel after being in the queue for a certain amount of time. This channel is invoked at intervals.

### 39.1.6 QMGR Management and Tailoring

The QMGR is managed mostly through the MTA console interface. However, there are several options you can give when starting up the QMGR to change the mode of operation. These are listed here, in approximate order of usefulness:

`-m`: This switch sets the default maximum number of channels that can be run simultaneously. This parameter needs to be set carefully (see below).

`-c seconds`: This switch sets the default time to cache a channel that has failed. It defaults to 5 minutes. The cache value is multiplied by 1.5 to obtain a delay for failed MTAs, and multiplied by 2 for failed messages. Successive failures will multiply this value up to some maximum.

`-D`: This switch starts up the QMGR with all channels disabled. This is most useful to allow controlled startup of channels. Once started in this mode, channels can be gradually enabled via the MTA console.

`-d hours`: This switch sets the time between successive runs of the debris channel. This is the channel that removes extraneous bits of messages, etc. Its default value is about six hours.

`-l hours`: This switch sets the time between successive runs of the load channel. This channel is run at intervals to check consistency between the image of the queue in memory and that on disk.

**-t hours:** This switch sets the time between successive calls to the timeout channel. This channel is run at intervals to time out messages that have been in the queue too long.

**-C:** Do not change directory to the queue directory.

**-b:** Do not run in the background, stay in the foreground.

**-T file:** Use this file as the pp *tailor* file.

**-X:** Turn up the debugging.

The QMGR also responds to various signals (where available). A SIGTERM signal will cause the QMGR to gracefully shutdown. This is the same as QMGR control option. A SIGUSR1 signal will increase the debugging level and a SIGUSR2 will reset the level, or decrease it. All other signals default to their normal actions.

The loading on a given machine varies and it is controlled mainly through the maximum number of channels variable. Consequently, it is important to get this factor correct, otherwise response will suffer.

The main adjustable parameter is the maximum number of channels that can be run at any one time. This parameter should be set with care. It can be set by the above-mentioned flag at QMGR start time, or can be modified dynamically through the use of the MTA console. This parameter should be used in conjunction with the per channel maximum number of processes. The QMGR has a number of built in heuristics as to how useful running several channels at once is. This will be overridden by the per-channel maximums, so they should be used sparingly. Suitable cases for imposing a per-channel maximum are the following:

- Channels which run very quickly. Such channels are usually reformatters that do their job quickly. Allowing only one or two instances of these channels can help loading in some cases. These channels can create a load on the machine as they have no external influence and run as fast as the machine will let them.

- Special network channels. If you have a channel that uses a dedicated resource, then this may be a candidate for setting a maximum on. Such a resource might be a modem or a non-multiplexed line. Clearly, if there is only one logical stream that a channel can use, starting multiple instances of such a channel is pointless.

Cases that should generally not have a per-channel maximum are the following.

- Network channels. Unless you have an amazingly fast network and instantaneous response from remote hosts, network channels do not usually create too much load. They tend to be self-throttling, as they spend much of their time waiting for I/O to complete or for response from the remote host.

- QMGR special channels. Such channels as QMGR-load and timeout are special to the QMGR and will only be invoked one at a time.

The maximum number of channels defaults to three, which is a reasonable number for a small machine that is doing other things besides mail. If you are running a dedicated mail server you will probably get better throughput with a larger number. However, it is worth spending some time watching what happens and increasing and decreasing this number via the MTA console to get a reasonable value. If you specify a value of 10, for instance, you may end up just wiping out any trace of performance on your machine, as the machine will just be thrashing between processes. On the other hand, 10 channels talking to 300 baud modems will probably not be noticeable. Once you have determined a reasonable value, add this to your pp.start script using the -m switch detailed above.

To begin with it is recommended that the default configuration with no per-channel maxima is used and that it is run for a while before adjustment is made.

## 39.2 MTA Console

The MTA console is a management tool that can be used to monitor and/or control a QMGR. This tool uses the Athena widget set on top of X11 release 4.

### 39.2.1 The MTA Console's Display

The MTA console's display has two modes, the *monitor* mode and the *control* mode. Toggling between these modes is done via the appropriate button.

The top section of the display is common to both modes. This section contains a box within which the states of all the channels are displayed.

The *state* of an entity (channel, MTA or message) represents how "bad" that entity is, compared to the upperbound on "badness" (maximum badness). The badness of an entity can reflect various things like number of messages on that entity or the age of the oldest message on that entity. Section 39.2.4 describes what badness represents, how badness is calculated, and how this calculation can be tailored.

#### The Monitor Mode

The *monitor* mode provides a passive display of the overall state of the QMGR.

In this mode, the lower part of the display presents an ordered list of the states of the channels. The list is ordered on the basis of comparative badness. The list is laid out vertically with the worst state channel at the top.

The states of the "n worst state" MTAs on each channel are displayed to the right of the channel they are on. They are ordered on the basis of comparative badness with the worst state MTA being display directly to the right of the channel. How many of the MTAs on a channel are actually displayed depends on the heuristic being employed. The MTA console has a number of possible heuristics. These are described in Section 39.2.2.

#### The Control Mode

The *control* mode allows the user to focus on particular channels, MTAs or messages and control their passage through and their behaviour in the QMGR.

The amount of control the console can invoke depends on how the console connected to the QMGR. There are two types of connection the QMGR allows, unauthorised and authorised. With an authorised connection, the console can control the QMGR by disabling entities, enabling entities and so on. With an unauthorised connection, the console has no control over the QMGR. To get an authorised connection, the user has to specify a name and password when he or she requests the connection.

In the *control* mode, the lower part of the console's display presents information on the entity the user has focused on and allows the user to focus on other entities.

### 39.2.2 Configuring The MTA Console

This section details how the MTA console may be configured by users to suit their own individual tastes. There are three static mechanisms that can be used for this configuration:

1. command line arguments
2. user defaults
3. application defaults

As well as these static mechanisms, the MTA console contains a configuration menu. This menu can be used dynamically to configure many of the options described below.

#### Totals Configuration

The MTA console displays the total number of messages and the total volume of messages in the queue. It also indicates how full the queue is by comparing these totals with specific maximum values. These maximum values can be statically tailored on the command line (e.g., `-number 1000000` and `-volume 100000000`) or in the X defaults (e.g., `MTAconsole.totalnumber: 1000000` and `MTAconsole.totalvolume: 100000000`) The values can also be tailored from the badness tailoring as described in Section 39.2.4. The default values are, for volume of messages, 1000000 and, for number of messages, 10000.

### Colour Configuration

On a colour screen the MTA console will display entities of significantly different badness as different colours, with the colour ranging from green for entities with low badness to red for entities with high badness. The number of colours the console will use can be statically tailored from the command line (e.g., `-ncolours 20`) or in the Xdefaults (e.g., `MTAconsole.ncolours 20`). The console will use a range of 10 colours by default.

### Static Connection Configuration

The user must specify which QMGR to attempt to connect to. Usually this is done dynamically from the connect popup. However it can be done statically from the command line (e.g. `-Queue trellis`) or in the X defaults (e.g., `MTAconsole.connectHost: trellis`). If the QMGR to connect to is statically specified, the MTA console will automatically attempt to open an unauthorised connection to the specified QMGR.

### Confirmation Configuration

Certain of the MTA console's commands request confirmation via a popup. This feature can be turned off dynamically from the confirmation menu or statically from the command line (e.g., `-NoConfirm`) or in the X defaults (e.g., `MTAconsole.confirm: false`).

### Heuristic Configuration

When in monitor mode, the MTA console displays some of the MTAs on each channel. There are different heuristics that the console can use to decide how many MTAs to display for each channel. These heuristics are:

**`line based`:** This heuristic limits the display of MTAs on each channel to a specific number of vertical lines. This number can be tailored dynamically from the configuration menu or statically on the command line (e.g., `-downLines 6`) or in the X defaults (e.g., `MTAconsole.maxvert: 6`). The default value is 4.

**`percentage based`:** This heuristic displays a specific percentage of the MTAs on each channel. The percentage to display is calculated by multiplying the badness of the channel (expressed as a percentage of the maximum badness) by a constant percentage. This constant percentage can be tailored dynamically from the configuration menu or statically on the command line (e.g. `-percent 70`) or in the X defaults (e.g. `MTAconsole.percentage: 70`). The default value for this constant is 50.

There is a lower bound on the number of MTAs displayed using this heuristic. The MTA console will endeavour to ensure that the number of MTAs displayed for each channel is at least the lower bound. This lower bound can be tailored dynamically from the configuration menu or statically on the command line (e.g. `-lowerbound 15`) or in the X defaults (e.g. `MTAconsole.lowerbound: 15`). The default value for this lower bound is 20.

**`all`:** This heuristic instructs the MTA console in monitor mode to display all the MTAs on each channel.

**`channelonly`:** This heuristic shows only the information about the channels with no MTA information. This is useful when the QMGR has many messages loaded into it and so refreshing the display takes a while.

The choice of heuristic can be changed dynamically from the configuration menu or statically on the command line (e.g. `-heuristic all`) or in the X defaults (e.g. `MTAconsole.heuristic: all`). The line-based heuristic is used by default.

### Configuration of Timeouts and Retries

There are various timeouts and retry intervals associated with the MTA console. These can be configured or disabled from the configuration menu and are as follows:

**auto-refresh timeout:** If no activity occurs on the connection between the MTA console and the QMGR during a specified interval, the console will consult with the QMGR and automatically refresh the information on display. This particular timeout interval can also be configured on the command line (e.g., `-refresh 3m30s`) or in the X defaults (e.g. `MTAconsole.refresh: 3m30s`). The default interval is 5 minutes. Note: to stop the console hogging the QMGR's resources, a minimum value for this interval is enforced. This minimum is 30 seconds.

**inactive timeout** If the console is in *control* mode and no user input has been received during a specified interval, the MTA console automatically toggles to the *monitor* mode. The default interval is 10 minutes.

**reconnection retry interval** If the connection between the MTA console and the QMGR breaks, the console will attempt to reconnect to the QMGR. After an unsuccessful reconnection attempt, the console will wait for a specified time and then try to reconnect again. The intervals between reconnection attempts increases in duration by a specified increment up to a maximum interval. The initial duration of the wait interval, the increment added to the interval after each unsuccessful reconnection attempt and the maximum interval can all be set dynamically from the configuration menu. This menu can also disable the reconnection mechanism and/or the increasing duration.

### 39.2.3 The Effect of the Mouse Buttons and Keys

This section describes how a user can use the mouse buttons and the keyboard to operate the MTA console. The following tables show the effect of the command buttons that can be found on the MTA console.

**Top row of buttons**

| Button | Effect |
|---|---|
| `Refresh/Reconnect` | Refresh the data or reconnect to the QMGR. |
| `quit` | Exit the console program. |
| `connect/disconnect` | Connect to or disconnect from the QMGR. |
| `control/monitor` | Change between the two modes. |
| `configuration` | Set various parameters. |
| `Qmgr control` | Perform global QMGR control. |

**Channel buttons**

| Button | Effect |
|---|---|
| `info` | Display information about the channel. |
| `disable` | Disable this channel. |
| `enable` | Enable this channel. |
| `clear delay` | Clear any delays on this channel. |
| `add delay` | Specify a delay. The channel will wait this time before starting again. |
| `downward force attempt` | Invoke this channel now if possible, clearing any delays and those messages and MTAs waiting on this channel. |

**MTA buttons**

| Button | Effect |
|---|---|
| `info` | Display information on this MTA. |
| `disbale` | Disable this MTA. |
| `enable` | Enable this MTA. |
| `clear delay` | Clear any delays for this MTA. |
| `add delay` | Specify a delay before next retry. |
| `force attempt` | Clear any delays for this MTA, an similarly for the channel this is on. |
| `downward force attempt` | Clear delays for this MTA and those of any messages on this MTA. |

**Message Buttons**

| Button | Effect |
|---|---|
| `info` | Display information about this message . |
| `show all` | By default only information on ten messages is shown. This button will show all messages on this MTA/channel. |
| `freeze` | Stop this message being delivered. |
| `thaw` | Allow this message to be delivered (this is the opposite of freeze). |
| `clear delay` | Clear the next delivery attempt time. |
| `add delay` | Set a next delivery attempt time. |
| `force attempt` | Try and deliver the message now by clearing all delays associated with this message. |

Here are the effects each button has when pressed within the MTA console's display. It is based on a three-button mouse. Different configurations are tailorable through the X defaults mechanism for other hardware.

**`left hand button`:** If this button is pressed while the cursor is over one of the many *command* buttons in the console, that command is invoked.

If the console is in monitor mode and the left-hand button is pressed while the cursor is over the area occupied by the display of an entity, the console toggles to control mode, focuses on that entity, and displays information about the entities directly below it. For example, if in monitor mode the left-hand button was pressed while the cursor was over the area occupied by the channel `x400out84`, then the console would toggle modes, make `x400out84` the current channel and display information about the MTAs currently on that channel.

If the console is in control mode and the left-hand button is pressed while the cursor is over the area occupied by the display of an entity, then the console focuses on that entity and displays information about the entities directly below it. For example, if in control mode the left-hand button was pressed while the cursor was over the area occupied by the channel `x400out84`, then the console would make `x400out84` the current channel and display information about the MTAs currently on that channel.

**`middle button`:** If the console is in monitor mode and the middle button is pressed while the cursor is over the area occupied by the display of an entity, the console toggles to control mode and focuses on that entity.

If the console is in control mode and the middle button is pressed while the cursor is over the area occupied by the display of an entity, the console toggles

| Accelerator | Command | Prerequiste |
|---|---|---|
| Meta + R | Refresh | |
| Meta + Q | Quit | |
| Meta + D | Disconnect | |
| Meta + C | Connect | |
| Meta + M | Toggle Modes | |
| Meta + F | Configuration | |
| Return | Ok | A popup must be on display |
| Control + C | Notok | A popup must be on display |
| Meta + H | Toggle Heuristic | The configuration popup must be on display |
| Meta + A | Toggle Authorisation | The connect popup must be on display |

Table 39.1: MTA Console Accelerators

the focus on that entity (i.e., if the focus at that level is not on the entity, the focus is set on that entity. However, if the focus is already on that entity, the focus is unset).

`right button:` This button has a similar effect in both modes. If it is pressed while the cursor is over the area occupied by the display of an entity then the information displayed relating to that entity is refreshed and redisplayed.

There are various "accelerators" installed in the MTA console. These are key presses that allow the user to invoke commands that would otherwise have to be invoked by moving the cursor to a specific area on the screen and then pressing one of the mouse buttons. The accelerators installed in the console all provide alternative ways to invoke some of the commands represented by *command* buttons. Some have prerequisites for use. Table 39.1 shows the accelerators, their prerequisites, and the commands they invoke. This table has two modifier keys that must be held down together with the other keys mentioned in the accelerator for that accelerator to work – the *Meta* key and the *Control* key.

Several of the popups have various text boxes into which a user can type. At any one instant only one of these boxes can have the keyboard focus (the box with the keyboard focus gets the text the user types in). This is indicated by the text box with the focus having a border around it. All other text boxes will have no border. There are accelerators installed in the MTA console to allow the user to change the keyboard focus. The up arrow key when pressed will change the focus to the box above the one currently with the focus. The down arrow key when pressed will change the focus to the box below the one currently with the focus. The tab key has the same effect as the down arrow key. If the left-hand button on the mouse is pressed when the cursor is over one of the text boxes, that text box gets the focus.

### 39.2.4 Badness

The *badness* of an entity (channel, MTA or message) is a value used to compare the state of one entity with that of another. This comparison is used through out the MTA console to order the displayed lists of entities, to choose which colour to display that entity in, and so on.

The badness of an entity is calculated from the sum of up to four factors.

`number:` The number of messages on an entity.

`volume:` The volume of messages on an entity.

`age:` For channel and MTA entities, this is the oldest message on the entity. For message entities, this factor is the age of the message itself.

`last:` The last successful attempt on an entity.

Each factor has a specific upperbound and these upperbounds are tailorable (this is described below). In the badness summation, the factors are expressed in terms of percentages of their respective upperbounds. So if the upper bound on the number factor is represented as *ub_number* and similarly for the other factors then the badness summation would be calculated as follows: $(number/ub\_number)*100+(volume/ub\_volume)*100+(age/ub\_age)*100+(last/ub\_last)*100$, or, put more concisely, $\sum^{factors}(factor/ub\_factor)*100$.

#### Tailoring of Upperbounds

When the console connects to a queue, it builds a database of tailoring entries. It can get the information for the database from any of three sources. The file specified in the connect popup, the hardwired defaults and the X defaults. Entries in the file override equivalent entries in the defaults. The file specified in the connect popup should be relative either to the current directory, a full path name, or the home directory.

An entry in this database has the form:

```
<key> ":" <value>
```

The `key` is a tuple indicating which channel, or type of channel and which type of entity on that channel the tailoring information in the value relates to. The channel or channel type and the entity are separated a "-". The entity must be one of:

```
chan
mta
msg
```

| Tailor File Values | | |
|---|---|---|
| type | access | Key |
| in | mts | mtsin |
| out | mts | mtsout |
| both | mts | mtsboth |
| in | mta | mtain |
| out | mta | mtaout |
| both | mta | mtaboth |
| in | | mtsin |
| out | | mtsout |
| both | | mtsboth |
| shaper | | internal |
| warn | | internal |
| delete | | internal |
| qmgrload | | internal |
| debris | | internal |
| timeout | | internal |

Table 39.2: Tailor File Entries to Console Keys.

If the tailoring information is related to a specific channel, then the channel's name must be before the -. For example, if "822local," "x400in84," and "p2explode" are all names of channels, then the following are valid keys that can be used in the database: "822local-chan," "x400in84-mta," and "p2explode-msg".

If the tailoring information is related to a type of channel then the type of the channel appears before the -. The type of a channel is constructed from the `type` of that channel given in the *tailor* file and the `access` of that channel also in the *tailor* file. Table 39.2 gives all the types of channels that can be used in keys and how they are constructed. Some valid keys of this form are "mtaboth-chan", "passive-msg", "internal-msg."

When the console searches through the database, it searches first for keys with the specific channel name in them (i.e., "channelname-entity"). If this fails, it searches for keys with the channel type in them (i.e., "channeltype-entity"). This second search will never fail as there are default entries for all possible channel types.

The `value` is a comma-separated list of expressions. These expressions are of the form `keyword<upperbound`, where keyword is one of:

```
age
vol
num
last
```

and upperbound is a number and an optional letter representing a unit. The possible units are

h: Hour (number * 60).

d: Day (number * 24 * 60).

k: Kilo (number * 1000).

M: Mega (number * 1000000).

Note that if one of the four keywords is missing from a value, the associated factor is ignored in the badness summation.

Figure 39.1 shows an extract from the MTA console's hardwired defaults.

```
#define default_mtsboth_chan \
        "mtsboth-chan:age<2h,vol<1M,num<500,last<2h"
#define default_mtsboth_mta \
        "mtsboth-mta:age<2h,vol<1M,num<500,last<2h"
#define default_mtsboth_msg \
        "mtsboth-msg:age<2h,vol<1M"

#define default_mtain_chan \
        "mtain-chan:last<2h"
#define default_mtain_mta \
        "mtain-mta:last<2h"
#define default_mtain_msg \
        "mtain-msg:last<2h"

#define default_passive_chan \
        "passive-chan:age<20,vol<1M,num<10,last<20"
#define default_passive_mta \
        "passive-mta:age<20,vol<1M,num<10,last<20"
#define default_passive_msg \
        "passive-msg:age<20,vol<1M"
```

Figure 39.1: Extract From the Console's Tailoring

## 39.3 Line Console

The line console provides similar functionality to the control mode of the MTA console. The main difference between the two tools lies in the fact that the line console does not work on top of the X-windowing system and so can be used to manage the QMGR from a terminal or from the comfort of your own home over a modem connection.

The line console has a three level hierarchical view of the queue and its contents. These three levels are channels, MTAs, and messages. The prompt specifies which level the user is currently studying and is constructed from the names of the entities chosen in the levels above. For example, if the user was examining the MTAs on the channel `822tous` the prompt would be `822tous.mta`.

Within a level, the user can use UNIX regular expressions (*regex* (3)) to specify the entity or entities he or she is interested in. This allows easy group control. For example to disable all the X.400 protocol channels, the user would type the command "disable x400". For each channel whose name matched the regular expression "x400", the line console would then ask the user to confirm that he or she wants to disable that channel.

Note that when moving down a level in the hierarchy, the user must specify an expression that matches a unique entity at the current level.

### 39.3.1 Line Console Commands

This section provides a brief overview of the commands the line console provides.

`set` This command is used to set one of the line console's variables, e.g., `set pager=off` or `set user=foo`. Currently the variables you can set are `pager`, `tailorfile`, `authorised` and `user`.

If no arguments are given with the set command, the current settings of the variables are printed.

`status` This command prints out the overall status of the QMGR currentlt connected to.

`connect` This command connects to a specified QMGR. The line console will prompt for the name of the QMGR and, if attempting to connect in authorised mode ("authorised=yes"), a password to connect with.

`disconnect` This command disconnects the line console from the QMGR.

`quit` This command quits from the line console.

`list` This command lists all the entities on the current level with badness greater than zero [1].

If the command is given with the argument "all," entities with zero badness are also displayed.

[1]badness is calculated and tailored as with the MTAconsole

`info` This command displays information relating to all entities which match the given regular expression.

`refresh` This command updates the line console's database form the QMGR.

`down` This command moves the line console to the level below the current level in the hierarchy. Note that to do this a regular expression which matches a unique entity from the current level must be specified.

`up` This command moves the line console to the level above the current level in the hierarchy.

`next` This command selects the next entity in the current list and displays the information relating to that entity. If no entity is currently selected, the first entity on the list is selected.

`previous` This command selects the previous entity in the current list and displays information relating to it. If no entity is currently selected, the last entity is selected.

`current` This command allows the user to select a given entity. The regular expression given must select only one entity.

The remaining commands are only available if the user connects to the QMGR in authorised mode.

`enable` Enables processing for entities which match the given expression.

`disable` Disables processing for entities which match the given expression.

`delay` Delays matching entities for a specified amount of time.

`clear` Clears any delay on matching entities.

`belowclear` Clears and enables any entities below the matching entities.

`aboveclear` Clears and enables any entities above the matching entities.

`quecontrol` Performs an overall control on the QMGR. The valid controls are `abort`, `terminate`, `restart`, `rereadQueue`, `disableSubmission`, `enableSubmission`, `disableAll`, `enableAll`, `increasemaxchans`, and `decreasemaxchans`.

Note that there is a simple redirection facility in the line console. This facility allows a user to redirect the output from the commands `list`, `info` and `status` into a file. This can be either as an append operation or as an overwrite operation. To invoke this facility follow the usual command with a redirect symbol and a file name, e.g.:

```
status > /tmp/foo
info 822 >> /tmp/foo
list >> /tmp/foo
```

The > symbol represents the overwrite operation, and the >> symbol represents the append operation.

# 39.4 Checkup Procedures

Additional procedures exist for querying the queue directly about the status of the system. However, their prime importance is as development tools; the MTA console should be the main source of information for the system administrator.

## 39.4.1 ckchan

The *ckchan* tool prints out information on the state of currently active channels and is invoked as follows:

```
ckchan [-v] <channelname> ...
```

*ckchan* prints out information on the specified channels. If no channels are specified, *ckchan* prints out information on all the channels currently active.

The presence of the -v flag on the command line instructs *ckchan* to output a verbose form of information.

If given a -s flag, the program only shows a summary of the information.

Warning: on even a moderately-sized queue, this process runs fairly slowly.

## 39.4.2 ckconfig

The *ckconfig* tool performs various checks on the configuration of PP including confirmation that:

- All the required directories are in place and have appropriate permissions.
- All the channels and filters described in the *tailor* file reference programs in the appropriate directory (*chndfldir*).
- All the tables described in the *tailor* file reference files in the appropriate directory (*tbldfldir*).

By default *ckconfig* will prompt for correction of any configuration errors it identifies.

*ckconfig*'s behaviour can be altered by the following command line flags:

-f: (*force*) *ckconfig* will attempt to automatically correct configuration errors.

-v: (*verbose*) *ckconfig* will display correct configuration information as well as displaying configuration errors.

-n: (*no execution*) *ckconfig* will perform all its checks and report back the results. No automatic correction will take place and the user will not be prompted for corrections.

It is worth running this program at intervals and after every change you make to PP.

### 39.4.3 Checking of Addresses

It is sometimes useful to check out addresses with and without the whole system being invoked. To this end two utilities are provided.

#### Ckadr

PP provides a tool, *ckadr*, to check whether an address is acceptable to the mail system. Note that this tool does not do any of the PP authorization checks, so an address may be acceptable to *ckadr*, but PP may still refuse it due to authorisation criteria.

If the address is acceptable, *ckadr* will display how the address was parsed and how PP will deliver to this address. For example:

```
pac
Address parsing succeeded
pac -> (rfc822) p.cowen@cs.nott.ac.uk
    -> (x400)
  /I=p/S=cowen/OU=CS/O=NOTT/PRMD=UK.AC/ADMD=GOLD 400/C=GB/
Delivered to sheriff.cs.nott.ac.uk by 822-local
```

If the address is not acceptable, *ckadr* will display how far it got in the parse of the address and why it failed to find the address acceptable. For example:

```
/S=foo/OU=CS/O=NOTT/PRMD=HOL/ADMD=GOLD 400/C=GB/
Address parsing failed
Reason : Unknown PRMD HOL
Parsing gave this:
/S=foo/OU=CS/O=NOTT/PRMD=HOL/ADMD=GOLD 400/C=GB/ ->
  (rfc822) foo@CS.NOTT.HOL.gold-400.gb
/S=foo/OU=CS/O=NOTT/PRMD=HOL/ADMD=GOLD 400/C=GB/ ->
  (x400) /S=foo/OU=CS/O=NOTT/PRMD=HOL/ADMD=GOLD 400/C=GB/
```

If *ckadr* is invoked with command line arguments (other than its own command line flags), it will attempt to parse these arguments as addresses. Note that if any of the addresses have whitespace in them, they should be quoted to avoid being split up into separate arguments.

If *ckadr* is invoked with no command line arguments, it will read from the standard input until the end of that input. Each line of input is parsed as though it were an address.

The behaviour of *ckadr* can be modified with the following switches:

-r: Treat all addresses as 822 format addresses. This is the default behaviour.

-x: Treat all addresses as X.400 format addresses.

Note in most cases, *ckadr* will correctly parse an X.400 address even if you say it is an 822 address and vice versa. However there are some cases where this is not so, therefore be careful when using *ckadr* and different formats of addresses.

-n: Check the address without expanding aliases.

-p: Check the address and allow parsing of percent symbols in the route.

-a: Normalise all domains.

-l: Normalise domains with the USA ordering (littlendian) preferred.

-b: Normalise domains with the UK ordering (bigendian) preferred.

-0: recognise USA domain ordering *only*.

-1: prefer USA domain ordering.

-2: recognise UK domain ordering *only*.

-3: prefer UK domain ordering.

The above values relate to the numerical values used internally to specify which domain ordering to use. By default, *ckadr* will recogise USA domain ordering ONLY.

### Probes

PP provides a tool, *probe*, which checks whether or not a message would be acceptable either locally or to a remote mail system.

A message probe attempts to transit the message transfer system network to its destination. On arrival at its destination or at a place where it can no longer be delivered (either because of errors or because a gateway through which the network beyond does not support probes is reached) a delivery report will always be returned. No message is ever delivered to a recipient as a result of a message probe.

The returned delivery report informs of the future successful or unsuccessful delivery of a message, having the same parameters as those specified within the previously generated message probe.

Within PP, the delivery report can be generated at either the remote end or locally. The exact location of the generation will depend on how the channels are specified within the PP *tailor* file.

If an outbound channel supports message probes, then it should have

```
probe=y
```

specified as one of its parameters in the *tailor* file. If this parameter is not specified than the default

```
probe=n
```

is taken. If probe=y is set against any outbound channel, then the delivery reports are generated remotely for any message probes outbound through that channel. It is assumed that the remote sites, reached via that outbound channel, will reply to the message probes. If, however, the parameter is set to probe=n, then the delivery reports will be generated locally, and this fact is recorded within the delivery report.

Note that the information within a delivery report could sometimes prove erroneous. For example, a remote recipient name (e.g James.Hacker) in an X.400 address needs clarifying, but the outbound channel associated with that recipient is set to probe=n. If the X.400 address is parsed correctly, then a successful delivery report is generated locally, regardless of whether or not the name of the recipient (e.g James.Hacker) is a valid one at the remote end. Thus it is necessary that the probe parameters are set correctly in the *tailor* file for *probe* to work correctly.

Note also, that only the X.400 channels support message probes, so any probing done of a non-X.400 site would have the delivery report generated by a gateway. Thus an X.400 remote user probing a recipient at a non-X.400 site, reachable via the local PP mail system, would have a PP generated delivery report. Once again the information within the delivery report could prove erroneous, if the remote recipient's address is parsed correctly but the recipient name is invalid.

*Therefore for message probes to work absolutely correctly, probing must be carried out between X.400 sites only.*

The *probe* message generation program can be called in 2 ways:

- With command line arguments. It will attempt to parse the specified arguments before generating a message probe.
- Without command arguments. It will prompt on standard output and read on standard input until all the information has been received, before generating a message probe.

With the following options:

-t: Interprets the remaining arguments up to the next switch as "To:" Recipients.

-s: Specifies the size (in bytes) of the future message.

-e: Specifies one or more body part types within the future message. The list of types should be separated by a ",".

-u: Specifies a user agent identifier. This should be a maximum of 16 characters.

-i: Requests implicit conversion.

-a: Allows alternate recipients.

## 39.5 Dealing with Errors

To identify reasons for failure, it is necessary first to figure out which program is failing. This is not always easy as there are many programs involved in PP and at any one time, several of them may be interacting.

For a message submission that fails, it is rarely the inbound channel that is the problem, though obviously this can be the case sometimes. Most likely is that there is a problem in *submit*, so examining the *submit* log is likely to be a good starting point. It is also rare (but not unknown) that the problem is a bug in *submit*. The most likely causes initially are that you have one of the following wrong:

- The *tailor* file has things specified incorrectly. Most of the common problems here are missing formatters, badly specified channels, and missing directories. The *ckconfig* will help solve some of these.
- Another very likely cause is that the tables are wrong. This can be checked to a degree by use of the *ckadr* program. This allows addresses to be entered and the tables interrogated to determine the actions for that address. If you alter the tables, do not forget to run *dbmbuild* or else change the relevant table to linear mode.
- Worth checking, although less likely, is whether *submit* is installed properly with the correct setuid bit on (it should be mode 4755 or similar).

On outgoing channels, it is more likely either an error in one of the channels, a queue file that is incorrect, or an inconsistency between the QMGR and the queue on disc.

If the QMGR is running but not delivering anything, check to ensure the following:

- That the channels in question are enabled (check this via the MTA *console* program).
- That the *pptsapd* is running.
- That the channel programs exist in the right place, with the right modes (*ckconfig* will check most of these).

Remember, if you add channels or tables to the *tailor* file, then you will need to restart both the QMGR and the *pptsapd* programs.

If you wish to monitor the progress of the PP system through the logs in a dynamic way, it may be worth using the *ntail* program supplied in the *tools* directory. This program is much like running the UNIX *tail* (1) command with the `-f` flag on several files at once.

## 39.6 Managing Tables

As described in Section 37, there are a number of tables that PP requires. For a site of any size, the generation of these tables is likely to be substantially automated.

Manual generation will probably only be used by very small sites. Local tables, such as *aliases*, *users*, *local channel*, *list channel* or *authorisation* files will come from local sources. The system manager will be able to generate these easily. In the longer term, support for local information by use of the OSI Directory is to be expected.

For now, the tables needed for X.400 routing (the *or* table and X.400 channel tables) must be manually generated. This is an indication of the immaturity of this technology.

### RFC 1148 Mapping Tables

RFC 1148 mappings should be global. Therefore, it is desirable to use standard tables as far as possible. Two approaches are possible:

1. UCL (and later the UK Gateway service at ULCC) will maintain and make available RFC 1148 tables in PP format. FTAM will probably be the preferred mode of access.
2. There are scripts to take the RARE WG1 format tables and generate PP format tables from these. The ambiguous and dubious mappings are avoided by the simple expedient of ignoring all mappings which relate to a single domain component.

The first method is preferred, until the RARE tables are updated at a realistic interval (preferably on a continuous basis, which can be pulled each day).

### Domain and Channel Tables

There are some support tools to help generate the *channel* and *domain* tables, for domain-based information. Note that the *channel* table is used for both X.400 and domain bindings.

For *domain* and *channel* tables, it is important to understand the use of these when defining mechanisms to build them. The steps that are taken for resolving a domain address are as follows:

1. Look up the domain of the address in the *domain* table. Note:
   - Domains are in US order.
   - With `mta` and `local` entries, there maybe a third component. If there is a third component then this indicates the number of levels of subdomain permitted ($* \equiv \infty$).
2. Look up the domain name derived from the domain table in channel table. The RHS of the channel table gives a list of host/MTA pairs which may be used. If the MTA is null, the originally specified MTA will be used.

Two basic strategies for generating these tables are described.

**Internet:** This assumes that SMTP is used, in the context of domain nameservers. The tables are used to identify a part of the domain tree which will be passed to the SMTP channel. Use of DNS is confined to this channel.

**NRS:** Here, UK NRS tables are used to point valid NRS domains at JNT Mail channels.

Simple sites will be able to use one of these strategies directly. More complex sites will need to add additional information.

### Generation of the domain table

When building a domain table, it is useful to start by building a variant which only has entries for fully qualified domain names and the partial domain names that are known. The *abbrev* tool can be used to create the required `synonym` entries for abbreviated forms of domain names.

The domain table is compiled from one or more sources:

**Local Name:** Your own domain name, and alternates are needed. For example:

```
cambridge.ac.uk:mta =
cam.ac.uk:synonym cambridge.ac.uk
```

**NRS data:** The NRS data can be converted directly into the PP domain format by use of the *c-nrs* program[2]. The file *pp.dmn* created by this program should then be concatenated with the other generated domain data before being processed by the *abbrev* tool.

**Internet:** A list of top level domains which you wish to be passed to the SMTP/DNS channels should be given. For example:

```
edu:mta = 1:*
gov:mta = 1:*
com:mta = 1:*
mil:mta = 1:*
```

Note that the partial rules are `1:*`, thus preventing `edu`, `gov`, `com` and `mil` being recognised as valid domains by themselves.

**Other known domains:** Other known domains (e.g., those associated with local UUCP links) should be added in. For example:

```
iconet.uucp:mta =
inset.uucp:mta =
```

Once all the data has been collected, including all your local hosts and domains, it should be passed through the *abbrev* program. This arranges for all reasonable abbreviations of domains to be added. An example input might be the following:

[2]To obtain a copy of this, contact Piete Brooks at Cambridge Computer Laboratory (pb@cl.cam.ac.uk)

```
cs.nott.ac.uk:mta =
cs.ucl.ac.uk:mta =
stc.co.uk:mta =
widget.uucp:mta =
```

The syntax of the *abbrev* command is `abbrev domainname...` and it reads from the standard input and writes to the standard output. One domain name should be the fully formed local domain. Other arguments can be used to generate abbreviations for other domains. When given the above as input and the command

```
abbrev cs.nott.ac.uk uucp
```

the output produced is

```
cs.nott.ac.uk:mta =
cs.nott.ac:synonym cs.nott.ac.uk
cs.nott:synonym cs.nott.ac.uk
cs:synonym cs.nott.ac.uk
cs.ucl.ac.uk:mta =
cs.ucl.ac:synonym cs.ucl.ac.uk
cs.ucl:synonym cs.ucl.ac.uk
stc.co.uk:mta =
stc.co:synonym stc.co.uk
widget.uucp:mta =
widget:synonym widget.uucp
```

### Generation of the Channel Table

The channel table is also generated in two stages. The input is as follows.

**Local domain:** This is not needed.

**NRS data:** The file *pp.chan* generated by the *c-nrs* program is used directly.

**Internet:** The list of valid domains is given, with the channel indicated. For example:

```
edu:(smtp)
gov:(smtp)
com:(smtp)
mil:(smtp)
```

**Private links:** These should be added manually. For example:

```
widget.uucp:widget.uucp(uucp)
```

Note that the key "widget.uucp" must be the same on each side of the table.

**Application relays:** Known domains, reached indirectly, can be added. For example:

```
foobar.uucp:widget.uucp()
```

This says that foobar.uucp is reached indirectly through widget.uucp.

In the second stage, the program *tjoin* is run to collate and reformat these input data into their final form. This stage is essential if the input contains application or top-level relays, and performs the following functions:

- "Unrolling" application relays, so that the installed tables specify the correct first hop.
- Where an MTA can be reached by multiple channels, sorting these into the preferred order. A direct connection will always be preferred to an application relay.

*Tjoin* input allows the following syntaxes:

**mta:mta(channel):** Specifies to contact `mta`, call `mta` using channel `channel`. Both `mta` parameters should be the same

**mta:mta1():** To contact `mta`, call `mta1` using the channel associated with `mta1` which should be specified elsewhere in the *channel* table. This is the application relay format.

**mta:(channel):** To contact `mta` call `mta` using channel `channel`. This form is appropriate for domain nameservers.

An example of the functions that *tjoin* does is shown here. The input of

```
stc.co.uk:(smtp)
uucp:uucphost.stl.stc.co.uk()
ac.uk:psshost.stl.stc.co.uk()
win.icl.stc.co.uk:erbert.uucp()
erbert.uucp:erbert.uucp(uucp)
psshost.stl.stc.co.uk:psshost.stl.stc.co.uk(smtp)
uucphost.stl.stc.co.uk:uucphost.stl.stc.co.uk(smtp)
```

would give as final output the table:

```
ac.uk:psshost.stl.stc.co.uk(smtp)
erbert.uucp:erbert.uucp(uucp)
psshost.stl.stc.co.uk:psshost.stl.stc.co.uk(smtp)
stc.co.uk:(smtp)
uucp:uucphost.stl.stc.co.uk(smtp)
uucphost.stl.stc.co.uk:uucphost.stl.stc.co.uk(smtp)
win.icl.stc.co.uk:erbert.uucp(uucp)
```

## 39.7 Adding New Users and MTAs

To add new users to the tables is best done in an automated way, generating the list from some master table perhaps or a system database.

To add a user, for example "J.Soap" with login id "joe" using the local channel, the following is required:

1. Add an entry to the *alias* table to map "joe" into "J.Soap."

   ```
   joe:synonym J.Soap
   ```

   This step is not required if you do not want to refer to Joe other than by the UNIX login id.
2. Add an entry to the *users* table to specify which channel to deliver Joe's mail by.

   ```
   J.Soap:822-local
   ```

   If you run a number of MTAs locally, then add the machine name after the channel.
3. Add an entry to the local channel table to give the delivery details.

   ```
   J.Soap:joe
   ```

   Optionally add the home directory and the mailbox if required.
4. To make the changes have immediate effect, run *dbmbuild*. It is not necessary to restart any of the daemon programs.

## 39.8 Adding Filters, Shapers + EITs

### 39.8.1 Adding A New Encoded Information Type

If you wish to add a new encoded information type, then some editing of the *tailor* file is necessary.

Suppose we wish to add a new body type "binary" which we want to be able to submit and have converted to ia5 before transmission.

1. Add a new body type to the list of body types in the *tailor* file.

   ```
   bodypart     binary
   ```

2. Now specify which outbound channels can handle such a body part by adding this type to the bptout list associated with the channel. If no outbound channel will be delivering this type then this step is unecessary. This is the case for binary.
3. To allow *submit* to work out how to convert from binary to ia5 it is necessary to add a new reformatting channel, such as the following:

   ```
   chan bin2ia5   prog=fcontrol, type=shaper, bptin=binary,
                  bptout=ia5, info="uuencode binary",
                  show="Binary -> Text"
   ```

This specifies that to convert input bodypart type `binary`, to output body type `ia5` the channel *fcontrol* should run the process uuencode `program` with standard input from the `binary` body part and standard output into the `ia5` body part.

In practise, it might be better not to call *uuencode* directly, but wrap it up in a shell script; we could then print out some preliminary remarks instructing the recipient how to unwrap the binary part.

Now, when *submit* receives a message which has flagged that it contains a body part of `binary`, it will be able to convert that part into `ia5`, which most output channels can deal with.

### 39.8.2 Adding a New Content Type

Adding a new content type for PP to relay is similar in style to adding a new encoded information type. The steps that need to be taken are dependent on whether conversion is involved or not.

If no conversion is involved, then to add a new content type such as `p22-encrypted`, for instance, would simply consist of registering that content type with an outbound channel. This is done by adding a new channel with the `content-out` part set to `p22-encrypted`. In this case, *submit* will pass the message straight through, unaltered, providing the recipient is reachable via that channel.

If conversion is required, then two things are necessary. The first is to add a new unflattening channel which is capable of splitting the message into component parts. Secondly, the component parts must be able to be reformatted into whatever is required on the outbound channel.

For example, suppose we have a new message content called "whizbang". This consists of a "whizbang" specific header and a standard `ia5` body part. To allow the type of mail to be input, the following would be required.

- An exploder channel that can split up "whizbang" format mail into its components.

  ```
  chan WBexplode     prog=WBexplode,type=shaper,
                     content-in=whizbang,
  ```

  This channel is defined to split up the message into two components, a file `hdr.wb` and a body part `1.ia5`.

- The new encoded information type `hdr.wb` needs to be registered in the tailor file

  ```
  headertype wb
  ```

- The `ia5` body part is okay as it stands, but to relay the message to X.400 or RFC-822 the header will need converting, therefore a filter to convert `hdr.wb` into either `hdr.822` or `hdr.p2` will be necessary. Only one need be written, because if *submit* has a `hdr.822` it can convert it to a `hdr.p2` using the *822top2* channel. Such a channel definition might look like this:

```
chan wbhdr-2-822 prog=wbto822,type=shaper,hdrin=wb,
                 hdrout=822,
                 show="WhizBang to 822 Header converter"
```

# 39.9 The Day–to–Day Running of PP

## 39.9.1 How to Start Up the PP System

Each time the UNIX machine is started up, the *rc.local* script in your UNIX system is executed. An entry for PP should be placed in *rc.local*. This entry should refer to a script which starts up various programs related to the running of PP. Typically this script is similar to *pp.start* (see appendix B) which starts up:

- QMGR: The queue manager which runs as the PP userID.
- *pptsapd*: The PP TSAP Daemon which also runs as the PP userID.
- *smtpsrvr* (optional): The SMTP listener which runs as the superuser. This is only necessary if:
    1. You are using the SMTP protocol.
    2. You are not running SMTP from *inetd* (see Section 36.8.1 on page 404 for details of this).
- *tsapd* (optional): is necessary if you are expecting incoming X.400 messages. This is assumed to be part of the general ISODE configuration; see *isode-gen* (8) for details.

Normally, these programs will run without interruption unless something serious happens, such as the machine going down. But if necessary you can always stop them by using the UNIX *kill* command. You can restart them by running the script manually or by invoking the programs separately, then letting them run in the background.

## 39.9.2 What to Run Each Night

In addition to running *pp.start* whenever the machine starts up, there are other things you should run regularly, ideally each night.

For example, if you build the PP tables from other sources, such as the NRS database, local system databases or other external sources, then running *dbmbuild* each night is a useful thing to do.

All the nightly routines can be run from a shell script, conventionally named something along the lines of *pp.night* (see appendix C for an example).

The sequence of operations should be :

- Archive the day's logs and remove outdated logs (see Section 39.9.3 on page 484).
- Collect statistics.
- Import new table source data files if necessary.
- Build new tables.
- *dbmbuild.*

### 39.9.3 Saving Logs

Saving logs depends very much on the individual policies for each site. For many cases the logs can just be set to truncate themselves when a suitable size is reached. Alternatively, if you are more concerned about keeping the information you should backup the logs each night. Two important exceptions to these general rules above are the *oper* log and the *stat* log.

The *oper* log should under normal conditions be empty, or at least very small. For this reason it is worth checking this overnight and perhaps mailing it to the postmaster if it contains anything.

The *stat* log can be processed to show statistics. There is a program in the *tools* directory call *statp.* This program processes the *stat* log file into a more structured format that is suitable for processing with *awk* (1). A sample awk script is supplied which shows the sort of output that can be produced from this.

## 39.10 Examining the PP Queue

Occasionally there may be problems encountered by PP that cannot be resolved by normal means, and it will be necessary to look at the queue directory to find out what is going wrong. This section is a brief guide to this.

The PP Queue is composed of two directories, *addr* and *msg*. An item in the queue is identified by a file in the *addr* directory with a unique name. This file is text encoded, and has information which corresponds approximately to P1 functionality. In the *msg* directory, there is a directory of the same name as the queue file, and contains the message. There is a subdirectory *base*, which contains the message as it arrived, and other directories, prefixed with the string *base.*, which contain transformed versions of the message content. There are also files *report.**, containing text encoded delivery reports associated with the message.

Each message content is a (possibly degenerate) directory tree. This hierarchy represents the structure of a message, with each body part being represented by a single file. Subdirectories represent forwarded IP messages. This structure is to allow for straightforward transformation of messages. When a message is converted, the body parts not affected are linked, rather than being copied.

An example queue file is shown in Figure 39.2.

```
Start-of-MsgEnvPrm
Message-type User-Mpdu
Message-size 269
Return-interval 168
Content-type p2
Encoded-info EncTypes="hdr.p2,ia5"
Priority non-urgent
cont-return true
Inbound-channel list
Inbound-mta "cs.nott.ac.uk"
MsgId string="trellis.cs.981:30.07.90.12.10.44" Country=GB
        Admin="GOLD 400" Prmd="UK.AC"
Trace mta="trellis.cs.nott.ac.uk" Country=GB Admin="GOLD 400"
        Prmd="UK.AC" arrival="Thu, 30 Aug 1990 12:10:44 +0000" action=0
        End-of-block
dl-exp-history "/S=private/OU=CS/O=NOTT/PRMD=UK.AC/ADMD=GOLD 400/C=GB/"
        "" "Thu, 30 Aug 1990 12:10:44 +0000"
Queued-time "Thu, 30 Aug 1990 12:10:44 +0000"
Start-of-MsgEnvAddr
Origs rno=000 status=done reform-done=000 outchan=dr2rfc
        outmta="cs.nott.ac.uk" ext-id=0 resp=false mta-rreq=basic
        usr-rreq=basic type=822 orig=private-request
        x400="/S=private-request/OU=CS/O=NOTT/PRMD=UK.AC/ADMD=GOLD 400/C=GB/"
        rfc="private-request@cs.nott.ac.uk" End-of-addr
Recip rno=001 status=pend reform-done=002
        reform-list="p2explode,p2to822,822touk,822flatten"
        outchan=822-local outmta="trellis.cs.nott.ac.uk" ext-id=1
        resp=true mta-rreq=basic usr-rreq=basic type=822
        eits="ia5,hdr.822-uk" content=822 orig=pac
        x400="/I=p/S=cowen/OU=CS/O=NOTT/PRMD=UK.AC/ADMD=GOLD 400/C=GB/"
        rfc="p.cowen@cs.nott.ac.uk" End-of-addr
```

Figure 39.2: Example of Address File

### 39.10.1 Delivery Reports

The basic operation of a channel is discussed in Section 36.9 on page 414. Delivery Reports are text encoded, using a format similar to that used for text delivery. Reports are stored as files in the message directory, with name `report.<n>`, where n is the PP number for the lowest recipient to which the DR refers. Where a DR refers to multiple recipients, all except the lowest are marked to done in the queue, and the first is marked to dliv.

An example text-encoded delivery report is shown in Figure 39.3.

```
Msgid string=DR020905-900816141523Z Country=gb Admin=" " Prmd=interspan
Trace mta="bells.cs.ucl.ac.uk" Country=gb Admin="gold 400" Prmd="uk.ac"
        arrival="Thu, 16 Aug 1990 14:15:32 +0000" action=0 End-of-block
Trace Country=gb Admin=" " Prmd=interspan
        arrival="Thu, 16 Aug 1990 14:15:23 +0000" action=0 End-of-block
Report-Hdr-End
Recip-No 1
DR-Failure Unable-To-Transfer Unrecognised-ORName
Arrival-Time "Thu, 16 Aug 1990 14:14:59 +0000"
Reported-Recipient-End
Report-End
```

Figure 39.3: Example Delivery Report Format

### 39.10.2 Receipt Notifications

These are handled by the UA, and are thus beyond the scope of PP. Mappings to RFC-822 are done according to RFC 1148.

### 39.10.3 Warnings

There are hooks to support warnings from the MTA to the message originator, typically of slow progress of a message through the MTS. This will be added in due course, by use of a new (private) protocol (to be specified). It is hoped also to provide a mechanism to query remote MTAs.

# Appendix A

# Example of the Tailor File

What follows is a suggested layout for the pp runtime tailor file. As the file is read in by most programs it is best if the number of long comments is kept to a minimum.

---

```
###################################################
#
# Tailor file for PP
#
###################################################

###################################################
#
# The following variables will need tailoring
#
###################################################
#
# The loc_dom_mta is the host that the MTA will reside on and execute from
# It is a fully qualified domain name and represent the physical machine
#         Examples might be
#                 cheetah.nyser.net
#                 violet.berkeley.edu
#                 john.cs.nott.ac.uk
#
loc_dom_mta       lancaster.xtel.co.uk
#
# The Sitename is what the rest of the world sees you as. This is typically
# a domain shorter than the full domain name. It is the name used to represent
# your site or group as a whole. This name normally hides the individual
# machine names
#         Examples might be
#                 berkeley.edu
#                 nyser.net
#                 cs.nott.ac.uk
#
loc_dom_site      xtel.co.uk
#
# The postmaster should include the local site name
```

```
# e.g., postmaster@berkeley.edu or postmaster@cs.nott.ac.uk
#
postmaster          postmaster@xtel.co.uk
#
# The pplogin should be the username of the owner of pp.
#
pplogin             pp
#
# The qmgrhost should be the same as the name found in isoentities file.
# This can be the same as loc_dom_mta name
#
pptsapd_addr        LOCAL-ETHER=lancaster+20001
qmgrhost            lancaster
#
# The local or name should be the name of your site in X.400 terms.
# This is attribute value based, and starts with organisational units and
# works up to country. If you are unsure, leave it with just a country
# component, e.g., "/C=GB/"
#
loc_or              "/o=xtel/prmd=X-Tel Services Ltd/admd= /c=GB/"
###################################################################
#
# That is the end of the things you must tailor - the rest are
# probably ok - but you should check.
#
###################################################################

delim1              "\1\1\1\1\12"
delim2              "\1\1\1\1\12"
#returntime 36
dap_user            "c=GB@o=X-Tel Services Ltd@cn=lancaster@cn=pp qmgr"


authchannel         free
authloglevel        high
wrndfldir           warnings
#submit_addr        lancaster:pp-submit

# Body types

headertype          822 822-jnt 822-us p2 822-uk p22 ipn g3fax
bodypart            ia5 dmd odif g3fax ipm voice


#  **-- Mapping tables --**
#
# All of these table MUST have the names given here
tbl       aliases             show="Aliases:  mapping -> local id",
                              flags=dbm
tbl       users               show="Users:  mapping local id -> disposition",
                              flags=dbm
```

```
tbl     domain          show="Mapping domain key ->full domain/MTA",
                        flags=dbm
tbl     or              show="Mapping O/R Address -> MTA",flags=dbm
tbl     channel         show="Binding MTA -> Channels",flags=dbm
tbl     or2rfc          show="RFC 987:  X.400 -> RFC 822",flags=dbm
tbl     rfc2or          show="RFC 987:  RFC 822 -> X.400",flags=dbm
tbl     rfc1148gate     show="Gateways that perform RFC 1148 conversions",
                        flags=dbm
tbl     auth.channel    show="Authorisation:  channel policy",flags=dbm
tbl     auth.mta        show="Authorisation:  mta based",flags=dbm
tbl     auth.user       show="Authorisation:  user based",flags=dbm
tbl     auth.qmgr       show="Authorisation:  qmgr control",flags=dbm
# **-- Channel tables --**
#
# Needed by individual channels, not submit
tbl     local           file="ch.local",
                        show="local id -> uid + home dir",
                        flags=dbm

tbl     x400in84        file="ch.x400in84",
                        show="MTA -> connect info",flags=linear
tbl     x400out84       file="ch.x400out84",
                        show="X.400(84) connect info -> MTA + other info",
                        flags=linear
tbl     x400in88        file="ch.x400in88",
                        show="MTA -> connect info",flags=linear
tbl     x400out88       file="ch.x400out88",
                        show="X.400(88) connect info -> MTA + other info",
                        flags=linear
tbl     shell           file="ch.shell",
                        show="info for shell chan"
                        flags=dbm
tbl     list            file="ch.list",
                        show="Lists:  distribution lists",
                        flags=dbm
tbl     uucp            file="ch.uucp"
                        show="UUCP: rfc822 -> uucp",
                        flags=dbm
tbl   fax               file="ch.fax",
                show="FAX: mappings and info",
                flags=linear
tbl     mslocal         file="ch.mslocal",
                        show="Message Store:local id -> user id,home directory",
                        flags=linear

chan    822-local               prog=local,
        show="Local Delivery channel",type=both,
        sort="user time",adr=822,adr-order=uspref,
        hdrin=822,hdrout=822-us,
        bptin=ia5,bptout=ia5,
        content-out=822,table=local,access=mts,chanout=dr2rfc
```

```
chan    xua          show="XUA Submission Channel",type=in,
                     access=mts,adr-order=ukpref,
                     adr=x400,
                     chanout=dr2rfc

chan    x400in84     prog=x400in84,show="X400 inbound",type=in,
                     content-in=p2,adr=x400,
                     adr-order=ukpref,intable=x400in84,chanout=x400out84

chan    x400in88     prog=x400in88,show="X400 inbound (1988)",type=in,
                     content-in=p22,adr=x400,
                     adr-order=ukpref,intable=x400in88,chanout=x400out88

chan    x400out84    prog=x400out84,show="X400 outbound",type=out,
                     adr=x400,adr-order=ukpref,
                     content-out=p2,
                     hdrout=p2,
                     bptout="ia5,g3fax,odif",
                     table=x400out84

chan    x400out88    prog=x400out88,show="X400 outbound",type=out,
                     adr=x400,adr-order=ukpref,
                     content-out=p22,
                     hdrout=p22,
                     bptout="ia5,g3fax,odif",
                     table=x400out88

chan    mslocal      prog=mslocal,show="MS local delivery",type=out,
                     hdrout="p22",
                     bptout="ia5,g3fax,voice",table=mslocal,
                     sort="user time"

chan    smtp         prog=smtp,show="with SMTP (PP)",type=both,
                     adr=822,adr-order=usapref,chanout=dr2rfc,
                     bptout=ia5,hdrout=822-us,content-out=822,

chan  gb-janet    prog="greyout -P",show="via JANET with NIFTP (PP)",
                     type=both, adr=822,adr-order=ukpref,
                     hdrout=822-jnt,
                     bptout=ia5,chanout=dr2rfc,
                     content-out=822,info=janet
#                    mta=much.cs.nott.ac.uk,

chan    gb-pss       prog=smtp,key=ipss,
                     show="via PSS with NIFTP (PP)",type=both,
                     adr=822,adr-order=ukpref,chanout=dr2rfc,
                     bptout=ia5,hdrout=822-jnt,
                     content-out=822,mta=much.cs.nott.ac.uk

chan  fax         prog=G3Fax, show="Fax channel",type=both,
```

```
                content-in=p22, hdrout=g3fax, bptout=g3fax,
                            chanout=dr2rfc,table=fax,
 info="in=/dev/ttyb,out=/dev/faxout,softcar,debug,master=adam@xtel.co.uk"

chan   faxyuch        prog=G3Fax, show="Fax channel",type=both,
                            content-in=p22,
                bptout="g3fax,ia5", chanout=dr2rfc, table=fax,
                info="in=/dev/ttyb,out=/dev/ttyb,master=faxmaster"

chan     dirlist              prog=dirlist,show="Directory List channel",type=both,
                              chanout=dr2rfc,adr=x400,adr-order=uspref,
                              sort="user time"

chan     list                 prog=list,show="List channel",type=both,
                              adr-order=uspref,info="linked",
                              table=list,chanout=dr2rfc,sort="user time"

chan     uucp                 prog=uucp-out,key="uucp-out,rmail",
                              show="UUCP channel",type=both,
                              adr=822,adr-order=ukpref,table=uucp
                              info="uux=/tmp/uux,host=nott-cs",chanout=dr2rfc

chan     dr2rfc               prog=dr2rfc,show="Dr2rfc channel",type=both,
                              adr=822,adr-order=ukpref,
                              bptin=ia5,hdrin=822,
                              info="return=all",
                              content-out=822

chan     shell                prog=shell,type=out,access=mts
                              show="Shell channel",
                              table=shell,sort="user time",
                              bptout=ia5,hdrin=822-uk, content-out=822

# QMGR special channels (load/manage/clean)

chan     qmgr-load            prog=qmgr-load,show="Loading the QMGR",
                              type=qmgrload,info="5";

chan     msg-clean            prog=msg-clean,show="Removing finished message"
                              type=delete

chan     trash                prog=trash,show="Removing trash"
                              type=debris

chan     timeout              prog=timeout,show="Timeout messages"
                              type=timeout

#  **-- shaper channels --**

#  Flatteners
```

```
chan    p2flatten       prog=p2flatten,show="Structured message -> P2",
                        type=shaper,content-out=p2

chan    822flatten      prog=rfc934,type=shaper,content-out=822

chan    p22flatten      prog=p2flatten,show="Structured Message -> P22",
                        type=shaper,content-out=p22

#   Unflatteners

chan    p2explode       prog=p2explode,type=shaper,content-in=p2

chan    p22explode      prog=p2explode,type=shaper,content-in=p22


# Header Filters
chan   822tofax     prog=fcontrol,type=shaper,
               hdrin=822-us,hdrout=g3fax,
 info="hdr2fax -from $(400sender) -to $(400recip) -subject $(ua-id) \
  -table $(table) -outmta $(outmta)",table=fax,

               cost=20
chan    822touk         prog=fcontrol,type=shaper,
                        hdrin=822,
                        hdrout=822-uk,
                        info="rfc822norm -jnt -bigend"
chan    822tojnt        prog=fcontrol,type=shaper,
                        hdrin=822,hdrout=822-jnt,
                        info="rfc822norm -jnt -bigend -jntsender $(822SENDER)"
chan    822tous         prog=fcontrol,type=shaper,hdrin=822,
                        hdrout=822-us,
                        info="rfc822norm -822 -littleend"
chan    822top2         prog=RFCtoP2,type=shaper,hdrin=822,conv=1148
                        hdrout=p2,cost=10,
                        show="RFC1148 RFC 822 -> P2"
chan    822top22        prog=RFCtoP2,type=shaper,hdrin=822,conv=1148
                        hdrout=p22,cost=10,
                        show="RFC1148 RFC 822 -> P22"
chan    p2to822         prog=P2toRFC,type=shaper,hdrout=822,conv=1148,
                        hdrin=p2,cost=10,
                        show="RFC1148 P2 -> RFC 822"
chan    p22to822        prog=P2toRFC,type=shaper,hdrout=822,conv=1148
                        hdrin=p22,cost=10,
                        show="RFC1148 P22 -> RFC 822"
chan    p22top2         prog=fcontrol,type=shaper,hdrout=p2,hdrin=p22,
                        show="P22 to P2 downgrade",
                        conv=conv,cost=10,info="P22toP2"
#identity map
chan    p2top22         prog=fcontrol,type=shaper,hdrout=p22,hdrin=p2,
                        show="P2 to P22 upgrade",cost=1,
                        info="/bin/cat"
```

```
# Body part filters

chan    g3faxtotxt        prog=fcontrol,type=shaper,bptin=g3fax,
                          bptout=ia5,info="removebp G3Fax",
                          show="Fax -> Text mapper",cost=100,conv=loss
chan   txttofax     prog=fcontrol,type=shaper,bptin=ia5,
               bptout=g3fax,
                          info="ia52fax -table $(table)",table=fax,
#                         info="ia52fax -table $(table) -display trellis:0",table=fax,
               show="ia5 -> g3fax mapper"
chan   voicetotxt         prog=fcontrol,type=shaper,bptin=voice,
                          bptout=ia5,info="removebp Voice"
                          show="Voice -> Text mapper",cost=100,conv=loss

#  **-- Logging for the rest of the prog --**
#
authlog level=notice, size=400
operlog level=notice, size=400
normlog level=notice, size=400, sflags=zero

822flatten       normlog  file=filter
p2flatten        normlog  file=filter
822touk          normlog  file=filter
822tous          normlog  file=filter
dr2rfc           normlog  file=filter
fcontrol         normlog  file=filter
odif2txt         normlog  file=filter
p2explode        normlog  file=filter
rfc822norm       normlog  file=filter
trash            normlog  file=filter

822top2          normlog  file=rfc987
p2to822          normlog  file=rfc987

list             normlog  file=lists

qmgr             normlog  file=qmgr
qmgr-load        normlog  file=qmgr

smtp             normlog  file=smtp
smtpsrvr         normlog  file=smtp
greyout          normlog  file=greyout
gb-janet         normlog  file=greyin
submit           normlog  file=submit dflags=close

local            normlog  file=local
msg-clean        normlog  file=msg-clean

x400in84         normlog  file=x400in84,level=pdus
x400in84         isodelog rtsaplevel file=rts,level=all
```

```
x400in84        isodelog ssaplevel file=ssap,level=all
x400out84       normlog  file=x400out84

x400in88        normlog  file=x400in88 level=trace level=pdus
x400out88       normlog  file=x400out88

p7server        normlog  file=p7server level=all

xfax            normlog  file=fax
xfaxd           normlog  file=fax #level=all
G3Fax           normlog  file=fax
hdr2fax         normlog  file=fax
ia52fax         normlog  file=fax

#isodelog       rtsaplevel file=rts           level=all
pptsapd         normlog  file=pptsapd,        dlevel=notice
dirlist         normlog  file=dirlist
mslocal         normlog file=mslocal
xprobe          normlog file=probe level=trace,level=pdus
p7server        isode ns_enable off
xua             isode ns_enable off
libmsattr                isode ns_enable off
submit          isode ns_enable off
```

Figure A.1: An Example Tailor File

# Appendix B

# Example of the PP Start Script

What follows is an example of a script which is run to start the PP mail system.

```
#! /bin/sh

# SMTP running under inetd
#cd /usr/pp/pp/lib/chans
#if [ -f smtpd -a -f smtpsrvr ]; then
#       (./smtpd `pwd`/smtpsrvr smtp > /dev/null 2>&1 ) &
#       echo -n ' smtp'
#fi

cd /usr/pp/pp/lib
su pp <<EOF
echo -n ' pp.startaspp :  '
if [ -f pptsapd ]; then
        echo -n ' pptsapd '
        pptsapd > /dev/null 2>&1
fi
if [ -f qmgr ]; then
        echo -n ' qmgr '
        qmgr > /dev/null 2>&1
fi
echo '.'
EOF
```

Figure B.1: An Example Start Script

# Appendix C

# Example of the PP Script Run Nightly

What follows is an example of a script which is regularly run to keep the PP mail system up to date.

---

```
#! /bin/sh

PATH=/crg/pp/bin:/crg/pp/cmds/tools:/usr/local/bin:/usr/ucb:/bin:/usr/bin:/usr/5bin:
export PATH
#
# Shell script run nightly to collect up things etc.
#
set -x
cd /crg/pp
L=logs
T=tables
STATDIR=/crg/pp/logs/statistics

exec 1> $L/pp-nightly.log 2>&1

freespace . 2000 || { echo NO space left on device; exit 1; }

#Save the stats files
if [ -f $L/stat ]
then
        DATE=`date +%h-%d.%T`
        [ -d $L/tmp ] || mkdir $L/tmp
        mv $L/stat $L/tmp/stat.$DATE
fi

# And then once a week...
if [ `date +%w` -eq 0 ]
then
        YDATE=`date "+%h-%d-%y`
        [ -d $STATDIR ] || mkdir $STATDIR
```

```
        if pstat $L/tmp/* /dev/null | bin/stat.awk > $STATDIR/stats.$YDATE
        then
                echo 'Sucessful - removing old files'
                rm $L/tmp/*
        fi
fi

# This should be first building command, as it updates the DERFIL2 file
echo 'building the PP tables'
(cd tables; make install)

# update the niftp stuff
echo 'building the niftp database'
(cd niftp; make )

echo UPDATE complete
```

Figure C.1: An Example Nightly Script

# Appendix D

# Obtaining X.400 Tables

The following tables are necessary for correct X.400 operation. These tables should be obtained from UCL. The tables are:

**or:** The O/R Table.

**rfc2or:** The RFC 822 to O/R mapping table

**or2rfc:** The O/R to RFC 822 mapping table.

**rfc1148gate:** The RFC 1148 known gateways file.

These tables can be fetched in a number of ways.

**FTP:** If you have access to Internet FTP then use anonymous FTP to cs.ucl.ac.uk [128.16.5.31] to retrieve the files from the directory *pp-tables/*. For example:

```
% ftp cs.ucl.ac.uk
Connected to bells.cs.ucl.ac.uk.
220 bells.cs.ucl.ac.uk FTP server (SunOS 4.0) ready.
Name (cs.ucl.ac.uk:pp): anonymous
331 Guest login ok, send ident as password.
Password:
230 Guest login ok, access restrictions apply.
ftp> get pp-tables/or or
...
ftp> get pp-tables/or2rfc or2rfc
...
ftp> close
%
```

**FTAM:** If you have access to FTAM on Janet, PSS or the Internet, you may obtain the tables from UCL using one of the following:

- Janet DTE 00000511160013 with TSEL 259 (ascii-encoded)

- PSS DTE 23421920030013 with TSEL 259 (ascii-encoded)
- Internet address cs.ucl.ac.uk ([128.16.5.31]) port 102 with TSEL 259 (ascii-encoded)

Use the "anon" user-identity and retrieve the files in the *pp-tables/* directory. For example:

```
% ftam ucl
user (ucl:pp): anon
ucl... connected
ANONymous user permitted, access restrictions apply
ucl> get pp-tables/or /tmp/or
ftam: unstructured text file transfer
ftam: 5792 bytes received in 5.88 seconds (0.96 Kbytes/s)
...
ucl> close
%
```

**NIFTP:** If you run NIFTP over the public X.25 or over Janet, and are registered in the NRS at salford, you can use NIFTP with username "guest" and your name as password, to access UK.AC.UCL.CS to retrieve the files found under `<pp-tables>`. For example:

```
% cpf '<pp-tables>or'@uk.ac.ucl.cs or
%
```

**MAIL:** The files may be obtained by mail by sending a suitable query to the address `info-server@cs.ucl.ac.uk`. This query should consist of a message body with the lines:

```
Request: pp-tables
Topic: or
Topic: rfc2or
Topic: or2rfc
Topic: rfc1148gate
```

E.g.:

```
% mail info-sver@cs.ucl.ac.uk <<EOF
Request: pp-tables
Topic: or
Topic: rfc2or
Topic: or2rfc
Topic: rfc1148gate
EOF
%
```

# Appendix E

# Testing PP — the MTS User Interface

A special user interface known as *mu* is provided as a general tool to help test *submit* and consequent operations in PP. Setting defaults in the *mu.defaults* file allows a minimum number of message-specific parameters to be provided. It may be used to resubmit a modified text-encoded file taken from the queue.

## E.1 Overview

The message submission tool MU takes input from the command line, from a defaults file *mu.defaults* if present in the working directory, and otherwise from the default command directory `cmddfldir` and then any other files specified with `-file` flags. A full summary of the flags to MU is given in Table E.1 on page 506. Any command line option may be placed on a line within an input file. MU calls its command line parser recursively when it encounters a line starting with `'-'` (flagchar). Any line starting with `'#'` (commentchar) is ignored. Otherwise, all lines are offered to the various *submit* input routines in turn for incorporation into PP's internal message structures (*prm_vars*, *Qstruct* and *addr*). Any line which returns an error code (`rp_isbad`) from all these routines is assumed to be in error.

The input lines which specify assignments as specified in queue (5) may be received in any sequence, and inputs may override earlier entries. Any value may also be assigned on the (original) command line with `-value v1 v2` ...up to the next flag.

If input files are nested, input lines from the nested file are processed before the remainder of the file containing the `-file` specifier. The default file is parsed first (*mu.defaults* unless overridden with a `-default` flag on the command line), then any `-file` specified files from the command line, finally `-value` specifications from the command line. Body part files may be specified with `-body` commands, either on the command line or embedded as with other commands.

MU uses PP's standard logging: additional logging messages generated by –0 –1 –2 –3 flags are output to a channel (`muout`) which defaults to `stdout` unless flag `-logfile` is specified. Note that output may be rerouted in the course of processing input files. The flag –5 allows these messages to be appended to the nominated logfile, rather than replacing it.

In addition to the llog_trace and llog_debug calls associated with flags `-0` and `-1` shown below, there are some other llog_fatal and llog_exceptions calls. Note that functions `list_args` and `show_args` (in *argh.c*) do not generate llog events. MU accepts a number of debug flags `-0`, `-1` etc.; currently these are used as follows:

| flag | function |
|---|---|
| -0 | Log to *muout* progress messages, and pplog(llog_trace ...). |
| -1 | Log to *muout* command files as they are processed, and pplog(llog_debug ...). |
| -2 | List to *muout* body part files as they are io_tdata'ed. |
| -3 | List to *muout* structures prior to *submit* io_ calls. |
| -4 | Abort prior to *submit* io_ calls. |
| -5 | Append to logfile rather than overwrite. |

MU accepts `-body` part file names with any arbitrarily long pathname. The full path is used:

1. To open the file and check its length. Two fatal errors are detected :

   a. `unable to read body part %s.`

   b. `body part %s is null file.`

2. To open the file in order to pass its contents to *submit* with a series of *io_tdata(buf,length)* calls. Again, failure to open is reported:

   `unable to open body part for reading %s.`

3. To pass a name for *submit* to use in the queue. *submit* generates a message directory to match the supplied pathname. Thus:

   `-body 4.ipm/hdr.822uk` — generates :

   usr/spool/pp/queues/msg/msg.annnnnn/base/4.ipm/hdr.822uk

If a reserved character "*" (filemarkchar) is embedded in the `-body` pathname, MU strips all characters up to and including the "*' from the pathname before passing to *submit*. This allows MU to distinguish between the path used to find the file(s) and that required within the message. Thus:

```
-body nest1/nest2/*3.ipm/1.ia5
```

generates:

```
/usr/spool/pp/queues/msg/msg.annnnnn/base/3.ipm/i.ia5
```

The "*" is removed for purposes (1) and (2) above. The character '*' may also be placed in the pathname to a directory to truncate the pathname passed on to *submit* from a `-tree` command; in the same way as for `-body` specification.

Because the line parsing routines used in MU are exactly those in *submit* itself, any values/options which are acceptable to *submit* will also be accepted by MU (but in any sequence ).

To illustrate :

```
mu  -- -0 -file test1 -body b1 /tmp/jtaylor/messdir/*b2 \
       -default new.defaults -value MsgiD Country=US
```

will read from "`new.defaults`", (processing any "`-flag`" specifiers it contains ), then from file "`test1`" finally setting a new country US to override any file-specified value. The `-0` flag turns on progress messages and "`--`" will list the flag table. During submission, files "b1" and "b2" will be transmitted individually.

# E.2 User Input

The reserved character "$" (TOKENCHAR) is used to indicate that the user should input a value to replace the "$", unless the line is a comment line or the "$" is immediately followed by a second to escape a real $ symbol. The portion of the input line up to and including the "$" is displayed on screen, then a carriage return delimited string is input to replace the "$". The substituted line is scanned for further unpaired "$" characters. When all have been replaced, if the flag `-confirm` has been specified, the user input will be re-displayed awaiting user confirmation or cancellation with "y" or "n". The line is then offered to the *submit* input routines. Any error will cause the input portions to be re-prompted *unless* the flag `-nofix` has been specified, in which case MU will ignore the error and continue.

To allow repeated user input, for example, of multiple recipient lines, another reserved character "*" (repeatchar) may be placed at the start of a line to indicate repetition. If this character appears at the start of a line which contains no unpaired "$" characters, an error

```
error : no TOKENCHAR(s) in REPEAT line - REPEATCHAR ignored
```

is reported. Otherwise, user input takes place as before, terminated by a null input (just a carriage return) on any substitution field in the line. Repeat lines are stripped of the "*" character before passing to the *submit* input routines.

An example command line:

```
mu  -confirm -file a1 -nofix
```

where file a1 contains:

```
# Start-of-MsgEnvPrm
-body hdr.822
-body 2.ia5
# $$ implies $
-file level$$
Message-type User-Mpdu
# $ symbols in comments are ignored
Inbound-channel 822-local
Inbound-host UK.AC.UCL.CS
Content-type $
Encoded-info EncTypes=iA5Text
Priority $
PerMsg-Flags disclose-recipients
PerMsg-Flags return-contents
MsgId string $
Start-of-MsgEnvAddr
*Recip type=822 orig=$@uk.ac.ucl.$ End-of-addr
```

will prompt for `Content-type`, `Priority`, `MsgId string`, and two components from `Recip` lines until a null input. Each input line must be confirmed with "y", but any errors will be disregarded. Section delimiters such as `Start-of-MsgEnvAddr` are redundant, since MU accepts control lines in any order, but are benign.

# E.3 MU Internals

MU uses the argument handling routine **argh** and can therefore accept any unambiguous prefix for a flag specifier. (See separate document.)

MU has no knowledge of the significance of any input line other than that it is valid for *txt2prm*, *txt2q* or *txt2adr*. The one exception to this is that, to allow a recipient to be specified before the originator, each potential address line is tested against `"Origs."` (Because the originator is held in a separate structure from the recipient list, and *io_wadr* needs to have `AD_ORIGINATOR` or `AD_RECIPIENT` passed to it explicitly.) Second and subsequent `"Origs"` lines are treated as errors.

After processing all inputs, a sequence of procedure calls to are made to *submit* the message (as outlined in Part IX). Thus (summarised) :

Each procedure call returns a status in the error structure `RP_Buf` which is displayed as follows:

```
io_init(rp);      /* initialisation */
io_wprm(&prm,rp); /* write management parameters */
io_wrq(&q,rp);    /* per message parameters */

ap = ad_originator;           /* originator */
io_wadr(ap,AD_ORIGINATOR,rp);
ap = ad_recipient;
do {                          /* list of recipients */
   io_wadr(ap,AD_RECIPIENT,rp);
   ap = ap->ad_next;
   } while ( ap != NULL );
io_adend(rp);                 /* terminate address list */

if((p=next_arg("body",argv)) != NULL) {
   io_tinit(rp);              /* prepare for body part(s) */
   do {
      io_tpart(p,FALSE,rp);   /* prepare one body part */
      loop_data(p);           /* transmit with io_tdata() /*
      io_tdend(rp);           /* end one file */
   } while(p=next_arg("body",argv));
}
io_tend(rp));  /* complete message */
io_end(type);  /* terminate session with submit */
```

Figure E.1: io_ Interface

| Flag | Purpose |
|---|---|
| default | override mu.defaults |
| file | input from file(s) |
| value | command line specification of value |
| body | body part file name(s) |
| tree | directory name(s) |
| confirm | wait for y/n after $ substitution |
| nofix | ignore errors resulting from user input |
| logfile | re-route output messages to file |
| help | list flag table analysis |
| – | same as –help |
| ! | dummy next flag to terminate sequence ( future use ) |
| 0 | debug (see above) |
| 1 | debug |
| 2 | debug |
| 3 | debug |
| 4 | debug |
| 5 | debug |

Table E.1: Summary of MU flags

```
RP_ERROR error_number error_string.
```

Such errors abort the submission.

# Appendix F

# QMGR Protocol

This appendix contains the ASN.1 description of the QMGR protocol.

```
-- qmgr.ry - Qmgr operation definitions

Qmgr
DEFINITIONS ::=
BEGIN

IMPORTS MPDUIdentifier FROM QmgrP1;

-- EXPORTS everything


-- PORTS
qmgr-use OBJECT
      PORTS { newmessage[S],
                  readmsginfo[S],
                  msginfo[C],
                  channelinitialise[C],
                  processmessage,
                  channelbegin[S],
                  readqueue[C],
            channelread[S],
                  channelinfo[C],
                  channelcontrol[S],
                  mtaread[S],
                  mtainfo[C],
                  mtacontrol[S],
                  qmgrstatus[S],
                  readchannelmtamessage[S] } ::= id-pt-qmgr-use


activeChannel OBJECT
            PORTS { channelinitialise,
                        processmessage [S] }
      ::= id-pt-activeChannel
```

```
passiveChannel OBJECT
                PORTS { processmessage[S],
                        channelbegin[C] }
        ::= id-pt-passiveChannel

submitProcess OBJECT
        PORTS { newmessage[C] }
        ::= id-pt-submitProcess

queueReadProcess OBJECT
        PORTS { readqueue[S] }
        ::= id-pt-queueReadProcess

managementUA OBJECT
                PORTS { processmessage[C],
                        readmsginfo[C],
                                msginfo[S],
                        channelread[C],
                                channelinfo[S],
                                channelcontrol[C],
                        mtaread[C],
                                mtainfo[S],
                        mtacontrol[C],
                                qmgrstatus[C],
                                readchannelmtamessage[C] }
        ::= id-pt-managementUA

-- OPERATIONS

                                        -- new message arrived
                                        -- Submit -> QMGR
newmessage OPERATION
        ARGUMENT MsgStruct
        RESULT NULL
        ERRORS { congested, protocol }
        ::= 0

                                        -- read a message
                                        -- Console -> QMGR
                                        -- QMGR -> QMGR
readmsginfo OPERATION
        ARGUMENT ReadMessageArgument
        RESULT MsgList
        ERRORS { congested, protocol }
        LINKED {msginfo}
        ::= 1

                                        -- QMGR -> Console
                                        -- Incremental update
msginfo OPERATION
```

```
        ARGUMENT MsgList
        ::= 10

                                        -- processes a message
                                        -- QMGR -> Channel
processmessage OPERATION
        ARGUMENT ProcMsg
        RESULT DeliveryStatus
        ERRORS { congested, protocol }
        ::= 2

                                        -- start up a channel
                                        -- Channel -> QMGR
channelbegin OPERATION
        ARGUMENT FilterList
                                -- type of message requested
        RESULT FilterList
                                -- what you are going to get
        ERRORS { congested, protocol }
        ::= 3

                                        -- read the entire queue
                                        -- QMGR -> Q reader
readqueue OPERATION
        ARGUMENT NULL
        RESULT MsgList
        ERRORS { congested, protocol }
        ::= 4

                                        -- read a channel
                                        -- Console -> QMGR
                                        -- get info at channel level
channelread OPERATION
        ARGUMENT UTCTime
        RESULT ChannelReadResult
        ERRORS { congested, protocol }
        LINKED {chaninfo}
        ::= 5

                                        -- QMGR -> Console
                                        -- Incremental update
chaninfo OPERATION
        ARGUMENT ChannelReadResult
                                -- info on ALL channels
        ::= 11

                                        -- control a channels behaviour
                                        -- Console -> QMGR
channelcontrol OPERATION
        ARGUMENT ChannelControl
        RESULT PrioritisedChannelList
```

```
        ERRORS { congested, protocol, noSuchChannel, illegalOperation,
                authenticationFailure}
        ::= 6

                                        -- read about a mta
                                        -- Console -> QMGR
mtaread OPERATION
        ARGUMENT MtaRead
        RESULT PrioritisedMtaList
        ERRORS { congested, protocol, noSuchChannel }
        LINKED {mtainfo}
        ::= 7

                                        -- QMGR -> Console
                                        -- Incremental update
mtainfo OPERATION
        ARGUMENT PrioritisedMtaList
        ::= 12

                                        -- control a mta
                                        -- Console -> QMGR
mtacontrol OPERATION
        ARGUMENT MtaControl
        RESULT MtaInfo
        ERRORS { congested, noSuchChannel, mtaNotInQueue,
                authenticationFailure}
        ::= 8

                                        -- control a message
                                        -- Console -> QMGR
msgcontrol OPERATION
        ARGUMENT MsgControl
        RESULT NULL
        ERRORS { congested, protocol, noSuchChannel, mtaNotInQueue,
                authenticationFailure}
        ::= 13

                                        -- QMGR -> Channel (process)
channelInitialise OPERATION
        ARGUMENT Channel
        RESULT NULL
        ERRORS { congested, protocol, noSuchChannel}
        ::= 9

qmgrControl OPERATION
        ARGUMENT QMGRControl
        RESULT NULL -- always works
        ERRORS { congested, protocol, authenticationFailure}
        ::= 14

readChannelMtaMessage OPERATION
```

```
        ARGUMENT MsgRead
        RESULT MsgList
        ERRORS { congested, protocol, noSuchChannel, mtaNotInQueue }
        ::= 15

qmgrStatus OPERATION
        ARGUMENT NULL
        RESULT QmgrStatus
        ERRORS { congested, protocol }
        ::= 16
-- ERRORS

                        -- congestion at the responder
congested ERROR
        ::=             0

                        -- unknown channel
noSuchChannel ERROR
        ::=             1

                        -- unknown operation
illegalOperation ERROR
        ::=             2

                        -- operation on mta makes no sense
mtaNotInQueue ERROR
        ::=             3

                        -- error in the protocol
protocol ERROR
        ::=             4

authenticationFailure ERROR
        ::=             5

-- Bind Arguments

BindArgument ::= CHOICE {            -- structure used in association request
        noAuthentication [0] NULL,
        weakAuthentication [1] WeakAuthentication
        }

WeakAuthentication ::= SEQUENCE {
        username [0] IA5String,
        passwd   [1] IA5String OPTIONAL
        }

BindResult ::= SEQUENCE {
                result[0] ENUMERATED {      -- result from the association request
                        acceptedLimitedAccess(0), -- accepted limited access
                        acceptedFullAccess(1)     -- accepted full access
```

```
                },
                information[1] IA5String OPTIONAL,
                version[2] IA5String OPTIONAL
        }


BindError ::= SEQUENCE {
                reason[0] ENUMERATED {
                        badCredentials(0),          -- dont know this person
                        congested(1)                -- some system problem
                },
                information[1] IA5String OPTIONAL
        }

-- DATA TYPES

Mta ::= IA5String

Channel ::= PrintableString

Priority ::= ENUMERATED {low(0), normal(1), high(2)}
                        -- Internal priorities COULD be different
                        -- to external ones

UAContentId ::= PrintableString

ContentType ::= PrintableString

EncodedInformationTypes ::= SEQUENCE OF PrintableString

QID ::= PrintableString

User ::= IA5String
                        -- QMGR just sees users as strings.
                        -- This is 822 or /= X.400 syntax
                        -- The caller must get the right form!


ReadMessageArgument ::= SEQUENCE {
                filters  FilterList,
                interval UTCTime OPTIONAL
                        -- interval for control of the LINKED operation
                }

MsgList    ::= SEQUENCE {
                msgs SEQUENCE OF %[ type_Qmgr_MsgStructList %]
                        MsgStruct,
                deleted SEQUENCE OF %[ type_Qmgr_QidList %] QID OPTIONAL
                }

ProcMsg ::= SEQUENCE {
```

```
        qid QID,
        users UserList,
                              -- if USER 0, do all outstanding DNs
        channel Channel  -- Channel to apply
                  -- must be same for each user!
                  -- Warning and Expiry channels have "special" behaviour
}

Control ::= CHOICE {
                  stop [0] NULL,
                  start [1] NULL,
                  cacheClear [2] NULL,
                  cacheAdd [3] UTCTime }

ChannelControl ::=  SEQUENCE {
                  channel [0] Channel,
                  control [1] Control
                  }

MtaControl ::= SEQUENCE {
                  channel [0] Channel,
                  mta [1] Mta,
                  control [2] Control
                  }

MsgControl ::= SEQUENCE {
                  qid [0] QID,
                  users [1] UserList,
                  control [2] Control
                  }

UserList ::= SEQUENCE OF RecipientId

RecipientId ::= INTEGER

MsgStruct ::= SEQUENCE {
        messageinfo          [0] PerMessageInfo,
        recipientlist        [1] SEQUENCE OF %[ type_Qmgr_RecipientList %]
                                     RecipientInfo
                             -- only recipients with responsibility bit set
                             -- AND originator (recipient 0)
                             -- The originator is needed for DRs
        }


PerMessageInfo ::= SEQUENCE {
        queueid              [0] QID,
        mpduiden             [1] MPDUIdentifier,
        originator           [2] User,
        contenttype          [3] ContentType OPTIONAL,
        eit                  [4] EncodedInformationTypes OPTIONAL,
```

```
        priority              [5] Priority,
        size                  [6] INTEGER,
                              -- size in bytes
        age                   [7] UTCTime,
        warnInterval          [8] INTEGER,
        numberWarningsSent [9] INTEGER,
        expiryTime            [10] UTCTime,
        deferredTime          [11] UTCTime OPTIONAL,
        uaContentId           [12] UAContentId OPTIONAL,
        errorCount            [13] INTEGER OPTIONAL,
        inChannel             [14] Channel OPTIONAL
        }

ProcStatus ::=        SEQUENCE {
        enabled               [0] BOOLEAN,
        lastAttempt           [1] UTCTime OPTIONAL,
        cachedUntil           [2] UTCTime OPTIONAL,
        lastSuccess           [3] UTCTime OPTIONAL
        }

RecipientInfo ::= SEQUENCE {
        user                  [0] User,
        id                    [1] RecipientId,
        mta                   [2] Mta,
        channelList           [3] SEQUENCE OF %[ type_Qmgr_ChannelList %] Channel,
        channelsDone     [4] INTEGER,
                                          -- Number of channels processed
                                          -- If EQUAL to the number of channels,
                                          -- this implies DN is still pending
        procStatus            [4] ProcStatus OPTIONAL,
        info                  [5] IA5String OPTIONAL }


FilterList ::= SEQUENCE OF Filter

Filter ::= SEQUENCE {
        contenttype           [0] ContentType OPTIONAL,
        eit                   [1] EncodedInformationTypes OPTIONAL,
                              -- message must have only specified types
        priority              [2] Priority OPTIONAL,
                              -- messages of this priority and above
        moreRecentThan        [3] UTCTime OPTIONAL,
        earlierThan           [4] UTCTime OPTIONAL,
        maxSize               [5] INTEGER DEFAULT 0,
                              -- size in bytes
        originator            [6] User OPTIONAL,
        recipient             [7] User OPTIONAL,
        channel               [8] Channel OPTIONAL,
        mta                   [9] Mta OPTIONAL,
        queueid               [10] QID OPTIONAL,
        mpduiden              [11] MPDUIdentifier OPTIONAL,
```

```
        uaContentId          [12] UAContentId OPTIONAL }

ChannelReadResult ::= SEQUENCE {
        channels             [0] PrioritisedChannelList,
        load1                [1] INTEGER DEFAULT 0,
        load2                [2] INTEGER DEFAULT 0,
        currchans            [3] INTEGER DEFAULT 0,
        maxchans             [4] INTEGER DEFAULT 0}

PrioritisedChannelList ::= SEQUENCE OF PrioritisedChannel

PrioritisedChannel ::= SEQUENCE {
        channel    ChannelInfo,
        priority Priority }

ChannelInfo ::= SEQUENCE {
        channel                [0] Channel,
        channelDescription [1] PrintableString,
        oldestMessage          [2] UTCTime,
        numberMessages         [3] INTEGER,   -- not including DRs
        volumeMessages         [4] INTEGER,        -- bytes
        numberActiveProcesses [5] INTEGER,
        status                 [6] ProcStatus,
        numberReports    [7] INTEGER,
        direction              [8] BITSTRING {
                inbound (0),          -- supports inbound traffic
                outbound (1)          -- supports outbound traffic
                                      -- both bits on => does both
                                      -- both bits off is internal
                },
        chantype               [9] ENUMERATED {
                mta (0),              -- is an MTA level channel
                mts (1),              -- is an MTS level channel
                internal (2),         -- is an internal channel (formatter etc)
                passive (3)           -- responding channel?
                },
        maxprocs               [10] INTEGER DEFAULT 0,
        numberMtas             [11] INTEGER DEFAULT 0

        }

MtaRead ::= SEQUENCE {
        channel Channel,
        time UTCTime OPTIONAL
        }

MsgRead ::= SEQUENCE {
        channel Channel,
        mta Mta,
        time UTCTime OPTIONAL
        }
```

```
PrioritisedMtaList ::= SEQUENCE OF PrioritisedMta

PrioritisedMta ::= SEQUENCE {
        mta MtaInfo,
        priority Priority }

MtaInfo ::= SEQUENCE {
        channel             [0] Channel,
        mta                 [1] Mta,
        oldestMessage       [2] UTCTime,
        numberMessage       [3] INTEGER, -- not DRs
        volumeMessages      [4] INTEGER,
        status              [5] ProcStatus,
        numberDRs           [6] INTEGER,
        active              [7] BOOLEAN DEFAULT FALSE,
        info                [8] IA5String OPTIONAL
        }

DeliveryStatus ::= SEQUENCE OF IndividualDeliveryStatus


IndividualDeliveryStatus ::= SEQUENCE {
        recipient [0] RecipientId,
        status        [1] ENUMERATED {
                                -- The QMGR should treat the following
                                -- as successful. In the latter cases
                                -- a DR is processed in conjuction
                                -- with a different recipient
                success (0),
                successSharedDR (1),
                failureSharedDR (2),

                                -- The next set are treated by the
                                -- QMGR as now having to send a DR
                negativeDR (3),  -- negative DR
                positiveDR (4),         -- positive DR


                                -- the final set are different types
                                -- of transient failure, needing
                                -- different QMGR retry strategies
                messageFailure (5),-- temp failure on the Message (e.g.
                                -- protocol temp reject)
                mtaFailure (6),         -- MTA failure (e.g. couldn't connect)
                mtaAndMessageFailure (7) -- Both (e.g. connection bust)
                },
        info[2] IA5String OPTIONAL
        }
```

```
QMGRControl ::= SEQUENCE {
        op [0] QMGROp
        }

QMGROp ::= ENUMERATED {
        abort (0),
        gracefulTerminate (1),
        restart (2),            -- as if from cold
        rereadQueue (3),   -- but don't discard current information
        disableSubmission (4),  -- Don't let processes submit
        enableSubmission (5),
        disableAll (6),
        enableAll (7),
        increasemaxchans(8),
        decreasemaxchans(9) }


QmgrStatus ::= SEQUENCE {
        boottime            UTCTime,
        messagesIn          INTEGER,
        messagesOut         INTEGER,
        addrIn              INTEGER,
        addrOut             INTEGER,
        opsPerSec           INTEGER,        -- * 100
        runnableChans       INTEGER,        -- * 100
        msgsInPerSec        INTEGER,        -- * 100
        msgsOutPerSec       INTEGER,        -- * 100
        maxChans            INTEGER,
        currChans           INTEGER,
        totalMsgs           INTEGER,
        totalVolume         INTEGER,
        totalDrs            INTEGER
        }
END
```

Figure F.1: QMGR ROS

# Bibliography


[Dun] Kevin J. Dunlap. *Name Server Operations Guide for BIND.* University of California, Berkeley. BSD 4.3 Release.

[Kil88] S.E. Kille. PP - a message transfer agent. In *IFIP WG 6.5 Conference on Message Handling Systems and Distributed Applications*, pages 115–118. North Holland Publishing, October 1988.

[Kil89] Stephen E. Kille. Mapping between X.400(1988)/ISO10021 and RFC822. Request for Comments 1148, DDN Network Information Center, SRI International, July 1989.

[Mar85] Marshall T. Rose and Einar A. Stefferud. Proposed Standard for Message Encapsulation. Request for Comments 934, DDN Network Information Center, SRI International, January 1985.

[RC87] Marshall T. Rose and Dwight E. Cass. ISO Transport Services on top of the TCP. Request for Comments 1006, DDN Network Information Center, SRI International, May 1987.

[Ros86] Marshall T. Rose. *Changes to the Rand MH Message Handling System: MH #6.5 for 4.3BSD UNIX*, May 1986. MH documentation set.

[Ros88] Marshall T. Rose. Post Office Protocol — Version 3. Request for Comments 1081, DDN Network Information Center, SRI International, December 1988.

[Ros89] Marshall T. Rose. *The ISO Development Environment: User's Manual.* The Wollongong Group, 5.0 edition, March 1989.

# Part X

# PP Manual: Programmer's Guide

# PP

## *Volume 2: Programmer's Guide*

Julian Onions
X-Tel Services Ltd

# Preface

This part describes the PP programming interface, and covers:

- Submission of messages such as might be used by a user agent.
- Submission of messages as by a protocol channel.
- Writing channel programs.

It also explains the major data structures used in PP and the conventions such as logging and initialisation.

# Chapter 40

# General

## 40.1 Overview

There are certain approaches taken by PP processes. These are described here to facilitate emulation by new processes. These are not strict guidelines, but following existing practises will usually be easier and make upgrading the software less painful.

## 40.2 Initialisation

All PP programs generally start by calling one or more initialisation routines. This may vary depending on what the channel needs to know. This initialisation does various things, amongst which are:

- Reading global parameters from the tailor file.
- Initialising the logging packages.
- Handling of signals.

The normal method of initialising a process is to call the following routine very early on (usually one of the first things):

```
sys_init (name)
char *name;
```

This routine does most of the initialisation required. The argument is usually the value of `argv[0]`, which is used in the logging initialisation to record the name of this program.

## 40.3 Runtime Tailoring

The runtime tailoring for PP is complex, as there are many parameters that can affect the operation of the system. The main things tailored are pathnames to locate

| | |
|---|---|
| LLOG_NONE | Not logged |
| LLOG_FATAL | Fatal errors |
| LLOG_EXCEPTIONS | Exceptional events |
| LLOG_NOTICE | General information |
| LLOG_PDUS | Printing of Protocol Data Units |
| LLOG_TRACE | Program Tracing |
| LLOG_DEBUG | Full debugging |
| LLOG_ALL | All Values |

Table 40.1: Logging Levels

commonly used programs; file names and directories; or the more complex tailoring to define such things as channels and tables. See Part IX for the full detail.

To add new items to be tailored, it is necessary to add some code to the parsing routines. For simple additions, it is necessary only to modify the tables and the switch statement in the file *pp/Lib/tai/tai_sys.c*. More complex tailoring is best done by creating a separate procedure, possible in a new file. Such additional tailoring should not be undertaken lightly as it will make the new version of PP incompatable with existing and new versions.

## 40.4 Logging

All logging works through a standard package. This package includes features to limit the log files and to notify administrators of errors. The logging has some structure too it and the following are the general rules used when programming PP.

### 40.4.1 Logging Levels

The logging package takes a bit mask of values to log. This is compared with the current setting of the logging level and then certain values are logged. The levels available are shown in Table 40.1. The values `LLOG_NONE` and `LLOG_ALL` are special: the first is no logging at all, the latter sets all bits in the bitmask.

### 40.4.2 Logging Structures

There are three log structures used in PP. The structures themselves are defined in the include file *isode/logger.h*. These structures are of type `LLog *` and are the following:

| Structure | Usage |
|---|---|
| `log_norm` | Normal logging |
| `log_oper` | Critical Operator message |
| `log_stat` | Statistical and Authorisation |

These structures are rarely used explicitly. With few exceptions, the logging macros described below use the `log_norm` structure.

### 40.4.3 Logging Macros

There are several macros defined to aid in the use of logging. The definitions of these macros can be found in the include file *ll_log.h*. These macros may be used in the following way:

```
PP_LOG (level, (format, arg1, arg2 ...))
int    level;
char   *str;
```

This macro is used for most of the non-debugging logging. The arguments to this call are as follows:

`level`: One of the logging levels specified above. However, as there are macros provided for fatal errors and debugging, it is usually only the values of `LLOG_EXCEPTIONS` and `LLOG_PDUS` which are used as the argument here. The `LLOG_EXCEPTIONS` is used to log failures that are not critical. The `LLOG_PDUS` level is used to trace any protocol exchanges – using the `PP_PDUS` macro if suitable.

`format`: This is a printf-like format string which together with any arguments *must* be enclosed in brackets as shown. The `format` and any number of optional args produce the logging message.

The next macro is a more general macro which allows logging of system error messages to be attached to the basic log message.

```
PP_SLOG (level, what, (format, arg1, arg2 ...))
int  level;
char *what;
char *format;
```

This is similar to the PP_LOG macro, but the extra argument if not null ensures that operating system call failures are logged as well. This macro should be used where it is suspected that a system call has failed.

`level`: The logging level.

`what`: A string which if not the null pointer logs the system error.

`format`: A printf-like format string.

For more urgent cases of logging, the following macro is provided:

```
PP_OPER (what, (format, arg1, arg2 ...))
char    *what, *format;
```

This macro is used for logging of extreme problems. It should only be used for errors that require operator intervention. These errors typically end up in a separate log as well as the normal log and are always logged at the LLOG_FATAL level. It is assumed that the system administrator will look through this log frequently and will immediately take action on anything found there. The arguments are:

`what`: This is a string which is used to construct a system error message. This should only be present if a system call is suspected of failing. Otherwise the constant NULLCP should be used.

`format`: This string is used as a printf like syntax to produce the message together with optional arguments as in the case of PP_LOG. Again, this parameter and any arguments *must* be enclosed in brackets as shown.

Another logging call is provided for statistical and authorisational data:

```
PP_STAT ((format, arg1, arg2 ...))
char    *format;
```

This macro is used for logging statistical information. It should be used where useful to record statistics like number of messages and times, etc. Its arguments are printf like, and *must* be enclosed in the double brackets as shown.

```
PP_NOTICE ((format, arg1, arg2 ...))
char    *format
```

This macro is used to record interesting events in protocol exchanges. It should be used so that the basic flow of a program may be observed, without undue amounts of log file space or extra machine load. Common logging events should be: connecting to a host, terminating a connection, and the transfer of a message.

```
PP_TRACE ((format, arg1, arg2 ...))
char   *format;
```

This macro is used throughout the source code to trace the calling of functions and the general flow of the programs and libraries. It logs the information at the LLOG_TRACE level, and this macro is dependent on the value of the PP_DEBUG define. If this is not defined then the PP_TRACE macros are not compiled in. The arguments are identical to the PP_STAT macro.

```
PP_DBG ((format, arg1, arg2 ...))
char   *format;
```

This macro is similar to the PP_TRACE macro, except it logs at the level of LLOG_DEBUG and will not expand to anything unless PP_DEBUG is defined and has a value greater than 1 (usually PP_DEBUG_ALL). This macro should be used for very detailed tracing, or where large amounts of logging are likely to be generated.

```
PP_PDU ((fnx, pe, text, rw))
IFP    fnx;
PE     pe;
char   *text;
int    rw;
```

This macro is for logging of ASN.1 protocol data units (PDUs). It is only compiled in if PP_DEBUG is PP_DEBUG_SOME or greater. The arguments are as follows:

fnx: A function to print out the PDU. This should be a function constructed by the printer option of pepy.

pe: The presentation element to print out.

str: An explanatory string, usually the name of the PDU.

rw: A flag indicating the direction the PDU is going. Set to PDU_WRITE to indicate the pdu is being written and PDU_READ to show it is being read.

Non ASN.1 protocol exchanges can be logged with the PP_LOG macro at the LLOG_PDUS level.

If other logging calls not described here are needed, they can be constructed from the more general SLOG macro described in the ISODE manual. Use of this feature is discouraged.

## 40.5 Code Location

The code to PP is arranged in a hierarchy of directories. This is a brief tour around the structure.

### 40.5.1 Library Code

Much of the PP system is in the library code. This is found in the directory `Lib/` under the top directory of the PP distribution. The library itself is split into several subdirectories. These are as follows:

**addr/:** The RFC 822 address parser library. This contains ways to manipulate and process RFC 822 addresses.

**format/:** This directory contains support routines for formatting messages.

**io/:** This directory contains most of the routines concerned with writing out and reading in structures. It is generally used for reading in structures and writing them out.

**or/:** This directory has a set of routines for manipulating O/R addresses.

**parse/:** This directory contains the code to do the generic parsing of addresses. It contains the general interface to X.400 and RFC 822 addresses.

**pp/:** This directory contains many of the basic PP specific routines such as manipulation of structures, PP structures, and the flattening and unflattening of these structures.

**qmgr/:** This directory contains the code required to interface with the QMGR process.

**table/:** This directory contains routines for accessing the databases used by PP for routing, aliases and the like.

**tai/:** This contains the routines responsible for reading and parsing the *tailor* file.

**util/:** This directory contains some generally useful common procedures.

**x400/:** This directory contains support routines for X.400 handling.

### 40.5.2 Core Programs

The next major directory to be considered is the `Src/` directory. This contains the core programs required by PP. These are:

**MTAconsole/:** This is the source code for the X-based MTA console program. It monitors the overall running of PP.

**submit/:** This is the source for the submission process. All messages entering the queue go through this process.

**qmgr/:** This is the source for the QMGR process.

`pptsapd/`: This is the source for the pp tsap daemon. This is the process that runs the channels invoked by the queue manager.

### 40.5.3 Other Directories

The are the following other directories which have some significance.

`h/`: Contains all the public header files used in the PP system.

`doc/`: Contains the documentation on PP.

`man/`: Contains manual pages on the PP programs.

`Uip/`: Contains some user interface programs for submitting messages to PP.

`Tools/`: Contains several programs useful for building up parts of the PP system or verifying it.

`Chans/`: The channel programs can all be found under the directory `Chans/`.

# Chapter 41

# Message Submission

## 41.1 Overview

This chapter describes the procedural interface for message submission. This interface reflects the submission interface of both the message transfer abstract service and the MTA abstract service. It is therefore used for:

- User interfaces submitting messages (message transfer abstract service).
- Inbound channels submitting messages (MTA abstract service).

It is a generalised interface, with aspects beyond X.400, but it is broadly targeted for X.400 usage. The general function of the interface is as follows:

1. Initialise submission.
2. Initialise Message (per-message parameters).
3. Handshake on addresses.
4. Transfer one or more body parts.
5. Final handshake to lock message into the queue or abort.
6. Goto 2, until no more messages.
7. Terminate submission.

## 41.2 The io_ Interface

The `io_` interface is the full interface to PP. All routines have the prefix `io_` and all return some type of status indicating success or failure.

### 41.2.1 Major Structures

The following are the key structures used in submission. These structures should be filled in and passed over to *submit* by the procedures defined below.

### Channel Lists

A channel list is the structure used to keep channels and hosts. It is defined in file *list_rchan.h* and the structure is shown in Figure 41.1

```
typedef struct list_rchan {
        char                *li_mta;
        CHAN                *li_chan;
        AUTH                *li_auth;
        struct list_rchan   *li_next;
} LIST_RCHAN;
#define NULLIST_RCHAN       ((LIST_RCHAN *)0)
```

Figure 41.1: Channel List Structure

The use of the structure members are:

**li_mta:** The MTA name as a character string.

**li_chan:** The associated channel structure.

**li_auth:** Authorisation parameters. This should not normally be filled in.

**li_next:** The next element in the list.

There are several routines to manipulate such structures.

A new list element can be created by using the routine `list_rchan_new`. This is defined as:

```
LIST_RCHAN *list_rchan_new (mta, chan)
char *mta;
char *chan;
```

The parameters to this call are:

**mta:** The name of the MTA. This parameter is copied intop heap storage.

**chan:** The name of a channel. This is converted to a channel structure internally.

A new structure can be added onto the end of a list, or if the list is empty can be set as the first element by a call to `list_rchan_add`. This is defined as:

```
void list_rchan_add (base, new)
LIST_RCHAN **base;
LIST_RCHAN *new;
```

The linked list structure can be freed by calling `list_rchan_free`, which is defined as:

```
void list_rchan_free (list)
LIST_RCHAN *list;
```

Two other useful routines are those to convert a string into a channel structure. The first one is a simple string to structure routine:

```
CHAN *ch_nm2struct (name)
char *name;
```

This converts from the given name into a channel structure, or returns `NULLCHAN` if there is no match.

For inbound channels when filling in the queue structure with inbound parameters it is necessary first to allocate a channel list with one of the above functions, but not to fill in the channel part of it. This should be filled in with the routine:

```
CHAN *ch_mta2struct (name, mta)
char *name, *mta;
```

This routine returns a channel structure based on a name and an MTA. This allows the particular channel to be selected dependant upon the MTA the message is received from. This allows the channel pairing to take place.

### Encoded Information Types

Encoded information types are used in several places in PP. They are kept internally as a linked list of strings which contain either the name of the information type, or a string representation of an object identifier. The structure is shown in Figure 41.2.

```
typedef struct list_bpt {
        char                *li_name;
        struct list_bpt     *li_next;
} LIST_BPT;
```

Figure 41.2: Encoded Information Type Structure

There are some support routines to help construct these lists. A new structure can be allocated with a value stored in help space by using the function `list_bpt_new`. This is defined as:

```
LIST_BPT *list_bpt_new (value)
char *value;
```

A linked list structure can be duplicated by using `list_bpt_dup`. This returns a separate duplicate list. It is defined as:

```
LIST_BPT *list_bpt_dup (list)
LIST_BPT *list;
```

A new element may be added to the end of a list, or become the first member if the list is empty, by calling `list_bpt_add`. This is defined as:

```
void list_bpt_add (base, new)
LIST_BPT **base;
LIST_BPT *new;
```

A list may be searched for a particular type of element by using `list_bpt_find`. This returns either the first matching entry or `NULLIST_BPT` if no such element is found.

```
LIST_BPT *list_bpt_find (list, item)
LIST_BPT *list;
char *item;
```

Finally, a linked list may be deallocated up by calling the routine `list_bpt_free`:

```
void list_bpt_free (list)
LIST_BPT *list;
```

### Management Parameters

The management parameters are defined in the file *prm.h* and the structure is shown in Figure 41.3. These values are set before each message submission to change the general policies of *submit*.

There are two support routines for manipulating this structure. The first, `prm_init`, initialises the structure to its default state. The second, `prm_free`, frees off all allocated variables within the structure.

```
void prm_init (pp)
struct prm_vars *pp;

void prm_free (pp)
struct prm_vars *pp;
```

The use of each of the members of this structure are:

**prm_logfile:** A logfile to be used for this specific message.

**prm_loglevel:** A logging level to be used for this message. It should be one of the levels of logging specified in *ll_log.h*.

```
struct prm_vars {
        char    *prm_logfile;
        int     prm_loglevel;
        int     prm_opts;
        char      *prm_passwd;
};
```

Figure 41.3: Management Parameter Structure

**prm_opts:** A set of options to control *submit*. This should be one of the following:

| Value | Meaning |
|---|---|
| PRM_NONE | No options |
| PRM_ACCEPTALL | *submit* should accept bad recipient addresses and generate error reports itself |
| PRM_NOTRACE | *submit* should not generate Received: or Via: lines. |

**prm_passwd:** A password to authenticate the local user's submission (not used as yet).

### The Per-Message Information

The per-message information is defined in the file *q.h* and the structure is shown in Figure 41.4. Only the fields which should or may be filled in by interface programs are described in detail. The rest are calculated by *submit* if necessary.

```
typedef struct Qstruct {
        int             msgtype;            /* Type of message */
#define MT_UMPDU          1
#define MT_DMPDU          2
#define MT_PMPDU          3

/* -- MTS Parameters */
        long            msgsize;            /* Size of message */
        UTC             defertime;          /* Deffered time */
        UTC             latest_time;
        char            latest_time_crit;

        char            nwarns;             /* Number of warning msgs to send */
        int             warninterval;       /* Interval between warning msgs */
        int             retinterval;        /* Interval after which return mail */
        char            *cont_type;         /* Content type of message */
#define CONT_822S       "822"     /* 822 default type */
```

```
#define CONT_P2S            "p2"        /* p2 default string */

          EncodedIT         encodedinfo;        /* Encoded information type */
          int               priority;           /* Priority of message */
#define PRIO_NORMAL           0
#define PRIO_NONURGENT          1
#define PRIO_URGENT           2

          char              disclose_recips;
          char              implicit_conversion;
          char              alternate_recip_allowed;
          char              content_return_request;

          char              recip_reassign_prohibited;
          char              recip_reassign_crit;

          char              dl_expansion_prohibited;
          char              dl_expansion_crit;

          char              conversion_with_loss_prohibited;
          char              conversion_with_loss_crit;

          char              *ua_id;             /* UA content id */
          char              *pp_content_correlator;
                                                /* PP preferred string form  */
          struct qbuf       *general_content_correlator;
          char              content_correlator_crit;
                                                /* ASN.1 uninterpreted */

          FullName          *originator_return_address;
          char              originator_return_address_crit;

          int               forwarding_request;
          char              forwarding_request_crit;

          struct qbuf       *originator_certificate;
          char              originator_certificate_crit;

          struct qbuf       *algorithm_identifier;
          char              algorithm_identifier_crit;
                            /* content confidentiality */

          struct qbuf       *message_origin_auth_check;
                                      /* also for Probe */
          char              message_origin_auth_check_crit;

          struct qbuf       *security_label;
          char              security_label_crit;

          int               proof_of_submission_request;        /* boolean */
          char              proof_of_submission_crit;
```

```
        Extension       *per_message_extensions;

        ADDR            *Oaddress;              /* Orig addr - linked list */
        ADDR            *Raddress;              /* Recip addrs - linked list */

/* -- MTA AS Parameters */
        LIST_RCHAN      *inbound;               /* Inbound MTA/Channel */
        MPDUid          msgid;                  /* Message ID */
        Trace           *trace;                 /* Trace info */
        DLHistory       *dl_expansion_history;
        char            dl_expansion_history_crit;

/* -- PP calculated parameters */
        UTC             queuetime;              /* Time that message was enqueued */
        UTC             departime;              /* Time that message left the queue */
} Q_struct;
```

Figure 41.4: Queue Structure

The queue structure controls most of the per message parameters. There are a number of utility routines to help manipulate these structures.

The routine `q_init` can be used initialise an empty structure. The routine `q_free` can be used to free off allocated fields within the structure.

```
int q_init (qp)
Q_struct *qp;

int q_free (qp)
Q_struct *qp;
```

Typically an inbound channel will only fill in one or two parameters, most can be safely defaulted unless required. It is important to set the inbound parameter and to fill in the list of encoded information types and possible the content type. The rest are all optional.

The elements of the queue structure are now described. Some elements have an associated flag with the name ending with `crit`. This refers to an element in the structure with a similar name. This element indicates what the criticality constraints on the element are. Values for the settings of these are shown in Table 41.1. These values may be logically or'd together to set several critical values.

**`msgtype`:** The type of message being submitted. This should be one of the following:

| Value | Meaning |
|---|---|
| MT_UMPDU | Normal message |
| MT_DMPDU | A delivery report |
| MT_PMPDU | A Probe |

| Value | Meaning |
|---|---|
| CRITICAL_NONE | Not critical |
| CRITICAL_SUBMISSION | Critical for submission |
| CRITICAL_TRANSFER | Critical for Transfer |
| CRITICAL_DELIVERY | Critical for Delivery |

Table 41.1: Criticality Codes

The q_init routine defaults this value to MT_UMPDU.

**cont_type:** The content type of the message. This should be one of the defined types; normally one of the following:

| Value | Meaning |
|---|---|
| "rfc-822" | An RFC 822 content |
| "p2" | A P2 1984 content |
| "p22" | A P2 1988 content |

As these values are common, they are available via the following string variables.

```
extern char *cont_822;
extern char *cont_p2;
extern char *cont_p22;
```

An empty content implies that the message will be submitted in structured form (usually the default for RFC 822 messages).

**encodedinfo:** A list of encoded information types. This should include all the encoded types that are in the message, and should be a member of the list defined in the bodypart tailor variable. Although any encoded information type present in the bodypart list is allowed, PP knows about some special cases. These are:

| Value | Meaning |
|---|---|
| "ia5" | An Ia5 (ascii) body part |
| "hdr.822" | An RFC 822 header |
| "hdr.p2" | A P2 1984 header |
| "hdr.p22" | A P2 1988 header |
| "hdr.ipn" | An IPN header |

These definitions are available in the external variables as follows:

```
extern char *hdr_822_bp;
extern char *hdr_p2_bp;
extern char *hdr_p22_bp;
extern char *ia5_bp;
```

The following variables can all be safely defaulted to those initialised by `q_init`, but can be varied as required.

**`defertime`:** The time the message should wait for before being delivered (for deferred delivery): optional.

**`latest_time`:** The latest delivery time this message should be delivered by.

**`nwarns`:** The number of warning messages to be sent if the message is delayed.

**`warninterval`:** The interval of time between successive warnings.

**`retinterval`:** The time to wait before returning the message as undeliverable.

**`priority`:** The priority associated with the message. This takes one of the following values:

| Value | Meaning |
|---|---|
| PRIO_NORMAL | The default |
| PRIO_NONURGENT | A low priority message |
| PRIO_URGENT | A high priority message |

**`disclose_recips`:** A true/false flag indicating whether recipients should be disclosed.

**`implicit_conversion`:** A true/false flag indicating if implicit conversion can be performed.

**`alternate_recip_allowed`:** A true/false flag indicating if the message can be sent to an alternate recipient.

**`content_return_request`:** A true/false flag indicating if the message content should be returned on delivery failure.

**`recip_reassign_prohibited`:** A flag indicating if the recipient may reassign the message to a new recipient.

**`dl_expansion_prohibited`:** A flag indicating if the message may not be expanded into a distribution list.

**`conversion_with_loss_prohibited`:** A flag indicating if conversion is allowed even if it loses information.

**ua_id:** The user agent ID. This is a string that identifies the message to a user agent.

**pp_content_correlator:** The internal version of the content correlator.

**general_content_correlator:** The content correlator of the message.

**originator_return_address:** The postal return address of the originator.

**forwarding_request:** An indication of whether the physical forwarding address should be returned to the originator.

**originator_certificate:** This element conveys the certificate of the originator when secuure messaging is being used.

**algorithm_identifier:** An indication of the encryption algorithm used for message encryption.

**message_origin_auth_check:** This element allows MTAs and recipients to authenticate the message origin.

**security_label:** A label indicating the security policy.

**proof_of_submission:** An indication of whether proof of submission is required.

**per_message_extensions:** A holder for any additional elements of the message.

**Oaddress:** Should be empty for submission.

**Raddress:** Should be empty for submission.

**inbound:** The inbound channel/mta pair This is important as this controls authentication and authorisation.

**msgid:** The MTS identifier of this message (P1 level).

**trace:** The trace fields.

**dl_expansion_history:** A trace of the distribution lists this message has been expanded by.

### The Address structure

The address structure contains all the information about each address. The structure is defined in the file *adr.h*. The same structure is used for both Recipient and Originator address. The structure is shown in Figure 41.5. There are a number of support routines that help construct addresses.

The routine `adr_new` creates a new address structure with some of the values filled in. This structure is the minimum necessary set of values to submit a recipient. To create an Originator, the responsibility bit `ad_resp` should be set to false, and the status (`ad_stat`) should be set to `AD_STAT_DONE`. The routine is defined as:

```
ADDR *adr_new (str, type, rno)
char *str;
int type;
int rno;
```

The arguments to this call are

`str`: The address in string format, either RFC 822 or the string form of the O/R name.

`type`: This is the type of address; it should be one of the values suitable for `ad_type`.

`rno`: The recipient number. Set this to 0 if you do not care about this value.

The routine `ad_init` will initialise an `ADDR` structure to its default values. It is defined as:

```
void adr_init (ap)
ADDR *ap;
```

The routine `adr_add` adds an address onto the end of a linked list of addresses, or allocates the first node if the list is empty.

```
void adr_add (base, new)
ADDR **base;
ADDR *new;
```

The routine `adr_tfree` frees a list of addresses freeing of all allocated elements and the structures themselves.

```
void adr_tfree (ap)
ADDR *ap;
```

The routine `adr_free` frees off all the allocated elements within a single address structure but does not free the structure itself.

```
void adr_free (ap)
ADDR *ap;
```

```
typedef struct ad_redirection {
        struct ad_redirection *rd_next;
        char      *rd_addr;             /* O/R Name */
        char      *rd_dn;               /* Distinguished Name */
        int       rd_reason;
#define RDR_RECIP_ASSIGNED      0
#define RDR_ORIG_ASSIGNED       1
#define RDR_MD_ASSIGNED         2
} Redirection;

#define AD_ORIGINATOR           1
#define AD_RECIPIENT            2

typedef struct     adr_struct {
        int             ad_no;          /* recipient number */
        int             ad_status;      /* recipient status */
#define AD_STAT_UNKNOWN         0
#define AD_STAT_PEND            1
#define AD_STAT_DRREQUIRED      2       /* DR required */
#define AD_STAT_DRWRITTEN       3       /* DR written */
#define AD_STAT_DONE            4
        int             ad_rcnt;        /* reformatters done count  */

        /* -- MTS Service Parms */

        char            *ad_value;      /* address-original */
        char            *ad_dn;         /* Directory Distinguished Name */
                                        /* QUIPU string encoding */

        int             ad_usrreq;      /* user-report-request bit */
#define AD_USR_NOREPORT         0
#define AD_USR_BASIC            1
#define AD_USR_CONFIRM          2
#define AD_USR_NONE             3
        int             ad_explicitconversion;      /* explicit conversion */

        int             ad_type;        /* address-type */
#define AD_X400_TYPE            1
#define AD_822_TYPE             2
#define AD_ANY_TYPE             3

        char            *ad_orig_req_alt; /* originator requested alternate */
                                        /* recipient - std encoded */
        char            ad_orig_req_alt_crit;

#define AD_RDM_MAX      4
        int             ad_req_del[AD_RDM_MAX];    /* requested delivery method */
#define AD_RDM_NOTUSED  -1
#define AD_RDM_ANY      0
#define AD_RDM_MHS      1
```

```
#define AD_RDM_PD          2
#define AD_RDM_TLX         3
#define AD_RDM_TTX         4
#define AD_RDM_G3          5
#define AD_RDM_G4          6
#define AD_RDM_TTY         7
#define AD_RDM_VTX         8
        char               ad_req_del_crit;

        char               ad_phys_forward; /* boolean - is physical */
                                            /* forwarding allowed */
        char               ad_phys_forward_crit;

        char               ad_phys_fw_ad_req;
        char               ad_phys_fw_ad_crit;
                                            /* boolean - request for phys */
                                            /* foward address */

        int                ad_phys_modes;
        char               ad_phys_modes_crit;
#define AD_PM_ORD          0x1
#define AD_PM_SPEC         0x2
#define AD_PM_EXPR         0x4
#define AD_PM_CNT          0x8
#define AD_PM_CNT_PHONE 0x10
#define AD_PM_CNT_TLX      0x20
#define AD_PM_CNT_TTX      0x40
#define AD_PM_CNT_BUREAU           0x80
#define AD_PM_MAX          0x80

        int                ad_reg_mail_type;
        char               ad_reg_mail_type_crit;
#define AD_RMT_UNSPECIFIED         -1
#define AD_RMT_NON_REG             0
#define AD_RMT_REG                 1
#define AD_RMT_PERSON              2

        char               *ad_recip_number_for_advice;
        char               ad_recip_number_for_advice_crit;

        OID                ad_phys_rendition_attribs;
        char               ad_phys_rendition_attribs_crit;

        int                ad_pd_report_request;
        char               ad_pd_report_request_crit;
#define AD_PRR_UNSPECIFIED -1
#define AD_PRR_UNDELIV_PDS         0
#define AD_NTF_PDS                 1
#define AD_NTF_MHS                 2
#define AD_NTF_BOTH                3
        Redirection        *ad_redirection_history;
```

```
        char            ad_redirection_history_crit;

        struct qbuf     *ad_message_token;
        char            ad_message_token_crit;

        struct qbuf     *ad_content_integrity;
        char            ad_content_integrity_crit;

        int             ad_proof_delivery;
        char            ad_proof_delivery_crit;
                                /* boolean.  Is proof of delivery */
                                /* requested */

        /* -- MTA Service Params (calculated for MTS AS) */

        int             ad_extension;           /* extension-id */
        int             ad_resp;                /* responsibility bit */
        int             ad_mtarreq;             /* mta-report-request bit */
#define AD_MTA_NONE             0
#define AD_MTA_BASIC            1
#define AD_MTA_CONFIRM          2
#define AD_MTA_AUDIT_CONFIRM    3

        /* -- This may be supplied as a hint  but might get changed */

        int             ad_subtype;             /* address-subtype */
#define AD_NOSUBTYPE            0
#define AD_JNT                  1
#define AD_REAL733              2
#define AD_REAL822              3
#define AD_X400_84              4 /* Use this if compatible */
#define AD_X400_88              5


        Extension       *ad_per_recip_ext_list;
                                        /* bucket for new and private */
                                        /* odds and sods */

        /* -- parameters calculated by PP */
        /* -- Note: the outbound mta is held in ad_outchan -- */

        char            *ad_r400adr;            /* x400-addr */
        char            *ad_r822adr;            /* rfc-addr */

        char            *ad_content;            /* outgoing content type */

        LIST_RCHAN      *ad_fmtchan;            /* reformatting channels */
        LIST_RCHAN      *ad_outchan;            /* outbound channel structure */
        LIST_BPT        *ad_eit;                /* outgoing eit's */
```

```
        /* -- from here onwards extra PP specific info -- */
        /* -- Diagnostics for any address parsing failures -- */

        int             ad_parse_stat;      /* address parsing err status */
        int             ad_reason;          /* DR reason failure */
        int             ad_diagnostic;      /* DR diagnostic code */
        char            *ad_add_info;       /* DR supplementary info */

        /* -- Address Control File offsets for fixed length variables -- */

        off_t           ad_no_offset;          /* offset param for recip number */
        off_t           ad_stat_offset; /* offset param for recip status */
        off_t           ad_rcnt_offset; /* offset param for reformat next */


        struct adr_struct   *ad_next;
} ADDR;
```

Figure 41.5: Address Structure

Only the non-internal fields are described here:

**ad_extension:** The extension identifier for this address.

**ad_status:** The status of this address, one of:

| Value | Meaning |
|---|---|
| AD_STAT_PEND | for recipients awaiting delivery |
| AD_STAT_DONE | for recipients not to be delivered to |

**ad_dn:** The distinguished name component of the address.

**ad_usrreq:** This maps to the X.400 user request bits. It has the one of the following values:

| Value | Meaning |
|---|---|
| AD_USR_NOREPORT | No delivery reports requested |
| AD_USR_BASIC | Delivery failutes should be reported |
| AD_USR_CONFIRM | Deliveries should be confirmed |
| AD_USR_NONE | Undefined value |

**ad_explicitconversion:** Is explicit conversion required. It should be one of the values defined in Table 41.2.

**ad_type:** The address type. This is one of the following values:

| Value | Meaning |
|---|---|
| AD_X400_TYPE | An X.400 format address |
| AD_822_TYPE | An RFC 822 format address |
| AD_ANY_TYPE | An address in any of the above formats |

| Value |
|---|
| AD_EXP_NONE |
| AD_EXP_IA5_TEXT_TO_TELETEX |
| AD_EXP_TELETEX_TO_TELEX |
| AD_EXP_TELEX_TO_IA5_TEXT |
| AD_EXP_TELEX_TO_TELETEX |
| AD_EXP_TELEX_TO_G4_CLASS_1 |
| AD_EXP_TELEX_TO_VIDEOTEX |
| AD_EXP_IA5_TEXT_TO_TELEX |
| AD_EXP_TELEX_TO_G3_FACSIMILE |
| AD_EXP_IA5_TEXT_TO_G3_FACSIMILE |
| AD_EXP_IA5_TEXT_TO_G4_CLASS_1 |
| AD_EXP_IA5_TEXT_TO_VIDEOTEX |
| AD_EXP_TELETEX_TO_IA5_TEXT |
| AD_EXP_TELETEX_TO_G3_FACSIMILE |
| AD_EXP_TELETEX_TO_G4_CLASS_1 |
| AD_EXP_TELETEX_TO_VIDEOTEX |
| AD_EXP_VIDEOTEX_TO_TELEX |
| AD_EXP_VIDEOTEX_TO_IA5_TEXT |
| AD_EXP_VIDEOTEX_TO_TELETEX |

Table 41.2: Table of Explicit Conversion Values

**ad_orig_req_alt:** The originator requested alternate recipient, if supplied.

**ad_req_del:** The requested delivery method. This is an array of delivery method alternatives.

**ad_phys_forward:** If physical forwarding is allowed.

**ad_phys_fw_ad_req:** A request to supply the physical forwarding address of the recipient.

**ad_phys_modes:** Specifies the type of delivery required.

**ad_reg_mail_type:** The type of registered mail in use.

**ad_recip_number_for_advice:** The number for advice to call for delivery.

**ad_phys_rendition_attribute:** The physical rendition attributes for the address when transfered to the postal service.

**ad_pd_report_request:** An option to supply a physical delivery report.

**ad_redirection_history:** The redirection history for this address.

**ad_message_token:** A security parameter for message tokens.

**ad_content_integrity:** A content integrity check parameter.

**ad_proof_delvery:** Proof of delivery is requested.

**ad_resp :** The responsibility bit. This should be set to either TRUE or FALSE.

**ad_mtareq:** This maps to the X.400 MTA report request bits. It should be set to one of the following:

| Value | Meaning |
|---|---|
| AD_MTA_NONE | Undefined value |
| AD_MTA_BASIC | Generate Delivery failures |
| AD_MTA_CONFIRM | Generate Delivery confirmations |
| AD_MTA_AUDIT_CONFIRM | Generate full trace confirmations |

**ad_subtype:** The subtype of the address if appropriate. This is only used for RFC 822 addresses at present. The values are:

| Value | Meaning |
|---|---|
| AD_NOSUBTYPE | No particular sub type |
| AD_JNT | JANET style address |
| AD_REAL733 | RFC 733 style address |
| AD_REAL822 | RFC 822 style address |

**ad_pre_recip_ext_list:** A list of extension attributes.

**ad_value:** This is the address submitted.

**ad_next:** The link to the next address if they are in a linked list.

### 41.2.2 Reply Value Structure

The reply value buffer structure is shown in Figure 41.6. This is used in all handshakes with *submit* to return a status and an explanatory string.

The structure here is:

**rp_val:** The value returned; this is one of those defined in *retcode.h*.

**rp_line:** An optional explanatory string.

### 41.2.3 Procedure Calls

The submission interface is procedural and has a handshake at most of the interaction points. This interaction is reasonably complex but allows the submission to be flexible; this interface can be used to validate address as well as to submit message.

Most of these routines return a set of codes as defined in *retcode.h* to indicate success or failure of the operation. The codes indicate detailed status and are shown in Table 41.3. Two macros are useful for determining the general status of the reply. The behave as though they were defined as:

```
int rp_isgood (code)
int code;

int rp_isbad (code)
int code;
```

where "code" is the return code. The macros return boolean values of `TRUE` if the code is generally good or bad respectively.

Along with other parameters, these routines usually take an `RP_Buf` structure which is updated with the code and an explanatory string if the routine fails in some way.

#### Initialisation

To initialise the submission system it is first necessary to call the routine `io_init`:

```
int io_init (rp)
RP_Buf *rp;
```

This call initialises the submission by either invoking *submit* as a child process or by connecting to a *submit* daemon. It returns a good or bad status, and fills in the `rp` structure if the response is bad.

```
typedef struct rp_bufstruct     /* for reading reply strings */
{
    unsigned char      rp_val;
    char               rp_line[256];
} RP_Buf;
```

Figure 41.6: Reply Structure

| Value | Meaning |
|---|---|
| RP_DONE | General purpose done value |
| RP_OK | General purpose OK value |
| RP_MOK | Message accepted |
| RP_MAST | Master side |
| RP_SLAV | Slave side |
| RP_AOK | Address OK |
| RP_HOK | Host OK |
| RP_AGN | Temporary failure |
| RP_TIME | Timeout |
| RP_NOOP | No op |
| RP_EOF | End of file |
| RP_NET | Network failure |
| RP_BHST | Bad host interaction |
| RP_DHST | destination connection broke |
| RP_NIO | Network I/O problem |
| RP_NS | Temporary nameserver failure |
| RP_FIO | File I/O problem |
| RP_FCRT | File creation problem |
| RP_FOPN | File opening problem |
| RP_LIO | Local I/O problem |
| RP_LOCK | Resource locked |
| RP_MECH | Mechanism failed |
| RP_NO | General purpose failure |
| RP_BAD | General purpose failure |
| RP_PROT | General protocol failure |
| RP_RPLY | Bad reply code |
| RP_NAUTH | Bad authorisation |
| RP_NDEL | Couldn't deliver |
| RP_HUH | Parse error |
| RP_NCMD | No such command |
| RP_PARM | Bad parameter |
| RP_UCMD | Unknown command |
| RP_PARSE | Address parse error |
| RP_USER | Unknown user |

Table 41.3: Return Codes

### Message Management Parameters

The first set of parameters to negotiate with *submit* are the management parameters. These are defined in the structure in Figure 41.3 on page 539. This structure is passed over using the `io_wprm` routine:

```
int io_wprm (prm, rp)
struct prm_vars *prm;
RP_Buf *rp;
```

The parameter structure is often only sparsely filled (or even empty), as the default values assumed are usually correct for most common submissions.

### Per-Message Parameters

The next stage is the per-message parameters. This is achieved by filling in a `Q_struct` structure and passing it to *submit*. Once the structure is complete it can be written to *submit* using the `io_wrq` routine:

```
io_wrq (qp, rp)
Q_struct *qp;
RP_Buf *rp;
```

### Originator and Recipient Addresses

After the general parameters have been passed by the above routines, the send is passed over in the standardised address structure. The call to achieve this is the `wr_adr` routine:

```
int io_wadr (ap, type, rp)
ADDR *addr;
int  type;
RP_Buf *rp;
```

The type parameter is either `AD_ORIGINATOR` or `AD_RECIPIENT`. First the originator address is passed over and checked followed by the list of recipients. This is then followed by each of the recipient addresses. In this way, each address is checked and any failures can be pinpointed.

When all the addresses have been submitted, the address list is terminated with the call:

```
int io_adend (rp)
RP_Buf *rp;
```

This concludes the preliminaries, and the body of the message can be transferred.

### Body Part Submission

The body parts presented are dependent on the type of message being transferred. To initialise for body part submission, the following function is called:

```
io_tinit (rp)
RP_Buf *rp;
```

This initialises for text submission.

Following this call it is necessary to initialise for the first body part. This is done by:

```
int io_tpart (name, link, rp)
char    *name;
int     link;
RP_Buf *rp;
```

The name is the name of this part, for an RFC 822 body part it is usually something like `hdr.822` and `2.ia5` for the two parts of the message. For X.400, it is more often just a single file p2 or similar with the whole of the message in. The link parameter is a Boolean value to indicate whether the name is actually a secret link to another file in the queue to be linked with *link* (2); this is only for use by special channels and normally will be rejected by *submit*. If the link is false, then the data stream is read for the body part contents.

All Data is passed with the following routine:

```
io_tdata (buffer, length)
char *buffer;
int  length;
```

The buffer is a pointer to an array of characters of length `length`, which are written into the file created by the `io_tpart` call.

Once the body part has been written, the data stream is terminated by the call:

```
io_tdend (rp)
RP_Buf  *rp;
```

which closes the stream and returns the status in rp.

### Termination

Once all the body parts have been passed over the message is finally submitted with the following call:

```
io_tend (rp)
RP_Buf  *rp;
```

This puts the message into the queue and allows it to be delivered.

Finally, the whole session with *submit* can be terminated using the `io_end` call. The termination can either be graceful, or a program can, upon detecting an error, call an abort to the submission process at any time with this function:

```
int io_end (type)
int type;
```

The `type` parameter is set to one of the following:

| Value | Meaning |
|---|---|
| OK | The submission is successful |
| NOTOK | The submission should be aborted |

### 41.2.4 Example

An example interaction with submit is shown in Figure 41.7.

```
submit_message (orig, recips, fp)
ADDR    *orig;
ADDR    *recips;
FILE    *fp;
{
        RP_Buf  rps, *rp = &rps;
        char    buf[BUFSIZ];
        ADDR    *ap;

        if (rp_isbad (io_init(rp)))
                error ();

        if (rp_isbad (io_wprm (prm, rp)))
                error ();

        if (rp_isbad (io_wrq (q, rp)))
                error ();

        if (rp_isbad (io_wadr (orig, AD_ORIGINATOR, rp)))
                error ();

        for (ap = ad_recipients; ap; ap = ap -> ad_next)
                if (rp_isbad (io_wadr (ap, AD_RECIPIENT, rp)))
                        error ();

        if (rp_isbad (io_adend(rp)))
                error ();

        if (rp_isbad (io_tinit(rp)))
                error ();
```

```
        if (rp_isbad (io_tpart ("hdr.822", FALSE, rp)))
                error ();

        while (fgets( buf, sizeof buf, fp))
                if (rp_isbad (io_tdata (buf, strlen (buf))))
                        error ();

        if (rp_isbad (io_tdend(rp)))
                error ();

        if (rp_isbad (io_tpart ("1.ia5", FALSE, rp)))
                error ();

        while (fgets (buf, sizeof buf, stdin))
                if (rp_isbad (io_tdata (buf, strlen (buf))))
                        error ();

        if (rp_isbad (io_tdend (rp)))
                error ();

        if (rp_isbad (io_tend (rp)))
                error ();

         io_end(OK);
}
```

Figure 41.7: Example Interaction with Submit

## 41.3 The RFC 822 Interface

PP provides a full service interface, most of which is not needed by RFC 822-based systems. A simplified interface is provided on top of the `io_` interface. This interface is characterised by procedure calls with the prefix pps_ for PP simple interface.

It assumes a large number of default parameters and does not allow for much variation. It does provide an easy route for constructing */bin/mail*-like programs and can be used within programs to fire off system generated messages. This interface runs as a state machine, and the procedures must be called in the correct order to get the correct results.

All routines return the constant `NOTOK` on failure and `OK` on success. The `NOTOK` is unrecoverable, and the interface must be started again from the beginning. All routines in addition take an `RP_Buf` pointer which is updated if the call fails. This may be used to give better diagnostics.

## 41.3.1 Initialisation

To initialise this interface, a client program calls the pps_init routine. This attempts to initialise the association with *submit*.

```
pps_init (subject, rp)
char    *subject;
RP_Buf  *rp;
```

The parameters to this routine are:

**subject:** the subject line of the message, the constant NULLCP may be used if no subject line is required.

**rp:** An RP_Buf structure pointer that is updated if the call fails.

The errors produced by this call are usually the result of some deep system problem, such as failing to connect with the *submit* process.

## 41.3.2 Addresses and Headers

To supply recipient addresses for the message, the routines pps_adr, pps_to and pps_cc are called. The pps_adr supplies a new address to the system for this message. Use of the pps_to and pps_cc routines switches the status of the address between that of primary recipient and secondary recipient (i.e., the To and CC header lines).

```
pps_adr (address, rp)
char    *address;
RP_Buf *rp;

pps_to(rp)
RP_Buf *rp;

pps_cc(rp)
RP_Buf *rp;
```

The arguments are:

**address:** The recipient address as a legal RFC 822 format address.

**rp:** An RP_Buf structure pointer that is updated if the call fails.

The possible errors from these calls usually arise from the failure to call pps_init. The pps_to and pps_cc calls are entirely optional and may be interspersed with the pps_adr calls in any order.

Finally, when the addresses have all been submitted, the address phase is ended by calling pps_aend.

```
pps_aend (rp)
RP_Buf *rp;
```

At this stage, other headers may optionally be added by the pps_hdr routine. This is normally not necessary as the header fields To, Cc, From, and Date will automatically be generated.

```
pps_hdr (name, contents, rp)
char    *name,
        *contents;
RP_Buf *rp;
```

If the message is only being submitted to one recipient, there is a shorthand form which replaces the routines from pps_init up to and including the pps_tinit call. This routine, pps_1adr, is occasionally useful for submitting error reports to the system administrator or similar.

```
pps_1adr (subject, address, rp)
char   *subject,
       *address;
RP_Buf *rp;
```

The parameters to this routine are:

**subject:** The subject of the message. As above this can be the constant NULLCP for no subject.

**address:** The RFC 822 format recipient address

### 41.3.3 Text Submission

To add the body of the message, the routine pps_tinit is called first to initialise for text. This terminates the header part of the message and prepares for the text to be submitted.

```
pps_tinit (rp)
RP_Buf *rp;
```

The text is then submitted in two ways. The first method is as a sequence of null terminated character strings using the pps_txt routine. The second method is by passing an open file descriptor to the routine pps_file.

```
pps_txt (string, rp)
char *string;
RP_Buf *rp;

pps_file (fp, rp)
FILE *fp;
RP_Buf *rp;
```

The parameters to these calls are:

**string:** A null terminated string of characters.

**file:** A stdio file stream opened for reading. This is read up to the end of file.

These calls may be freely intermixed in any fashion.

### 41.3.4 Termination

To finally submit the message, it is necessary to call the routine pps_end. This terminates the interaction for this message and resets the state.

```
pps_end (status, rp)
int status;
RP_Buf *rp;
```

The status parameter is either OK if the submission is satisfactory and NOTOK if the submission is to be aborted. The NOTOK version may be called at any point to abort the submission and return to the pps_init state.

## 41.4 Debugging

Most of the debugging can be done through the logs. Typically turning the logging levels to include trace and debug will give large amounts of information and will slow the processes down considerably! The system should not normally be run with full logging for these reasons.

The use of the PP_TRACE and PP_DBG macros described in Section 40.4.3 on page 529 are very useful for inclusion in program text. the PP_TRACE should be used to indicate the flow of control. Usually a PP_TRACE call is included in each significant procedure call and typically displays the procedure name and any useful information about procedure arguments.

The PP_DBG macro is used anywhere that very detailed tracing might be needed such as printing out individual variables or similar. In particular, library routines usually use this macro to log tracing, as this sort of logging is not required as often as the tracing in programs.

The PP_NOTICE call should be used when interesting events happen to allow the progress of the program to be monitored.

The PP_PDUS macro and the LLOG_PDUS logging level should be used to log any protocol exchanges that might be of interest.

# Chapter 42

# Channels

## 42.1 Overview

This chapter describes the interface which provides the message delivery aspects of the message transfer abstract service and MTA abstract service. The major component of this is a set of routines for accessing the PP queue. As these routines are usually used in the context of a channel process, their usage is illustrated in various types of channel. There are also additional functions to facilitate reformatting/conversion.

The following types of channel are supported:

- Protocol outbound channel (MTA AS delivery).
- Local delivery channel (MT AS delivery).
- Local pickup channel (MT AS delivery).
- Remote TWA channel (MTA AS delivery).
- Reformatters.

## 42.2 The Queue Interface

### 42.2.1 Major Structures

The major structures in use for reading the queue are the following:-

- The parameter structure described in Figure 41.3 on page 539.
- The queue structure described in Figure 41.4 on page 539.
- The address structure described in Figure 41.5 on page 546.

There is also a separate set of routines and structures for interacting with the queue manager. This interface makes use of the structures defined in Figure 42.1.

```
struct type_Qmgr_ProcMsg {
   struct type_Qmgr_QID *qid;

   struct type_Qmgr_UserList *users;

   struct type_Qmgr_Channel *channel;
};

struct type_Qmgr_DeliveryStatus {
      struct type_Qmgr_IndividualDeliveryStatus *IndividualDeliveryStatus;

      struct type_Qmgr_DeliveryStatus *next;
};

struct type_Qmgr_IndividualDeliveryStatus {
   struct type_Qmgr_RecipientId *recipient;

   integer     status;
#define int_Qmgr_status_success     0
#define int_Qmgr_status_successSharedDR  1
#define int_Qmgr_status_failureSharedDR  2
#define int_Qmgr_status_negativeDR       3
#define int_Qmgr_status_positiveDR       4
#define int_Qmgr_status_messageFailure   5
#define int_Qmgr_status_mtaFailure       6
#define int_Qmgr_status_mtaAndMessageFailure      7

   struct          qbuf     *info;
};
```

Figure 42.1: Channel / Queue Manager Interface Structures

These structures are derived from the queue manager ROS specification given in Appendix F of Part IX.

### 42.2.2 Basic Access

The basic access provided to the queue is through a set of library calls. There are several classes of routines which can be divided up into queue manager interaction, address file processing routines and message body routines. Most of the operations described here are only useful for outbound channels.

#### Queue Manager Interaction

The queue manager interaction is normally handled by a single procedure, `channel_control`, which manages the session with the QMGR and calls the appropriate routines on receipt of ROS operations.

```
int channel_control (argc, argv, initfnx,
                     procfnx, endfnx)
int    argc;
char   **argv;
IFP    initfnx;
struct type_Qmgr_DeliveryStatus   *(*procfnx)();
IFP    endfnx;
```

The arguments are as follows:

**argc/argv:** The argument count and vector, normally copied from the `main` procedure. These are used to recapture the state of the association as outbound channels are normally run under the *pptsapd* (8) daemon.

**initfnx:** An initialisation function. This is called to initialise the channel and inform it of its name.

**procfnx:** A function called for each QMGR process message operation.

**endfnx:** A function called when the session with the QMGR is terminated. The constant `NULLIFP` may be used if this function is not required.

The `channel_control` function invokes its own error handlers and does not normally return.

The two functions `initfnx` and `procfnx` shown above are the key to the channels operation. The initialisation function should be defined in the following way:

```
int   initfnx (arg)
struct type_Qmgr_Channel *arg;
```

The function should then decide whether the given channel argument is sensible for this channel and return one of the constants `OK` or `NOTOK`. This function is normally only called once by the QMGR, but in cases where the same program can run as a number of channels it may be called subsequently to reinitialise the channel to a different mode of operation.

The process function is the one that does the real work of the channel. It should be defined like this:

```
struct type_Qmgr_DeliveryStatus *processmessage (arg)
struct type_Qmgr_ProcMsg *arg;
```

The function should then attempt to process the given message for the given recipients. This usually involves first reading the address control file given as part of the structure passed.

When the processing of the message has finished, the function should return a pointer to a list of recipient numbers together with a status field. This structure is the `type_Qmgr_DeliveryStatus` structure. This specifies for each recipient whether the operation was a success or failure. The status values are:

**int_Qmgr_status_success:** The operation was successful, the next processing stage can be considered.

**int_Qmgr_status_negativeDR:** The message has failed, and a delivery report *must* be written.

**int_Qmgr_status_positiveDR:** The message has succeeded, and a confirmation is required. This *must* be written out.

**int_Qmgr_status_successSharedDR:** The message has suceeded and a delivery report is to be sent. However, the delivery report will be sent as the result of processing another recipient.

**int_Qmgr_status_failureSharedDR:** The message has failed, and a delivery report should be sent for this recipient, but this will be sent as the result of another recipients actions.

**int_Qmgr_status_messageFailure:** The message has temporarily failed; other messages on the same channel may succeed and this message may succeed later at a second attempt.

**int_Qmgr_status_mtaFailure:** The remote MTA is not responding: the attempt should be retried at a later time. Further messages on this channel to this MTA should not be considered at this attempt.

**int_Qmgr_status_mtaAndMessageFailure:** This is an indication that there was a failure whilst transferring the message to the MTA. This channel should be attempted again in the near future.

To aid in setting these values, a set of support routines is provided in the library. These routines all update the global variable deliverystate which is suitable as a return value for the process function. Note, however, that the value of int_Qmgr_status_permanentFailure is "sticky"; this value may be set, but once set cannot be overwritten by these routines. This is because normally when an address is marked with this status, a delivery report is written out and the message is updated accordingly (see Section 42.2.3 for routines to write out delivery reports). To set the status then to something else would confuse the queue manager. The routines are as follows:

```
struct type_Qmgr_DeliveryStatus *delivery_init (users)
struct type_Qmgr_UserList *users;
```

This routine initialises the structure. It does by allocating an element for each of the users passed in the argument. The single parameter is the list of users passed over by the QMGR.

```
struct type_Qmgr_DeliveryStatus
       *delivery_setstate (rno, val, reason)
int  rno, val;
char *reason;
```

This routine sets the value of the given recipient number to the indicated value in the global structure (with the above proviso). It also includes a string indicating the reason for failure, if failure occurred. This string is passed back to the QMGR for display by the MTAconsole. It should be set to the constant NULLCP if the recipient was handled successfully or no diagnostic reason is available.

```
struct type_Qmgr_DeliveryStatus
       *delivery_setallstate (val, reason)
int  val;
char *reason;
```

This routine sets all users' status to the given value. This is useful when a connection cannot be established, for instance, and all recipients must be put in the same state (again, the above proviso about delivery reports holds). The reason field is the same as above.

Occasionally it may occur that a permanent failure is received but it is not possible to write a delivery report (e.g., a full disk). In this case the address file should not be updated and the DR status should be set to message failure (the next retry should also give a DR and then hopefully a report can be written). To aid in resetting these variables the following procedure is useful.

```
struct type_Qmgr_DeliveryStatus
       *delivery_resetDRs (val)
int     val;
```

The argument is the state to set the DR values to (nearly always `int_Qmgr_Status_messageFailure`).

The termination function, if used, should be defined as follows.

```
int endfuction ()
```

This routine is used to close down anything required before exiting the program. The calling routine will execute this function before sending the final disconnect to the QMGR and exiting.

### Address File Routines

The address file reading is usually the first operation a channel does on receiving the instruction to process a message. This is usually achieved by first building up the name of the message file to be read in from the queue id, and then invoking the procedure `rd_msg`.

```
int rd_msg (msg, prm, qp, ad_sndr, ad_recip, ad_count)
char  *msg;
struct prm *prm;
Q_struct *qp;
ADDR  **ad_sndr,
      **ad_recip;
int   *ad_count;
```

The parameters are:

**msg:** The address control file.

**prm:** The message parameters.

**qp:** The message queue structure.

**ad_sndr:** the originator of the message.

**ad_recip:** The list of recipients of the message.

**ad_count:** A count of the number of recipient addresses.

The routine returns a status to indicate success or failure. As part of its operation it locks the address file to prevent simultaneous access by other channels.

When the message has been processed, the lock *must* be released by calling the function `rd_end`.

```
int rd_end ();
```

If the messages status changes in some manner, the address file must be updated. This is achieved by one of the following functions.

```
int wr_ad_status (ap, type}
ADDR *ap;
int type;

int wr_ad_rcntno (ap, rcnt)
ADDR *ap;
int  rcnt;
```

The wr_ad_status routine is used to update the status of the address. This can take one of the following values.

| Value | Meaning |
|---|---|
| AD_STAT_PEND | The address is pending |
| AD_STAT_DONE | The address has been finished with |

The wr_ad_rcntno is used to update the reformatter count variable.

### Message files

There are a number of routines to allow a channel to iterate through the set of message files to deliver. First in this set is a function to allow location of the relevant directory. This function maps a given queue id as given by the QMGR into a directory basename with the message files in relating to a given address. It is used as follows:

```
int qid2dir (qid, ap, exists, cpp)
char   *qid;
ADDR   *ap;
int    exists;
char   **cpp;
```

The arguments to this are

qid: A character string containing the queue identifier.

ap: The address that is being processed.

exists: A flag, this should be TRUE if the directory should exist, and FALSE if it doesn't matter.

cpp: A character pointer that is assigned the resulting directory name.

The function will return OK on successful completion and NOTOK on failure.

The next operation is typically to visit each of the message files in turn. This is handled by the following routines.

```
int msg_rinit (dir)
char *dir;
```

The argument here is:

dir: The directory base of the message (usually obtained from a call to qid2dir).

This function returns the usual OK/NOTOK status.

Following this, the function msg_rfile is called repeatedly until it returns RP_DONE to obtain each of the files composing the message.

```
int msg_rfile (buf)
char *buf;
```

The argument is:

buf: A pointer to a character buffer (of size FILNSIZE) which is filled in with the file name if the call succeeds..

Finally, when all files have been processed, or if the operation is to be aborted, the function msg_rend is called:

```
int msg_rend ()
```

### 42.2.3 Delivery Notifications

Delivery reports should be written out by a channel when it is clear that the message cannot be delivered or if the message has been delivered and confirmation is requested. The routine set_1dr is then used to set the appropriate status in the address structure:

```
int  set_1dr (qp, ad_no, msg, reason, diag, str)
Q_struct *qp;
int       ad_no;
char     *msg;
int       reason;
int       diag;
char      *str;
```

The arguments to this function are as follows:

qp: A pointer to a queue structure representing the message. The queue structure should have the address components filled in (this is normally the case).

| Reason | Meaning |
|---|---|
| DRR_NO_REASON | No reason is given for the failure (should not be used normally) |
| DRR_TRANSFER_FAILURE | Unable to transfer the message to the destination |
| DRR_UNABLE_TO_TRANSFER | There is a problem with the message that causes the failure |
| DRR_CONVERSION_NOT_PERFORMED | A conversion is required and cannot be done |
| DRR_PHYS_RENDITION_NOT_PERFORMED | Can not print the message in the required format |
| DRR_PHYS_DELIVERY_NOT_PERFORMED | Physical delivery of the message didn't work |
| DRR_RESTRICTED_DELIVERY | The recipient subscribes to a restricted delivery service. |
| DRR_DIRECTORY_OP_UNSUCCESSFUL | A required directory operation failed |

Table 42.1: Reason Codes

**ad_no:** The address number that this report is for.

**msg:** The queue name of the message being processed.

**reason:** A reason code for the message failure. This should be chosen from one of those in Table 42.1 on page 569.

**diag:** A diagnostic code for the message failure. This is supplementary information to the reason code. It should be one of those values given in Table 42.2 on page 570.

**str:** A character string which records the reason for the failure. This should be something that describes the failure. This field should always be filled in with something appropriate.

| Diagnostic | Meaning |
|---|---|
| DRD_UNRECOGNISED_OR | The sender or recipient name is unknown |
| DRD_AMBIGUOUS_OR | The sender or recipient name is ambiguous |
| DRD_MTA_CONGESTION | Problems with the MTA (catch all!) |
| DRD_LOOP_DETECTED | A loop has been detected in routing |
| DRD_UA_UNAVAILABLE | The user agent is not available |
| DRD_MAX_TIME_EXPIRED | The message was not delivered before the specified delivery time |
| DRD_ENCINFOTYPES_NOTSUPPORTED | The encoded information types are not supported at the destination |
| DRD_CONTENT_TOO_LONG | The message is too big to be delivered |
| DRD_CONVERSION_IMPRACTICAL | The conversion required by this message is not sensible |
| DRD_CONVERSION_PROHIBITED | The conversion required for delivery is prohibitied |
| DRD_IMPLICITCONV_NOTREGISTERED | The implicit conversion required can't be performed |
| DRD_INVALID_PARAMETERS | There is a problem with the message parameters |

Table 42.2: Diagnostic Codes

When calling this function the routine should return to the QMGR one of the following variables:

| Qmgr code | When Applicable |
|---|---|
| positiveDR | For the first recipeint with a positive delivery report |
| successSharedDR | For subsequent recipients with positive delivery reports |
| negativeDR | For the first recipient with a negative delivery report |
| failureSharedDR | For subsequent recipients with negative delivery reports |

Once the recipients have been marked with `set_1dr`, the last step necessary is to write out the actual delivery report by calling `wr_q2dr`. This is defined as follows:

```
int wr_q2dr (qp, msgid)
Q_struct *qp;
char *msgid;
```

The arguments to this function are:

**qp:** A pointer to the queue structure representing the message with the address components filled in.

**msgid:** The queue id for this message.

This function will then write out the reports and update the queue entries with their new status.

### 42.2.4 Successful Delivery

A successful delivery is recorded in the stat log. This is done by the routine `wr_q2dr` if a positive delivery report is required. Alterntively, if no report is required, the delivery is noted with the function `wr_stat` which is called as follows.

```
int wr_stat (ap, qp, msg, size)
ADDR *ap;
Q_struct *qp;
char *msg;
int size;
```

The parameters to this are:

ap: The address that has been successfully delivered.

qp: The queue structure for this message.

msg: The queue name for this message.

size: The size in bytes of the message delivered. This may be different from the size in the queue file.

When a message has been delivered successfully, it is necessary to check several things. These are:

1. If a positive delivery report was requested, one should be composed with `set_1dr` and `wr_q2dr`.
2. Otherwise, the status should be updated to `AD_DONE` with a call to `wr_ad_status`.
3. The QMGR return status should be updated to either `int_Qmgr_Status_success` or `int_Qmgr_Status_positiveDR`.
4. If `wr_q2dr` is not necessary (there was no request for positive delivery reports). A call should be made to `wr_stat` to indicate in the statistics that successful delivery has been achieved.

### 42.2.5 Verification and Trust

Channels are trusted processes, and as such should respect this trust. As far as possible they should check that the data they are being given is reasonable. This includes the following:

- That the channel name and type is reasonable for this channel.
- That the address requested to be processed exists and is ready to be processed (e.g., it has passed through all reformatters).
- That the type of address is correct for this type of channel (e.g., RFC 822 for smtp or X.400 for X.400 channels).
- That the message is not locked by another channel.
- That the channel is the same as the channel given in the address structure.

For common outbound channels and filters these checks are encapsulated in the functions, `chan_acheck`, `lchan_acheck` and `chan_dcheck`.

These calls are similar in function; one checks the address is okay to process for filters and outbound channels; the second is for local channels; and the last is for channels that can handle delivery reports. They are called in the following way:

```
int chan_acheck (ap, mychan, first, mta)
ADDR *ap;
CHAN *mychan;
int first,
char **mta;
```

The arguments are as follows:

**`ap`:** The address to be checked.

**`mychan`:** The channel that is doing this checking.

**`first`:** If this is the first address to be checked. This is used to determine if the mta parameter can be changed.

**`mta`:** The MTA this should connect to. If the constant `NULLVP` is used, the mta parameter will not be filled in or checked. If the mta is the address of a pointer with `NULL` contents then it will be updated if required. If the mta is a pointer to a string, then it is checked that the mta does not change unless the `first` flag is set. This ensures for channels that batch messages to the same host, that all addresses in this message are destined for the same MTA.

It returns either the constant `OK` or `NOTOK`. If `NOTOK` then the `deliverystate` is updated in a suitable way. If `OK` then the address should be processed, and the `deliverystate` updated accordingly.

The function `lchan_acheck` is almost equivalent, except in place of the `mta` parameter is a user.

```
int lchan_acheck (ap, mychan, first, user)
ADDR *ap;
CHAN *mychan;
int first,
char **user;
```

The last function is similar but suitable for channels that can handle delivery reports (such as X.400).

```
int dchan_acheck (ap, asp, mychan, first, mta)
ADDR *ap, *asp;
CHAN *thechan;
int first;
char **mta;
```

The only difference for this call is that an address structure referencing the originator must be passed in as the second parameter.

# 42.3 Example Usage

## 42.3.1 Outbound Channels

Presented here is a skeleton of an outbound channel. This structure is not required, but is a common way of achieving the results.

```
main (argc, argv)
int     argc;
char    **argv;
{
        sys_init (argv[0]);   /* init the channel – and find out who we are */

        dirinit();            /* get to the right directory */
#ifdef PP_DEBUG
        if (argc > 1 && strcmp (argv[1], "debug") == 0)
                debug_channel_control (argc, argv, chaninit, process, endproc);
        else
#endif
                channel_control (argc, argv, chaninit, process, endproc);
        exit (0);
}

static int chaninit (arg)
struct type_Qmgr_Channel *arg;
{
        char    *p = qb2str (arg);

        if ((mychan = ch_nm2struct (p)) == (CHAN *)0)
```

```
                err_abrt (RP_PARM, "Channel '%s' not known", p);
        exam_init (mychan);
        free (p);
        return OK;
}

static int endproc ()
{
        if (cur_host)
                exam_close (OK);
}

static struct type_Qmgr_DeliveryStatus *process (arg)
struct type_Qmgr_ProcMsg *arg;
{
        struct prm_vars prm;
        struct type_Qmgr_UserList *up;
        Q_struct        Qstruct, *qp = &Qstruct;
        int     retval;
        ADDR    *ap,
                *ad_sendr = NULLADDR,
                *ad_recip = NULLADDR,
                *alp,
                *ad_list = NULLADDR;
        int     ad_count;

        if (this_msg) free (this_msg);

        this_msg = qb2str (arg -> qid);

        PP_TRACE (("process msg %s", this_msg));

        bzero ((char *)&prm, sizeof prm);
        bzero ((char *)qp, sizeof *qp);

        (void) delivery_init (arg -> users);

        retval = rd_msg (this_msg, &prm, qp, &ad_sendr, &ad_recip, &ad_count);

        if (rp_isbad (retval)) {
                PP_LOG (LLOG_EXCEPTIONS, ("rd_msg err:  %s", this_msg));
                return delivery_setall (int_Qmgr_status_messageFailure);
        }

        sender = ad_sendr -> ad_r822adr;


        for (ap = ad_recip; ap; ap = ap -> ad_next) {
                for (up = arg ->users; up; up = up -> next) {
                        if (up -> RecipientId -> parm != ap -> ad_no)
                                continue;
```

```
                                if (chan_acheck (ap, mychan,
                                                ad_list == NULL, &cur_mta) == NOTOK)
                                        continue;
                        }
                        if (up == NULL)
                                continue;

                        if (ad_list == NULLADDR)
                                ad_list = alp = (ADDR *) calloc (1, sizeof *alp);
                        else {
                                alp -> ad_next = (ADDR *) calloc (1, sizeof *alp);
                                alp = alp -> ad_next;
                        }
                        *alp = *ap;
                        alp -> ad_next = NULLADDR;
        }

        if (ad_list == NULLADDR) {
                PP_LOG (LLOG_EXCEPTIONS, ("No recipients in user list"));
                rd_end ();
                return deliverystate;
        }

        deliver (ad_list, qp); /* do what is required */

        rd_end();

        return deliverystate;
}


static void dirinit()       /* Change into pp queue space */
{
        if (chdir (quedfldir) < 0)
                err_abrt (RP_LIO, "Unable to change directory to '%s'",
                                                quedfldir);
}
```

Figure 42.2: Example Outbound Channel

## 42.3.2 Address Parsing

Occasionally it is necessary for a channel to parse or manipulate an address. Most channels can get away without needing this however. Some of the basic parsing routines are given here.

The basic interface to parsing is **ad_parse**. This takes an address and attempts to parse it according to the given type and domain ordering. It is called as:

```
int ad_parse (ap, rp, order)
ADDR *ap;
RP_Buf *rp;
int order;
```

The parameters are:

**ap**: The address structure with the address to be parsed in the ad_value structure member. The address type should be set in ad_type.

**rp**: A reply structure which is updated with the results of the parsing.

**order**: The expected order of the domains. This is one of the following:

| Value | Meaning |
|---|---|
| CH_USA_ONLY | US order domain only |
| CH_USA_PREF | US order prefered (UK will be tried) |
| CH_UK_ONLY | UK order domains only |
| CH_UK_PREF | UK order prefered (US will be tried) |

This routine returns an RP code which can be checked with rp_isgood to see if the address was parsed. If it fails, a suitable error will be written in the RP_Buf structure.

Once an address has been parsed and validated by ad_parse it is often necessary to get the "other" form of address (e.g., X.400 if it is an RFC 822 address). There are two routines that will add the correctly encoded alternate address:

```
void x400_add (ap)
ADDR *ap;

void rfc822_add (ap)
ADDR *ap;
```

When delivering to local addresses it is often necessary to reduce a global address down to a user of the system. The routine ad_getlocal can be of use here. This routine takes an address and returns just the local part of it if any, else NULLCP. It is called as follows:

```
char *ad_getlocal (addr, type)
char *addr;
int type;
```

The arguments are:

**addr**: A string-encoded form of the address; either an RFC 822 address or an RFC 1148 encoded X.400 address.

**type**: The type of address, either AD_X400_type or AD_822_type.

### 42.3.3 Local Pickup

This style of channel has not yet been written.

### 42.3.4 TWA Channel

This style of channel has not yet been written.

### 42.3.5 Delivery Reports

A typical interface to the delivery report functions is shown in Figure 42.3.

```
...
  {
          char buffer[BUFSIZ];

          (void) sprintf (buffer, "Address %s failed for reason %s",
                          ap -> ad_r822adr, rstr);

          (void) delivery_set (ap -> ad_no,
                               int_Qmgr_status_permanentFailure);
          set_dr (qp, ap -> ad_no, msg_name,
                  DRR_UNABLE_TO_TRANSFER,
                  DRD_UNRECOGNISED_OR, buffer);
  }
...
```

Figure 42.3: Example Delivery Report Generation

## 42.4 Formatters and Converters

Formatters and converters can run in two ways. Generally the simple filters work on single files, the complex filters work on several files at once. The majority of filters should be of the simple kind.

### 42.4.1 Simple Converters

The simple converters are programs that read from the standard input, do some formatting, and write the result to the standard output. This type of formatter is invoked by the filtercontrol program, `fcontrol`.

These simple filters should return a suitable exit status to confirm that the conversion completed successfully. They follow the standard UNIX[1] tradition of returning 0 on success and anything else on failure.

[1] UNIX is a trademark of AT&T Bell Laboratories.

These filters may be anything from simple shell/awk/sed scripts to more complex *C* programs.

### 42.4.2 Complex Filters

More complex formatters are necessary if the formatting needs to convert more than one file. This is the case for formatters that change the directory structure, or combine several files into one. These formatters require more work, but are similar to the channel programs in their operation. The QMGR interface is in fact identical. The only real difference is in the `qid2dir` routine used to locate the directory. The starting directory is found using the normal `qid2dir` routine. The destination directory is found using the same routine, but first incrementing the formatter count in the address structure, and then calling the routine with the flag set to `FALSE`. The formatter should however place its output in a temporary directory which will then be renamed to the destination directory if the transformation is successful. This allows for failure at any point in the reformatting.

# Part XI

# PP Manual: User's Guide

# PP

## *Volume 3: Users Guide*

Pete Cowen
X-Tel Services Ltd

Julian Onions
X-Tel Services Ltd

# Chapter 43

# Introduction

This manual is concerned with the user-visible tools associated with PP. Other tools which are management oriented or system related are described in other parts of this manual.

Most of the work of a message transfer system is not visible to the user, who typically interacts with some intermediary (user agent or UA). As such this manual is a collection of the tools and interfaces that are directly visible to the user. Conceptually, they may be considered as a part of the UA, which for convenience and performance are implemented as a part of the MTA.

The main components of this part consider the following:

**`local delivery`:** Local delivery is one of the more obviously noticeable parts of PP to the user. This is where the message leaves the transfer system and enters the user's domain. As such, this interface is tailorable to a considerable degree. PP does not restrict the user to a given delivery program, but can be configured on both a per recipient and a per message-type basis. This is conceptually a user agent function, but it is often more efficient to do this operation at the user agent/MTA boundary.

**`distribution lists`:** Maintenance and use of distribution lists is another area where the end user is directly involved. This verges on administration, but is administration that can be delegated to given users for each list. The areas discussed here are the administration of distribution lists and the information associated with such lists.

**`user oriented management`:** There are certain administrative functions that it is useful to make available to end users. These include checking the progress of individual messages and checking the validity of addresses and usernames.

Much of the information presented here is often available in the online UNIX[1] manuals but usually in a much less verbose format. These are listed here:

[1]UNIX is a trademark of AT&T Bell Laboratories.

*chkmf* (1) Check the *.mailfilter* syntax.

*ckmail* (1) Check status of your mail.

*flagmail* (1) Notify a server program of new mail.

*mail* (1) A very dumb mail submission program.

*malias* (1) Show what mailing lists expand to.

*mlist* (1) Distribution list maintenance program.

*ttyalert* (1) Alert of new mail on the terminal.

*xalert* (1) Alert of new mail in an X window.

*resend* (1) Resubmit a message to more recipients.

*strip_addr* (1) Remove comments and extraneous parts from an RFC 822address.

*mailfilter* (5) Brief description of the *.mailfilter* syntax.

# Chapter 44

# Local delivery in PP

The local channel is the mechanism by which PP delivers mail to users. There may be several of these channels tailored to specific mailbox formats. A user may have more than one local channel associated with him/her where this is useful, such as having two formats of mail (e.g., X.400 and RFC 822) delivered in different ways.

## 44.1 Local RFC 822-based Channel

The RFC 822 local channel has considerable control over the delivery of the message. In particular, the channel has a particular search path which is followed when the message is attempted to be delivered. If the message is considered delivered, or rejected by any one of these methods, then the further methods of delivery are attempted. The later methods of delivery are only attempted if the earlier ones are inconclusive. (This does not apply to the *.mailfilter* processing which normally processes the entire file.)

1. If the user has a *.mailfilter* file in his/her home directory and the file is owned by that user and not writable by anyone other than that user, the commands within that file are obeyed. The syntax is defined in Section 44.1.1. If the user does not have a *.mailfilter* or the actions in it do not deliver, reject, or temporarily fail the message, the next method is attempted.
2. If there is a system defined *.mailfilter* then the commands in that are obeyed. Again if this does not exists, or the actions are not conclusive, the next method is tried.
3. If the above two methods appear inconclusive, the message is written to a file in a well-defined place (system configured) surrounded by delimiters.

### 44.1.1 Format of the .mailfilter File

The *.mailfilter* file allows quite complex processing of incoming messages to be performed. The format takes the form of a small interpreted language in which expressions can be tested and evaluated prior to performing actions. In particular conditional actions are the most useful.

The language is defined more formally in the grammar given in Figure 44.2. However, a more gentle introduction is given here with some examples of usage.

### Commands

There are two basic commands that can be performed on a message. These commands can be performed any number of times so the message can be delivered in several places and/or to several processes.

The first command is `file`. This command takes an argument which is a string and the result is to attempt to copy the message surrounded by delimiters into the given file. This might be as in one of the following examples:

```
file "mailbox";
file "/archive/mailbox";
```

A variant of this is the `unixfile`. This writes into the given file, but in sendmail or traditional UNIX-style format; i.e., with a header line stating `From`.

```
unixfile ".mail";
```

Note that all statements in the *.mailfilter* file must be terminated with a semicolon (";").

The second basic command is `pipe`. This command starts up a process and writes the message into it as standard input. This is shown in the next example.

```
pipe "rcvstore +inbox";
pipe "lpr -p -Ppostscript";
```

The system can tell if these commands have succeeded by the following methods. If the file writing works then a flag `delivered` is set to indicate success. Similarly, if the exit status from a pipe is zero, the delivery is considered a success and the flag updated. Additionally, as programs may report temporary failure, this is supported. A program may return a temporary failure by exiting with a value between 1 and 127, in which case the delivery attempt is aborted and retried at a later date. An exit status greater than 127 is taken as permanent failure.

Sometimes, though, you may wish to run a command and ignore the results; that is, to have the system not update the status of the delivery. This can be achieved by setting a variable as described later, but for simplicity, if you precede the command with the keyword `ignore`, then no notice will be taken of the return status.

```
ignore pipe "echo hello";
ignore file "/dev/null";
ignore pipe "rcvalert 'you have new mail'";
```

One last feature of these commands, header variables (described below) may be substituted in the strings associated with these commands. These are not too useful for `file` commands, but can be useful as arguments for processes. Care must be taken that appropriate quoting of these is done in case they contain special characters. As any string containing a "$" is substituted, a $ must be inserted by doubling it, e.g., "$$". If you require a quote """ character in the string, it must be preceeded by a backslash character: "\".

Normally, the commands are interpreted by `/bin/sh -c <command>` but if the *822-local* channel is running in restricted mode, the command is directly executed.

### Conditional Expressions

The real power of the *.mailfilter* comes with conditional expresssions. These allow the user to select particular rules depending, for instance, on certain attributes of the message.

The most basic form of condition is an `if` statement with a simple comparison. This allows you to compare two strings for equality. This takes the form of one of the following:

```
if ( <string1> == <string2> )
    <expression> ;

if ( <string1> == <string2> ) {
    <expression1> ;
    <expression2> ;
}

if ( <string1> == <string2> )
    <expression> ;
else if ( <string1> == <string3> )
    <expression> ;
else
    <expression> ;
```

These examples show a number of things. First, where you can have a single expression, you may have several expressions by enclosing them in braces[1]; this is an example of a compound expression.

Second, by use of the else statement, default actions can be taken. Finally, the `else if` allows a multi way branching construct.

Conditional expressions may also contain Boolean operators. The list is described below.

[1]Any resemblance to the *C* programming language is entirely intentional!

| Operator | Meaning |
|---|---|
| `==` | Is equal to |
| `!=` | Is not equal to |
| `&&` | Logical and |
| `\|\|` | Logical or |
| `!` | Logical not |

The conditional construct begs the question "what conditions can be tested?" These are discussed in the next section.

### Variables

There are two basic types of variables that can be accessed:

1. System variables. These are variables maintained by the *822-local* channel and may be updated after actions are taken.
2. Header fields. When delivering a message, all the current header fields are available for examination.

The system variables are the simplest and there are very few of these. The most used system variable is `delivered`. This variable normally contains the status of the delivery attempt. This is what the system thinks the state of your message is. This may be one of the following values.

| Value | Meaning |
|---|---|
| TRUE | The message has been delivered |
| OK | The same as above |
| FALSE | The message has not been delivered |
| PERMFAIL | The message has permanently failed to be delivered. A delivery report should be sent back if required. |
| TEMPFAIL | The message has failed to be delivered for some temporary reason. Another attempt may succeed. |

This may be used in conditional expressions to test for delivery, or in expressions to reset the delivery state. For example:

```
if ( delivered == FALSE) file "foo";

if ( delivered != TRUE ) file "bar";

# If not delivered - reject the message
if ( delivered == FALSE) delivered = PERMFAIL;
```

Another system type variable is PATH. If this variable is assigned a value, then it is placed in the environment as the default path. This is used to search for commands when executing pipe commands. It is initially set to nothing and the user's shell default search path is used.

Note: This variable is not used if the 822-local channel is configured in restricted mode.

The second class of variables, which are more useful for automatic filing and delivery, are the variables derived from the messages header. These variables evaluate to the contents of the particular field, or to the null string if there is no such variable. These variables can be compared against quoted strings, but such usage is not generally useful. Such comparisons require exact matches including white space with the exception of letter case not being significant. These variables are distinguished by always starting with a dollar symbol ("$") followed by the field name in parentheses. (e.g., `$(to)` or `$(from)`).

Much more useful is comparison against a regular expression. The regular expressions used are those in *regexp* (3). These match against substrings of the fields by default and more complex patterns can be built up. Regular expressions must always appear on the right hand side of the expression and are delimited by slash marks ("/"). An example of such usage shows the real power of the *.mailfilter* file:

```
if ( $(from) == /namedroppers/ ||
     $(from) == /bind/) pipe "rcvstore +mailadmin";
else pipe "rcvstore +inbox";
```

Finally, there are some variables that may appear to be header fields but which are actually derived from other sources. These are:

| | |
|---|---|
| `size` | The size of the message in bytes as a string. |
| `return-path` | The original sender of the message. |
| `mailbox` | The mailbox file associated with this user. |
| `recipient` | The address of this recipient. |
| `userid` | Either the username or userid of this recipient. |
| `groupid` | The group id of this recipient. |
| `channelname` | The name of this delivery channel. |
| `hostname` | The name of the host. |

### Other Features

There are a few other features that can be used in the *.mailfilter* file. These are summarised below:

`exit`: This statement exits the processing of the *.mailfilter* file. With no argument it exits with the current value of the `delivered` variable. If an argument is given, then that is taken as the success or failure of thedelivery attempt. The argument should be one of OK, TEMPFAIL, PERMFAIL or a variable that evaluates to one of these.

print: Normally, this statement does nothing and is ignored. However when running the checking program, it will echo its arguments on the standard output. This may be useful in debugging.

#: This symbol starts a comment, which finishes at the end of the line.

### 44.1.2 Examples

The following are some simple examples of *.mailfilter* files.

This first example shows just a simple delivery making use of the MH *rcvstore* (1) utility:

```
pipe "rcvstore +inbox";
```

The next example shows slightly more complex behaviour, whereby some mail-filtering occurs, and an alert is posted:

```
if ($(to) == /jpo/)
pipe "rcvstore +to";
else
pipe "rcvstore +inbox";
ignore pipe "flagmail -s $(size)";
```

A more complex example of a *.mailfilter* file is shown in Figure 44.1.

The grammar is specified in Figure 44.2 on page 601.

## 44.2 Mailfilter Checkup Tool

As writing *.mailfilter* files can be error prone, a tool to check that the contents conform to the language is provided. This is invoked with a given filename and a message on the standard input. The file is parsed and then interpreted and the actions appropriate for the given message are indicated.

```
ckmf ~/.mailfilter < msg
```

It is *strongly* recommended that you check your *.mailfilter* file each time it is modified. This will certainly pick out syntax errors and the like, however it will not discover errors such as the following which may be common causes of problems:

```
PATH="/usr/local/lib/mh:/usr/local/bin:/usr/bin:/bin:/usr/ucb";
folder = FALSE;
if ($(to) == /jpo/ || $(to) == /onions/) {
        pipe "rcvstore +to"; folder = "to";
} else if ($(sender) == /bind-request/) {
        pipe "rcvstore +bind"; folder = "bind";
} else if ($(sender) == /mailgroup/) {
        pipe "rcvstore +janet/mailgroup"; folder = "janet/mailgroup";
} else if ($(sender) == /namedropper/) {
        pipe "rcvstore +mail/namedroppers"; folder = "namedroppers";
} else if ($(sender) == /pp.*-request/) {
        pipe "rcvstore +pp"; folder = "pp";
}
if (!delivered) {
        pipe "rcvstore +inbox";
        if (!delivered) {
                ignore pipe "flagmail -f 'DELIVERY FAILED'";
                exit (TEMPFAIL);
        }
        folder = "inbox";
}
if (folder)
        ignore pipe "flgamail -s $(size) -e '$(folder): '";
```

Figure 44.1: Example .mailfilter File

- Unable to find the program to be run (not in search path).
- The process that is executed aborts. This may be because some things in the environment are missing. If this is the case it is best to wrap the process in a shell script. Alternatively, the process may expect the standard input/ouput be connected to a terminal. This is difficult to get around.

An example run of *ckmf* might look like this:

```
john% ckmf ~jpo/.mailfilter < /dev/null
pipe into process 'rcvstore +inbox'
pipe into process 'flagmail -s 0 -e 'inbox: ''
Result: delivered OK
john%
```

## 44.3 New Message Notification

PP provides a couple of simple tools for alerting the user of new messages arriving. Both methods share a lot of common features (and code, for that matter).

The basic idea of the notification is to run a process from the delivery process which reads the message, extracts some information, formats it, and then gives it to the user. This may be either by displaying this formatted information on the user's terminal, or on a client of an X Window System[2] display.

There are four processes involved. They are:

**`xalert`:** This process runs as a client of an X windowing system server. It displays messages sent to it by *flagmail*. If it detects that the X windowing system is not in use, it captures messages and displays them on the terminal.

**`flagmail`:** This process gathers the data from the message, formats it and attempts to pass it to *xalert* (or a similar process obeying the same protocol). If it fails it emulates the *ttyalert* program.

**`ttyalert`:** This process gathers data from a message and simply displays it on the user's terminal if logged in. It is only intended for large sites where all people use the same host.

**`ttybiff`:** This process runs in the background normally. It displays messages sent to it by *flagmail*.

This program's use is deprecated as the functionality is subsumed by *xalert*. It will probably not appear in future releases.

Both *flagmail* and *ttyalert* use the same method of preparing and formatting the data to be displayed. This is done by using a format string to indicate how the information should be laid out. The format string can contain verbatim text, header fields, and other attributes of the message.

Fields within the format string are indicated by percent (%) symbols. The general format bares some relationship to the *printf* (3) format:

```
%[digits]string
```

The digits are optional and indicate how large the field should be padded out to or truncated to. The string is any message field, or one of a set of special fields. The case of the string is not sensitive.

The special fields are:

| Field | Meaning |
|---|---|
| `body` | The first few characters of the body of the message |
| `size` | The size in bytes of the message |
| `extra` | A special field set on the command line |
| `from` | the from field is treated in a special way |

[2]The X Window System is a trademark of the Massachusettes Institute of Technology

The **body** field is the first few characters of the body with all new lines removed and multiple white space compressed to single spaces.

The `size` is set on the command line by the use of an optional flag. This is usually done in the *.mailfilter* file by use of the `$(size)` variable.

The `extra` field is used to allow simple changes to the default format string. This just allows a simple flag to adjust the output from the default format string rather than rewriting the format string. If not set, it defaults to the value `NEW:␣`.

The `From` field is treated slightly specially, in that if there is a name component in front of the opening angle bracket, then the rest of the field is ignored.

The default format string is the following:

```
%extra(%size) %20from %subject << %50body
```

This gives output something like the following

```
NEW: (3402) Steve Kille  Re: state of unix-niftp? << I
```

The whole output line is truncated to the number of characters set on the command line (defaulting to 80). This allows the later parts of the string to be large, in the assurance that they will get chopped off if they exceed the given size.

An example usage in a *.mailfilter* file might look like the following:

```
if (delivered)
    ignore pipe "flagmail -s $(size)"
```

See the example in Figure 44.1 on page 593 for a more complex example of usage.

### Flags

Both *flagmail* and *ttyalert* respond to a number of command line options to change the behaviour. These are:

**-d:** Runs the program in a debugging mode. This stops the program from running in the background. Only useful if you are trying to debug the program.

**-e string:** Sets the `extra` variable. This is used to override the default extra information which is normally `NEW:`.

**-f format:** Sets the entire format string to the given string. This is how you override the internal format string with something entirely different.

**-s size:** Sets the message size parameter.

**-w width:** Sets the default output line width. The line produced will be truncated to this width (default 80 characters).

**-x:** Forces the use of protocol. In this mode it will not try and do its own notification if it fails to notify a server.

In addition the *flagmail* program has two other options to tailor the interaction with *xalert* or other servers.

**-h hostfile:** Use the given file to read the host and port to communicate with. This overrides the default of *.alert* in the home directory.

**-p number:** Use the following number to override the UDP port found in the file.

*xalert* has only some command line switches. These are:

**-filename hostfile:** use the given file to write the host and port number in instead of the default (*.alert*).

**-user username:** *xalert* filters out requests destined for the given user. Normally it will not receive messages destined for another user, but this will change *xalert*'s idea of the current user anyway.

**-port number:** Set the UDP port number to the given number. The default is to choose a random unused UDP port.

**-s:** Only print to the standard output; do not display on all this user's login sessions.

**-t:** Do not attempt to use the X system.

**-x:** Allow use of X (default).

**-w width:** Use this width when displaying messages on the terminal.

In addition it takes all the standard X command line arguments.

*ttybiff* supports the following flags similar to *xalert*:

**-f hostfile:** use the given file to write the host and port number in instead of the default.

**-u username:** as for *xalert*'s -username switch.

**-p port:** as for *xalert*'s -port switch.

**-s:** only display on the standard output, not on other terminals where the user is logged on.

### 44.3.1 Use of flagmail with xalert and ttybiff

*Xalert* works with *flagmail* or *ttybiff* to provide the notification. *Flagmail* is responsible for building up the format string and sending it to either *xalert* or *ttybiff*. This is achieved using a UDP connection. *flagmail* contacts the server program by looking for a file with a hostname and UDP port in (by default *.alert*). If this exists then it attempts to contact a server on that host to display the message. If either of these steps fails, then it reverts to the behaviour of *ttyalert* except that there is a delay while it waits for UDP timeouts to occur.

The *.alert* has the format

```
<hostname> <udp-port-no>
```

*flagmail* will use this information to contact the remote process, which can be any process which understands the *flagmail* protocol.

The *xalert* program is just a simple display process that displays the messages sent by *flagmail*. It displays these message in a text widget which is scrollable. There are three buttons:

`Quit`: which does the obvious thing.

`Clear`: which clears the message window.

`Reset`: which rewrites the *.alert* file; it is used if two xalerts are started or the *.alert* file is removed.

The *ttybiff* attempts to locate the user in the same manner as *ttyalert* or, if that fails, to display the message on the standard output.

### 44.3.2 Examples

Here are a few examples of use.

First, the simple notification that should be put in the *.mailfilter* file:

```
ignore pipe "flagmail -s $(size)";
```

This does the most basic notification. If more control is required over the displayed message more complex strings can be built up:

```
if ($(subject) == /request/) {
    file "request-mbox";
    ignore pipe "flagmail -s $(size) -e REQUEST";
}
```

Finally, if you are adventurous, you might like to play with the format of the message given. For instance:

```
ignore pipe
 "flagmail -s $(size) -f '%5size %15from (%20subject) **%body'";
```

This would give an output in the following format for a typical message

```
1023  Julian Onions   (Re: Delivery Report ) ** Also
```

## 44.4 Automatic Vacation Notices

PP provides a simple program to notify originators that the recipients will not read their messages for some time. This is typically installed when the recipient is expecting to be unable to read mail for some time, such as going on vacation.

The program, *rcvtrip*, is installed in the *.mailfilter* file in a fashion similar to the following.

```
ignore pipe "rcvtrip"
```

The program reads the message and checks to see if the recipient is mentioned directly in either the `to` or `cc` line. If so, and the originator has not been replied to in a similar style before, then a reply is composed. This consists of some standard text, followed by the contents of the file *tripnote* in the user's home directory.

There are several flags to this program.

**-F:** Always reply to the user, even if the message is not sent directly to this user.

**-e value:** Set the exit code depending on this value. A value of 0 means the program always exits with failure (the default). If the value is 1, the exit code is always good. A value of 2 will give an exit status according to the following table:

| Condition | exit code |
|---|---|
| A message was sent | 1 |
| A message was not sent as this sender has already received a message | 2 |
| A message was not sent as this message was not sent directly to this user | 3 |
| A parse error was found | 4 |
| Anything else | 99 |

**-f:** Set the text of the from field (defaults to `MESSAGE AGENT`).

**-l file:** Set the database to this filename (default *triplog*).

**-n:** Use this file as the text of the message to send back after the standard preamble (default *ttripnote*).

-s: Use this file to determine the user's signature (default *.signature*).

-t text: Modify the preamble to use this line (several of these may be given).

-u user: Pretend to be this user when answering.

## 44.5 Forwarding Mail

There is a simple program which will forward mail to other recipients. This is called *resend*. This program takes a message as standard input with extra recipients given on the command line. The program will then submit the message as a `resent` message. The new recipients will appear in the `resent-to` and `resent-cc` lines as appropriate.

There are two flags that control the operation of this program:

-t: The next recipients should be specified as `Resent-To:` recipients.

-c: The next recipients should be specified as `Resent-Cc:` recipients.

-u username: Pretend to be this user (subject to authorisation checks).

## 44.6 Delivery Tools

There are one or two small tools that are provided to help with delivery processing.

### 44.6.1 strip_addr

The *strip_addr* utility takes a list of addresses either on the command line or on the standard input and issues those same addresses in a basic form. In particular all address comments are removed as are name and list constructs. This utility may be useful in processing mail where only the basic address is wanted.

*strip_addr* takes two optional flags. These are:

-p: Interpret the % character as a routing construct. If this flag is not present, the % character will be taken as just another character.

-r: Strip out routes as well.

An example of use might be:

```
strip_addr 'Julian Onions <jpo(thats me)@there.com>'
jpo@there.com
```

### 44.6.2 flock

The *flock* utility takes a single file followed by a command. The file is first locked in the current PP locking style, and then the command is executed. When the command exits, the file is unlocked and *flock* exits with the returned status of the command.

```
<statementlist> ::= <statement>
                  | <statement> <statementlist>

<statement> ::= <expression> ";"
                  | ";"
                  | "print" <prexp> ";"
                  | "if" <condition> <statement>
                  | "if" <condition> <statement> "else" <statement>
                  | "{" <statementlist> "}"

<condition> ::= "(" <expression> ")"

<expression> ::=  "(" <expression> ")"
                  | <expression> "==" <regex>
                  | <expression> "!=" <regex>
                  | <variable> "=" <expression>
                  | <expression> "==" <expression>
                  | <expression> "!=" <expression>
                  | <expression> "||" <expression>
                  | <expression> "&&" <expression>
                  | "!" <expression>
                  | [ "ignore" ] "file" <string>
                  | [ "ignore" ] "pipe" <string>
                  | "exit" [ <expression> ]
                  | <field>
                  | <variable>
                  | <string>

<prexp> ::= <expression>
                  | <prexp> "," <expression>

<string> ::= quoted string of characters (e.g., "abced")

<variable> ::= list of characters of the form [a-zA-Z_][a-zA-Z0-9_]*

<field> ::= "$(" list of characters and - ")"

<regex> ::= "/" regular expression (see regexp(3)) "/"
```

Figure 44.2: Grammar for the .mailfilter File

# Chapter 45

# Distribution List Maintance

PP provides an interactive tool for maintaining distribution lists, *mlist*. This tool allows you, the user, to view, modify and generally manage the members of a given list. What you are allowed to do to a list depends on the access rights set on that list.

The access rights for a list are set when the one of the managers of that list first uses *mlist* to manage the list. There are four modes of access rights:

**free:** Anyone can add or remove members of the list.

**public:** Anyone can add themselves to or remove themselves from the list.

**private:** Only managers of the list can add or remove members;

**secret:** Only managers of the list can view or alter the members of a list.

If you are a manager of a list, the access rights are bypassed and you are given *free* access to the list.

## 45.1 What you can and cannot do with *mlist*

For all modes of access except *free*, the maintainance of the list is done via a series of questions. For example:

```
You (pac) are not in this list
Do you wish to be added ? [y/n]
```

With *free* access, the maintainance is done via a menu of options.

**add:** A list of possible mail addresses is expected with this option (either following the add command or on the next line). *mlist* checks that each address is a valid mail address and that the normalised address does not already exist in the list. Addresses that pass both these tests are added to the list.

**remove:** A regular expression is expected with this option. Any address that matches this expression is a candidate for removal from the list. *mlist* asks the user whether each candidate should be removed.

**find:** As with the *remove* option, a regular expression is expected. Any address that matches the expressions is printed out.

**verify:** This option goes through the list checking that each member is a valid mail address.

As well as these maintainance options, there are a few inspection options

**print:** This option prints out all the information concerning the list. This information consists of all the members of the list, the list moderator's mail address, and the user ids of the moderators of the list.

**list:** This option displays all the lists known to the local PP system. Each list also has a short description of its purpose.

**help:** This option displays all the options that are available to you.

If the list you require does not exist, there is one further option, `create`. This option prompts you for all the details of the list you require and posts them to the postmaster. If the postmaster decides to grant you this list, he or she will then do the appropriate administration to create the list. Once the postmaster has done this, you can use *mlist* to manipulate the list.

If you have done this and the list you requested now appears in the output of the `list` option but *mlist* still thinks it does not know about that list, then it is possible that the postmaster overlooked creating an empty file to contain the list when he or she was adding the list to PP's tables.

## 45.2 How *mlist* can run

*mlist* takes each list specified on the command line in turn, and enables you to modify it. If no lists are specified on the command line, *mlist* enters a loop. Within this loop, you choose the lists you wish to modify. When you have finished modifying the required lists, you can choose to `quit` the loop and exit *mlist*.

*mlist* can take several command line arguments:

**-user 'username'** This specifies the username one wants to be known as when altering lists. Only priviledged users can use this flag.

**-uid 'userid'** This specifies the user Id one wants to be known as when altering lists. Only priviledged users can use this flag.

**-order 'domain order'** This specifies the preferred domain ordering to use when parsing addresses. This can be specified as:

**usa** usa domain ordering ONLY.

**uk** uk domain ordering ONLY.

**usapref** usa domain ordering preferred.

**ukpref** uk domain ordering preferred.

The default is usa domain ordering only.

### 45.2.1 *malias*

The *malias* tool is a passive version of *mlist*. Using the *malias* tool, you can only view the members of specified lists. You are unable to modify, in any way, the contents of a list.

# Chapter 46

# Miscellaneous Utilities

There are a number of small utility programs provided with PP that may be of interest to end users. These are described here.

## 46.1 A /bin/mail Replacement

PP comes with a very simple user interface for submitting messages. It has approximately the functionality normally assumed by */bin/mail* except that reading mail is not supported, only submission. That is, it takes a list of addresses on the command line and reads the body of the message on the standard input. By default all the addresses are marked as `To:` recipients. The command has a few options; each option stays in force until overriden.

**-t:** The following arguments, up to the next flag, are `To:` addresses.

**-c:** The following arguments are `Cc:` addresses.

**-s:** The following arguments are text for the `Subject:` line.

This program is most useful in scripts and programs as a simple way of sending a message.

## 46.2 Message Status Checkup

PP provides a tool, *checkmail*, that connects to an MTA and finds out about messages related to the user.

There are two flags to alter *checkmail*'s behaviour.

**-a:** This flag prompts *checkmail* to find out about messages to and from the user. By default, *checkmail* only finds out about messages from the user.

**-h MTAname:** This flag prompts *checkmail* to connect to the named MTA. By default, *checkmail* attempts to connect to an MTA running on the local machine.

Here are two example displays from the *checkmail* tool:

```
john% xcheckmail -h sheriff
Please wait while attempt to connect to sheriff....connected
The messages from pac on sheriff are as follows:
msg.aa03130 is pending delivery to p.pat@cs.nott.ac.uk

john% xcheckmail -h sheriff -a
Please wait while attempt to connect to sheriff....connected
The messages to or from pac on sheriff are as follows:
msg.aa03130 is pending delivery to p.pat@cs.nott.ac.uk
msg.aa03140 is from  P.Pat@cs.nott.ac.uk
```

# Index

## *The Artech House Telecommunications Library*

Vinton G. Cerf, *Series Editor*

*A Bibliography of Telecommunications and Socio-Economic Development* by Heather E. Hudson

*Advances in Computer Systems Security: 3 volume set,* Rein Turn, ed.

*Advances in Fiber Optics Communications,* Henry F. Taylor, ed.

*Broadband LAN Technology* by Gary Y. Kim

*Codes for Error Control and Synchronization* by Djimitri Wiggert

*Communication Satellites in the Geostationary Orbit* by Donald M. Jansky and Michel C. Jeruchim

*Current Advances in LANs, MANs, and ISDN,* B.G. Kim, ed.

*Design and Prospects for the ISDN* by G. DICENET

*Digital Cellular Radio* by George Calhoun

*Digital Image Signal Processing* by Friedrich Wahl

*Digital Signal Processing* by Murat Kunt

*Digital Switching Control Architectures* by Giuseppe Fantauzzi

*Digital Transmission Design and Jitter Analysis* by Yoshitaka Takasaki

*Disaster Recovery Planning for Telecommunications* by Leo A. Wrobel

*E-Mail* by Stephen A. Caswell

*Expert Systems Applications in Integrated Network Management,* E.C. Ericson, L.T. Ericson, and D. Minoli, eds.

*Handbook of Satellite Telecommunications and Broadcasting,* L. Ya. Kantor, ed.

*Innovations in Internetworking,* Craig Partridge, ed.

*Integrated Services Digital Networks* by Anthony M. Rutkowski

*International Telecommunications Management* by Bruce R. Elbert

*Introduction to Satellite Communication* by Bruce R. Elbert

*International Telecommunication Standards Organizations* by Andrew Macpherson

*Introduction to Telecommunication Electronics* by A.Michael Noll

*Introduction to Telephones and Telephone Systems* by A. Michael Noll

*Jitter in Digital Transmission Systems* by Patrick R. Trischitta and Eve L. Varma

*LANs to WANs: Network Management in the 1990s* by Nathan J. Muller and Robert P. Davidson

*Long Distance Services: A Buyer's Guide* by Daniel D. Briere

*Manager's Guide to CENTREX* by John R. Abrahams

*Mathematical Methods of Information Transmission* by K. Arbenz and J.C. Martin

*Measurement of Optical Fibers and Devices* by G. Cancellieri and U. Ravaioli

*Meteor Burst Communication* by Jacob Z. Schanker

*Minimum Risk Strategy for Acquiring Communications Equipment and Services* by Nathan J. Muller

*Mobile Information Systems* by John Walker

*Optical Fiber Transmission Systems* by Siegried Geckeler

*Optimization of Digital Transmission Systems* by K. Trondle and G. Soder

*Principles of Secure Communication Systems* by Don J. Torrieri

*Principles of Signals and Systems: Deterministic Signals* by B. Picinbono

*Private Telecommunication Networks* by Bruce Elbert

*Quality Measures and the Design of Telecommunications Systems* by John H. Fennick

*Radiodetermination Satellite Services and Standards* by Martin Rothblatt

*Setting Global Telecommunication Standards: The Stakes, The Players, and The Process* by Gerd Wallenstein

*Signal Theory and Processing* by Frederic de Coulon

*Techniques in Data Communications* by Ralph Glasgal

*Telecommunications: An Interdisciplinary Text,* Leonard Lewin, ed.

*Telecommunications in the U.S.: Trends and Policies,* Leonard Lewin, ed.

*Telecommunication Systems* by Pierre-Girard Fontolliet

*Television Technology: Fundamentals and Future Prospects* by A. Michael Noll

*Terrestrial Digital Microwave Communications,* Ferdo Ivanek, ed.

*The ITU in a Changing World* by George A. Codding, Jr. and Anthony M. Rutkowski

*The Law and Regulation of International Space Communication* by Harold M. White, Jr. and Rita Lauria White

*The Manager's Guide to the New Telecommunications Network* by Lawrence D. Gasman

*The Telecommunications Deregulation Sourcebook,* Stuart N. Brotman, ed.

*Traffic Flow in Switching Systems* by G. Hebuterne

*Troposcatter Radio Links* by G. Roda

*Voice Teletraffic System Engineering* by James R. Boucher

*World Atlas of Satellites,* Donald M. Jansky, ed.

www.ingramcontent.com/pod-product-compliance
Lightning Source LLC
Chambersburg PA
CBHW081123180926
51611CB00004B/37